THINK TANKS

THINK TANKS

THINK TANKS

Paul Dickson

NEW YORK

Atheneum

1971

To Nancy

ACKNOWLEDGMENTS

Most of the research for this book was completed while studying under a University Fellowship for Reporters from the American Political Science Association. I am greatly indebted to the Association for the time and resources which it contributed through the Fellowship toward the completion of this work.

The profiles of the think tanks which appear in the book were prepared primarily through interviews and the examination of reports prepared by the think tanks themselves. Several people within the institutions investigated worked especially hard to make sure that I got to talk with the people I wanted to see and helped me get my hands on the reports I needed. For this type of help I would like to thank Peter Madison of the RAND Corporation, Wayne Boucher of the Institute for the Future, William F. Arnold of Environmetrics, and Kathleen Manion of Arthur D. Little Inc.

ACKNOWLEDGMENTS

Others I would like to thank are: Professor S. McKee Rosen of George Washington University, who generously gave me much advice on sources; Joseph C. Goulden, who helped me get the project started; and Ray Connolly, Robert Skole and William Hickman, who suggested ideas and approaches which have been used in the book.

Above all, I would like to thank my wife, Nancy, who spent many days reading, correcting, and suggesting improvements for the book.

I am responsible for the information in the book as well as for the opinions set forth, which, of course, do not necessarily represent those of the people I have acknowledged for their help.

PAUL DICKSON

CONTENTS

THINK TANKS

THINK TANKS

I

INTRODUCTION: THE CLEAN FACTORIES

As you pass them by, they beg to be forgotten. Most are clean glass-and-concrete affairs set in man-made landscapes. They neither pollute the air with smoke nor foul the water with industrial waste. Those that don't look like dull boxes set down beside a highway are even less obtrusive, taking up part of a high-rise office building or filling an urban row house or suburban estate.

Only inside do they give up their bland disguises. Inside one of them, in Cambridge, Massachusetts, four small separate teams go to work each morning: one, synthesizing marijuana in a laboratory in order to isolate the effects of its active ingredients; another, putting the final touches on a plan to restructure the Jesuit order in America; the third, developing a sanitary napkin that will dissolve when flushed down a toilet; and the final team, trying to manage the revitalization of a Midwestern community. Across town, inside another, a team of six calling itself a "task force" is working up a long-range plan to create a working class New Town out of an urban slum.

Far away, in Menlo Park, California, on one floor of a third such place, a twenty-eight-member community calling itself the "Augmentation Research Center" is attempting to push man's use of the computer to its furthest application as an extension of the human brain. This effort, now ten years old, has led to the claim by the group that it has learned to live with, not just use, computers. Down the hall from this group, another team of about the same size is experimenting with artificial intelligence by teaching and learning from a mobile automaton—or, in layman's terms, one of the world's first true robots. On another floor of the same building, a suite of offices has recently been vacated by thirty-two researchers who have just delivered to the Governor of Alaska a planning guideline for the future of his state. A few blocks away, a permanent team of about fifteen has determined, over the last few years, that between now and the year 2000 there are eleven possible alternative futures for the United States. All but several of these futures promise that things will get worse, and the team is now trying to figure out how to guide the nation toward those few positive alternatives where things get better.

Outside Washington, D.C., in another of these clean factories behind secure doors, a group of analysts is fighting the wars of the 1990's in a $50,000 Strangelovean game room to see who wins, why, and with what weapons. One of the ten wars they fight over and over again takes place in northern Norway and pits the United States, Norway, West Germany, and Denmark against the U.S.S.R., East Germany, Poland, and Finland. Closer to home, another of their oft-played secret wars is an American civil war fought in the year 1990. Not far away, in downtown Washington, another type of game is being played. These games are public, and their object is to save American cities from further deterioration. The harsh, unflinching judge of these efforts to stave off urban decay is a computer.

A team belonging to a new one of these remarkable centers, on Madison Avenue in New York, has just perfected a chemical gimmick that it calls "slippery water." By reducing friction and turbulence, it enables 60 percent more water to come out of a standard fire hose and makes that water travel twice as far as it would normally. This organization believes it can take significant steps to improve the quality of life in New York City and is getting things rolling with minor steps like "slippery water," which, for example, should help the economy and effectiveness of the New York City Fire Department.

Elsewhere around the country, teams are refining nuclear policy, dreaming up new weapons, mapping out development schemes for emerging nations, inventing new flavors for foods, preparing advisory memos for the President, and trying to save whole industries. There are hundreds of these places where each year thousands of teams tackle tens of thousands of projects. These clean factories have come to be called "think tanks." Like so many other broad labels, think tank oversimplifies, but it is the best term anyone has yet devised to describe a unique class of institution that has proliferated in America since World War II.

Although there are many of them overseas and there will surely be more, at this point in history think tanks are an overwhelmingly American phenomenon. To understand them and their growing yet generally unrecognized impact on the American landscape, it is essential to survey the empire within the nation of which they are a part. This empire has helped make them, has conferred upon them an elite status, and insures their perpetuation. The size, importance, and richness of this empire is staggering. Its prosaic name is Research and Development.

II

THE RESEARCH
EMPIRE

---

1. $150 Billion Symbol

Sweat, Sweat Glands, Sweating—Eccrine Sweat Gland Activity and Racial Differences in Resting Skin Conductance . . . Finger-Sweat Prints in the Differentiation of Low and High Incentive . . . The Effect of Manual Labor and Perspiration on Blood and Tissue . . . The Physical and Chemical Properties Affecting the Water Balance in Confined Spaces . . . Reflex Responses of Human Sweat Glands to Different Rates of Skin Cooling . . . Palmar Sweat Gland Activity . . . Sweat Loss and Fluid Intake of Mine Workers and Industrial Laborers . . .

—A sampling of the scores of federally funded research projects on sweat. A more complete list available from the Clearinghouse for Federal Scientific and Technical Information

Nerve gas, Salk vaccine, the moon landings, and the digital computer are all dramatic symbols of America's dedication to research. But not one of them gives a true feeling for its volume or its boundaries. It would be impossible to get a true feeling for its immensity with any one fact or in any one place, but one can get some idea of it at a sprawling, drab federal building nestled between housing developments in Springfield, Virginia. It is called the Clearinghouse for Federal Scientific and Technical Information and has all the charm of a mammoth dry-cleaning plant. It is the focal point for the collection and dissemination of the most popular and sought-after government-sponsored research and development reports. Created in 1950 and greatly expanded in 1964, it is where federally supported technology is for sale. Housed here is a collection of millions of copies of over 600,000 separate research reports, to which 50,000 new titles are added each year. Over three million copies of these reports are sold each year.

This warehouse/library for American research includes in its collection reports on "Temperature Distribution of an Idealized Ice Cap," "Performance of Miniature Pigs After Partial Body Irradiation," "The Impact of Social Change in Developing Countries," "Decisionmaking on Farms in Middle Sweden," "Improved Propylene Copolymer Dielectrics for Communications Cable," "Environmental Effects of Nuclear Weapons," and "Counterinsurgency in Vietnam: Some New Alternatives." The Clearinghouse has everything, from research on how to conduct psychological warfare to reports on improving swimming-pool filters, researched, seemingly at least, in quadruplicate and from almost every angle. Seven new reports on swine were added in 1969, and five more on the same subject came in during the first six months of 1970.

The Clearinghouse, however, is an imperfect indicator, because its collection is selective. It covers only a small fraction of the government research effort and does not include research supported by private industry, universities, and state and local government. Moreover, even though it is the largest single outlet for federal research it is just one of many competing entities that move research reports; among the others are the Government Printing Office, the Defense Documentation Center, government journals, and the information and publications divisions of the more than fifty agencies and departments with major research programs.

Besides giving weight to the traditional assertion that Washington's biggest export is paper, all these reports, studies, and surveys resulting from federal research are testament to the nation's com-

7

mitment to research and development, or, as it is most commonly referred to, R&D. Paced by the federal government, this commitment to R&D is no less strong in industry, universities, foundations, private research institutions, and state and local governments. R&D is not a general term. It has an official definition provided by the National Science Foundation, which says it is the total of three activities: (1) *basic research*—the exploration of the unknown. Sometimes called nondirected research, it has its motivating influence in the desire to pursue knowledge for its own sake. Charles E. Wilson, President Eisenhower's first Secretary of Defense, called it what you do when ". . . you don't know what you're doing." An example would be a chemist working with a compound simply to find what is not known about that compound. He is looking for something but does not know what. (2) *applied research*—research directed to satisfying a stated need, such as finding a cure for a disease or discovering new ways to make planes fly faster. It draws on basic research and normally generates additional knowledge. To continue with the example of the chemist, he would be entering the realm of applied research when he started trying to see if his compound would have, say, an effect on curbing a specific disease. (3) *development*—the systematic use of basic and applied research for the creation and production of tangible objects (from serums to spacecraft), systems, methods, and materials. It normally includes design and experimentation of a product or process but never production of it. If, for example, our chemist were to find that his compound had potential as an antimalarial drug, then its development would include the refinement of the compound, its testing and preparation for producing it in mass quantities.

In the last decade $150 billion has been spent on these three activities, and they have been conducted by the federal government itself in its laboratories and offices; colleges, universities, and nonprofit research outfits and foundations; and industry, both for itself and for the government. Its supporters have also been varied, but the biggest contributor has been the federal government, which has provided about two-thirds of the funds spent. Most government research has been contracted for and conducted by industrial firms, while government laboratories, universities, and other nonprofit institutions have done about a third of it.

Considering that the annual national R&D budget in the United

States is larger than the total budget used to run medium-sized nations, it is no exaggeration that R&D is an immense apparatus. Just how immense and influential it is, however, cannot be expressed in terms of billions of dollars, or in the statement that it employs over one million people; it requires odd facts and comparisons to demonstrate. For example:

The total amount spent on R&D from the American Revolution through the end of World War II is less than the current annual expenditure.

Of every eight scientists who ever lived seven are alive today.

The U. S. now spends more annually on space research, just one element of the R&D budget, than it cost to run the whole government in 1927.

2. *Building the Empire*

> . . . *the growth of science is something very much more active, much vaster in its problems, than any other sort of growth happening in the world today . . . the density of science in our culture is quadrupling during each generation.*
>
> —From Derek J. DeSolla Price, *Science Since Babylon*

It started in 1832, when the Secretary of the Treasury, confronted by pesky steam boilers that kept exploding in American steamboats, contracted with the Franklin Institute of Philadelphia for a study of the problem. Since then, the government has been paying for more and more outside brainpower each decade.

The most phenomenal growth, of course, has occurred in the period from the late 1940's to the present. Federal R&D expenditures were $250 million in 1940, slightly less than a billion in 1948, hit $3 billion in 1957, jumped to $8 billion in 1960, and have zoomed to over $16 billion a year in the 1967–1971 period. President Nixon's

9

fiscal 1972 R&D budget request, considered relatively "austere," totaled $16.7 billion.

R&D now gets into every nook and cranny of the federal apparatus and is so far-reaching that it usually takes the National Science Foundation several years to determine just how much was spent and by whom. The extent to which everyone has gotten into the act is shown by the fact that in early 1970 it was determined that twenty-two agencies and departments were doing oceanological research and no less than sixty elements of government were involved in environmental research programs. The giant R&D spenders are the Pentagon, NASA, the Atomic Energy Commission, and the Department of Health, Education and Welfare, but there are scores of other agencies, offices, and commissions that also count their research money in millions. Ferreting through the fiscal 1971 budget request one can find, for example, that the Post Office has asked for $96.6 million to research items ranging from new automated mail handling equipment that scans, reads addresses, and sorts letters to new safety devices for mail trucks; or that a total of $27.9 million is scheduled for research into weather-forecasting techniques or that $34.5 million is slated for the National Institute for Dental Research to study specifics, ranging from new materials for filling cavities to oral cancer. Even the controversial Commission on Obscenity and Pornography had its R&D budget—which in fiscal 1970 hit $1.3 million—to determine through surveys, tests, and studies, the effects of pornography in America.

While federal R&D is large and likely to get larger in the years ahead, it still accounts for only somewhat more than half the nation's total R&D commitment. Two recent estimates showed the dollar size of all U.S. R&D in 1969: a study by the Battelle Memorial Institute, itself a research organization, pegged it at $25.9 billion, and a survey conducted by McGraw-Hill Publications came up with $27.17 billion. An early 1971 study made by the magazine *Industrial Research* predicted R&D expenditures of $28 billion before the year was out. Although there has been a leveling off of R&D in the last three or four years, due, among other things, to the burden of the Vietnam war and attempts to contain the growing federal budget, many predict that the pattern of growth will show no signs of slowing over the long run—and several predictions indicate that R&D will double in the next decade.

Future increases will not just be federally sponsored if the recent past is any guide, because local government and industry have been upping their antes by sizable percentages. Two facts from recent National Science Foundation surveys are indicative: local government R&D went from $20.3 million in 1966 to $28.8 million in 1967, and industry-sponsored R&D increased 114 percent between 1957 and 1966, from $3.4 billion to $7.3 billion.

A variety of factors have produced the phenomenon of growing R&D since World War II. Some can be traced to specific trends and events, such as Soviet success in launching Sputniks I and II. This feat was in large part responsible for touching off U.S. military and civilian space programs as well as for giving impetus to research in other areas, ranging from defense to education. The Sputniks alarmed America and caused the government to take a new look at institutions, ranging from the army status of forces to the quality of elementary education. The nation responded by authorizing billions more in R&D—specifically, expenditures went from $3 billion in 1957, the year of the Sputniks, to $15 billion by 1964. Research aid to universities spurted upward during the period, as did budgets for research into all forms of education. Other real and imagined threats from the cold war, along with the desire to maintain military supremacy led to burgeoning R&D expenditures, as did many smaller events, such as the sharp decline in the production and sale of coal, which brought about the creation of the Office of Coal Research and the beginnings of a modest research effort on coal mining and potential new uses for coal. In recent years, recognition of a variety of social and environmental ills has brought about the start of new research. Rising crime rates, for instance, have led to research into law-enforcement techniques and new police equipment.

Science and technology have more and more become wards of the federal government since World War II. Simply, a government policy has evolved holding that it will act as both benefactor and director of scientific efforts in the nation. Such a step was an outgrowth of World War II, when the government drew heavily on the scientific community to wage war. It was dramatically shown during the war years that science could contribute mightily to the nation's security, and ever since the government has continued to look upon science and technology as activities deserving its support. The federal attitude that prevails to this day is well stated in a report to Presi-

11

dent Roosevelt issued in 1945 by Vannevar Bush, the scientist who led the wartime Office of Science Research and Development, which said: "It has been basic United States policy that Government should foster the opening of new frontiers. It opened the seas to clipper ships and furnished land for pioneers. Although these frontiers have more or less disappeared, the frontier of science remains. . . . Moreover, since health, well-being and security are proper concerns of Government, scientific progress is, and must be, of vital interest to Government. . . ." Although a strong supporter and director, the government has limited its own role in the actual performance of research, a point that is exemplified in the Apollo program in which NASA's role was to orchestrate closely the efforts of about a thousand R&D contractors.

Another factor that has always fed growth of R&D is the simple one that progress demands it. If one wants a new missile, mumps vaccine or mousetrap the road to it is R&D. Moreover, the theme of progress does not require that a specific goal be established before research is funded. Basic research is often called "seed money" because even though it is geared to no specific result, new knowledge and techniques will probably germinate from it later to solve new problems or bring about new advances. A study released by the National Science Foundation in 1969 shows how this faith pays off. The study—named TRACES for Technology in Retrospect and Critical Events in Science—takes a number of important recent discoveries, such as the video tape recorder, and traces them back to their origins in the indefinite realm of basic research. The origins of the items in the work range from the relatively recent 1920's, when the technology needed to discover the oral contraceptive pill was being developed, to the 1860's, when scientists were laying the theoretical groundwork for the electron microscope.

Finally, a very strong factor contributing to the growth of research is that R&D inevitably produces more complex and costly R&D. Since the fruits of R&D are technology, ideas, knowledge, and products, it is obvious that research and development open the door for more research. DDT, for example, was the result of research. Later, widespread use of DDT sent other researchers to find out what effect it was having, and their negative findings are largely responsible for the fact that still other researchers are now laboring to find new means of controlling insects. Similarly, the invention of the computer has opened major R&D areas. Not only are researchers working on more sophisticated computers and uses for computers, but the computer itself has become a major research tool. Perhaps the single most dramatic example, however, is the airplane. Today close to $4 billion a year is being spent in the U.S. on aerospace R&D, yet the original "R&D" cost of getting the Wright brothers plane off the ground was just a few thousand dollars. In the 1920's a prototype aircraft could be researched and developed for about $10,000, in the 1930's the average jumped to the $600,000 level, in the 1940's it hit several million for each new kind of plane, and by the mid-Fifties it cost between $10 million and $20 million. The R&D costs on the supersonic transport had been estimated $1.4 billion—before Congress decided to stop running up that tab. One can go to virtually any pile of research reports, whether they be in theoretical physics or political science, and find one thing that most of them have in common: the suggestion at the conclusion that the findings presented indicate the need for more research. While one of the reasons for such suggestions may well be the self-justifying and self-perpetuating effort to attract more grants and contracts, "more research" is a reasonable conclusion in most cases.

As its volume and areas of interest grew, so too did the cost of R&D. Research is a multibillion-dollar industry that has moved a long way from the inventor tinkering in his basement or the un-supported university physicist. Inflation has had a lot to do with the increase, but so has the complexity of the work and the amount needed to support the researcher in terms of staff and equipment, such as computers and electron microscopes. In 1963 the average cost per R&D scientist working in space research was $54,400 per year; that rose to $62,000 per year in 1966 and is now estimated to be in excess of $70,000. The rising cost of research was pointed out in a staff report of the House Committee on Government Operations, which cited a particular research survey conducted in 1947 for the government at a cost of slightly over $9,000 and went on to report that a similar restudy of the same topic by the same firm in 1967 was going to cost $150,000.

The national effect of this mammoth effort has been enormous. A vaccine for German measles, the space program, freeze-dried coffee, solid-state electronics, color TV, lasers, LSD, the high-speed computer, automation schemes, the H-bomb, new breakfast cereals,

Xerography and war contingency plans are just a few of the spectacular explosion of end products that have resulted from post-World War II R&D. Along with this very large and very mixed bag of products and discoveries an empire has emerged. New jobs, unprecedented financial support for colleges and universities, boosts to regional economies, and—most dramatic—thousands and thousands of new firms and institutions testify to its permanent and growing status.

3. Surveying the Empire

> There is a place outside of time and space, although its influence on people's lives is very great. The name of that place is Expertland, the residents are called Experts, and they speak a language known as Expertese. The inhabitants are multiplying rapidly and spreading far beyond their original borders. It appears possible that they may eventually occupy all the world.
>
> —From Robert Sommer, Expertland

The largest class of R&D institutions is that of private companies, both independent and attached to larger companies. Their growth in the "technically rich" metropolitan areas of the nation has been astonishing. The Washington, D.C., area is a good case in point. In 1950 there were forty-eight private R&D and scientific firms in the area, by 1956 there were 107, and in 1967 there were 339 firms with 44,445 employees and a payroll of $360 million a year. Then between 1967 and 1969 the total number more than doubled once again. By November 1969 there were just about 700 firms with an annual payroll of $585 million. And there is no end in sight, because at the 1969 annual meeting of the Metropolitan Washington Board of Trade it was predicted by a member of that group's Science Industry Committee that by 1975 there would be 1,500 firms with a total annual payroll of over a billion dollars.

As impressive as these figures are, one needs to ride some of the suburban Washington highways to become aware of what they mean. R&D firms are popping up everywhere with housing tracts and shopping centers to support them. Not too long ago Washington was known as a "one company" town, but that image is quickly disappearing as these new firms appear with such names as Exotech, Entron, TRACOR, Versitron, Universal Dynamics, Vertex, Geonautics, General Kinetics, Cosmic, Dynalectron, Tele-Signal, Galaxy, Systematics, and hundreds more all connoting high technology.

Rounding out the R&D profile of the area are universities such as American University, George Washington University, and the University of Maryland, which have been well stocked with research money; a corps of individuals who serve in the R&D force as consultants and independent researchers; at least half a dozen personnel agencies specializing in the placement of R&D workers; and forty government research laboratories in the area with a total employment of close to 50,000.

The R&D boom around Washington and other major metropolitan areas offers testimony that bright young men can get into the business on a shoestring and get their enterprises moving with little more than some hustle and an insight into what kind of R&D the government and big companies are supporting. Indeed, this ease of entry is the subject of a publication of the U.S. Small Business Administration called *Small Business and Government Research and Development.* This handbook for the space-age Horatio Alger tells you how to get a firm started, how to get your first contract, and how to keep getting contracts. With unbureaucratic candor it starts by noting how informally and easily such firms are begun and how one goes about cultivating contacts. It starts by telling us: "The research-oriented firm is usually started by one man who is technically trained—generally as an engineer, physicist or chemist—or who is a specialist as the result of his experience." And it goes on to stress, point-blank, the most important element in landing the first big contract: "Continuous personal contact with the staff of contracting agencies is also a means of keeping informed about Government R&D contracts. The importance of such contacts is illustrated by a comment sometimes voiced that 'you are already out of the running if you first learn of a possible contract through a proposal request.' As in other aspects of business life, personal contacts are important." All of this vocational straight talk is backed up by a section entitled "Case Histories" in which four nameless one- and two-man operations emerge as major companies as a result of federal R&D contracts. Similar case histories abound in each major R&D industry area. For example, Flow Laboratories Inc. of Rockville, Maryland, began in 1962 when its founder got a $3,000 contract from the National Institutes of Health; seven years later the firm employed 300 and had sales of over $4 million per year. The Merle Thomas Corporation got started when Merle Thomas, a professor at George Washington University in Washington, was urged to bid on a contract to analyze data from satellites. He got that contract and shortly thereafter landed a $500,000 Navy research contract. The company and its 175 employees now offer a number of R&D services, from scientific consulting to something they call "statistical engineering."

While the Washington area serves as a good example it is not unique. In suburban Boston over 300 R&D firms have appeared along Route 128 alone. There are scores more in Cambridge and downtown Boston and many more are starting to crop up along the recently completed Route 495, which the area Chamber of Commerce has already dubbed the "platinum pike." Just as much of the growth in Washington can be attributed to nearby federal agencies, much of Boston's boom can be traced to the concentration of projects and brains at Harvard and the Massachusetts Institute of Technology. The massed technological know-how in the area recently led to the *Boston* magazine's claim that each morning between 7:30 and 9:00 the automobiles on Route 128 contain nearly one quarter of the electronics brain power in the nation. California is the leading state in the nation in R&D with its largest concentration in the suburbs of San Francisco and in the so-called "aerospace alley" that runs along the coast through Los Angeles to San Diego. In its last regional survey of R&D, the National Science Foundation found that almost 40 percent of all federal research money going to industry ended up in California. The New York City area is considered to be the largest single metropolitan center for R&D, with pockets of research institutions dotting the city itself as well as locations in suburban New Jersey, Connecticut, Long Island, and Westchester County.

In the 1950's and early 1960's it was said that the R&D industry was like a giant seesaw with all the weight on either coast. While

16

there is still some truth to this image, additional weight has since been placed in locations like Dallas, Chicago, Denver, Houston, Phoenix, Milwaukee, St. Louis, and Boulder. As an industry it is an attractive one for an area; in the parlance of regional developers, it scores high on the "three B's"—bucks, brains, and beauty—and rates well on the accompanying "three S's" of beauty: sight, sound, and smell. To be more specific, jobs, positive economic and cultural impact, handsome buildings with less pollution than most industries, prestige and new affiliations for local universities (including subcontracts, consulting jobs, and part-time teachers) are just some of the attractions that drive regions to solicit R&D firms—a trend that can be verified by scanning the "regional advertising" placed by development commissions in magazines and journals serving the R&D industry.

Even though the industry is actively sought as a stable element in a region, it is not immune to periodic setbacks as the nation's priorities change. A rapid build-up of space-related R&D in the "space crescent"—the arc extending from Cape Kennedy to Houston—was later followed by a quick slowdown when most of the research for the Apollo program had been completed. Employment related to the manned space program went from a peak of 300,000 in 1966 to 118,500 at the time of the Apollo 11 launch, with most of the reduction being made in the R&D force. Because of the versatile nature of R&D firms, however, such setbacks are not always as drastic as they might seem. Unlike other types of companies, an R&D firm can reprogram its computer, hire a few new specialists, change its name from ABC Space Systems to ABC Ocean Sciences or ABC Educational Development, and be back in business. Anyone scanning the notices of the Securities and Exchange Commission, where such changes are noted, will detect that quite a few firms have dropped "space" or a word relating to space or the military from their titles in the last few years and replaced it with the name of a specialty with greater financial promise or a more general name. Of course, new needs are not just met by changes in the emphasis of existing outfits. For every new shift or, for that matter, anticipated or hoped-for new shift in technological emphasis, new organizations are established to serve it. In the Washington, D.C., area, for example, recent cutbacks in defense and space research have been accompanied by a push in such areas as computer applications, medical and biosciences, "health delivery," urban problem-solving, and environmental research—all areas that entrepreneurs are willing to bank on as having future payoffs. To cite one older example, President Johnson's War on Poverty created a small "poverty industry" in the nation. In the Washington area alone over 100 companies specialized in some form of research, study, analysis, or evaluation of the poor and the various programs in the antipoverty field. Even today with poverty programs not that well funded, the Office of Economic Opportunity in 1971 has requested a budget of $78.8 million for R&D. Looking ahead, serious proposals for a National Oceanographic Agency, or "wet NASA," to conduct a multibillion-dollar program of undersea exploration have many of these firms at work establishing competence in one or more areas of marine research.

As an industry, one of R&D's main characteristics is its vagueness. Unlike most other multibillion-dollar industries—steel, automobiles, construction, or aircraft—R&D is difficult to pin down. While Detroit can say how many cars it produced in a year and the petroleum industry can cite barrels pumped, the results of any year's R&D are hard to evaluate. The only reasonable barometer is to say how much money was spent—a quantitative gauge for a qualitative activity—and even that takes years to determine exactly. Similarly, while everybody knows how many automobile manufacturers there are or can quickly find how many oil companies exist, nobody can say for sure how many R&D firms there are. Outfits constantly form, fold, merge, are acquired or are spun off from larger firms. For example, the Control Data Corporation has picked up at least four smaller firms in the Washington area in the last few years even as employees of this same company have created their own firms. Sometimes, when research leads to a product idea that is so good the researchers want to produce it, an R&D firm ceases its research and becomes a production company. This transformation is quite common in computer and plastics research. In short, it can be said that this is a unique industry in which the number, variety, and direction of its institutions are always in flux. As an official of a West Coast research firm said, when asked how many R&D outfits were in his state, "Trying to count the number of R&D firms in California would be about as hard as counting the number of birds."

The most recent well-researched attempt to come up with an estimate was arrived at by the National Science Foundation, which in 1969 determined that there were 11,355 R&D companies in the nation in 1967. Leveling off of research funding probably makes the estimate still fairly accurate.

Just as the number of R&D companies has grown considerably in the last decade, there has also been a boom in the world of university and other nonprofit research centers and institutes. A good barometer of this growth is the number of entries placed in the *Research Center Directory*, a publication of the Gale Research Company of Detroit, which lists nonprofit permanent research centers in the U.S. and Canada. In 1965 it listed slightly more than 3,200 of them, the 1968 total was 4,508, and in the November 1969 supplement the total had gone up to 5,329.

Most of the centers listed in the directory are affiliated with universities, and a glance through the heavy volume reveals that most major universities have in their midst at least a dozen such affiliated outfits (almost always called centers or institutes). These nonprofit centers range from small, esoteric operations manned by two or three Ph.D.s to large, multifaceted research factories employing hundreds or, in rare cases, thousands, such as MIT's Lincoln Laboratory. The work they do can be directed to very specific areas of interest or can be in the general business of problem-solving for a fee. In the former category, for example, is the University of South Florida with such operations as the Institute for Studies of Leisure and the Institute on Aging. The former looks at various aspects of leisure in America, such as the sociology of dog and horse tracks or the impact of leisure time on politics; the latter explores various aspects of gerontology, including the effects of retirement villages on their inhabitants. Elsewhere there are institutes devoted to such specialties as animal noise, religious communications, magnets, soybeans, the impact of computers on privacy, ESP, and electronic music. Any one university offers a wide range of specific subject areas for its research arm. At the University of Maryland the roster includes the Computer Science Center, the Institute for Fluid Dynamics and Applied Mathematics, the Institute for Molecular Physics, the Natural Resources Institute, the Child Study Institute, and the Bureau of Governmental Research.

While the Gale directory lists permanent research groups, there is no national accounting of the temporary research and study groups constantly emerging, but the national total must be huge. According

19

to a Library of Congress study, the legislative and executive branches of the federal government created 132 new study groups and commissions between 1965 and 1969, ranging from the President's Task Force on Telecommunications to the National Advisory Committee on Libraries. Within a few weeks of taking office, President Nixon had added ten new study commissions to the 169 already in operation solely to assist the President. In one banner week in June 1970 Mr. Nixon created five new study commissions, ranging from one on campus unrest to one on the supply of plywood and softwood, which brought the total that he had created to over forty. In addition, there are uncatalogued scores of commissions, study panels and the like advising federal agencies, state governments, cities, and trade groups.

Counting all the private companies, research centers associated with colleges and universities, government laboratories, commissions and research adjuncts to major companies, a conservative estimate is that there are at least 17,000 research entities in the United States. Among these, the relative degree and types of power each possesses is obviously highly varied. The company researching new consumer products or the institute studying animal noise has a distinctly limited kind of power. So too do the R&D firms with missions to carry out specific improvements in, say, rocket fuels. Astronomical research centers make significant contributions, but these are seldom earthshaking for the generations now living. Basic research groups have a certain degree of power but primarily in terms of the long-term future when their discoveries will have an impact. But there is one class of institution that, because of the role it plays in this vast R&D empire, can be considered the most powerful sector of the whole enterprise: think tanks, which perform research on matters relating to policy and the application of technology.

III

THINK TANKS

---

1. For the Want of a Horse . . .

Technology and experience have now reached the point where it is possible to design and construct craft which can penetrate the atmosphere and achieve sufficient velocity to become satellites of the earth. . . . In making the decision as to whether or not to undertake construction of such a craft now, it is not inappropriate to view our present situation as similar to that in airplanes prior to the flight of the Wright brothers. . . . Though the crystal ball is cloudy, two things seem clear: 1. a satellite vehicle with appropriate instrumentation can be expected to be one of the most potent scientific tools of the Twentieth Century. 2. The achievement of a satellite craft by the United States would inflame the imagination of mankind, and would probably produce repercussions in the world comparable to the explosion of the atomic bomb.

—Excerpts from *Preliminary Design of an Experimental World-Circling Spaceship.* Issued by the RAND Corporation, May 2, 1946.

Throughout the British Army in the early days of World War II, one of every six men manning the standard gun crew had nothing whatever to do. This bit of information came to light when a team of civilian researchers was dispatched into the field to look at and suggest improvements for military operations. One of their first tasks was to examine the gun crew. In short order they detected that one man had precisely no visible function. Inquiring as to his role, they were told that he was there to handle the horses. Horses? But there were no horses! Well, perhaps not, but there surely had been horses: the ones that drew cannon for British troops in the days up into World War I.

The discovery in fact brought about the end of a horseman in the British gun crew, but more important this nonheroic little war story was told and retold in military circles throughout the Western world and is, in fact, still told today because it explains the genesis of a new discipline within R&D that retains its original title: operations research. The story also serves to begin the explanation of why a unique group of institutions began, grew, and flourished in postwar America.

From its modest beginnings, operations research was quickly developed in Great Britain and the United States during the war as a formalized scheme for applying quantitative analysis to military operations. It was based on the concept that complicated systems involving men and machines operating in a given environment exhibit relatively stable characteristics. The volume of traffic crossing a city bridge, for example, during a given hour of a given day of the week usually experiences only minor variations from week to week just as, in a military example, the average percentage of depth charges which were dropped by Allied navies that hit German submarines was relatively stable from month to month. Once such quantifiable situations are identified, the principles of operations research come into play. Classically, there are three stages in operations research. First, the behavior of the system is carefully described, then the behavior is analyzed by constructing models or theories of operations which, finally, are used to predict the effects on the system that would result if it were changed or modified. In one simple but classic wartime application it was found through statistical analysis of submarine "kills" by depth charge that by slightly altering the depth at which the explosion occurred, the chance of nailing a submarine was greatly improved.

In the United States, during the war a corps of civilians—mostly scientists and engineers—was mobilized to fight on the technological front. On relatively short notice this group had developed such specific items as the atomic bomb, radar, and the proximity fuse. Also they had developed and refined the new analytical technique of operations research that had been successfully employed to increase the effectiveness of air defense, bombing, and naval operations. At the end of the war, when this corps was starting to break up, the military decided it wanted to retain some of the gifted personnel permanently to develop military technology in the years ahead, and, more specifically, it wanted to continue to nurture operations research. With this end in mind, in late 1945 General H. H. "Hap" Arnold, Commanding General of the Army Air Forces, suggested and got approval for an arrangement between the Douglas Aircraft Company and the Air Force that would create a unique experimental institution to be called Project RAND. The acronym was for Research ANd Development originally, but as things got moving it became apparent that it was almost entirely a research outfit, so it has been suggested, not altogether puckishly, that it more aptly stood for Research And No Development. Project RAND was set up as a department of Douglas under an initial $10 million contract.

It got moving in 1946 with the stated mission of conducting ". . . a program of study and research on the broad subject of intercontinental warfare other than surface," which would include recommendations of "preferred techniques and instrumentalities" to the Air Force. The Project RAND staff was immediately given the task of looking into new and unexplored areas for the military. Its first major work was a study entitled *Preliminary Design of an Experimental World-Circling Spaceship*. Although satellites were then considered to be mainly the province of science-fiction writers, the 1946 document was a detailed appraisal of the possibilities of scientific satellites and space exploration prepared by a team of fifty analysts. Because the study was remarkably prophetic it later brought considerable prestige to RAND. The findings of that report laid the groundwork for further study which prepared the United States for its unmanned ventures into space. (RAND's space studies have been prophetic on more than one level. Guessing in mid-1957 as to when Sputnik I would be launched, it missed the exact day by two weeks.) Other early RAND studies covered such pioneering areas as the use of rocket engines for strategic weapons (missiles), nuclear propulsion, the theory of games

23

as it applies to warfare, new concepts in air defense, new aircraft design, metal fatigue, and high-energy radiation. One early operations research analysis of the range of aircraft and how that range could be improved led to the Air Force's adoption of inflight refueling for military aircraft. Another early RAND study led to the production of considerable quantities of the metallic element titanium, thereby promoting widespread use of the element in aviation and space and the creation of a whole new metallurgical industry. Within its first year RAND began adding political scientists, economists, and psychologists to its staff so that its thinking would not be limited just to the physical sciences.

By 1948 pressure was growing to separate RAND from the Douglas Company. According to J. R. Goldstein, one of the founders of Project RAND and now a RAND vice president, a variety of factors were building as "causes for divorce." Other defense contractors objected to the fact that the planning arm of the Army Air Force was attached to one of its competitors. Douglas, on the other hand, believed that because of RAND the Air Force was bending over so far backward not to put Douglas in a preferred position that the company would, in fact, suffer by losing contracts. There was also some chafing between Douglas and its Project RAND employees. Although RAND was virtually sealed off from the parent company for reasons of security, RAND employees had to obey Douglas' rules and regulations, which extended all the way down to where and when one could drink coffee. Such rules were a constant source of irritation for the Project's thinkers. Fortunately, the Air Force was satisfied by the two-year-old project and was ready to let it stand on its own feet. Money was raised—including a crucial $100,000 and strong backing from the then nascent Ford Foundation—and the RAND Corporation emerged as a nonprofit independent enterprise in 1948. According to its Articles of Incorporation, it was formed "To further and promote scientific, educational and charitable purposes, all for the public welfare and security of the United States of America."

As the RAND Corporation grew, it became apparent to its sponsors that the experiment had worked. Not only was part of that corps of wartime scientific talent held together, but it was providing the military with a certain caliber and kind of thinking that it felt it could not buy elsewhere. It offered long-range thinking on a broad variety of matters not available in the regular halls and chambers of government whose operatives gear their thinking to day-to-day needs and emergencies. So, too, it was judged that an entity like RAND was more convenient and manageable than a university center, where such difficulties as maintaining security and bridging strongly maintained departmental lines to put together large teams of interdisciplinary researchers presented all too many problems.

Now over twenty years old, RAND has grown to a staff of over a thousand and is currently receiving about $30 million a year to think for its many sponsors, among whom the Air Force is still the largest. Its lifetime product has been about 11,000 reports and incalculable consultations, briefings, and meetings.

RAND is also the most famous and one of the most important in that elite group of American R&D institutions known as think tanks. There were entities that could justifiably be termed think tanks in existence before RAND (such as the Franklin Institute of Philadelphia or Arthur D. Little Inc. of Cambridge) but it was not until RAND's arrival on the postwar scene that the movement really got rolling. RAND became the pre-eminent model for scores of organizations devoted to modern policy-making and the brokerage of technology.

2. Paper Prophets

> *As custodians of a rare and precious national commodity—brains—the Think Tanks have a serious responsibility to see that this commodity is used wisely and productively in coping with some of the most important problems of our nation and society.*
>
> —General Maxwell D. Taylor, from a paper entitled "Case Study of a 'Think Tank.'" The Institute for Defense Analyses (November 1968)

Ron Batiste is a tall, lanky black man who claims that a stint in Las Vegas as a reporter immunized him from being taken aback by great concentrations of wealth and symbols of affluence. Yet not too long ago when he went to work for the System Development Corporation, a large think tank in Santa Monica, California, as a public-relations man, he found he was still not prepared.

"When I first got here, I really couldn't get over the fact that this place did sixty million dollars a year in business, but you could put all that we produced in a year—and I mean all of it—on this table," he says, pointing down to the small luncheonette-sized table from which he is drinking coffee. He adds, "Even Vegas didn't get me ready for that." His reaction is not typical only of newcomers to think tanks; veterans as well are struck by the preposterously high value of their paper. Holding up a single elongated sheet of paper, Herman Kahn—head of the Hudson Institute and probably the most famous man in the think-tank field today—giggles and says, "See this? It's worth three million dollars."

"Paper alchemy" is the term that is used (most often waggishly but nonetheless accurately) to describe the phenomenon. It is this production of valuable paper that links all the diverse institutions known as think tanks. They produce few tangible goods other than paper. Their major product is thought research usually reduced to written reports or studies that are policy alternatives, evaluations, designs, theories, suggestions, warnings, long-range plans, statistics, predictions, descriptions of techniques, tests, analyses or, simply, new ideas. What is not reduced to paper is usually presented orally in a lecture, briefing or informal conversation. When a new product, such as a serum or a piece of equipment, emerges from a think tank, it is only the original offered for copy, production, and distribution by others. One of the tangible innovations that has come from the RAND Corporation, for example, is an item known in the computer industry as "the RAND tablet." It is an electronic plate or "tablet" on which one can communicate graphs, diagrams and notes to a computer by jotting them down with a stylus. Although invented by RAND, the tablet is not produced by RAND.

Though most people agree that think tanks "think," produce paper and do not produce products in the normal sense of the word, the term "think tank" is ill-defined, subjective, and debated. First employed as a nickname for the brain along with "think box" in the 1940's, according to several slang dictionaries it took on a new meaning in the early 1960's when it first appeared in magazines and newspapers as a description for RAND and other similar civilian military research groups. The term seems to have had genuine popular appeal as a description for a variety of activities generally regarded as constructive. In early 1969, for example, when Senator Edmund Muskie was talking about readying himself for the Presidency he talked of creating two special staffs which he called "think tanks" that would advise him on international and domestic issues. A 1969 story in the Washington *Star* about a weekend session where young people met to discuss important issues was billed as a think tank. The term is often used to describe all R&D firms, as both *Forbes* and the Washington *Post* have done in articles on the R&D industry. On the other hand, there are those who use the term quite specifically. In government circles, for example, it is used to describe only a handful of federally sponsored institutions, such as RAND. While such periodicals as *Barron's*, *Newsweek*, and *Business Week* use the term to describe a wide variety of institutions, others like *The Economist* and the *Wall Street Journal* use it sparingly. With this multiplicity of definitions in mind, it comes as no surprise that estimates as to their number range from forty (as reported in *The Economist*) to 400 (a 1967 New York *Times* estimate) to "thousands" (from the Washington *Post*).

To further confuse the problem of definition, most groups that are think tanks don't like the term, while, in contrast, pretentious little research groups often invoke the term to look important. In the case of the big think tanks the term is considered limiting and confusing, perhaps even demeaning. Among the most common criticisms leveled: (A) It sounds too passive or, as it is often put, "ivorytowerish." (B) It connotes nonaccomplishment—that is, it makes one think of a place where thinking is an end in itself with little impact on policy and events. (C) It produces confusion as to the goal of the outfit. At RAND, for example, one of its public-affairs men says, "Hardly a day goes by without a letter coming in from someone asking us to think about something for them. For some reason the term makes a lot of people think we're sort of an institutional 'Dear Abby.'"

Since the term is so vague, an operational definition that makes a clear distinction between what is and what is not a think tank is in order before the detailed exploration that follows. How then does one differentiate a think tank from other R&D organizations?

First, there is no set pattern of financial objectives or affiliation. A think tank can be for profit or nonprofit; supported by the government, part of the government, completely free of the government or supported by a number of institutions including the government; or independent or tied to a larger company or university. A think tank must, however, be a permanent entity as opposed to a study commission or special group with a temporary assignment.

The crucial determinant is its role. The primary function of a think tank as the term is used here is neither traditional basic research, applied research, or development—although all three are commonly performed in think tanks—but to act as a bridge between knowledge and power and between science/technology and policy-making in areas of broad interest. They are closer to being agents of new knowledge and discovery than creators of new knowledge. As a RAND official explains the role of his corporation, "We are something like middlemen who find, assemble and interpret knowledge for its ultimate consumers, who, in our case, are mostly the government." A currently popular term for this role is "policy research" or research that produces ideas, analysis, and alternatives relevant to people who make policy. It contrasts to traditional science and R&D, which normally produce scientific knowledge for other scientists and researchers.

Finally, a think tank has several general characteristics that, taken together, help to set it apart. It is oriented to scientific methodologies, such as operations research, but is by no means limited to scientific issues. Because of the nature of the problems it faces and the techniques it employs, a think tank is invariably multidisciplinary—that is, it is seldom limited to professionals from one field while working on any given project and will almost always use a team of experts from a number of fields on large long-range projects. Although it has strong links to the scientific and technical communities, it also has strategic ties to the outside world whether it be the government, industry, or, in some cases, the public. Generally, a think tank has a relatively large degree of freedom in both defining the problem it is attacking and in making formulations and recommendations. To give a specific example, a think tank would seldom be called upon to design an improvement in radar for the military but would be called upon to look at military technology in the next decade and offer ideas including some on possible new developments in radar technology or, to continue the example, to determine the need for a new type

28

of radar, where radar installations should be located, how to operate radar for maximum efficiency, how to use radar in decision-making, and how to train men to use it. A think tank would thus be more interested in "radar policy" than in the actual equipment. Generally, then, think tanks are concerned with a variety of broad areas—as in RAND's case, from weapons systems to poverty policy—or in the broadest aspect of a single area such as naval operations in the case of the Center for Naval Analysis, a private think tank serving the U.S. Navy. Because of their broad mandates and their access to policy-makers, a final characteristic of think tanks is that they are pacesetters for much of the rest of the research world. Think tanks are more likely to help change goals and directions that are quite likely, in turn, to dictate the research orders given to other R&D entities.

To summarize this broad and subjective definition, the best general yardstick for separating a think tank from other R&D outfits is the size of its mission and mandate and the people it serves. A cancer research center, a large firm designing electronic equipment or an astronomical observatory are all R&D entities but none is a think tank. On the other hand, a group that is doing research for the government on educational policy for the future, a firm that is advising industry or government on new scientific techniques or a group of scholars who have institutionalized themselves to study the future of technology or democracy are all think tanks. Two distinctly different kinds of think tanks are both researching problems of the environment: the recently established Walden Research Corporation of Cambridge, Massachusetts, and the Overview Corporation of Washington, D.C. The first offers to government and industry a variety of services in the field of pollution research, including community air-quality planning, pollution prediction, economic evaluations of pollution problems and solutions, meteorological modeling, and consulting on the problems of pollution. Overview, in contrast, is a group headed by former Secretary of the Interior Stewart L. Udall and was organized to work and consult with those in power in a range of fields relating to environment in the broadest sense including urban design, pollution abatement, new towns, regional planning, wilderness preservation, housing renewal, and transportation planning. Though relatively narrow, the scope of what these two organizations are attempting to do sets them apart from a firm designing new filtration devices for cleaning water or a university center working to discover the exact chemical reactions present in smog, both of which are simply R&D groups.

According to this broad definition, out of the thousands of research groups in the United States about 600 qualify as think tanks. The general classes of think tanks may be categorized as follows:

Approximately seventy-five think tanks attached to the federal government by annual contract. Officially termed "Federal Contract Research Centers," they are contracted-for adjuncts to agencies of the government. Most of them have been created by either the executive or legislative branches. RAND, the Office of Education's Center for the Study of Advanced Educational Administration, and NASA's Bellcomm Inc. are examples. As one Defense Department official suggests, "They are continuous, close relationships not unlike those that film stars have with their analysts."

A dozen or so think tanks within the government created for long-range planning and studies of future alternatives. The Army's Institute for Land Combat and the White House Goals Research Staff are two of them.

Leading independent or university-affiliated nonprofit institutions and organizations devoted broadly to the natural and social sciences. About 200 of the more than 5,000 nonprofit research groups would qualify. The Stanford Research Institute, the Hudson Institute, the Battelle Memorial Institute, and the Research Triangle Corporation are prominent examples.

Approximately 300 profit-making firms that consult, study, conduct surveys, make recommendations, perform applied research, and, generally, think for a fee. They are reminiscent of the *condottieri* bands of medieval Italy who offered skilled soldiers to the highest bidder. These twentieth-century outfits offer teams of "brains" in much the same way. The Planning Research Corporation, Arthur D. Little Inc., the System Development Corporation, General Electric's TEMPO group, and Operations Research Inc. exemplify this group.

Finally, there is a handful of truly independent, nonprofit, self-determining think tanks that exist to explore a single subject or point of view. Their clients are their "publics," and rather than take support and direction from industry or government they rely on themselves and their mostly private supporters, including individuals and foundations. Among these are the Center for the Study of Democratic Institutions, the Brookings Institution, the Institute for Policy

Studies, and the Center for the Study of Responsive Law.

Today, think tanks represent a wide variety of institutionalized thought. The phenomenon has grown quickly and in all directions. It seems that almost every conceivable interest group in the nation has or has had at least one think tank working for it. Politically, for example, there are think tanks ranging from conservative groups, such as Stanford's Hoover Institution on War, Revolution and Peace and Georgetown's Center for Strategic and International Studies, to Washington's Institute for Policy Studies or Boston's Cambridge Institute, both well to the left of center. While most think tanks owe their survival to federal support, others, such as Robert Hutchins' Center for the Study of Democratic Institutions, refuse federal money as a matter of principle.

Just as their individual diversity is great, so is the diversity of things they do. Nuclear contingency plans, development schemes for emerging nations, new ideas for preventing and fighting crime, plans for revamping the nation's schools, new mixes of strategic weapons, stinging rebukes to federal agencies, and nuclear safeguards are some of their paper products. Moreover, they are not restricted to major issue-oriented projects but contribute to the commonplace as well— HoJo Cola, the Lark filter, much of the design of Expo 67, a list of considerations for the location of Disneyland, certain aromas and flavors, freeze-dried foods, and those computer-readable letters and numbers that appear on everybody's checks are all results of think-tank research.

The approach to problem-solving that created the think-tank explosion in the 1950's and 1960's is still very much with us. It would seem that every time a problem is recognized or a need is felt, somebody in government, industry or a university starts thinking about incorporating an intellectual center to deal with that problem or need. As soon as the Office of Economic Opportunity got on its feet, it created the Institute for Research on Poverty, just as the Office of Education started creating think tanks for educational research in the early 1960's when the push was on to improve the quality of American education. Some of the most important think-tank proposals now being considered or which are in the process of being created include:

CALRAND: A proposal advanced by Jesse Unruh and other California legislators for an organization to tackle a variety of governmental problems for their state. A consultant's study of the idea has been completed, and Unruh says that the concept " . . . holds great promise for California government and for government in other states." Currently the RAND Corporation is working for the state of California on several contracts and hopes they will lead to the creation of a think tank for the state. Meanwhile, New York City has established a think tank in cooperation with RAND called the New York–RAND Institute, which went into operation in April 1969. Other cities and states are considering the formation of think tanks for working on their particular problems.

Regional Pollution Research Centers: One of several current proposals for environmental think tanks, this idea was recently suggested to the White House by leaders of thirty universities. The concept calls for the establishment of three or four regional centers to study the social, legal, and engineering aspects of all forms of pollution. Other proposals range from that of a Congressional push to establish a series of university-based Water Resources Research Institutes to a strongly supported resolution from Washington Senator Warren Magnuson to establish a World Environmental Institute, which, as he puts it, would serve ". . . to aid all the nations of the world in solving their common environmental problems of both national and international scope."

Congressional Science Policy Advisory Group: Among others, the Science Policy Research Division of the Library of Congress has recommended in its report "Technical Information for Congress" that a research and advisory organization be formed to alert Congress to potential hazards involved in new technology and to spot promising areas that need additional Congressional attention. This is one of the latest of several suggestions and formal proposals that have been made to set up some form of science policy think tank for Congress. The most intriguing idea for such a group was suggested in March 1969 by Jerome B. Wiesner, former science adviser to President Kennedy and now president of MIT. During Senate hearings centering on technology and Congress, Wiesner suggested that Congress needed to set up a sophisticated group to analyze military proposals. He dubbed it "anti-RAND" because it would serve as a counterbalance to the sophisticated analysis and support the military gets through its think tanks, such as RAND.

The Office of Goals and Priorities Analysis: An idea supported by various members of Congress calls for setting up an independent think tank to provide Congress with detailed data and analysis on national goals, resources, and priorities. A bill to create this organization was introduced in the Senate in December 1969. It is one of several proposals for groups that would think about national priorities.

The Inter-American Social Development Institute: Authorized by Congress in late 1969, this outfit will exist as a semiautonomous corporation of the State Department. It will act as a special center to encourage development of democratic institutions in South America. It is charged with the job of undertaking broad research and planning work in South American affairs.

An East-West Think Tank: Soviet and American representatives have been holding discussions on the establishment of a large, internationally staffed think tank to study the common problems of industrialized societies. The nucleus of the group would be about 400 professionals who would concentrate on such universal problems as pollution, housing, education, and mass transportation. Deliberations on the idea have been going on privately since 1966 and were revealed in late 1969 in *Science* magazine. The prime U.S. negotiator for the organization has been McGeorge Bundy, president of the Ford Foundation, while Herman Gvishiani, vice-chairman of the Soviet State Committee for Science and Technology, has led the negotiators from the U.S.S.R.

National Institute of Education: A 1970 announcement from President Nixon called for an entity financed at $40 to $50 million annually to tie together research and recommendations in the field of education. In May 1970 the RAND Corporation was contracted with to study the idea and propose how to implement it.

In addition to these and dozens of other governmental ideas there are countless private ideas afoot. The Washington-based Institute for Policy Studies is attempting to start satellite think tanks around the nation and was recently instrumental in setting up a first, the Cambridge Institute. Others are operating in Berkeley and Atlanta. General Electric's TEMPO, one of the few think tanks attached to a private corporation, is in the process of setting up similar think tanks jointly with groups in Japan and England. Several universities—the University of California at Irvine and Brown University, among them—are planning policy research groups.

The urge to create think tanks seems to be gaining ground in other nations as well. Some are established and others are on their way. In early 1970 the Prime Minister of Canada was given a proposal by a study group led by Ronald S. Ritchie of Imperial Oil Limited for a public policy research institution to serve the government. Similarly, the Prime Minister of Israel is considering a RAND-like entity for her country formally proposed under the title of the Israeli Institute for Policy Analysis. In addition, there are reports of new think tanks in the works in Norway, Denmark, Japan, Germany, and France.

The last few years have seen the creation of scores of many quite unique think tanks such as the Institute for the Future, the first major "futurist" think tank; the Urban Institute, the first interagency think tank working for the Government; the Stockholm International Peace Research Institute, one of the earliest institutional attempts to research peace; the New York–RAND Institute, the first think tank in the service solely of a city; Ralph Nader's Center for the Study of Responsive Law, the first consumer think tank; the Institute of the Black World, the first black think tank; UNITAR (for the United Nations Institute for Training and Research), the UN's recent start to create an international think tank; and CARA (the Center for Applied Research in the Apostolate), a recently established independent group that does policy research for entities within the Catholic Church.

The growing number, strength, and diversity of think tanks, coupled with the gargantuan commitment to R&D, raise important issues for the nation. First, what is this mammoth research effort buying for the future—and in what order? Second, how good is the quality of thought developed by R&D? These questions apply to both the think tanks and the whole research empire to which they belong. These two questions are most dramatic and relevant when addressed at the federal level, for it is here that they relate most directly to the direction and quality of life throughout the nation. Furthermore, R&D on the federal level is most open to challenge simply because it is paid for by and supposedly geared to the needs of all the nation's inhabitants. Finally, there is a third question that must be scrutinized: How much power is held by these diverse think tanks that sit atop the R&D empire—and what are the perils of ceding them that power?

34

I V

THE STATE OF THE EMPIRE

---

1. Priorities

> *. . . the time is upon us for a reordering of national priorities.*
>
> —The National Commission on the Causes and Prevention of Violence

Cancer, it is estimated, will kill a quarter of the 200-odd million Americans now living. One million have it now, and the latest statistics indicate that it presently claims 900 people a day. There is little question that the cure for this disease must ultimately come from the research laboratory; yet the amount spent for cancer research in fiscal year 1970 was only $173 million, which is about one-twentieth of the space research budget for the same year and about one-fiftieth of the amount spent for military research. In fact, one single unmanned 1969 NASA space experiment cost more than half the total research into cancer for the same year. Ironically, although that experiment—putting a monkey into orbit in a satellite—ran to more than $100 million and was billed as medical research. Many in the medical community pointed out that it was unnecessary because its aim of determining the effects of weightlessness of a monkey was

35

repeating, on a less relevant species, the same research that had been and was being carried out on man in the Apollo program. The low priority thus put on cancer research was probably best driven home by Dr. James T. Grace, Jr., director of the Roswell Park Memorial Institute, a leading cancer research group, in a speech before the National Cancer Society in 1970. He noted that if the fiscal 1970 budget was divided up by the number of people in the population, it would work out to a share of $964 for every man, woman, and child. Of this amount $395 goes for defense and of that $125 is spent on the Vietnamese war. In contrast, each American's share for cancer research amounts to 91 cents.

The comparative status of cancer research is just one illustration of the state of national research priorities. Despite the promises and claims to the contrary by politicians, extremely low priority is given not only to curing cancer but also to such projects as new ways to prevent narcotics abuse, to achieve peace through arms control, and to curb ever-increasing air pollution. In addition, research into such general areas as health services, housing, the problems of urban decay, saving the environment, and mass transportation are "also-rans," way down on the list. Where does it all go then? The National Science Foundation says that 85 percent of the government's R&D from 1967 through 1969 went for "national security"—that is, the amalgam of defense, nuclear, and space efforts.

In the vital area of arms control and disarmament the research budget for 1971 amounts to a mere one two-thousandth of the weapons research budget. The nation's research into the means of achieving peace amounts to little more than dabbling. Funds for research by the Arms Control and Disarmament Agency have skidded from $3.6 million in 1969 to an estimated $2.1 million in 1971. John A. Mathews, who heads a novel group advocating a Federal Department of Peace, has studied recent federal budgets for totals spent on researching peace by all parts of the government and finds it averages a paltry $2.6 million a year. Making the situation even more ludicrous are some of the contractors being paid to perform peace research: the Department of the Navy, the McDonnell-Douglas Corporation (one of the largest defense contractors), and the Army Materiel Command.

To further illustrate a seeming indifference to areas of grave social concern: Amounts going for research into the prevention of drug abuse have hovered around a million a year for the last few years, while in comparison the average research allotment for that perennial boondoggle, civil defense, has averaged over $5 million. R&D for civil defense is pumped into new designs for fallout shelters, evacuation plans and other schemes and paraphernalia that are almost totally ignored by the public, which, by contrast, is seriously concerned about the effects of narcotics on youth.

Despite all the political sound and fury being expended on pollution of the environment, the amount of money spent for air, water, and solid-waste pollution research is still less than one percent of the total federal research tab. In order for the R&D budget to inch over even the one-percent mark in the next few years there will have to be more public pressure on Congress and the Executive. After Congress appropriated $45 million for air-pollution research in the fiscal 1970 budget, the President asked for only $27 million for the fiscal 1971 budget—amounting to a cut of $18 million, accompanied by a lot of rhetoric on improving the environment. John R. Ehrenfeld, president of the Walden Research Corporation, summed up the frustration of a combatant in the war on pollution: "Who does Nixon think he's fooling? He's still spending more money on chemical warfare research than on air pollution, yet he tells us he's cutting the first and pushing the second."

With the effort of R&D focused mainly on military concerns and no strong priorities clearly established beyond that of national security, other stark comparisons and ironies are easy to find. Dr. Roger Egeberg, the government's chief adviser on health, has stated recently that the U.S. has become at best a second rate nation in health. The figures back him up: The U.S. ranks 14th in infant mortality rates in the world, 12th in maternal mortality, 11th in life expectancy for women, and 19th in life expectancy for men. Ahead of the U.S. in life expectancy are East Germany, Norway, Ireland, Japan, Bulgaria, Greece, Italy, Canada, and New Zealand. Things are as bleak in such areas as housing, urban planning, and environment, while our resources are heaped on efforts to develop antiballistic missiles, manned strategic aircraft, underwater long-range missile submarines, new destroyers, jet transports, and new spacecraft.

Dubious examples of technological "advance" and decline abound. Until a short time ago the Army was cultivating and stockpiling bubonic-plague bacilli as a weapon with the blessings of the same

Congress that, with hilarity, had voted down a measure to eradicate rats. Deadly nerve gases were being shipped with regularity on a railroad system that gets more dangerous every year—in fact, 1969 was the twelfth year in a row that train accidents went up. Western Electric, the production arm of AT&T, begins work as prime contractor on the Safeguard missile system at the same time that telephone service is rapidly deteriorating. More people have died on American highways than in all American wars combined, as Ralph Nader continually points out, usually adding, ". . . yet we spend less on highway safety research than it costs to build half a nuclear submarine." The Comptroller General has estimated that cost overruns on military weapons systems have totaled about $21 billion in the last decade, but only recently—after public disclosure of such overruns as the $2 billion extra for the C5-A jet transport—has Congress started to give the kind of careful scrutiny to military costs that it has normally reserved for research to help the poor, the blind, and the retarded.

The kind of values that these facts reflect has been a major cause of the malaise among social reformers in the late 1960's and will undoubtedly retard such nonmilitary efforts in the 1970's. At one level, concern is expressed in student outrage and upheaval over the American value system; at another, it is responsible for the common objection that begins, "If we can put men on the moon, why can't we . . ." and winds up with any one of a thousand valid purposes from curbing venereal disease to making a shoelace that can't break. Even NASA Administrator Thomas O. Paine has mentioned the irony of ". . . mankind watching two men scramble around the moon while standing knee-deep in garbage."

R&D is a particularly critical element in the battle over national priorities because it not only reflects our current priorities but largely determines what will be technologically feasible in the future. It thus has a powerful effect on the future quality of our lives and is a far better guide to the life we will lead in the decades ahead than all the rhetoric of politicians proclaiming a rosy tomorrow.

The moon landings have shown how much is possible if a great deal of thought, resources and dedication are channeled into any stated goal. The vast majority of Project Apollo money had been pumped into space R&D during the decade prior to the first landing. There is, however, a catch in invoking the Apollo/NASA example, because such new knowledge as is developed in such a program must be applied and directed in order to get anywhere. If not conscientiously applied, well-performed research can lead to a range of ends from a simple nonuse to a more insidious ruse—a way of dodging action under the guise of studying the problem. The latter device was recognized in a little-noticed suggestion in the report from the National Commission on the Causes and Prevention of Violence. It came from U.S. District Judge A. Leon Higgenbothem, who called for a national moratorium on commissions and new study units to probe the causes of racism, poverty, crime, and the urban crisis. The judge felt that there had been too much study and too little application of findings. Research and study as a substitute for action or application can be detected all over the federal landscape: millions in antipoverty money going into studies of the poor that are not being heeded, or study commissions looking into the findings of previous study commissions, and the like—a mountain of research findings being treated as an end in itself.

2. Quality

Q: Specifically, what are some of the examples of the Center's work?
A: Well, the Center staff members have resolved the conflict between teaching and research.
Q: How?
A: By doing neither.

—From *Science*, the magazine of the American Association for the Advancement of Science, in a satirical interview with a "Dr. Grant Swinger," identified as the director of Breakthrough Institute and Chairman of the Board of the Center for the Absorption of Federal Funds.

As in any other multibillion-dollar industry that offers the promise of a fast buck, hustlers, tycoons and those willing to sell their objectivity for a fat contract have been attracted into R&D along with the honest, hard-working researcher. While abuses exist throughout the R&D empire, they are again most noticeable at the federal level. Bad research is hard to control and detect. Much of it is delivered on paper in the form of a report that can be—and often is—slipped away in a filing cabinet by the bureaucrat who commissioned it. Major R&D projects that do not work out are simply canceled, though in the case of the Pentagon, for example, such a showdown can add up to quite a large sum of money wasted. During the period from 1954 to 1970, some sixty-eight major weapons projects were terminated; a total of $10.7 billion was invested in them before they failed, faltered, or were canceled.

The vast size of the federal research program and the tendency for agencies of government to be vague in describing their desires are just two of the reasons for bad research. The difficulty of just trying to wade through—let alone evaluate—the volume of paper generated by countless researchers and agencies has meant that few people in the federal government have taken a critical look at the quality of research. In some cases the role of the government goes beyond that of simply not detecting bad research to actually inspiring and rewarding it. The results in too many cases have been absurdly high expenses, producing waste, corruption, duplication, irrelevance, subjectivity, and, at the very least, lack of originality.

R&D money is being squandered in many ways, and the implications for both American science and society are serious. One of the least sinister forms of abuse is duplication, but it is no less costly than others. Bad communications, interagency rivalry, poor control, and carelessness have produced many double, triple, and quadruple efforts. The problem is so serious that the Library of Congress, the Department of Defense and the Department of Commerce are all working on computerized information retrieval systems that would help prevent the government from commissioning research that has already been done. (No one seems to have pointed out that the setting up of three antiduplication systems in itself brings up the question of duplication.)

A second widespread abuse is that of contracts and grants that are inappropriate to the mission of the sponsoring agency or are of generally dubious value. Although individually amusing and good filler material for newspaper columnists on slow days, irrelevant and absurd studies abound to an extent that it is far from amusing. The

Department of Health, Education and Welfare has commissioned and paid for things like "The Social History of French Medicine, 1789–1815"—a questionable effort in the first place and doubly so in view of that agency's constant reminder that not enough R&D money goes into such relevant areas as stroke prevention and cancer research. Of particularly dubious value was a project called "The Demography of Happiness," which cost a quarter of a million dollars and consisted of sending a team of researchers to Puerto Rico to find that wealthy people were, generally, happier than poor ones and healthy people are almost always happier than sick ones. While many, Senator George McGovern prominent among them, have pointed out that not nearly enough money is going into research and education in nutrition, two recent Department of Agriculture research contracts, together costing over $100,000, studied the history of the Canadian tobacco auction and the frayed shirt collar (its official description was ". . . to determine the effects of laundry variables on edge abrasion of durable press cotton garments"). The Space Agency has shelled out huge research sums for histories of itself and most of its divisions. Besides bringing up the question of whether history writing should be commissioned by its subject, such allocations are odd for an agency that keeps saying it does not have enough money for space flight.

In recent years the Department of Defense has emerged as the undisputed king of irrelevant research. The immense list includes studies of Northern grouse, Korean women skin divers, the nervous system of the Chilean squid, the aging process in rocks, the temperament of Italian men, "Communist Vulnerability to the Use of Music" (a study classified as *Confidential*), diarrhea in horses, psychological differences between tattooed and untattooed sailors, the economy of aborigines, witchcraft in the Congo, the role of facial expressions in communications, migratory animal studies, and—one that achieved much notoriety in Congress when it was revealed—a $600,000 contract with the University of Mississippi to determine the role that birds might play in wars. The last study called for scholars to investigate the use of chickens, crows and other birds to steer missiles, detect mines, conduct search-and-destroy missions, and other assorted tasks. The Pentagon's entry into social research and other forms of nonmilitary research has prompted Admiral Hyman G. Rickover to launch more than one verbal attack. He has labeled much of the work "a waste of taxpayers' money," has said that some of it has no conceivable military value, and has gone so far as to say that it has had an adverse effect on the nation's military posture. Testifying before the Joint Economic Committee of Congress in November 1968, he said of his fellow military men, "They are attracted to studies like mice to a granary. . . ." The irrepressible admiral added that because of the number of military studies piling up, he found himself thinking of the commission established by the Weimar Republic to find out why Germany lost World War I. "The commission found that a major cause of this defeat was the amount of paperwork required of the armed forces," said Rickover. "Toward the end they were literally buried in paper."

Even when the matter is well within the legitimate realm of military research, the Pentagon seems to find a way to generate unnecessary research, as in the case of 1969 Army contracts with two different firms to develop a bigger—just bigger, no change in design— canteen cup. These two contracts cost a total of $58,000. In too many cases large sums are paid for research on nonurgent $100 ideas.

Another common abuse was summed up by Representative Henry Reuss (D–Wis.), who, in conducting an investigation of the use of research in federal domestic programs, said, "Federal agencies have a tendency to withhold research findings critical of present performance or policies." Examples of this relatively recent form of public-opinion manipulation and censorship are common. During the Johnson Administration $650,000 worth of outside research critical of the controversial supersonic transport (SST) was suppressed by the Federal Aviation Administration by stamping it with an "Official Use Only" label. One of many cases of a similar nature uncovered by Ralph Nader and his "Raiders" appeared in their work *The Chemical Feast*, a study of food protection and the Food and Drug Administration. Nader's Raiders reported that safety studies of the food additive monosodium glutamate had been termed "confidential information" by the government and were not even available to a physician at the Albert Einstein College of Medicine who was doing research on the possible negative side effects of the additive. A percentage of the research conducted by most agencies is kept off the streets, in fact, at the Pentagon, the percentage of classified or "Official Use Only" research results is currently running to about 40 percent—some of it obviously necessary for security reasons but certainly nothing close to all of it.

In the same vein is research commissioned for little more purpose than giving support to an agency attitude or policy. This common abuse prompts interesting reactions. Says a vice-president of a major California research firm, "The government is a prime market for subjective research, and we try to guard against it. We turn down most of these jobs but occasionally feel we have to take one as a favor or else face the threat of not getting legitimate research work from that agency."

A final class of common abuses in government R&D stems from federal apathy and laxity. Robert A. Nelson, who until recently headed the Department of Transportation's research-oriented Office of High Speed Ground Transportation and who is now a Fellow at the Brookings Institution, feels that apathy may be the most subverting abuse of all. He strongly believes that the government is either too polite or too lazy to make anyone do over a worthless study. He says, "Our office has refused to pay for a study for over two years, all the time sending it back and telling the contractor to do it over until it was done right—and it still hasn't been done right. But this kind of action is all too rare." Nelson, who headed a large research effort, calmly estimates that as much as 50 percent of government paper studies may be worthless.

Rampant apathy is acknowledged by a former Food and Drug Administration official who tells how easy it is not to give a damn. Several years ago a research organization turned in to the Food and Drug Administration a $100,000 study on the agency's image. "I took one look at the study and saw that it was horrible," he says. "The researchers used loaded questions in their interviews with the public. On top of that, the results were in direct conflict with a fair labeling act that the Administration was pushing. I took the report, stashed it away in a desk drawer and hoped nobody would ask for it. Nobody ever did. As far as I know, that report is still stashed away in my old drawer."

Unfortunately, such abuses have been relatively free of criticism—even when the waste is blatant. In August 1967, for example, President Johnson appointed an expert-studded group to study U.S. communications policy, with particular emphasis on international communications. The major reason for the study was that the U.S. was to meet in early 1969 with over ninety governments to hash out the future of satellite communications. The President set a deadline of August 1968 for the group's report so that the U.S. would have plenty of time to use it in getting ready for the meeting. The group, called the Telecommunications Task Force, got moving in the winter of 1967. A research team was assembled and contracts were awarded to a variety of research institutions for studies. But the final report was still not ready by the time of President Nixon's inauguration. The task force was disbanded. The international meeting was held, and the U.S. fared badly because it did not have a clear-cut policy. The report has still not been officially released, although copies of it have been given out. Outside of a few members of Congress, nobody seemed very upset over the whole matter even though a million dollars was spent on studies toward a report that was not ready in time to serve its intended purpose.

These two issues of priorities and quality raised by the giant phenomenon of R&D are beginning to be faced by those in the research empire. For the first time since the beginning of the postwar R&D honeymoon science and technology are being forced to face the significance of their having gone public. Unbounded growth has slowed since 1968 as the over-all research budget has stayed at the $16–17 billion level, and though few doubt that it will rise again, the mark-time level indicates that increases are not automatic. Questioning of priorities in American research and its domination by military concerns is producing more and more questions from Congress, the press and public, especially students. Specific challenges are being launched as well. Persistence by a group of Senators led by Mike Mansfield, for example, led to legislation passed in 1969 stipulating that the military can commission research that is clearly related only to military objectives. Although there is still some question as to how military objectives will be defined, Congressional action has limited the unbridled research power of the Pentagon.

3. Power

> *Yet, in holding scientific research and discovery in respect, as we should, we must also be alert to the equal and opposite danger that public policy could itself become captive of a scientific-technological elite.*
>
> —President Eisenhower in his Farewell Address on January 17, 1961

As the number of think tanks continues to grow and more and more people look to them to solve problems, analyze policy and perform long-range thinking, their power necessarily increases—a power that is seldom challenged or questioned.

Since power is greatest at the federal level, the power of the think tanks that serve government is the strongest. So potentially powerful is the group of think tanks that serves the U.S. government that they have collectively been nicknamed "the shadow government." Perhaps the most trenchant comment made on this "shadow" concept came from former Presidential adviser Roger Hilsman in his book *To Move a Nation* when he said of the military-sponsored think tanks, "Although not accountable to the electorate, they have power and are just as much part of the governmental process as the traditional legislative, judicial and executive branches of government."

As a "fourth branch" of government, federally sponsored think tanks offer a fertile field for exploration. Take, for example, think tanks officially tied to the Pentagon by annual contract. Although there are significant differences in these outfits in size, orientation, and mission, all are nonprofit institutions with private directorates. Their unique quasigovernmental role allows them to borrow from both the federal and private worlds. Their employees are free from the strictures and lower salary structure of Civil Service, yet they have access to the innermost secrets of government. Officials of these think tanks play powerful roles as advisers in the corridors of the Pentagon and the State Department, despite the fact that neither

45

those agencies nor Congress has power to confirm, promote, or fire them.

The unique roles played by the Pentagon think tanks have made them instrumental in shaping and creating U.S. foreign and military policy, weapons systems, plans, tactics, and technology. Moreover, much of their work has been cloaked in secrecy or obfuscated in other ways with the result that very little scrutiny has been directed toward their increasing power. Remarkably, their analysts play crucial roles in conducting and planning war and determining the weapons America will build, yet they remain virtually anonymous when these decisions are authorized. On the strength of their alleged knowledge-ability they have been given great freedom to operate in a wide variety of political, social, international, and military areas—a power that has served to widen considerably the province of the military. The Pentagon think tanks have been staunchly defended by their military sponsors, yet those same sponsors have admitted time and again that they have very little control over them.

Just as these semigovernmental corporations are playing an important role in deciding military issues, so are think tanks attached to other agencies of government making other important determinations—President Nixon's welfare reform package, the current set of federal housing plans, and safety requirements for nuclear power plants are all examples of policies shaped and refined in think tanks.

In an assessment of the importance of the hundreds of think tanks in the United States, the federally sponsored ones offer only a starting point. Independent think tanks, not officially tied to the government, also need to be scrutinized. Many of them receive the bulk of their funds from the government, and, though not officially "sponsored" like RAND, they bring up the same questions of power, unchecked and unanswerable, evoked by the officially sponsored outfits. They advise in such diverse areas as transportation, natural resources, defense, and domestic welfare programs. Nor do they draw the line on policy and decision-making for the United States government. More and more, their analysis and planning is being performed for industry, governments of cities and states and foreign nations. In fact, there is probably no nation in the so-called free world that has not in its recent history had at least one American think tank working in its behalf in a role ranging from general adviser, such as the relationship that Algeria has with Arthur D. Little Inc., to the role of planner for a specific project, such as that of the Hudson Institute in mounting a major regional development plan for Colombia.

While think tanks play many roles—all worthy of investigation—an example that brings home their importance both now and in the future is the increasing interest in long-range forecasting and thinking about the future. This futurist-orientation has resulted from both the initiative of the tanks themselves and of the government. Several independent "futurist" tanks have emerged, and massive studies are under way on American life and technology in the future; and the new occupational category of "futurist" has evolved. Most Americans are unaware of the degree to which government and industry are working on the quality of life (in particular, war and technology) for the future. The Army, for example, has created a series of think tanks to examine the future of warfare.

What we must realize is that as institutions assume the formal role of casting about in the future, they dramatically increase their influence on that future. Simply put, if a think tank tells its sponsors and others willing to listen that X, Y, and Z will occur by the year 2000, then X, Y, and Z are more likely to occur as policy and technological goals adapt to those predictions.

Think tanks offer amazing potential for change, innovation, and a better future. Although a relatively new phenomenon, they have already had a great impact. Just considering the example of their role in creating important new products we find that synthetic rubber got an important start at the Mellon Institute, electrostatic copying or Xerography was developed at the Battelle Memorial Institute, magnetic tape recording grew out of work at the Illinois Institute of Technology Research Institute, and Arthur D. Little Inc. came up with the first successful process to manufacture fiberglass, to name a few such cases.

In an era of so many phenomena that are hard to comprehend, the think tanks are no exception. In the popular mind think tanks sometimes conjure up a nightmarish world of rampant technology geared to program humanity out of existence—and sometimes a gleaming world where the miraculous is put on a daily businesslike basis. Neither extreme is true, though there is an element of truth in each. Both the complexity of the phenomenon and the fact that, generally, think tanks maintain their privacy and serve without fanfare have led to misconceptions and surrounded them in mystery. The very

47

term "think tank" carries with it the aura of enigma—and perhaps even of conspiracy.

Their terrain extends from war to peace, from Dr. Strangelove to Dr. Salk, from harsh practicality to idealism, from hawkish retired generals to Ralph Nader, and from the most amazing Yankee ingenuity and innovation to the role of errand boy to the Establishment. What follows is an investigation of a small representative sampling of think tanks and think-tank activities in an increasingly pluralistic society. Given their roles as problem-solvers, innovators and planners in a complex, troubled, and problem-saturated era, think tanks are clearly worth thinking about.

V

MOTHER RAND

---

1. Balancing Terror

Oh, the RAND *Corporation is the boon of
    the world;*
They think all day for a fee.
*They sit and play games about going up in
    flames;*
*For counters they use you and me, Honey
    Bee,*
For counters they use you and me.

*They will rescue us all from a fate worse
    than death*
With a touch of the pushbutton hand.
*We'll be saved at one blow from the des-
    ignated foe,*
Who's going to save us from RAND?

> —RAND hymn, words and music by
> Malvina Reynolds, Copyright © 1961
> by Schroder Music Co. (ASCAP). Used
> by permission. This song was made
> popular by Pete Seeger. An anonymous
> RAND lyricist penned the following re-
> buttal, which appears in Bruce L. R.
> Smith's book *The RAND Corporation:*

*Oh, the folk-singing crowd is a boon to the
    world;*
They sing all day for free.

49

*They sit and sing songs, of injustice and
    wrongs;
For scapegoats they use you and me, Honey
    Bee,
For scapegoats they use you and me.*

*'Twould be nice if our life were only a song
And as simply resolved as a chord.
That it's not can't be missed; Russian
    bombs do exist;
It's the fact that folk-singers ignored, Dear
    Lord,
It's the fact that folk-singers ignored.*

A prime mover in initiating the ICBM program, an academy producing high-ranking bureaucrats, a developer of scores of military
innovations, a prime analyst for U.S. foreign policy-makers, an early
instigator in the space program, the most important corporate analyst
for American nuclear policy, a conceiver of the deterrence policy that
dictates American defense, and undoubtedly the most powerful research organization associated with the American military—these are
just some of the roles played by the RAND Corporation, yet some of
its people report with a smile, "There are still a lot of people who
think we make typewriters."

In contrast to those who think it so benign there are those who
darkly perceive it as part of a conspiratorial enterprise. RAND, so went
the story, was working for the Nixon Administration to investigate
the possibilities of canceling the 1972 General Election should radicals threaten to disrupt it. The story began with a report from the
Washington bureau of the Newhouse News Service in April 1970
and immediately appeared in six newspapers in the Newhouse chain.
Shortly after it showed up in New York's *Village Voice*, the Los
Angeles *Free Press*, the *Wall Street Journal*, and the Chicago *Sun-
Times*, thus turning the story into a full-fledged national rumor.
Within days of the original Newhouse report RAND found that it was
getting dozens of queries a day on the story not only from the press
but from members of Congress, professors, and just plain citizens
alarmed by the possibility of a Nixon coup in '72. RAND's president,
Henry S. Rowen, vigorously denied the story, and just to make sure
that there was not some half-truth in the story he ordered a compre-

hensive review of all of its work of the past three years to see if there might be anything that could have been construed or misconstrued as a basis for the rumor. The results of the search were negative.

The Administration, faced also with constant inquiry on the story, brought it into the open in June 1970. Presidential Assistant Daniel P. Moynihan dwelt on it at length in a commencement speech at Fordham University, pegging it a rumor that was symptomatic of the fact that mistrust of the government had reached "epidemic" proportions. By October a White House communications aide said the story was still alive but gradually dying because people were realizing that there was not one shred of evidence to support it. The author of the original Newhouse item had already told a reporter from the Washington *Post* that he had picked up the original as a rumor in New York City and had written it as a "speculative item."

The "election" story is not the first of its type that has circulated and caused RAND to be propelled into the spotlight. On August 8, 1958, Senator Stuart Symington touched off what was to be one of the silliest of many tempestuous outbursts to hit Congress in the 1950's when he introduced into the *Congressional Record* an article from the St. Louis *Post-Dispatch* stating that RAND was conducting studies that dealt with the possible surrender of the United States at some future point in her history. The allegation resulted in immediate Congressional outrage and, according to an article in the Washington *Post* that appeared during the excitement, so rocked President Eisenhower that he was reported to have been ". . . more excited than at any time since assuming the Presidency." In reality, the study, entitled "Strategic Surrender," had nothing to do with U.S. capitulation but was a critique of historical cases in which the U.S. had made the "unconditional surrender" of an enemy a requirement for ending hostilities. Despite denials by the Air Force and RAND of any study of American surrender, the Senate, after two days of animated discussion on nascent defeatism in American life, overwhelmingly passed legislation that forbade the use of federal money to study defeat or surrender in any circumstances. The regulation, which is still in force, stands as an inane monument to the dedication of legislators to keep defeat out of the national vocabulary.

Both those who view RAND conspiratorially and those dwindling few who associate it with the manufacture of business machines have been led to their assumptions partly because of the way RAND has chosen to act. It is a secretive institution that until recently has explained itself reluctantly. According to a man who formerly worked in RAND's public-relations office and who now fills a similar post for another think tank, its prevailing policy was long that of "minimal reaction"—or answering questions posed to it by outsiders but offering little else. As he summed it up, "RAND was probably the only corporation in America which really didn't want itself featured in a *Time* cover story." Although it has opened up considerably—for a number of reasons that will later become apparent—RAND is still thought of by many people as a powerful "supersecret" paramilitary institute.

RAND is located in two large pink buildings overlooking the beach in Santa Monica, California. Save for the lack of neon, it could pass for an outsized, somewhat sedate, flat-roofed oceanfront motel. Inside, the halls have all the charm of hospital corridors, although individual offices are generally nicely cluttered, rather as professors' offices are thought to look. Even though it is one of the most important military adjuncts in the nation, the impression one gets while visiting it is that it is more Palm Springs than Pentagon. Many of its staff swim on their lunch hour, dress is casual, and people are generally congenial and talkative. Though security is tight, it is subtle. There are no guns at the doors, as one finds at some other military think tanks—just friendly guards who make sure you have an escort before you go traipsing through the halls and who record entries and exits by mumbling names and times into tape recorders.

Although there are no students and there is strict security, there is more at RAND to suggest a university than a corporation. Its major departments have academic titles (engineering, social science, physics, mathematics, economics, environmental sciences, and so forth); it supports a major publishing program and is open day and night to accommodate researchers who choose to work erratic hours.

Most of RAND's work has been conducted under the original "Project RAND" contract with the Air Force, one of the most unusual and longest-lived contracts between the government and a private institution. The contract is unique in that RAND's duties under the contract are totally contained in a single statement calling for "a program of study and research on the broad subject of intercontinental warfare, other than surface, with the object of recommending to the Army Air Forces preferred techniques and instrumentalities for this purpose." That work statement from the original Project RAND contract is almost identical to the statement in the current contract, the only difference being that "Air Force" replaces "Army Air Forces." Even this very general statement, giving RAND considerable latitude, is not followed strictly and has been stretched to include work that has absolutely nothing to do with "intercontinental warfare." To give one of many such examples: In 1967 RAND used Air Force funds to conduct research into the subject of the problems of privacy in the computer age. Those at RAND contend that the almost total freedom they have been given by the Air Force has allowed them to make some of their most important discoveries. Its list of freedoms under the contract includes the authority to initiate research without being told to do so by the Air Force and the option of turning the Air Force down when it asks RAND to perform some specific bit of research—an option that has been exercised on such occasions as when the Air Force asks for a "nuts and bolts" study requiring, in RAND's opinion, little intellectual stimulation.

Since RAND emerged as a corporation in 1948 with a $3 million annual budget and about 300 employees, it has grown to a present level of over a thousand employees and an annual budget of over $25 million. As it was in the beginning, RAND's primary client is the Air Force, although today its Air Force work accounts for only about half the research program. In the late 1940's and early 1950's the Air Force was its exclusive client. Over the years it has attracted other military and federal clients, including various elements of the Pentagon, the Atomic Energy Commission, and NASA.

In the more than twenty years since it became a corporation it has produced over 11,000 books and reports as well as countless memoranda, briefings, and communications. This gargantuan outpouring of words has contained a great diversity of research and opinion which, taken as a whole and by any standard one may reasonably choose, has had a substantial impact on the way the nation thinks and does things. This influence was nicely summed up by Joseph Kraft in an article on RAND in *Harper's* in 1960: "Though little known, it has had an enormous impact on the nation's strategic concepts and weapons systems, and in one way or another it has affected the life of every American family."

Although RAND has had an impact on a variety of concerns, the overwhelming influence that it has had is in the military realm. In trying to assess the impact of RAND's work for the military, the outsider cannot approach a large body of that work because it is officially secret or otherwise not available for public consumption. RAND analysts are required to have top-secret security clearances, and the percentage of its total annual work that has been labeled secret has traditionally run to about 50 percent (although that percentage has come down some in recent years). This situation has interesting consequences when someone lacking clearance talks with RAND thinkers about their work, for in many conversations, whether it be on communications theory or foreign policy, there is a point where the RAND man puts up his wall by stating that he really can't go any further because the discussion is getting into a classified area. Ralph Lapp, the author-physicist who has written critically about America's strategic policies, says in reference to RAND's secrecy, "The worst thing about people from RAND is that you cannot talk with them. They shy away from debate and discussion on anything important to their work, insisting that security dictates that they shut up. What really bothers me about this is that many of them are associated with universities and they have helped usher in silence and secrecy to those institutions where such behavior should be alien."

Since secret work is just that, it is difficult to pinpoint the virtues or perils of the secrecy governing its activities; however, there are general examples of this type of work that come to light and give some idea of RAND's covert research. For instance, RAND has done extensive work in the area of nuclear proliferation in which it has monitored the economics, politics, and technology of nuclear development throughout the world. Most of more than twenty studies that have been completed in this area since the early 1960's are classified as secret. RAND has also conducted a variety of secret programs to develop technical items for the military, including a spin-scan camera for airborne reconnaissance applications, over-the-horizon radar, a "silent" aircraft for night surveillance work, and new bombing techniques. An example of an ongoing secret RAND job is the picking, revising, and updating of nuclear targets within the Soviet Union. In the same vein, it has done much classified work for the Air Force on the use of radioactive fallout as a "kill mechanism," with RAND attempting to resolve such specific problems as how can one bomb Red China and get maximum fallout there without getting it over Taiwan and Japan. Not all of RAND's secret work has been directly for the Air Force. It has done much work for the Atomic Energy Commission on nuclear weapon design and weapons effect. In this area at least one newly configured nuclear bomb with increased destructive power was inspired by RAND research and is now part of the U.S. arsenal. As an example of the kind of secret work RAND is likely to be doing at any given point, as of 1970 it was conducting a series of studies for the White House's Henry Kissinger and the National Security Council on a variety of foreign-policy issues—studies that RAND does not even formally acknowledge are being done. In the same vein, a group of RAND analysts in late 1968 delivered to Richard Nixon a secret "option paper" outlining his possible alternatives in Vietnam ranging from unilateral withdrawal to further escalation.

RAND's secret role in national policy issues is perhaps best illustrated in regard to the secret "Pentagon papers" first brought to public attention by the New York *Times* in June 1971. The team of thirty-five military and civilian analysts that put the forty-seven-volume report together was liberally sprinkled with men from RAND and, in fact, the total number of RAND analysts working on it was second only to the number of government men. It is also indicative of RAND's importance that of the four "legitimate" copies of the final report permitted outside of government, two were given to RAND for reference (the other two went to LBJ and Clark Clifford).

Among those working on the papers from RAND was the now famous Dr. Daniel Ellsberg, a long time RAND employee who had first begun working on national security problems at RAND from 1959 to 1964, when by his own admission he was a "hawk." He left RAND when he was tapped to join the elite group of RAND-heavy "whiz kids" brought in by McNamara to run the Pentagon, and remained there as an analyst until 1967, when he returned to RAND. It was during his stint with the Department of Defense that he made trips to Vietnam and his views on the war began to change radically. Back at RAND he was soon put on the team working on McNamara's study of U.S. involvement in Southeast Asia. His views on the war grew increasingly negative, and he began making his opposition public in 1969. He left RAND for MIT in 1970, after first smuggling out the "Pentagon papers."

RAND secrecy is not confined to reports but on occasion extends to conferences and meetings. In July 1953, for example, a series of meetings were held at RAND to determine the national and world-wide health hazards implicit in nuclear testing. One topic of great concern at the meetings was the hazards of radioactive substances (such as Strontium-90) and their effect on food. To this date the secret stamp has not been removed from the proceedings of those meetings. In 1970 Ralph Lapp referred to those meetings in a speech on environmental health at Iowa State University in this critical manner: "We have here an example of the Atomic Energy Commission, a single government agency, acting on its own in assessing a global health hazard. We are also witness to the obedience of some of the nation's greatest scientists in bowing to the will of the AEC."

Just as RAND conducts a great body of covert work that is almost impossible to assess, it also performs a body of work that is not worth examining. This is work of little or no consequence to the world at large but rather the academic concerns and amusements indulged in by the RAND staff because of the largess of others—notably the Air Force. In this category, it has examined such items as the price of bricks in the Soviet Union, surfing, semantics, Finnish phonology, the social groupings of monkeys, and an analysis of the popular toy-store puzzle "Instant Insanity" (in this particular analysis, the researcher worked out and revealed a mathematical procedure for putting it together).

Nonetheless, between the secret and the silly there is another body of work of unclassified information and information that has been declassified which provides more than enough information for gauging its military importance. The four major categories that best serve to illustrate RAND's martial impact on the nation and the roles that it has played are: tactics and strategy, new techniques and methodologies, international relations and technology. In each category a few of the many possible examples will help illustrate RAND's influence.

The most important job probably ever performed by RAND (or any other military think tank for that matter) in the area of strategic thinking began with a routine request for advice from the Air Force and led to the adoption of a new defensive posture for the United States. The RAND studies that brought this about have been referred to as the "new Gospel of Deterrence."

In 1951 the Air Force came to RAND asking for help in choosing locations for new air bases to be established overseas in the 1956 to

1961 period. The request was turned over to Albert Wohlstetter, a mathematician/economist who was to become one of RAND's top strategic analysts. Wohlstetter, who at first did not want to conduct the routine nuts-and-bolts study, finally decided to do it but not by attempting to answer the straightforward request for advice but rather by examining the assumptions inherent in the question itself. Over a period of a year and a half he and his staff analyzed the options open to the nation in positioning its strategic forces. They concluded that adding such bases was not only too risky (they reasoned that aircraft positioned overseas closer to the Soviet Union were too vulnerable to surprise atomic attack on the ground) but more costly, less of a deterrent, and more of a problem for U.S. international relations than an alternative plan. The alternative the team framed was to build more bases in the U.S. and supplement them with small overseas installations for refueling aircraft.

"R-244," the designation for the report, was delivered to the Air Force and supplemented by briefings and meetings on its contents. Its impact was tremendous. Not only were RAND's recommendations on the positioning of bases adopted (a decision the Air Staff later concluded saved over a billion dollars in construction costs alone) but it significantly changed American strategic thought. Before the study U.S. policy was geared to the first-strike capability or the ability to deter potential aggressors by their fear of an American first strike. The study, however, raised the concept of the second strike capability or the ability to survive an enemy's initial attack with enough strength to punish him. In sum, it served to shift American nuclear defense policy to one in which the U.S. would be able to score a win in a second strike even though almost everyone was dead from the first. The second-strike concept suggested in the report was accepted and is still the dominant tenet in American deterrence policy.

In this case RAND had turned a routine request into a major examination and revision of strategic policy. The study not only changed the Air Force but had a great impact on RAND itself. Speaking about the study before a meeting of the International Council for Scientific Management in 1968, Roger Levien, head of RAND's Systems Sciences program, listed four lessons that were either learned or verified from the "bases study" and to some extent from other studies of that era which have been incorporated into RAND's collective approach to problem-solving. First, it underlined the necessity for rephrasing the question being asked to see if the question was based on invalid or anachronistic assumptions. Second, it showed that detachment from day-to-day bureaucratic problems was of benefit to this type of inquiry—Wohlstetter and his team worked virtually uninterrupted for a year and a half. The third lesson was that projected future events should be a major factor in policy research. In the bases study the analysts took into account what they surmised to be the major technological, strategic, and economic considerations for the period in which the bases would go into operation and later. Finally, the work re-emphasized the need to be close to one's client when working on the client's policies. As Levien put it, ". . . the result of the study would have gone for nought if RAND did not have close and continuous relations with the Air Force." Since the results of the study went contrary to established doctrine, it was essential to RAND that it was close enough to the Air Force to convince it of the validity of the study while remaining independent of it.

Follow-up studies by Wohlstetter's group and others led to further policy shifts. One study recommended the "fail-safe" procedure for nuclear bombers which was adopted by the Strategic Air Command. Under this procedure U.S. bombers are given a leg up on their opponents by heading toward enemy targets on receipt of even ambiguous information, only to return automatically to their bases when they get to a predetermined "fail-safe" spot unless a specific order to go on and attack is given by the President. Wohlstetter also advocated and gained acceptance for the concept of "hardening" missile defenses by burying them in underground silos—an idea that supports the second-strike concept because it means that missiles would probably be able to withstand a first attack from an enemy.

In addition, the "new gospel of deterrence" largely fathered by RAND led to still other programs. Its work stimulated development of long-endurance military aircraft and nuclear-weapon-bearing Polaris submarines on the strength of its argument that such weapons systems were ideal deterrents because they were actually moving missile bases hard for a prospective enemy to locate. Another offshoot of RAND thinking was a new interest in civil defense. It was argued that if both Big Two powers expended their nuclear arsenals, the winner would be determined by the numbers of survivors, so that there was a certain threat of deterrence in protecting more civilians. Some RAND analysts advocated extensive civil-defense programs for just this reason.

The bases study and those studies it prompted were seminal to the whole think-tank movement and did more than anything else to propel RAND into prominence. The study and its consequences were reported in detail and with considerable awe in magazines from *Business Week* to *Harper's*, and a large segment of Bruce L. R. Smith's book *The RAND Corporation* is devoted to it. RAND speakers on the banquet trail still use it as a prime example of the corporation's capabilities.

The importance of the studies today remains intact. RAND analysts had coached a decisive move in the ongoing chess game still being played, now with pieces marked SS-9, MIRV and ABM. With the benefit of hindsight, the studies seem somewhat less remarkable than they did at first. Assuming that a surprise Soviet nuclear attack was a distinct possibility, RAND's suggestion was to jump from a first- to a second-strike capability or, simply, not to put all of the nation's nuclear eggs in the same basket. RAND was able to sell this conclusion to the military because it was logical and helped beef up American defenses. One wonders, if only rhetorically, how the military would have greeted suggestions for a winding down of the arms race.

Perhaps the prime reason RAND's discoveries do not inspire the awe they once did is the course of history. That the Russians did not push the button seems today less a function of American deterrence than the fact that they had no more thought of pushing the button than the United States did. That a surprise nuclear attack by either side seems less probable every day underscores the absurdity of continued rounds of arming and serves to cast doubt on the original assumption that the Soviets had anything to gain from thermonuclear war in the first place.

Recently Secretary of Defense Melvin R. Laird has been telling Americans that besides building new defensive missiles, the U.S.S.R. is strengthening its civil-defense program and refining plans for evacuating cities—a transparent effort to help fund new defensive missiles. As the costly weapons game enters a new round, older rounds, like the crucial one directed by RAND, seem paradoxically logical and absurd at the same time. If to some the brilliance of that "RAND round" fades with hindsight, it does not at RAND, whose personnel continue to coach the deadly game with its assumptions on the need for the game unshaken.

Another study with influence over military policy began in the late 1950's when RAND, on its own, initiated an inquiry to determine the possibility of accidental detonation of a nuclear weapon. Like many studies RAND has produced for the Air Force, it was not requested by the military but rather was the result of a hunch on the part of researchers at the corporation. The study focused on the possibilities of a nuclear warhead going off as a result of technical malfunction, sabotage or a mad or irresponsible human action. RAND not only found that existing procedures were such that malfunction and sabotage were distinct possibilities but that they were especially vulnerable to the irrational person who wanted to set off a nuclear weapon. Recommendations for new safety regulations were made and adopted along with suggestions that resulted in new personnel screening processes for military employees working with nuclear weapons (a set of procedures that the Air Force has awkwardly labeled its "human reliability program"). Finally, RAND's research led to the development of the "permissive action link," a device that makes it physically impossible to arm or detonate a nuclear weapon without a release signal from a remote source under the command of high ranking officials.

Other RAND contributions in this particular realm have led to a set of policies the Air Force uses in the management of its extensive spare-parts inventories; current policies on the use of Air Force reservists, including procedures for the call-up of reservists and policy on the mixture of reservists with regulars in active units; policy research for the North Atlantic Treaty Organization (NATO) in such areas as long-range planning, force planning, and nuclear policy which, in turn, have had an impact on the military policies of the pact nations; and studies that led to the conclusion that nuclear warheads could be carried by rockets, which in turn had an important bearing on the U.S. decision in 1954 to proceed with the Atlas ICBM program.

In RAND's strategic work there is no such thing as a monolithic institutional attitude toward the subject; however, there is a cluster of prevalent thought patterns. For one crucial thing, preventive war —or the one in which the U.S. attacks first—has been ruled out. As for the dangers of war, RAND functions on the belief that the peril of total war is real and the nation must be prepared to fight both that kind of war and limited ones with a great variety of weapons, including nuclear ones. In the RAND scheme of things, communications can never be underrated as a tool of modern warfare, and they could play an important role in bringing one to a quick close. Deterrence or the balance-of-terror situation is not only an acceptable but a preferred mode of defense.

While RAND has done much to advance the state of the art of modern warfare, it has done little exploring in the area of disarming the nuclear monsters of Frankenstein. Nor has it been able to cope with the very real contingency of stopping a war once it has begun. As is pointed out in the RAND-produced report on its own history, *The RAND Corporation: The First Fifteen Years*, published in 1963, "The unsolved problem of modern total war (if it should come) is that of how to stop it, quickly, once it is decided. It is tantamount to negotiating complete disarmament with a 24-hour deadline, or less." The statement is important, for it not only discloses RAND's characteristic bravado—challenging itself to dealing with the worst thermonuclear case—but underscores its responsibility for having contributed so much to making an unstoppable war possible and so little to the strategy of arms limitation or other peaceful alternatives.

A second class of RAND research no less important than its work in strategy and tactics is its pioneering of new approaches to policy research. Some of these techniques and methodologies were discovered during work on its many studies, while others have come from those who, from RAND's inception, have been given the primary responsibility of looking for new analytical techniques. Many of these techniques were discovered at RAND and further developed elsewhere, while others came from other research groups but were pushed and developed at RAND. Some are mathematical techniques, complex and difficult for the layman to comprehend in detail, while others are so firmly entrenched in common sense that they seem patently obvious. Together, these approaches have defined the RAND style and to a major extent have affected all other think tanks—even those in operation before RAND came into being—as well as almost every major agency of government and a large part of industry.

Scenario-writing is a now well-known technique largely developed at RAND as an aid to strategic thinking. It calls for a careful attempt to write an artificial script of future events as a means of provoking thought about as yet unraised policy questions. Advocates of scenario-writing see their technique as an aid to the imagination, a device which, they contend, forces one to consider realistic details rather than abstract concepts, raises possibilities that may not occur in normal analysis, sets up and forces one to think about future alternatives, and focuses on the interaction of events. Scenarios are meant to be neither accurate nor predictive. A classic scenario scripted for strategic thinking might begin with the accidental firing of a Soviet missile, winging its way to Chicago; it might end with the war being called off after the U.S. made a retaliatory strike.

Closely related is the technique of war games which was developed at RAND. In its most simple form it calls for assigning players to assume the role of a national entity, group, or decision-maker—such as Spain, the Catholic Church in Spain or the Secretary General of the UN—and playing those roles in reaction to a crisis. In a strictly military exercise contending forces may simply be designated as the Red and Blue armies. Games have been most often used at RAND as a form of contrived experimentation with conditions that cannot be feasibly simulated in the real world. In their simple parlor game form they are often used as a training device for officials to enable them to understand what to be prepared for in a crisis contingency—a particular form of training that was popular at the Pentagon and State Department during the Kennedy Administration. A typical simple game of this nature might start with a nuclear explosion in Utah, and the player representing the President of the United States does not know whether the incident was the result of planned alien sabotage, a malfunction, or the work of a home-grown screwball.

Some games are computer-based operations in which the actions of human decision-makers touch off calculations of such variables as optimum mixtures of forces or the number of casualties that would likely be produced by a certain action. For example, in a Department of Defense game called x RAY 2 being played at RAND in 1970, a series of teams located at various think tanks, military installations, and the Arms Control and Disarmament Agency were connected by a nationwide network of teletypes and computers. The game consisted of rounds during which crises and wars that could emerge in the late 1970's were acted out in order to determine how such variables as the technological ability, weapons, and the size and composition of forces of the major powers would influence their outcome.

Historically games have not only kept RAND analysts on their toes and suggested alternatives not thought of before but have played a role in the evolution of major policy decisions. A series of games begun during the 1950's examined the possible role of the Air Force in a war in the Middle East, while another series of games initiated during that period, called Project Sierra, dealt generally with the role of the military in limited wars. Together these two series of games served to cast doubt on the then prevalent doctrine of "massive retaliation" and presented graphic examples showing why the nation must be prepared for limited warfare as well—a realization that was adopted as part of defense strategy.

Computers have played an important role throughout the history of RAND which has been instrumental in introducing them to both military operations and military analysis. An example of a RAND-developed technique for problem-solving that has gained widespread application is called heuristic programming. Unlike routines where men or computers work independently on the solution of a program, this technique allows researchers to interact with the machines during the process by the use of convenient consoles and video display units. The technique was developed as computer-generated graphics became feasible allowing the researcher literally to see what the computer was doing and what information it had. In actual application, a researcher might scan certain data stored in the computer and then change that data to see what effect it has on the outcome of a problem previously solved by the computer. Another computer technique developed at RAND is computer modeling or the creation of a computer system to simulate the operation of another system that could be anything from a model of a human heart to that of a proposed weapons system. Such a capability opens the possibility of experimenting under conditions not available in real life.

RAND has also contributed a number of highly esoteric and sophisticated mathematical techniques such as linear programming, dynamic programming, problems scheduling, nonlinear programming, and the Monte Carlo method. This last method is a procedure for solving a group of physical problems by conducting a series of statistical experiments in which accuracy depends on the number of trials performed. Many mathematicians claim that the H-bomb could not have been developed anywhere nearly as quickly as it was without such an approach. At RAND these techniques have been applied in such areas as satellite-trajectory problems, the analysis of the atmosphere of other planets, the assignment of repairmen at missile sites, and the design of communications networks.

Still other RAND lines of methodological approach are the techniques of futurism and technological forecasting. The most famous of these is called Delphi, now very much in vogue in government, universities, and business. Delphi is a set of procedures used to poll experts to ascertain the possibilities of future occurrences.

The most important methodological contributions from RAND are those of program budgeting, cost-effectiveness analysis, and systems analysis.

The first technique, variously called program budgeting, policy-oriented budgeting, and the Planning, Programming and Budgeting System (PPBS), was introduced by RAND to the Department of Defense during the McNamara regime and has been extended throughout the federal government as the result of a decision by President Johnson in August 1965 to apply it to all government budgeting. PPBS is simply a procedure for thinking that is intended to force planners to use resources more effectively. Its major tenet is that in order to make a decision or frame an annual budget, one must think beyond the short term and decide whether possible decisions fit in with long-range goals. It requires one to think far into the future, delineate and state objectives, find better and cheaper ways of accomplishing goals, and question the costs and benefits of existing programs. When he ordered its implementation in government, President Johnson, who was particularly taken with the technique, noted that it requires the continual identification of national goals, forces selection of the most urgent goals, and heightens awareness of future as well as immediate costs. While this kind of thinking seems relatively elementary, it replaces the prior mode of thinking in which planning was more random and often predicated on annual needs rather than long-term goals.

Closely allied with program budgeting and similarly popular in government is the concept of "cost-effectiveness," or the application of economic analysis to decision-making. Used in long-range planning, the technique is concerned with objectives rather than objects and is applied where there are several courses of action possible to reach an objective. By analyzing the economics of alternative courses of action, the planner gains an idea of how to achieve his objective most economically.

Finally, there is the form of analysis that ties all of the other RAND techniques together. Called "systems analysis," it is the essence of the RAND style, which can be defined by its way of looking at things, its dedication to unearthing new techniques and methodologies, and the religion it makes of looking at problems in the light of more than one discipline. This form of analysis widely used today throughout the world, including by such major projects as the Apollo program, is essentially a broadening of the original World War II concept of operations research. Unlike operations research, which is applied to existing systems to improve them—such as in improving the accuracy of an aircraft in bombing—the more advanced form of analysis is applied to complex questions of choice among alternative future systems (e.g., what is the best system that can be built to fill the role of traditional bomber aircraft?). The difficulties, of course, become much greater when applying systems analysis since the analyst must start from scratch.

In practice, systems analysis is a complex, unstructured, untidy, and individualized way of looking at a new system—whether it be a new weapon or a systematic assault on malnutrition—in which analytic techniques ranging from mathematics to intuition are brought to bear. It is not a formal mode of analysis with prescribed dicta but rather a conceptual approach calling for the assemblage of a maximum range of disciplines and research skills to look at a single problem.

Another major area of RAND's work has been its production of international studies in such areas as politics, economics, and military affairs. This role as global researcher was neatly summed up in a *New Yorker* cartoon that showed two natives perched on a mountain ledge looking down at a well-dressed American with a briefcase with one native saying to the other, "Don't look now but here comes that pest from the RAND Corporation again." According to James F. Digby, who currently heads its international-studies program, RAND has the country's largest staff of experts working on international security research. There are very few areas of the world that the corporation has not studied since it began international research in 1948.

Its first job in this realm was a series of studies, undertaken in 1948, of the economic and military potential of the Soviet Union—an effort to probe into the Soviet mind that has continued to the present day. RAND was the pioneering American institution in the kind of Cold War scholarship that calls for intensive study of a

potential enemy from afar. One of the earliest studies in this area
sought to determine the guiding principles (or "operational code")
that directed Soviet political conduct in the world. On the assumption that Soviet politics were firmly rooted in the writings of Lenin
and Stalin, an intense analysis of all of their writings, along with a
historical study of the Soviet Union's actions, yielded a report entitled "The Operational Code of the Politburo." The report has been
used extensively by American diplomats in their attempts to fathom
the next move that Communists would make. To give a specific example, during the Korean truce negotiations at Panmunjon, the
report was used as a guide by the U.S.–United Nations negotiators.
The head of the team later said that it was "required reading for
every Allied negotiator" and that it closely predicted Communist, in
this case North Korean, conference-room strategy and tactics. Another early RAND work entitled "Soviet Military Doctrine" was the
first of its kind published in the West; another, produced by Margaret
Mead, looked at the Soviet national character.

During much of the early work focused on the Soviet economy,
RAND faced a tough challenge. Very little detail was filtering out of
Russia on its economy, and the little that did was suspected of being
let out for propaganda reasons. RAND assembled a staff of economic
experts who began constructing a reliable body of statistics and
estimates gleaned from such items as Russian documents captured
by the Germans which the U.S., in turn, captured from the Germans. RAND created what might best be termed a remote Soviet
economics bureau by constructing such factors as price, cost-of-living
and wage indices and estimates of actual ruble purchasing power.

Today RAND still casts profound looks at the U.S.S.R. from Santa
Monica. A current product of this ongoing scrutiny is a RAND journal
called *The Soviet Cybernetics Review* in which Russian advances in
electronics and computers are reported and analyzed. The journal
contains good examples of how academic intelligence work is conducted. In one typical footnote, for instance, the reader is told that
the existence of a particular piece of Soviet computing equipment
was revealed ". . . buried in tabular material in an obscure 1968
[Soviet] book on using computers in maritime transportation."

Similarly, RAND is one of the nation's most important centers for
collecting and analyzing information on mainland China. Its work
in this area began in 1955 and relies heavily on the same kind of

66

fine-toothed analysis of documents, reports, and periodicals as its work on the U.S.S.R. Typical of the kind of research assignment that RAND has undertaken on China are studies to determine the organization of the Peoples' Liberation Army and the technological abilities of Chinese industry. In a 1969 report, the result of an intense study of China's economy, the major revelation was that many recent Chinese claims of economic gain were overstated—according to RAND, the actual rate of annual economic growth, claimed to be nine percent, is closer to three percent.

Not all of its international work is based on remote scholarship. RAND's people in Vietnam have overseen some 2,400 intensive interviews with Vietcong prisoners and defectors. It performed this kind of work earlier with Chinese and North Koreans during the Korean War and with Soviet defectors in Germany after World War II. According to a RAND report, the Vietnamese interviews ". . . have provided U.S. policy makers with the most significant body of detailed information available on Vietcong motivations and attitudes." This Pentagon-sponsored attempt to understand the Vietcong—his morale, attitudes, tactics, and motivation—is classified, but as international-studies director Digby notes with a certain smugness, "Some day we hope that they will be available to scholars so that we can all have a better understanding of the war."

RAND's involvement with Southeast Asia has been extensive. From the beginning of U.S. involvement there, RAND analysts have studied the people, the way the war was being fought, and the weapons that were being used. True to its interdisciplinary character, its studies have ranged from mathematical analyses of bombing effectiveness to anthropological studies of the Montagnards along Vietnam's border. The collective result of this work has been a large body of material that has predominantly served to justify the war throughout its various stages. Indeed, its degree of involvement has made it more a participant of the war than a scholarly observer.

Among the many jobs that RAND has performed in this value-loaded area is its work on the organization of Vietnamese student movements with emphasis on motivation and organization. More than just a passive study, it served as the locus for a RAND-inspired student youth movement which in the summer of 1966 involved the use of 8,500 Vietnamese students who worked in pacification programs. Another type of work has been its continuing studies of the effects of

American military actions. One such study was discussed by the Washington *Post's* veteran Vietnam correspondent Stanley Karnow in a 1970 article: "The demand from Washington for rapid action sometimes meant that decisions were made without advance study and were justified afterward. In late 1964, for example, a RAND Corporation team was set up to assess the possible political repercussions of employing tactical U.S. air power inside South Vietnam. The team expected to produce 'preliminary' recommendations within a year. The bombings started long before that. The team thereupon endorsed the bombings with the somewhat contorted rationale that peasants blamed the Viet Cong for turning their villages into targets for air strikes."

One of RAND's most important recent Vietnamese studies appeared in 1970. Based on captured documents and interviews with prisoners, it predicted that approximately 100,000 South Vietnamese might be executed, if the Communists should take over the South. The study served as a major piece of supporting evidence for those advancing the idea that an American pullout would result in a "bloodbath." The estimate was used extensively by the Nixon Administration and Congressional opponents of quick withdrawal. The report was not without its critics, however, among them Senator George McGovern, who attacked it on such grounds as that it did not take into account international controls that would presumably follow a peace settlement or withdrawal and that it assumed the total failure of the Vietnamization program.

On the other hand there is evidence that RAND has on occasion delivered reports to the military on Vietnam that must have raised some eyebrows among its military patrons. A secret 1968 report informed the Pentagon of unsubstantiated reports from Vietnam that South Korean troops being used there were engaged in acts of terrorism against the South Vietnamese. This charge emerged in January 1970 in a Washington *Post* story along with the information that another think tank, Human Sciences Research Corporation, had reported the same finding in one of its secret reports. One of the researchers from the Human Sciences Research Corporation told the *Post*, "If we had spoken out then, I don't believe Mylai ever would have happened." Perhaps not, but it is worth noting that two independent scholarly organizations felt that their obligation in reporting the allegations of terrorism was limited to giving their reports to authorities who immediately made them secret.

While much of RAND's work has focused on the Communist world and areas of military activity, its analysts have also looked in detail at most other nations and regions. It has, for instance, done considerable work touching on virtually all aspects of life in Latin America, including detailed studies of such items as the area's military regimes, population growth, student activism, the policies of other nations toward Latin American countries, and the influence of the Catholic Church in that part of the world. Its importance as a U.S. analyst of Latin American affairs was suggested when Nelson Rockefeller made his publicized trip there for President Nixon in 1969. Before he left, three RAND analysts prepared a review for him of the major political and military issues affecting inter-American relations.

RAND has been one of the most important of a number of military think tanks carrying out foreign-policy research—a significant fact when one further realizes that the Department of Defense, not the State Department, is the major sponsor of foreign-policy research in the nation. Hearings before the Senate Foreign Relations Committee indicated that the amount spent for international research by the Pentagon in 1969 was over $65 million, while the State Department spent only $5 million, almost all of it for studies by the Agency for International Development. Notes RAND's Digby, "We've really never done much work for the State Department because until recently they've only spent about $125,000 a year on policy research"—less than some individual RAND international studies.

The final major realm in which RAND has made important military contributions is that of technology, a major element of RAND from its beginning. In the introduction of new structural materials its role has been highly useful. Beryllium and titanium and its alloys were first found to have valuable properties in research conducted by RAND engineers. Both have become major structural materials for aircraft, missiles, and spacecraft.

A good deal of its most important technological work has been in space programs. The RAND-produced document on unmanned satellites in 1946 was just the beginning of what proved to be a long series of studies that have figured prominently in the nation's exploration and exploitation of space. Work that began in 1952 led to the solution of the critical problem of nose-cone overheating during the re-entry of a returning space vehicle into the earth's atmosphere—a development not only essential to the space program but also critical to the success of the intercontinental missile. Another detailed study completed in the early 1950's showed that earth-orbiting satellites could serve as weather-observation platforms and suggested plans for designing and building them. These plans were used in the construction of the Tiros weather satellites that began going aloft in the late 1950's to generate television pictures of climatic conditions. Descendents of those satellites are orbiting today as part of the Commerce Department's environmental services program. Similar work at RAND led to the development of the Midas satellites, employed to detect and give early warning on missile launches, the SAMOS series of Air Force spy satellites, and the Discoverer satellites, the first to go into orbit and return their payloads to earth. RAND also helped the founders of the Communications Satellite Corporation (COMSAT) with the technical expertise needed to begin their program of commercial communications satellites. In addition, RAND performed much pioneering work in such specific areas as space power systems, trajectory calculation, launch reliability, and orbit stabilization.

An interesting and, depending on your outlook, either frightening or encouraging story behind some of RAND's most important space work is retold by J. R. Goldstein, the RAND vice-president who has been with the corporation from its inception, and suggests the value of RAND's early work in space. "During the early Eisenhower years research became sort of a dirty word," he recalls. "Secretary of Defense Charles Wilson decided in 1953 that the military could no longer support space research. Luckily, we had the freedom and the charter to use military money independently, so our people kept going with a low-key space research program that was to be of great benefit to the nation in 1957 when Sputnik revived America's interest in space." Ironically, Project Feed Back, the name for RAND's space research program, was highly praised by the Administration which had specifically forbidden military space research. Much later, in 1967, an Air Force Special Study Group set up to study the impact of Project RAND concluded that the "low key" program of space research was a good example of the valuable payoffs to be gained from funding completely free and independent research programs.

The innumerable projects conducted at RAND on the electronic digital computer have resulted in dozens of important individual contributions to cybernetics. Two typical examples serve to illustrate its impact in this area. First, it created two simple computer languages—called JOSS and SIMSCRIPT II—which, unlike their highly complex predecessors, can be used by nonexperts to tell a computer what operations to perform. SIMSCRIPT II is one of the most popular new computer languages—a short form of English that can be learned with a minimum of training. Similarly, the JOSS language can be learned in a few minutes and is uniquely suited to computer systems in which individual users are scattered and linked to a central computer by small consoles. A second area of innovation has been computerized communications networks. RAND's most important contribution in this area probably was the development of the "distributed network concept," a networking scheme capable of survival and continued operation during an attack even though parts of the system may be destroyed. Through the use of many small computers the RAND-designed system would continue to dispatch messages through the damaged network by the fastest surviving link. Elements of this adaptive concept are being incorporated into several military communications networks.

Basic to RAND's ability to complete its scores of highly sophisticated jobs is its ability to draw some of the most competent researchers in the nation. As a research haven, RAND offers scholars some unique opportunities and one major limitation. The limitation is that while the researcher is free in how he works, he has not been when it comes to what he is working toward. Save for certain civilian jobs, the RAND man must relate his work to military applications. Coming to RAND means giving up basic and academic research for work that is largely related to warfare.

Trading in one's academic freedom for a slot at RAND has its compensations. One is the heady business of power and being central to the policy-making process. As one analyst there points out, his thoughts on the Sino-Soviet split are likely to end up on the desk of the President of the United States or one of his top aides—a claim that few, if any, college professors can make. This feeling of potency and action is evident throughout the corporation whose people describe the RAND experience in terms of quick trips to Washington to consult with the Joint Chiefs of Staff, access to the highest offices of the State Department, and an atmosphere of dealing with major

71

issues on a day-to-day basis.

There is, moreover, the matter of resources. RAND has always been given the best and gotten it first. The fact that it had some of the earliest computers, years before major universities were to get them, was an enormous drawing card for those who correctly surmised that computer pioneers would soon be in great demand.

Still another major attraction is its continuing sense of being a novel institution. RAND is still thought of as an experiment by its staff, who often liken it to a latter-day Tennessee Valley Authority because both are unique federally related institutions. A related attraction is RAND's determination to create new techniques. It is one of the few institutions in America where year in and year out a major percentage of its funds have been applied to finding new ways to do things.

Added to these major attractions are a bundle of influential personal considerations. The pay is excellent, and RAND employees have never complained about their benefits. Analysts there supplement their incomes by teaching or acting as paid consultants to other military think tanks. RAND's location is attractive; Herman Kahn, now of the Hudson Institute, recalls that one of the reasons he was originally drawn to RAND was because it was close enough to the beach for a noontime dip. For the Ph.D. not all that excited by the American university as a place to work, RAND is an academic institution without students, faculty meetings, tenure battles, and the constant fiscal squeeze on laboratory space.

That the attractions of RAND outweigh its disadvantages for many is attested to by the fact that in some years more than 70 percent of Americans receiving their Ph.D.s in mathematics have applied there for a job. One of the problems RAND has encountered over the years is that of "dossier builders"—those who see a stint at the corporation as crucial to enhancing their professional credentials. This situation has accounted for some of RAND's turnover.

Turnover at RAND, however, is not just the result of the credentials race. At this academy of American policy, analysts often discover their and RAND's limitations and leave. As one former RAND analyst now working elsewhere on pollution control puts it, "Policy is not exactly like a make of automobile that is restyled each year. Everyone has heard of RAND's studies that have changed American policy, but when you get there you realize that for every one of these studies there are scores which have had no dramatic impact or were simply 'housekeeping' studies for the military done to help them resolve some minor logistics problem." Others add that there is a great deal of pressure at RAND to come up with the "big study"—pressure that makes university scholarship seem leisurely in comparison. RAND's two major objectives of advancing techniques of intercontinental warfare and stemming the threat of communism also take their toll. These objectives wear morally on some, seem confining to others, and are thought of as something of a bore by still others. Until quite recently one had to leave RAND if stemming urban decay came to seem more important than combating the Red menace.

Few who leave—or criticize RAND from afar—question its ability to do a good job for the military; rather, they challenge the underlying assumptions RAND takes to the job. If the major problem in America today is misplaced priorities, then RAND is part of the problem. RAND, for example, has never worked on the very real problems encountered by the elderly today in America, but it has sternly considered the hypothetical problem of the elderly after nuclear war. As disclosed in the 1970 book *Population Control Through Nuclear Pollution* by John Gofman and Arthur Tamplin (a former RAND analyst), RAND suggested in 1966 that survivors of nuclear attack would be best off without the old and feeble, and U.S. policy should be to abandon them. Concludes the cold-blooded RAND report: "The easiest way to implement a morally repugnant but socially beneficial policy is by inaction. Under stress, the managers of post-attack society would most likely resolve their problems by failing to make any special provision for the elderly, the insane and the chronically ill."

Outside of its walls, the RAND Corporation is many things to many people. To *Pravda* it is the "American academy of death and destruction." To many tradition-bound militarists it is a place where the old values and modes of military decision-making have been usurped by human computers who talk in terms not of courage, principle, and heritage but of quantifiable variables and cost-effectiveness. The political Left perceives RAND as a vital brain center for the military-industrial complex, inspiring costly new weapons, mapping out counterinsurgency plans and computing kill rations and "megadeaths." Intellectuals not part of the defense community view it with a skepticism born of their traditional concern with secret science and

73

the use of the intellect to advance the martial arts. Congressional doves see it as a power source for the military, while, paradoxically, their hawkish counterparts sometimes contend that it is sapping the vitality of the military with its charts, computer analyses, and technical mumbo-jumbo.

There are those who have tried to put the impact and importance of RAND in less parochial terms. Arthur M. Schlesinger, Jr., for example, writes in A Thousand Days that RAND techniques and ideas have given the government ". . . the means of subjecting the anarchy of defense to a measure of order." Harvard historian Roger Hagan was quoted in Atlantic in 1963 as summing up RAND as an influence that has ". . . increased public acceptance of nuclear war as a part of national policy." Professor Bruce L. R. Smith of Columbia University concludes in The RAND Corporation that RAND has contributed to the pluralism of the American governing system by offering another voice in the making of policy. Perhaps a less abstract way of evaluating RAND is to say that by its balanced way of quantifying, investigating, innovating, and intellectualizing it has been instrumental in transforming the Air Force from a cocky young postwar entity that had been an extension of the Army into full thermonuclear maturity, strength, and, at times, sophistication—a superpower in its own right. To the Pentagon as a whole, RAND has given new methodologies and defense concepts. Its military contribution has generally been to rationalize the irrationality of warfare, make the waging of it more efficient, and the ability of the nation to defend itself more effective. While this may be a fair judgment of RAND's past, it is increasingly obvious that it will not be more than a partial description of its future role.

2. RAND Today: From Missile Detection to Stroke Detection

Such topics as cancer research, how to take up the slack in employment if peace breaks out, the problem of juvenile delinquency and the galloping spread of neurosis—these are not for the group intellectual.

—Editorial in *The Nation* on RAND and other military think tanks in January 1959

In a real attack on the United States, not just real missiles but harmless decoys sent to draw off interception and fragments of the booster rockets from the real missiles are all likely to be heading toward a given target. A prime Pentagon problem has been the inability of existing defense hardware to distinguish among those real and illusionary threats and to find a way to prevent defenses from being expended on intercepting harmless junk. RAND thus undertook a series of studies on missile detection in the mid-1950's.

One avenue they decided to explore as a tool for detection involved the human eye and mind rather than an unassisted automatic device. Tests showed that men are unexpectedly successful in detecting decoys, and RAND researchers concluded that man's vision could be extended from the visual part of the spectrum to the infrared and radar regions and outperform any automatic device. RAND is still working on the problem of extending human vision for this military application. Its research on the human eye in general subsequently led to other projects, most of them outside the military area. The most important of the projects spun off in this manner could pave the way for a major innovation in preventive health—the stroke detection center.

The RAND stroke project is composed of a truly interdisciplinary team of seventeen professionals, including engineers, statisticians, systems analysts, an ophthalmologist, a cardiologist, a neuroradiologist,

75

and a bioengineer. The leader of the project and the team's young bioengineer, Joseph J. Sheppard, remarks, "Today in America there are about two million people who are alive and suffering to varying degrees from the effects of strokes. It is, along with cancer and heart disease, one of the three big killers, but unlike the other two more acute diseases, it leaves more disabled people. At least half of all stroke sufferers who don't die right away are left handicapped."

The project itself centers on stroke prevention and was inspired by the observation that many people who are later felled by strokes first exhibit minor signs such as eye troubles that show up well before the stroke itself. The work relies heavily on clinical research that indicates that three out of four strokes are not due to cerebral hemorrhages but rather to occlusive lesions to the carotid system—or, in layman's terms, most strokes are caused by deposits that block the arteries in the side of the neck. These deposits can be removed surgically, thereby preventing stroke in many cases. As Sheppard explains it, these findings have led to the conclusion that if these lesions can be detected early, they can be removed or treated so that the cause of many, if not most, strokes will have been removed.

The first major step in this program involves the development and testing of a detection unit or "stroke screening clinic." Work began on the development of such a clinic in 1968, and by mid-1970 most of the components of a prototype clinic had been assembled and, according to Sheppard, could be in test operation within a year. The test installation will be used on patients who have been referred to it by doctors who notice symptoms of stroke, such as the patient who has gone to an ophthalmologist with eye trouble that cannot be diagnosed as any known eye disorder. The clinic itself gives a series of atraumatic tests (i.e., a test that can be given without puncturing the patient's skin). The checkup begins with a review of the patient's medical history with particular attention to anything that might conceivably indicate stroke in his future, and then moves on to four technical procedures. They are: ophthalmodynamometry, which is a measure of the blood pressure in the carotid arteries; mediate auscultation, a stethoscopic examination of the carotid area that can detect the sound of turbulence in a partially blocked artery; funduscopy, or the examination of the rear interior of the eyes through retinal photography; and finally thermography, a photographic technique in which heat emissions of the head are recorded and will show the possible presence of arterial blocking by depicting the cooler areas, which are a strong hint that an artery is partially closed.

According to Sheppard, when the clinic is set up in the 1972–73 period it will be able to handle thirty to thirty-five people a day, with each person being screened in about an hour. It will be staffed by a professional nurse, two technicians, and a physician who would be on call. He says it will eventually become a "semi-automated" procedure with computers correlating many of the test results. The team hopes to be able to test a prototype unit for a year or longer to evaluate its usefulness and then, when it has proven itself, offer its design for others to copy. Sheppard says that at this point the team emphasizes that the clinic will neither locate all potential stroke victims nor will it necessarily lead to treatment that is effective; however, the members of the team do believe that the procedure will serve to weed out many who need to be treated to prevent strokes either by surgery or medication. In addition, such clinics will serve to collect data on strokes that may lead to further advances in preventing them.

This particular project serves on several levels as a symbol of the RAND Corporation today. First, it shows how RAND is able, as it has been in previous cases, to develop its research naturally from military technology to technology that can be used to solve civilian problems. Second, it displays RAND's particular ability to convene interdisciplinary teams and their utility in solving technical problems. Sheppard points out with considerable pride that the stroke project is one of very few large, truly interdisciplinary teams in America at work on a medical problem and adds that, without a variety of highly capable specialists, such complex projects would be impractical. It also shows the direction in which RAND is moving and where its vitality is today. In interview after interview at RAND, officials and staff members cite the stroke project and several other nonmilitary efforts as the most exciting and important work going on there currently. Finally, and perhaps most important, it shows that even the mighty RAND Corporation cannot readily contend with the illogical set of research priorities sanctioned today in America. The fact of the matter is that the stroke project has been slowed by lack of funds, has continually had to go begging, and survived its first phases only with the help of extra RAND Corporation funds and private donations. Sheppard added that outside consultants to the project had helped keep it alive by contributing their time for nothing. As he summed up the situation,

"Forgetting human misery for a moment, just the economic cost of stroke to this country is tremendous. A third of its victims are wage earners and it has been estimated that the cost of caring for those who have had strokes runs to about $3 billion a year. Although the government allots money for research into the rehabilitation of those who have been attacked by it, there is close to zero in funds for research into preventing strokes." Another RAND staff member who was not on the stroke project but well aware of its financial dilemma acidly remarked in private conversation, "If they could find a way to make stroke detection apply to the ABM program, they'd have the money they needed in a minute."

Today the RAND Corporation is like the mother whose child has grown and matured under her care, and she is now looking for a new direction in life as her child becomes less and less dependent on her. RAND is beginning to find that new direction as its work diversifies and its list of clients broadens. Although it has dabbled in nonmilitary work for some time, increasingly civilian institutions are seeking its services—a trend that RAND is encouraging. Its articles of incorporation dictate that it cannot go out and compete with others for research work, but it is allowed to accept or set up research arrangements with people who come to it. The Office of Economic Opportunity, for example, has asked RAND for research help on several occasions, and in 1969 the New York and American Stock Exchanges sought technical help from RAND in unjamming the paperwork mess that has crippled both exchanges in recent years.

Although its principal client is still the Air Force—the original Project RAND accounts for half its research program, while another 15 percent of its work goes for other military agencies—its civilian research had grown to 35 percent of all its activities in 1970. Its fifteen or so nonmilitary clients include the Ford Foundation, the National Institutes of Health, several private hospitals, the Carnegie Corporation, and the city of New York. Its unprecedented volume of civilian work has grown quickly in the last few years and is expected to continue to grow significantly in the future. Although this domestic nonmilitary work is still relatively minor to its total effort, it is extremely important to those at RAND today in terms of its future business and future importance to the nation. Asked to name the really exciting things now emerging from the corporation, RAND officials answer in terms of new techniques for solving urban problems, medical systems and the like. This excitement over nonmilitary work seems genuine enough, no doubt in part because these civilian projects are mostly geared to solving long-felt social problems. Furthermore, although few RAND people readily admit it, its military work is a shadow of its former self, much of it unstimulating replays of former triumphs. RAND is still working on the problems of military bases but it is now clerk's work—mechanical long-term studies of the utility of overseas bases, being conducted with an eye to future negotiations with host governments. It still conducts economic analysis for the Air Force, but much of it is concerned with trying to figure out how its client can live with stable or declining budgets rather than growing ones. Few studies are concerned with massive new systems. RAND is still a Russia- and China-watcher, but so are a lot of other institutions.

One of those who talks openly about RAND's new conception of itself is its forty-four-year-old president, Henry S. Rowen, a longtime RAND employee who worked on the Wohlstetter team that studied overseas bases. During the Kennedy years he left RAND as one of the "whiz kids" brought to the Pentagon by Secretary of Defense McNamara to become an Assistant Secretary of Defense. A friendly, outgoing man with a deceptively dour face, Rowen talks with unbureaucratic frankness and gives the impression of being an active, athletic man. Rowen acknowledges that RAND is clearly facing an important juncture in its history. "It is now hard to be at the cutting edge of national security problems," he says. "We're getting old and much of the action that groups like ourselves have practiced is moving from outside of government to the inside. The government has become much more thoughtful, if I can use that term in the sense that a think tank is thoughtful. There are now systems analysis groups throughout government, and though many of them have been stimulated by RAND, they have hurt RAND."

He stresses that RAND's strong desire now is to face new challenges in new areas, "although we have every intention of staying with military problems because those problems have not gone away." The new challenges are pervasive domestic problems like urban blight and an imperfect medical health system. Rowen adds that RAND has started its move in this direction and is refocusing its talents with speed. "Three years ago only about five percent of our work was in the domestic area, in 1969 it hit 20 percent, and for 1970 it will amount to 35 percent or more." The first "major breakthrough," according to Rowen, is an arrangement with the city of New York which has resulted in the establishment of the New York City–RAND Institute (see Chapter IX) and another breakthrough may be in the offing as a result of work RAND is beginning for the state of California. Rowen would like to see its work for California centered in an institution by itself, as has happened in New York City. Further, he believes that policy analysis groups like the New York Institute will have to be set up around the nation as a means of extricating local governments from the mess they are in. "Things are desperate," he says, "and most local governments simply don't even have enough competent people to figure out what resources they have let alone figure exactly what they need."

As Rowen points out, RAND is not precisely on the verge of beating itself into a plowshare, but indications abound that it is changing and emerging from its role as a closed paramilitary academy. Rowen himself talks about major nonmilitary roles that RAND might be able to play, such as mapping out *the* program to deal with the nation's environmental problems. Its international-studies director, James F. Digby, predicts that in the near future RAND analysts will be working for foreign governments and international agencies. He expresses the thought that RAND may be able to do a lot more good by helping other nations rather than studying them for the United States.

Even in its heavily military research areas, there has been at RAND some shift in emphasis away from Cold War partisanship. On the drawing boards next to studies of third-world insurgency, the effectiveness of counterinfiltration control in Vietnam, and the military potential of Communist China are such projects as a Ford Foundation-sponsored examination of possible solutions to the Middle East crisis, including the use of peace-keeping forces and demilitarized zones, and studies of population and birth control in underdeveloped lands for the Agency for International Development. In the strategic area along with its studies of total-war options and the effectiveness of air "interdiction" in Laos and Vietnam, RAND has been working on studies to background the U.S.'s team at the Strategic Arms Limitation Talks (SALT) and is working on the manifold problems of switching to an all-volunteer Army. Current RAND work in technology and methodology tends to focus more on improving the state of the art in such realms as the biosciences, neurology, cancer research, and ecology than in areas of military importance.

Another aspect of a changing RAND is evidence of doubts about military power and the whole effort in Vietnam that poke through a once virtually unified façade. Superficially, the growing disenchantment can be detected on the bumpers of the low-slung sports cars and economy imports that predominate in RAND's parking areas, where there is a considerable display of stickers like "How Many Vietnamese Fought in Our Civil War?" and "Vietnam: Love It or Leave it." More significantly it is detectable as terms like "new priorities" crop up in conversations with a frequency one would expect among a cluster of liberal Democrats. One of the more sensational examples of disaffection for the war at RAND occurred in December 1969 when six RAND analysts—including Daniel Ellsberg—sent identical letters to the New York *Times* and the Washington *Post*, which both papers printed. The letter said in part: "Now the American people are once again debating the issue of Vietnam, [and] we desire to contribute to that discussion by presenting our views which reflect both personal judgments and years of professional research on the Vietnam war and related matters. . . . We believe that the United States should decide now to end its participation in the Vietnam war, completing the total withdrawal within one year at the most. . . ." The long letter went on to list specific reasons for withdrawal that included frontal attacks on some of the Johnson–Nixon pet rationales, such as the domino theory, the negative international impact of a pullout, and the notion that the enemy was weakening. They argued that neither North nor South Vietnam wanted peace, and in the face of such intractability the only option for the U.S. was to get out. Not only were these six analysts not fired but their letter turned them into minor celebrities at America's best known think tank.

Needless to say, the most sensational crack in the façade was the public revelation of the "Pentagon papers." Their publication thrust RAND into a difficult position which immediately strained the relationship between it and the Pentagon. Since the documents which got to the press were copied by a RAND employee from a copy entrusted to RAND, its loyalty to the government and its security procedures were immediately challenged. As a result, both of RAND's copies of the forty-seven-volume report were recalled and all of its classified material was turned over to Air Force officers stationed at

RAND—a move that essentially took RAND's long-standing security clearance away. Adding to the strain of the Ellsberg incident was the fact that another ex-RAND analyst, Anthony J. Russo, chose to go to jail for contempt rather than answer a federal grand jury's questions about Ellsberg and the papers. After Ellsberg's public confession, Russo's action, and the security-tightening move by Secretary of Defense Laird, the mood around RAND was fearful. According to a report in the New York *Times* in June 1971, the majority of RAND's people were upset with the fact that not only had the "rules" of secret analysis been broken but that the long-term result might be a lessening of federal confidence in the institution and a subsequent loss of revenue. To be sure, there were still many at RAND in full support of the war, and to them Ellsberg's action was unpardonable.

The man with the responsibility of broadening RAND's thrust into nonmilitary areas is Gustave H. Shubert, a vice-president in his early forties. Like that of the corporation itself, his experience has been primarily in military areas, but Shubert is both optimistic about RAND's ability to contribute to civilian problem-solving and refreshingly skeptical of its ability to work miracles or to bring all of its famed techniques to bear on pressing domestic problems. He says, "I am afraid that too much faith is put in techniques like systems analysis, and if they are going to be applied to civilian problems, they are going to have to be used with care and sharply modified. One cannot think that current problems can be solved by rushing in a lot of engineers and computer experts to apply a lot of old strategic concepts." Shubert, like Rowen, believes that the area in which RAND may have its greatest future impact is in setting up satellite Project RANDs to help cities and states. Beyond California as a candidate for the first state think tank, he mentions both the city of San Francisco and the state of Illinois among other governments RAND has been talking with about possible long-term projects.

RAND's expeditions into nonmilitary realms has been even more significant than the fact that 35 percent of its support comes from civil sponsors, for many of these civilian projects are thus far small and not as generously financed as they may become in the future. To suggest the trend in one area, RAND was working on twenty-six health projects in 1970 besides the previously mentioned stroke project. Many of these projects offer potential benefits, no less significant than those promised by the stroke-prevention clinics. Its health projects show a diversity of approaches to and concerns about health that is typical of RAND's many-sided way of approaching a problem. Subjects under study run from intensely technical efforts, such as harnessing the power of the computer for medical research, to mundane but no less important matters such as new designs for hospitals with an eye to efficiency and patient comfort.

In charge of RAND's health program is M. A. Rockwell, a young man whose credentials are rare if not unique. He became interested in the medical applications of computers while working as a mathematician, and to give himself the skills he thought would be needed to marry cybernetics and medicine he took time out to enroll in and graduate from medical school. Rockwell characterizes the work of the health-programs section of RAND as being concerned with the "ecology of health." He explains that his department is working on the quality and efficiency of health care while striving to reduce the cost to patients and the financial strain on the health community itself—a community which he feels is on its way to financial bankruptcy unless sweeping changes are made.

The series of studies of the economics of health in America that Rockwell heads up amounts to an attempt to explain the meteoric rise in health-care costs and demands on the health-care system and to come up with remedial suggestions. One bit of information that has already surfaced in these studies is that the government vastly underestimated the costs and demands of the Medicare and Medicaid programs and still has no efficient means of determining the cost of future health programs. RAND is working for two Los Angeles-area hospitals—Children's Hospital and the Hospital of the Good Samaritan—on long-term projects to improve their organizations, operations, and facilities.

One intensely personal project being carried out is under the direction of a RAND pathologist whose wife contracted leukemia. In leukemia cases, there are four drugs which in combination can be used to keep the patient alive, but they must be given with great care, for they can kill the patient as quickly as the disease itself. Doctors normally administer the drugs as best they can in what Rockwell calls "a tough, crude balancing act between life and death." The RAND pathologist got mathematicians at the corporation to construct a computer model of a human with leukemia—in other words, as Rockwell puts it, "they gave the disease to a computer." By using the computer as a guinea pig for testing doses of the drug, the pathologist has worked out a regimen for the management of the drugs so that the trial-and-error aspects of the treatment are experienced by the computer and not the patient. Rockwell calls the work a "conceptual breakthrough" in the administration of drugs, and though in the case of leukemia it promises no cure, the concept does offer a possible system for keeping patients alive longer and in greater comfort, as it has done in the case of the wife of the RAND doctor. In other applications of computer modeling to medicine, RAND has constructed and is refining computers that simulate the lungs, kidneys, brain, blood system, and eye—a development that of course offers considerable possibilities for nonhuman medical experimentation.

Rockwell himself is heading a project aimed at improving the effectiveness of coronary care units and thereby improving the lot of the heart-attack victim. The project began with the realization that there was little reliable data available on the effectiveness of intensive-care units for heart-attack victims. Rockwell's group has collected extensive data on cardiac care from units in eighty hospitals throughout California. Thus far the work has yielded the largest file on heart patients ever assembled and has already led to some interesting findings. Among them are that some hospitals do better than others in caring for heart patients and may help improve care in those hospitals not doing as well; that many patients now receiving treatment in cardiac care units don't need it—a finding which points to the possibility that less expensive forms of care may be best for many patients; and that in many cardiac care cases intensive care has meant the difference between life and death.

As a final example of the kind of approach RAND is capable of making to a current social problem, its environmentalists are creating a highly complex computer model that will simulate the climatic changes occurring on the earth. This model will move more quickly than the actual climate of the earth and will be able to simulate a day in the meteorological history of the earth in twenty to thirty minutes. This feat will enable possible future decades of the earth's climate to be speeded up and simulated so that theories about our environmental future can be tested before it is supposed to occur. Is a new ice age in the offing, for example, as some have predicted, and what effect will a widely discussed Soviet plan to siphon off Arctic waters to irrigate Siberia have on the earth's climatic balance? As R. R. Rapp, head of RAND's environmental sciences group, puts it,

"We need devices to tell us what our environmental future is so that we can take action to prevent calamity. Like many in our field, we are worried about the future, and one of our worries is that we are in trouble unless we know what are the right things to worry about."

For all of RAND's collective brilliance—a characteristic even its most determined critics grudgingly grant—it has by its own admission fallen behind in perceiving and acting to solve the major problems facing the nation. It is now trying to catch up, and without question a new RAND is developing. Barring some unforeseen challenge to "national security" in the military sense, its once single-minded concern for that issue will soon become just one of many concerns about national security in the broadest, nonmilitary sense of the term. If RAND cannot make that conversion, then it knows it might as well go out of business. Or it could start making typewriters; after all, it has a built-in reputation.

3. Up from Santa Monica: Alumni and Apostles

> *"The military professionals dub these civilian interlopers into the national security arena "defense intellectuals," "RANDsters," "technocrats" and worse. General Thomas D. White recently declared that in common with other military men, 'I am profoundly apprehensive of the pipe-smoking, trees-full-of-owls type of the so-called defense intellectuals who have been brought into this nation's capital.'"*
>
> —*Business Week*, from an article entitled "Planners for the Pentagon"

"National resource" is the term that those at RAND like to use to describe their organization. Though self-serving, the term is appropriate because RAND has—for good or bad—been tapped for ideas, techniques, and services that have served the national purpose as defined in Washington. The term also works when applied to the roles it has played outside of its formal research responsibilities. To be more specific, RAND plays two important and not necessarily planned roles that have served to spread its particular gospel of policy research. It has been both an academy producing graduates who have moved in and out of government and an inspiration and, to varying degrees, a model for a large variety of other think tanks.

"McNamara's techniques were RAND's techniques," claims RAND's Goldstein, suggesting how from time to time its analysts are brought into government, either one at a time or en masse, to effect change. The example Goldstein cites is the most dramatic in RAND's young history—the one in which RAND supplied the rebellious faction that created the "McNamara Revolution" in the Pentagon. Charles J. Hitch, Pentagon comptroller, Henry Rowen, Assistant Secretary of Defense, and Alain Enthoven, Deputy Assistant for Systems Analysis, were the three most important figures brought in from RAND, but there were others. As *Business Week* commented in early 1961, when the RAND invasion was beginning, "Anyone looking for a line on the Kennedy Administration's defense policy soon finds the trail leading to a group of military economists, mathematicians, and statisticians and to Santa Monica's RAND Corporation." Their influence over the Department of Defense was mostly methodological as they introduced or further developed a range of RAND techniques and concepts like program budgeting, systems analysis, gaming, cost-effectiveness, and new procurement policies. During this period McNamara was quoted on several occasions as saying that the military had received from it in new ideas more than ten times what it had spent on RAND. As Goldstein sums it up, "It is really difficult to determine how good or bad the influence of our men was, but it was extensive." Other RAND men have filled high-ranking slots in the Bureau of the Budget, the Department of Health, Education and Welfare, and elsewhere. Similarly, RAND employees are used extensively on commissions, committees, task forces, and planning groups. The 1966 RAND Annual Report, for example, stated that some ninety staff members were holding down 269 advisory posts, with groups serving such entities as the White House, Department of Defense, Commerce Department, and the National Science Foundation.

More dramatic is RAND's role as prototype for other institutions. So common is the concept of a bureaucrat or problem-solver proposing "a RAND-like entity" to tackle an area of policy research that at RAND the facetious description often rendered for itself is that of "a RAND-like entity located in Santa Monica." As the first permanent military think tank, it was a source of inspiration (and doubtless some jealousy) in prompting the creation of the other military think tanks. It was the model for the first national think tank, the Urban Institute (see Chapter IX), and for the creation of other nonmilitary appendages of government.

Some of the ways in which RAND serves as prototype are quite basic indeed and not at all involved with the abstract concepts of policy sciences. A prime example is financing. One of the Ford Foundation's first large grants went to help the RAND Corporation emerge from its Douglas cocoon. Since then large foundations have played an active role in funding the start and continuation of think tanks. Ford money has been used to start scores of new think tanks, ranging from the Pentagon's secretive Institute for Defense Analyses to the fiercely antimilitary Institute for Policy Studies. The Ford Foundation is also an active, continuing supporter of a large variety of think-tank projects. If RAND is the mother of think tanks, the Ford Foundation must be considered the father.

In fact, RAND shares at least part of the credit for waking the nascent Ford Foundation. When RAND was trying to turn itself from a department into a corporation, it looked to a variety of foundations for support, but none of the major ones then in operation could help it out for a variety of policy reasons. As RAND's Goldstein recalls, the Ford Foundation was at that time just beginning to think about changing from a rather limited philanthropic organization to a major foundation and force in American life, and the men running Project RAND decided that they might be able to convince the foundation to part with some of its money. Their approach was carefully plotted. For example, when it was discovered that Dr. Karl Compton, one of the foundation's trustees, was traveling from New York to Boston by train, three RAND officials arranged to ride the same train to lobby for support. Finally, Ford decided to give RAND $100,000 and guaranteed it $300,000 in bank credit.

Another pattern established by RAND was that of obtaining continuing federal support in which, year in and year out, an agency promises the think tank relative freedom to pick projects and problems to solve.

While RAND has served as model for many think tanks, it has worked an even more direct and personal influence on the many institutions that were either formed by RAND itself or created by one or more of its employees. Alumni have founded such think groups as the Planning Research Corporation, TEMPO, the Institute for the Future, and the Hudson Institute. Two think tanks, the System Development Corporation and ANSER (for Analytic Services Inc.), were created by RAND but are no longer affiliated with it. Presently, the National Institute of Education, an idea advanced by President Nixon in early 1970 for a super research group to coordinate the nation's educational research, is being born under guidance of a RAND team under contract.

RAND's offspring are a mixed bag. ANSER, for example, is a small, relatively obscure, tight-lipped Air Force think tank which serves to provide its sponsor with information on advanced weapons. In contrast, the Planning Research Corporation is a large diversified outfit consisting of a parent company and seventeen subsidiaries and affiliated groups that among them do virtually everything. It has, for instance, planned the recent relocation of the obsolete London Bridge to the American Southwest as a tourist attraction, assessed the U.S. market for foreign candy sales, designed the new subway system for Buenos Aires, and is providing technical direction for several weapons systems.

Two of RAND's most illustrious and markedly different descendants are the System Development Corporation and the Hudson Institute. SDC is closely allied with the computer which it uses as a tool and which it has advanced as an element of federal systems. This close relationship with the computer does not necessarily exist at all think tanks. In fact, at the Hudson Institute, perhaps the best known of all the RAND spin-offs, its members often boast that its computing power is, with a gesture to the head, "all up here."

VI

. . . AND TWO OF
HER CHILDREN

---

1. Herman-on-Hudson

Scenario I—Successful Restoration of Soviet
Power
*1. Security breached: Soviet espionage net-
work picks up word of plot in Bucharest,
Prague*
*2. Confirmation from Soviet Agent in Bonn
Ministry of All-German Affairs, Quai
D'Orsay*
*3. Moscow alerts DDR (East German) old
guard*
*4. Soviets see DDR—keystone of their
East European security—threatened, consider options:*
    *A. Crush conspiracy directly (with neg-
        ative effects in "satellites," west)*
    *B. Move directly through DDR old
        guard*
5. Soviets choose proxy operation:
    *A. Old guard infiltrates modernist con-
        spiracy*
    *B. DDR agents agitate among national-
        ist elements in West Germany*
    *C. Entice 5–10 middle-echelon Bun-
        deswehr officers, officials in West*

German Ministry of Defense to "correspondence"

D. Deploy DDR (and Soviet) forces behind screen of maneuver

6. Modernists touch off East Berlin demonstration, riots spread through DDR

7. Berlin wall torn down: East and West Berliners mingle

8. DDR troops strike, suppress rioters, cross into West Berlin ("hot pursuit")

9. Berlin Garrison isolated, small-scale fighting with DDR troops

10. Garrison besieged in West Berlin center, suffers few casualties

11. USSR announces full support for regime in face [of] "provocation"

12. DDR, USSR disclose West German "complicity"

13. NATO allies angry at Bonn, disunited: US temporizes

14. DDR allows civilian evacuation West Berlin, offers compensation in 30-year bonds

15. Soviets reinforce

16. Declining West European morale: "Finlandization"; revived fear of West Germany in East, respect for USSR. . . .

Scenario IV—A US-Soviet Central War

1. As in Scenario I, but US and allies launch two-division attack along Berlin highway to relieve Berlin

2. Attack penetrates 50–60 kilometers into DDR

3. Soviets demand withdrawal NATO forces from DDR, threaten to use tactical nuclear weapons

4. Soviets use tactical nuclears, destroy NATO forces, Moscow issues call for mobilization

5. US responds in kind

6. *****

—Two of four scenarios based on the same series of events from a study for the Air Force by the Hudson Institute entitled "War Termination Issues and Concepts." Delivered June 1968.

The Hudson Institute is located on a hill in a bucolic setting overlooking the Hudson River at Croton-on-Hudson, about twenty-five miles from New York City. The spacious grounds contain seven buildings ranging from a small cozy cottage used for conferences to a dark, stone Gothic mansion which serves as Hudson's headquarters. Each building is of a distinctly different architectural style in accordance with a therapeutic theory held by the doctor who had originally put the estate together as a private mental hospital. Housed in this bizarre scramble of buildings is what must be considered the think tank at its most flamboyant.

Founded in 1961 by two men, it is now composed of about forty permanent fellows and relies on some 100 outside consultants. Though relatively small in size, Hudson evinces interests in a broad range of great issues, from thermonuclear protocol to developing whole continents, and the future of the Western world. Its first five years were devoted almost exclusively to defense policy research, but it is now drifting into a variety of new areas. The change to its present mix of about half military and half nonmilitary work was accompanied by a change in the motto of the Institute from "National Security—International Order" to the new "Policy Research in the Public Interest."

There is a certain unmistakable style to the institute fostered by Herman Kahn, its leader and director since inception. Kahn is unmistakably the most prolific, controversial, and outspoken of the "defense intellectuals" who emerged in the late 1950's and early 1960's. His influence over the institute has been such that the place has come to be known as "Herman-on-Hudson." The role he assumed as the man who was not afraid to let out all the stops when discussing nuclear war caused him to be called everything from courageous realist to nuclear bogeyman. His influence is everywhere at the institute, and it is all but impossible to engage in conversation with one of its Fellows without hearing references to "Herman." As one staff member puts it: "There are two institutions here: Herman and the institute. They go together like a great opera and a great star and one really can't perceive it all perfectly until he hears both." First, the opera.

There are only a few titles at Hudson, and staffers point proudly to the fact that Herman calls the black mail-deliverer "Walter" and Walter calls Herman "Herman." Dress is as casual as one prefers, and members are encouraged to set their own working hours and general *modus operandi*—an arrangement that staff members like to dwell on. George Wittman, an animated institute fellow working on a long-range study of the future, says, "We've made a conscious attempt to create a character here by scrupulously avoiding regular patterns."

Lack of traditional structure and stricture is just one of the unique facets of Hudson. It also has, for example, its own way of speaking. It has coined words of its own such as "doomsday machine," "mega-corpse," and "wargasm" (defined by one of the fellows as "when all of the buttons are pushed"). Then there are catch phrases and names for its approaches, many of them coined or popularized by Kahn, such as: "thinking about the unthinkable"—the motto for Hudson's insistence that it look at *every* alternative when considering an issue and not be afraid to do so; "expert amateur" (also referred to as "trained incapacity")—the role of the Hudson thinker in a world of experts; "scenario"—a RAND creation popularized by Hudson; and "surprise-free projection"—a prediction based on current trends, which is therefore not surprising. Also there are the big New York *Times* crossword-puzzle words that are used routinely at the institute, like "heuristic" (serving to stimulate investigation) and "propaedeutic" (pertaining to the conveying of preliminary instruction).

Another characteristic of Hudson is its proclivity to be bold, outspoken—and very general. Since the institute is in the center of many vital issues, this element of style produces startling, sometimes unnerving results. In making the rounds at the institute, one wonders if its staff members fully recognize that they are talking with someone from the outside world. Perhaps the best way to impart this aspect of Hudson is to offer a sample of the more colorful and outlandish statements offered during the course of a visit.

"We're the product of affluence," says Hudson fellow George Wittman on the institute's offerings, "and people with money come to us as an oracle because they can afford an oracle and, who knows, they may get something out of it." At another point he says, "If I were in a company and one of my men told me he was going to the Hudson Institute for a study, I'd probably fire him." Wittman on Kahn: "He's amazing. He puts people on to destroy their values and is not afraid to tell absolute lies just to see what happens. He must drive Henry Kissinger out of his mind."

Ray Wilson, a soft-spoken, polite, retired colonel who serves the institute as part of the administrative staff, comments on defense scenarios: "We've developed a large number of outbreak scenarios that are really plots which trace possible world events into the outbreak of hostility or nuclear war. One interesting thing we've found in developing these scenarios is that it's incredibly hard to get a major war started." Wilson says of the institute's work, "In general, our people are scornful of details in working on projects, which sometimes leads to problems."

Basil J. Candella, an outgoing chemical engineer and a veteran of most of Hudson's major international development projects, remarks of work he would like to do as a continuation of earlier work done for the city of New York: "We'd like to have a look at other things —ideally to be given a *carte blanche* from the city. If only I had a spectacular idea for Harlem, then I could work on it and then we might be successful in getting some money." Candella on pollution: "I'm not a purist in these matters. I'm a realist. Look at the Grand Canyon, one of the greatest environmental ravages around, and that was done by God. I'm not so sure we shouldn't be looking at ideas that seem impractical now but that may not be in the future. For example, perhaps we should think of piping our garbage into the Gulf Stream, which would feed the algae, which in turn would grow and offer us a new food supply. I'm working on an idea that may sound stupid, but it could take care of two big problems: saving the railroads and getting rid of our garbage. We could use the railroads to cart all our garbage to barren areas of the West where heat will boil off the water in the garbage. I'm working on the costs of such a plan." Candella offhandedly adds that the dried-out garbage could be used to "landscape" the plains.

Barry Bruce-Briggs, a young researcher who was trained as a historian (and who points out he could have been "the American Toynbee"), says of Hudson and the Pentagon: "Most real military innovation is made over the feelings of the uniformed officers by the so-called whiz kids and defense intellectuals. We've performed this role and for that reason our senior staff people are received at the highest level in the Pentagon like the Jesuit advisors who walked the courts of the Hapsburgs."

One staff member who uncharacteristically asked that his statement not be attributed to him had this to say about the staff's way of looking at things: "Herman would like to be advising God on how

93

to run the universe, and this is reflected in his choice of men who work at the institute—we are men, like him, who think big and refuse to be constrained by disciplines, preconceived notions, or the expected." He adds that, like Kahn, the average staff member comes from a lower-middle-class background, craves to be in on new ideas, and cannot tolerate fools, long-winded experts, or bureaucracies.

Just as Hudson has a characteristic style, so does it also have a distinct approach to policy research for its clients. Max Singer, an easygoing, soft-spoken attorney who is president of Hudson and one of its co-founders, explains the institute's role as researcher: "Most experts have very strong tendencies to perceive problems as, or turn problems into, technical problems within their own area of competence, giving relatively little weight to other aspects of the problem. The values applied by the expert are normally his own values or those fashionable at the moment in his profession or the element of his profession to which he belongs, not the values of the decision-maker whom he is advising. At Hudson we have a group of people who try to deal with this problem by being willing to 'play expert' for all the public policy problems we work on." Seen another way by Singer, the staff at Hudson tries to approach problems as "expert amateurs" —that is, the staff is expert at playing expert in whatever fields are relevant to the problems being examined. Singer, who actively participates in the research program, was involved in early 1970 in a $150,000 contract from the Division of the Budget of the State of New York which called for a five-month study of the state's policy toward drugs and drug abuse. Although neither Hudson nor Singer can claim previous experience in the area, Singer explains that this is how the institute moves. "I'm now working on this drug study," he says, "but after it's done, I may start in on an urban transportation project or something entirely different." He points out during another part of the conversation, "Whether we're working on drugs or nuclear weapons we are novices. We can always find experts to help us."

Using the drug study as an example, Singer outlines the three phases through which Hudson studies pass. "First," he says, "we inform ourselves: talking to people we know, reading the literature, talking to police, addicts, and ex-addicts. Secondly, we begin to formulate policy points of view. We develop ideas and shoot them down, learning how to defend the ideas that have merit. Finally, we

94

put it all together, offering the sponsor the alternatives we have come up with. As is our normal approach, in the drug study we will be looking at every alternative from the legalization of heroin to zealous enforcement of the law."

Although there has been a shift away from heavy defense orientation—defense work has run as high as 80 percent of Hudson's activity—it still accounts for about half of the work. Military work at the institute runs through many areas, most of it oriented to situations that don't—but might—exist. Their effort has been to shy away from urgent research in favor of longer-range futuristic military research, although, Hudson has done some work on Vietnam and the ABM system, both of which fall into the urgent category. According to its 1968 "Report to Members," a "substantial" amount of its military work is secret.

Some of its recent and current studies give an idea of the kind of thing Hudson thinkers dwell on for the military. A study in "War Termination" looked at the means for ending wars that might break out between the U. S. and China or the Soviet Union. Another recent study considered how information on nuclear force could be communicated—primarily for reasons of bargaining—during a war or in a period of intense crisis. One of Hudson's many contracts with the Office of Civil Defense examined "Post-Attack Social Organization," a series of projections on what America might be like after a nuclear attack. Other studies have been quite general in nature, covering such areas as "International Peacekeeping," "Stability and Tranquility Among Older Nations," a look at the possible uses of force in the 1970's, and an "Analytic Summary of U.S. National Security Policy Issues." Not all of the military work is done for the government. For example, Hudson has worked on a study for the Grumman Aircraft Corporation to forecast the technology of Navy planes for the period starting in 1985.

Recent work in a variety of nonmilitary areas shows what Hudson staff members refer to as its "diverse menu." The Space Agency commissioned Hudson to look at long-range planning methodologies for the space program—or as one of the seven who worked on the project summed it up, ". . . helping NASA try to figure out what to do for an encore." Coca-Cola is underwriting a Hudson analysis of the current situation and probable prospects for youth movements, adolescent rebellion, and youthful alienation. Hudson has conducted an analysis

95

of poverty programs for the U.S. Office of Economic Opportunity and has performed other studies for the U.S. Office of Education. The institute's range is further demonstrated by a sampling of the titles of some of its studies: "The Pros and Cons of a Japanese ABM," "The Utility of Protecting Gold from Nuclear Attack," "Groping for Perspective in Race Relations in the United States," "The Electric Car in Perspective," "An Arab-Israeli Nuclear War," "A Military and Police Security System for Vietnam," "Characteristics of Alternative Anti-Poverty Measures," and "Crisis Preparations for Post-attack Economic Recovery."

A major project that Hudson is beginning, which will take at least four years to complete, is entitled "The Future of the Corporation and Corporate Environment." One hundred U.S. and foreign corporations will co-sponsor the undertaking with such monoliths as Ford, General Motors, General Electric, IBM, Xerox, and Westinghouse among the participants. This study will be Hudson's major institutional effort in the near future.

Such varied studies are Hudson's major product and worth examining in more detail. Two of the most interesting areas are those of international development and thermonuclear warfare—the former emerging as a specialty of the house and the latter somewhat on the wane at Hudson.

On the international front, Hudson's most impressive credential is the fact that its work is actually being realized in a massive scheme in Colombia to create two huge lakes with a combined length of 120 miles. Called the Chocó Project, the plan emerged from Hudson in 1968; once completed, there will be two low dams across the Atrato and San Juan rivers that will create the two connected lakes—one linked to the Pacific Ocean and the other to the Carribean by canals and channels. The plan, which was paid for by the Colombian Ministry of Public Works, foresees new sources of hydroelectric power, the opening of the Chocó Valley for economic development, and better access to the oceans from the Cauca Valley, Colombia's prime industrial area. Hudson is not shy about its role in the plan. According to its "Report to Members," "It is not often that a small private organization can, with its first economic development study, touch off an idea that becomes one of the major programs of a country of Colombia's importance."

As a first excursion into large-scale national development, the Chocó project is an ambitious one—perhaps too ambitious. Hudson's sixty-page report on the project states that its concepts were developed in the period from March 1, 1968, to March 15, 1969, by four Hudson staff members. One can seriously question whether the time expended or the experience possessed by four men was adequate to raise the profound questions that should be asked before such a massive job begins. One who does more than question the project is John Sullivan, a staff man on the House Committee on Foreign Affairs who has spent time at Hudson and follows its programs. He says, "Generally, the institute gets hung up on techniques and exhibits little understanding of what those techniques lead to. The Chocó project is a good illustration. They've gotten very interested in the technique of making lakes but they haven't looked at the people the program will displace, its impact on the central government or what it will do to the environment."

Hudson has been studying "new approaches" to national development since mid-1964. Funded by private and government grants and Hudson research funds, a variety of other reports and suggestions on unique alternatives have been developed. The boldest notion is that of a system proposed in a Hudson work entitled "A South American 'Great Lakes' System." The concept advanced by the Hudson team calls for the construction of seven low dams to create five regional great lakes (or nine dams and seven lakes, if you count the Chocó project already under development). The plan projects new lakes to be located mainly in Brazil, Bolivia, Colombia, and Peru and dams to be erected on the Amazon (Peru and Brazil), Caqueta (Colombia), Mamoré (Brazil and Bolivia), and Guaporé (Brazil and Bolivia) rivers. The concept, according to the Hudson report, would have some—if not all—of the following effects:

Connect the nations of Brazil, Venezuela, Colombia, Peru, Bolivia, Paraguay, and Argentina through the interior of the continent.

Reduce current navigation difficulties and distances. Open new, well-drained land areas, currently inaccessible.

Stimulate trade between the industrial complexes of Buenos Aires and São Paulo and raw material producers of the north and west.

Act as a catalyst to continental and regional economic integration.

Train technicians of different nations to work together on projects with joint or common goals.

Focus foreign development efforts on tangible goals.

Produce major new activities on a large scale, such as electrical, timber, fishing, petroleum, and mining industries as by-products of the creation of artificial "Great Lakes."

While Colombia has begun work on its first two lakes, Hudson acknowledges that support for the vast plan is not universal on the continent. Its "Report to Members" points to Hudson's continuing interest in developing the Amazon: "It appears that very much the same pattern—cheap, low dams converting large, low and partially flooded areas into lakes, stabilizing the borders between land and water and improving water transportation throughout the area—can be followed in many other parts of South America. The most exciting possibility is a dam on the Amazon River in the vicinity of Monte Alegre or Obidos. We have been able, with the help of several of our members and consultants, to generally establish the feasibility of the idea, but such a project is too vast and too intimately bound up with the development of Brazilian history for us to take any further steps in the absence of Brazilian initiative."

Hudson's plan for turning the Amazon into a thousand-mile-long "Great Lake" was not only met with "absence of Brazilian initiative" but with some genuine hostility. It was first-page news in Brazil and produced outrage among certain Brazilian experts and officials. Ray Wilson, speaking for the institute, doesn't take the Brazilian reaction too seriously: "The idea prompted certain Brazilians to state that the idea would change the climate of the country, perhaps causing less rainfall. Others were concerned about what the lake would do to the area that would have to be drowned to create it. Their concerns are with a few villages, a city, parrots and stuff like that." Compounding the problem, says Wilson, was the fact that the Brazilians were not happy with Herman Kahn's comments on Brazil in his book *The Year 2000: A Framework for Speculation on the Next Thirty-three Years*, which essentially said that the country will not significantly develop by the year 2000. Says Wilson, "The result of all this is that Hudson is probably more famous in Brazil than it is in the United States." The Great Lakes work has been shelved for the time being.

While nobody can dispute the novelty of the Great Lakes idea, its depth can be questioned. Hudson's twenty-nine-page report on the concept, prepared by a staff of eight supplemented by consultants, is broad and without detail. It raises concepts galore but does not follow them through. It tells us, for example, that the scheme would result in a "major modification of continental economic geography" but does not tell us what that modification would be. Similarly, we are told that the creation of the five major lakes would make possible the creation of "countless" secondary and tertiary lakes, but keeps us in the dark as to how, where or to what purpose. Not even glancing reference is made to the question of what would happen to the people who now live in the areas Hudson would flood.

A more recent job performed in Africa by the institute offers a new technique christened "the flying think tank." The short $100,000 study, sponsored by a leading Portuguese manufacturing company, Companhia Unias Fabril (CUF), looked at the Portuguese colony of Angola. A "flying think tank" seeks to expose members of a team studying an area to the maximum information about it within a short period by flying them over the region in small airplanes. In the case of the Angola study, four light twin-engine aircraft were used to crisscross the country during a ten-day period in 1969. The teams that flew around Angola were multidisciplinary groups who met each evening to discuss what they had seen that day from the air and to plan flights for the next day.

Basil Candella, a resident engineer and pivotal member of Hudson's Angola team, did the advance work for the group and participated in all aspects of the mission. His feelings on the survey and his impressions of Angola roll out in staccato bursts. "We hear all this stuff about murder and war in Angola," he says, "but I didn't see any fighting. I'm told that two hundred Portuguese soldiers were killed there last year, but all I can figure is that they were killed falling off trucks." Or: "It is very fashionable to say that all white people should get out of Africa. The truth may be that it's very good that the Portuguese are there." He insists that too many social commentators are looking for "pure solutions," whether it be African colonialism or American racial integration. "Take school integration and see what the purists have done. The Southern governors came up with a gradual plan which—according to my calculations—would have had everything worked out by now. Instead of a tranquil situation, look what we have now!" Asked if there wasn't some question

99

in his mind about the morality of working on a project in Angola, a colony run by a distant dictatorship, he says, "Look at it this way—at least nobody's getting beaten up on the streets like they do in this country."

The completed study is contained in two volumes, one looking at the sociopolitical aspects of Angola's development prospects and the other at industrial and technical approaches to the colony's development. It is the full Hudson treatment replete with scenarios and alternatives. Scenarios include such specifics as a Congo-style scenario, a Rhodesian-style scenario, a white-federation scenario, and so forth. The four broad alternatives offered to Portugal for the colony are labeled "Business as usual" (continue present policies), "Business better than usual" (some fixing up and improvement), "Large-scale development with insurance" (development which would include projects that would be "take-over proof"—for example, a fishing industry with floating processing plants and facilities that could "sail away" in time of trouble), and, finally, "High-speed development" or the "Go Fast" scenario (which sees Angola emerging as the ideal African state).

Sandwiched into the reports are a lot of impressionistic thoughts, among them that the military situation will not deteriorate for the next ten to fifteen years, that there is a "happy" black-white atmosphere in the country, that the natives are not lazy, that there is little evidence of war, hostility or repression, and that, as one flyer puts it, he feels less threatened by Angolese blacks than Harlem blacks. All of these impressions, gathered by people who basically did nothing more than fly over Angola in airplanes, are presented along with a long essay from Kahn himself, who wasn't even on the tour. Kahn argues, among other points, that Portugal has been smeared by the Western press with articles that make Angola look ". . . like an armed camp." He tells Portugal how to sharpen up her image as a colonial power: "Portugal must go against the fashion of the day. The fashion of the day is militant black separatism. And one can make the same comment—there is absolutely no reason for trouble in this country [the U.S.] except fashion. But the fashion is there—it is set by the United States and Russia and black Africa today. It is a crazy fashion, but that is irrelevant." Kahn condones authoritarianism as a way to develop the nation and tells the Portuguese that they should not worry about black Africa or the United Nations. He also propounds on preventing trouble and getting rich at the same time; "It is possible to develop a country like Angola without disruption. You can use the tribal society, if you will, and get richer. You can bring in outside capital and control it."

What are some of the specific suggestions generated for Angola by the "flying think tank"? They include:

Development of large-scale oil-refining industry
Additional iron exploitation
Large-scale cattle operations
Special companies built on imported middle-class entrepreneurs
Creating a wine industry
Television
Creation of a Singapore-like electronic equipment assembly area
A territorial and border patrol (a Mountie-like outfit which, according to the report, would be an all-black elite that always gets its man)
Hunting industry—"black hunters" to lead safaris
Black 4-H clubs
Open immigration
Tourism
A public-relations and advertising campaign to spruce up Angola's image (says the report: "We should like to suggest selection of about ten noted firms . . . who would be asked to change the image of Angola. A token fee of $10,000 U.S. would increase their interest")
Regional development corporation for the Queve River
Damming the Congo River

As for the last suggestion, Hudson proposes three possible dam sites, any one of which would result in cheap electricity, the creation of an industrial port, and the first real "bridge" between a black African state (the Congo) and a European colony. The report modestly tags the proposal "The world's *most* exciting dam and port development project." Nor is this the only dam proposed. Its suggestion for a regional development corporation on the Queve River calls for the use of low inexpensive dams.

Hudson's attitude toward working for Portugal is unequivocal: It was a job to be done and it was done. In the final Angola report Kahn points out that an apology was given to the Institute's Members (analogous to its Board of Directors) for his taking the colonialist job, but he also defends it by pointing out that Hudson would not work for Rhodesia or South Africa, the difference being that Angola is an "assimilationist culture." (Before he can explain that in his essay, Kahn is off in another direction, calling Brazil the most racist nation in the world—a conclusion that few other than Herman Kahn have reached and one that fully measures up in simplistic thought with his comment that racial problems in the U.S. are a question of "fashion.") Hudson's antipathy to self-determination in Angola and its suggestions for perpetrating dictatorial rule display the mentality of Kahn's think tank at work. The institute clearly feels free to roam the world hunting for projects without having to worry about the political or moral repercussions of what it says or does.

Hudson's multifaceted blueprint for alternative means of keeping the Portuguese in power in Angola flies in the face of all those who have condemned Portuguese colonialism, including the United Nations, the Vatican, black Africa, and anticolonialists everywhere. Speaking for many, former Congressman Benjamin S. Rosenthal of New York, from his vantage point on the Subcommittee on Africa of the House Foreign Affairs Committee, typified Portugal's rule as ". . . one of economic exploitation, forced labor and the denial of fundamental human liberties." There are many specific conditions in Angola which support Rosenthal's contentions: Life expectancy is judged to be between twenty-eight and thirty-five years, one in three children die at birth, 95 percent of all black Angolese are illiterate, a South African-style passbook system is maintained for blacks who face terms at "correctional labor" for losing their books, and the native population is subject to forceable relocation by the Portuguese authorities. Even in Hudson's two-volume report, some of the reasons for the wide censure of Portugal are casually acknowledged—among them, "economic distress," "harsh governmental control," "forced labor," and "severe wage differences for black and white workers." Although Hudson stalwart Candella and the report itself assert that there is no war going on in the nation, the report also talks about 55,000 Portuguese troops in the area and mentions guerrilla forces, a rebel enclave in the north, and terrorist activities. One of the kinder things that can be said of the Hudson report on Angola is that it is contradictory.

The study is a telling example of the think tank at its most ideological. In this case, Hudson's politically Rightist predilection dictated taking the contract. It is safe to conclude, moreover, that Hudson would not have hired itself out to those trying to rid Angola of Portuguese rule. Though the Angola study is more obvious than many, it underscores the fact that Hudson, like most of America's think tanks, are political entities that, to varying degrees, do all but their most technological thinking along ideological lines. Just as RAND starts with the assumption of the need for ever-increasing nuclear power, Hudson starts with the assumption, in this case, of the need for Portuguese supremacy. Perhaps, because the military nurtured so many of America's think tanks, it is more common to find in them a predilection to the political Right rather than Left. In fairness, however, few show Rightward bias as blatantly as Hudson does.

Similarly, Hudson's study of Angola illustrates how political predisposition can influence think-tank methodology. The concept of a "flying think tank" is by definition a superficial means of examination, ideally suited to keeping aloof from the issues on the ground. Also, Kahn's part of the study, in which he defines future alternatives and supports Portugal's position, was created in his office on the Hudson River and serves as another example of how methodology is shaped in an ideological study. Predictably, the conclusions are also shaded. Part of Hudson's response to the outrages in Angola, for example, is to mount a public-relations campaign to spruce up its image.

The "flying think tank" is not a one-shot phenomenon. A similar mission was sent flying around Mexico's Yucatán peninsula, and Hudson would like to find other takers for overflights of underdeveloped parts of the world.

Not all of Hudson's studies yield earth-changing suggestions or alternatives, like damming the Congo, but many of them do:

A suggestion presented to the Pentagon for the Vietnam war suggested putting a moat around Saigon.

A series of investigations for the city of New York led to the suggestion that Welfare Island, a narrow strip of land in the East River extending from 50th to 85th streets, act as the main pillar or fulcrum for new bridges from Manhattan to Long Island to effectively give the city a new "center of gravity" around Long Island City and Greenpoint. The first stage of this undertaking would be to turn

Welfare Island into a new commercial and residential area. Hudson will continue to work on the idea, and its staff feels it may succeed. Mayor John Lindsay has already proposed turning the island into an auto-free residential community. Another Hudson study for the city looked at New York's underground resources and in conclusion called for a new underground tunnel system to avoid all above-ground repairs, a major source of traffic jams.

One series of studies that have come out of Hudson's almost $2 million in research contracts for the Army's Office of Civil Defense looked at the use of mines, caves, and tunnels as fallout shelters while other studies pondered every kind of national shelter system. No doubt its most bizarre—and one that Hudson concedes is extreme—suggestion would involve the creation of what almost amounts to a "spare United States" all underground. Film buffs will recognize this as one of the notions lampooned in *Dr. Strangelove.*

While the Hudson Institute is moving more and more into international development work, it is most famous for its unique studies of nuclear war. Ray Wilson explains its work for the Air Force in this area: "Most people think of nuclear war in terms of what we call 'wargasm'—or a situation in which everything is set off. But there could be another type of war in which less than a total stockpile or just a few nuclear weapons are expended. We're the only people who are looking at what you would do then if you were in the middle of such a war. We look at all the problems that we would face, such as pride—will the nations try to end it or will they try to show how tough they are? We look at all the spooky, ambiguous things that could happen if only one missile comes in and destroys the Grand Coulee Dam. What do we do then?"

An unclassified 1968 report called "War Termination Issues and Conflicts" provides a good example of this specialty of the house. Authored by Kahn and Hudson Fellows William Pfaff and Edmund Stillman, it is a 134-page treatise containing definitions, causes of war, outbreak and war-fighting scenarios, and the strategic, political, and social factors involved in such wars and their termination. As with other Hudson studies past and present, it has a distinct style. Things are neatly and precisely categorized—even things that can't be neatly and precisely categorized, such as: "The 6 Basic Thermonuclear Threats," "6 Ways to Hypothecate Forces in Stable Balance of Terror Environment," "17 Attack Options in a General War,"

"11 Possible Outcomes of Thermonuclear War," and so on. There are illustrative anecdotes and scenarios for just about every alternative, ranging from one that details how the U.S. will rot away to a third-rate power as a result of internal pressure and conflict to one in which the U.S. and China get into a nuclear war because the U.S. decides to attack North Vietnam. Some of the detailed projections are compelling enough to set any red-blooded hawk salivating. In the scenario describing nuclear war in China, for instance, after the U.S. makes the first nuclear strike, we are offered ". . . the United States detonates a one-megaton weapon at 500,000 feet above Peking as a demonstration, together with limited nuclear attacks on selected military targets. Simultaneously, the United States begins round-the-clock broadcasts and drops leaflets proclaiming that Chinese nuclear facilities and air defense have been destroyed. 'Your leaders have led you to disaster, nothing stands between the Chinese people and annihilation but the self-restraint of the United States.' "

Once the nuclear stage is set, the report discusses ways of terminating conflicts. Two major tactics explored are wars of "competitive mobilization" and "city avoidance and other sanctuary tactics and strategies." Competitive mobilization is based on the theory that if nuclear war seemed imminent or highly plausible, the United States could put everything into mobilizing itself—a state of readiness that would presumably provide superiority leading to ". . . either accommodation by the Soviets or, if it came to central war [or all-out war], an improved war outcome for the United States." The scenario runs like this: The Soviets provoke (for example, they take Berlin), and the U.S. responds by declaring war; but rather than attack, the U.S. begins a preplanned mobilization—costing an additional *trillion* in defense expenditures over the normal billions—to gain overwhelming superiority. The massive mobilization would include high altitude ABM's, missiles of all sorts, shelters, and mammoth armed forces (over six million by the end of a year's mobilization). This would go on until the crisis passed or war started in earnest. Implicit in this preposterous scheme is that the U.S. would be able to outmobilize the U.S.S.R. and that Russia would take no overt military action in the interim.

The second major tactic—city avoidance—aims at bettering the political and military outcome of nuclear war by attempting to limit civilian deaths. The chapter examining this notion opens with this paragraph: "We want to render nuclear forces, and by extension even nuclear war itself, more rational, which means making it more 'usable' as an instrument of policy." Making nuclear war more palatable and rational by better civil defense and the intentional hitting of fewer cities is a prime illustration of the motto "thinking about the unthinkable" that dictates thought at the institute and is the title of Kahn's best-known work.

The institute is not without critics in high places, although few are announced as such. Its proposals have raised some eyebrows in the Senate. Senator Thomas F. Eagleton of Missouri, for example, wrote to his constituents, "Recently . . . the Hudson Institute, perhaps the nation's best-known think tank, contributed the suggestion [to the Pentagon] that we dig a moat around Saigon. . . . I wonder how much that cost the taxpayers of Missouri?" Arkansas Senator J. William Fulbright, in an August 1969 speech, had similar words for the moat and also commented dryly on the plan to dam up the Amazon. "I understand," he said, "that it did not appeal to the Latin Americans." The General Accounting Office, Congress' financial watchdog, gave Hudson its strongest official slap when it investigated three Hudson contracts with the Army's Office of Civil Defense that cost $600,000 and yielded eleven reports, of which, the GAO reported, ". . . seven . . . were considered either to be less useful than had been expected or to require major revision." Three of the eleven Hudson reports were singled out for special criticism.

A study report "On the Rating of Blast Shelters" was criticized by the director, Systems Evaluation Division, as adding nothing to the state of the art; i.e., it added no new thoughts and failed to provide any information not previously known.

A study report on "A New Look at the Design of Low-Budget Civil Defense Systems" was returned by the then director, Systems Evaluation Division, to Hudson Institute for major revision because, among other things, it appeared to be "a rehash of old, if not tired, ideas."

A study report on "Deferred-Cost CD [Civil Defense] Options for Nuclear Crises" was criticized by the technical monitor, an operations research analyst, as not having sufficient depth to warrant general distribution.

Such criticism notwithstanding, the institute's relationship with the federal government is close and financially rewarding for Hudson

—and one in which Hudson is generally influential. For example, Hudson's thinking on Vietnam has been considered and reportedly adopted in part by the Nixon Administration. Hudson's Vietnam plan emerged from a series of studies on counterinsurgency the institute performed for the Pentagon. As presented in 1969, it called for the reduction of U.S. troops to between 100,000 and 200,000 by the end of 1971, reliance only on U.S. volunteers and a change in tactics away from casualty-producing large-unit sweeps through enemy areas to smaller patrol operations backed up with air strikes. Half of the American troops held in Vietnam would be kept in "reserve," out of the fighting, to be used in case of a large influx of North Vietnamese troops. The remaining troops would be used to support the South Vietnamese in tactical fighter squadrons, logistics units, long-range artillery batteries, and helicopter units. The plan was geared to making the war acceptable at home, cutting casualties and giving the U. S. a better chance of a peaceful settlement or a long-range shot at winning the war. According to an article in the New York *Times* on June 26, 1969, an Administration official stated that some of the Hudson plan ideas were "being woven into the fabric of our strategy."

To understand Hudson, one must attempt to understand the man who runs it. Herman Kahn describes himself as "an ex-physicist and half an economist." He is the author of seven books and countless articles. An irrepressible lecturer, he is given to exposing his ideas to audiences typically of bankers, industrialists, or senior military officers. His highest degree is a Master's in physics, which he received from the California Institute of Technology in 1948. The degree got him a job at RAND as a research analyst in the Physics Division, where he worked on problems in applied physics, mathematics, operations research, systems analysis, weapons design, and strategic warfare.

He and Max Singer founded the Hudson Institute in 1961 after Kahn left RAND. The founding came during the period when controversy over his first book, *On Thermonuclear War*, was still raging. The book, published in 1960 when he was still at RAND, was a 650-page treatise which bluntly discussed every aspect of nuclear war. The book was both warmly praised and sharply blasted. The *Scientific American* review said, "This is a moral tract of mass murder: how to plan it, how to commit it, how to get away with it, how to justify it." Max Lerner, on the other hand, said of it: ". . . it is Kahn's contention that we must take the possibilities of nuclear war 'seriously'

107

instead of throwing up our hands and refusing to think about it. Kahn is the first writer I have read who, on a massive scale and with thoroughgoing detail, faces the nature and consequences of thermonuclear war not as a paralyzing abstraction but in all its sizes, shapes, degrees, possibilities, probabilities."

With the book, concepts like "massive retaliation," "trading cities," "nuclear blackmail," and "postwar state" came out of the think tanks and inner circles of government and into the public arena. For the first time alternative possibilities were discussed in vivid detail in terms of millions of deaths and the consequences of those deaths (for instance, Kahn pointed out that a death toll of forty million Americans would require a twenty-year period before the economy could recover). It was intended as an antisimplistic approach to nuclear war. Kahn argued for neither disarmament favored by many on the political Left nor an all-encompassing nuclear umbrella and massive retaliation as urged by many on the Right but rather for civil defense and limited nuclear alternatives (one tactical alternative, "trading cities," was coolly discussed in terms of taking of one Russian city—rather than all of them—for, say, the accidental destruction of New York). It was no accident that *Fail-Safe* and *Dr. Strangelove* appeared on the heels of Kahn's book. Strangelove himself and Groteschele in *Fail-Safe*, both bitter spoofs on the "defense intellectual," were mostly inspired by Kahn and his thoughts.

On Thermonuclear War is still discussed in the closed community from which it sprang, and some at Kahn's alma mater, RAND, are still a bit overwhelmed by him and the book, though it is a decade old and its author visits Santa Monica only on occasion. Opinion at RAND ranges from the feeling that Kahn is hard to live down (or as one RAND researcher puts it, "Herman did us a disservice when he offered himself to the world through that book; he gave the impression that all of us were like him, not that there was one of him") to the feeling that he has a redeeming nerviness. As one RAND hand says: "He did what nobody else had the guts to do—he took the secret stamp off all of those estimates of nuclear destruction because he believed it was time for the rest of the nation to get in on our debates." The commentator adds, "You could say that his major contribution to the nation was giving everyone else the ammunition they needed to sort it out for themselves."

Since the book appeared, Kahn has kept himself in the eye of the storm. He is both a strategist for and a proponent of the ABM. His occasional pronouncements on Vietnam are hawkish though severely critical of how things have been and are being run. He still considers thermonuclear matters his turf and speaks out on them when the mood hits him. Of late, however, he is more and more interested in his role as a futurist—a prophet leading others of his ilk into investigations of the major trends the world will take over the next thirty years. Both his critics and defenders are legion, the former proclaiming him a global charlatan—a power-hungry W. C. Fields plumping his "snake oil" to the mighty; to the latter, he is possessed of a singular genius.

Herman Kahn is big—obese, actually. He is also engaging, witty, friendly, and frank to the point of making the rest of those at the institute seem guarded in contrast. Punctuated by occasional stammers, wheezing snorts and chuckles, his words flow rapidly and without the slightest trace of self-consciousness. Talking to him is not unlike talking with a hyperactive, oracular New York cab driver who has both a sense of where he's going and of what he feels he must communicate to you before the ride is over.

"When we started," says Kahn of Hudson's mission, "Max Singer and I had an idea that the first year we would put down on paper everything that a good Secretary of Defense would want to know, next year a good Secretary of State, next year a good President, the fourth year a good Secretary General of the United Nations, and the fifth year a good God. And then we'd quit."

"Well," he continues, "we started this in 1961. In 1966, Max pointed out that we were six years behind in the five year program. Now I would say we're very much into the second and third year of the program." Does this explain the de-emphasis of Hudson's military work? "Yes, if you've ever seen our charts of nuclear war, they're so much ahead of current practice that there is nothing to work on. I'm giving lectures tomorrow at the War College, but they're the same lectures I gave five years ago. Nothing new because they haven't caught up with us."

Kahn discusses Hudson's level of input in the federal government this way: "At RAND they try to go to the highest level they can and hit hard with a lot of pressure. At Hudson normally we put on no pressure and we hit, with a few exceptions, at the fifth level down. The reason for this is that when I'm dealing with a major or a colonel or a general or an undersecretary and I disagree with them, they don't take it badly; but at the top level when I disagree they look at it like it's treason. When the Nixon Administration came in we dealt with the Laird, Packard, Kissinger group, but it didn't work out for just that reason. I just found that it was too hard to push things, particularly over their objections, which became quite severe. We constantly go back to the fourth or fifth level—where a lot of decisions are made anyhow—whenever we try to go to the top. It's hard to deal with these people at the top unless you've got a lot of time to spend."

The subject of RAND pops up often in a conversation with Kahn. When asked if there is any other institution in the world like Hudson, he says that RAND used to be but isn't any more. As to the present-day RAND: "They haven't really done any significant work since 1960"—which is about when he left. As to the importance of RAND: "In the late 1950's it was all by itself a fourth branch of government. About one hundred people were advancing RAND's ideas on government and had a very powerful impact. In 1961, McNamara hired this group of people and it ended up that they were no longer persuading government but they'd taken over the government." At another point he says of RAND's advisers, "They're dangerous as all hell, especially for people who don't know what is going on. They really are dangerous since usually they're just a little more knowledgeable than the guys they're serving, but not enough to justify the amount of persuasion they have."

Kahn also explains the reasons for his leaving RAND to start the Hudson Institute. "I had gotten into a very serious fight with the president of RAND, Frank Collbohm, which lasted about two or three years. It was very funny. A lot of people think that the studies that were the basis for On Thermonuclear War were done on the order of RAND or the Air Force. It was actually done over the objections of both groups. The president of RAND had ideological objections to civil defense, as did the Air Force, and his objections were very personal—he was director of civil defense [programs] at Douglas and had done some very stupid things. In general, the Right was anti-civil defense before our study and the Left was pro-civil defense because civil defense cared about people—it was warm, human, soft. The Right didn't like the idea of being scared, so they opposed it. There had been several people at RAND who had gotten into serious trouble because of civil-defense studies due to the animosity of the president. But RAND was the kind of place where you could still do that kind of thing. The crucial event occurred when I was a member of the three-man group in charge of the strategic airpower project which tied up about one-third of RAND. I decided to do the civil-defense part of this study and I got some of the vice-presidents to blackjack the president by giving me permission to start it. At the time I did it, people said that this would probably be the end since the president wouldn't stand for it. Then I got into a series of fights with the president and, of course, I got pretty nasty. . . . It ended up with the president telling me that if I stayed at home at RAND and worked on what I was supposed to work on, then things would be fine. At that time I was the second highest paid guy, and if I'd stayed they probably would have given me the highest pay. I just didn't want to work under their restrictions, and then I decided to start something of my own invention. I just can't work around silly restrictions. I quit."

On the general topic of think tanks, Kahn exhibits genuine skepticism and seldom excludes Hudson from his generalizations. On their power he says, "They're very influential and very much out of Congressional control. I myself worry about them." He adds with some delight that sometimes he even scares himself. He thinks that President Eisenhower's farewell remarks about the military-industrial complex was really a reference to people like himself and places like RAND. Kahn's prediction for the future of think tanks is surprisingly negative: "I make the point that the 1970's will see unbelievable retrogression by these groups. The reason, I believe, is that in the 1960's most of the customers were quite hostile to this kind of work —certainly skeptical and at least a little hostile. You had to have good studies or they'd kill you. When I came to Washington ten or fifteen years ago, people were mad at me. Usually they'd let me in once and not let me back for three years. Under those circumstances, you really gave a careful talk. Now I'm invited all the time and nobody hurts my feelings. I can get away with any kind of crap—I could even just say 'crap' and get away with it. This is a field where it is very easy to be illusioned, biased, or stupid—and there are no cops any more. You know, these studies have to be interesting, bright, or creative. But if you don't have a cop or a harsh critic or a hostile audience, they fall apart. The good ones are works of art. Put it this way: Suppose I went out on the street and hired one hundred people to write poems and then published them—they'd be unbelievably second-rate. That's how the government is hiring think tanks these days. First, then, it's hard to be creative without a critic, and, secondly, it's very easy to be crooked."

Asked how he keeps Hudson from getting into trouble, Kahn says, "I make this point to my staff all the time—if you can't be honest, which is hard, be careful. Being careful is a good substitute for honesty." In evaluating specific studies by his own organization, Kahn varies between skepticism and hucksterism. The Hudson study of drugs for the state of New York he labels "Uncreative but competent." On the other hand, he calls the Welfare Island study for the city of New York very creative, largely because of its iconoclasm. Of the General Accounting Office's criticism of Hudson's civil-defense studies, Kahn says, "They picked out some of our best for criticism and missed others which were really poor. One of their strong points was that our work was not in accordance with the policy of the agency contracting for the studies, but that point is irrelevant because we were attacking those policies. I look upon their criticism as kudos for those studies." This comment fails to confront the main criticism made by the General Accounting Office—namely, that the ideas were not new.

As for his personal style, Kahn admits that he provokes on purpose. He says, "I do it but not just to be provocative. Some of the things I say have shock value, but the reason for it is not to shock but to clarify. It wakes them up and makes them think that what I'm saying might be true." He illustrates the point by explaining how he poses the question of fees to be paid Hudson by companies wishing to participate in a major upcoming study. "I was in Germany recently trying to get companies lined up for our big study of the future. I would tell them that for twelve thousand dollars paid to us, they could work for the Hudson Institute for free. It really bothered them when I said that, but there was truth in it. Only if they work on the study will they get anything out of it; otherwise they'd just pay the money for the study and when it was completed it would just sit on the shelf. If they work on it, then it means something."

Much of Kahn's conversation relates to his plans for Hudson's future, which is very much bound up with the study he was selling Germany—a major attempt to study the future, a program due to last several years and substantially expand the institute. One hundred companies are expected to sign on—seventy had by mid-1970—for what he terms ". . . the most important attempt yet to look at the future." The paradigm for the study—assumptions, definitions, conjectures, questions to be explored—is contained on a long piece of paper that he offhandedly points out is worth $3 million—his way of explaining how much of his and Hudson's thinking has gone into the work so far. The sheet is shorthand for the study, phrases, lists and what seem to be *non sequiturs*, but as he explains it several times, it begins to dawn on the listener that it really does encompass everything likely to go on during the final third of the twentieth century. Kahn thinks that as a basic document it will allow us to better understand what is to come by sharing a common frame of reference.

"We had a meeting in Paris and I had this document and held it up," he says, pointing to the sheet, "and said that it replaces the Bible, Shakespeare, Goethe, and Racine. They laughed and probably took me too seriously. Then somebody took issue and said what about Dante—this objector was an Italian—and I said, 'Okay, Dante too.' The point is if you understand every phrase, every line here, our shared understanding is unbelievably high and will be greater as the study goes on." Before it is all over, he explains, the study will have involved not only 100 major corporations but scholars, consultants, and governments from around the world.

To flavor its contents and get a feel for Kahn's shorthand, here is one of his lists, covering the long-term international trends he assumes are developing:

1. Increasingly sensate (empirical this-worldly, secular humanistic, manipulative, explicitly rational, utilitarian, contractual, epicurean, hedonistic, etc.) culture—recently an almost complete decline of the sacred & a relative erosion of "irrational" taboos, totems & charismas
2. Bourgeois, bureaucratic, and "meritocratic" elites
3. Accumulation of scientific & technological knowledge
4. Institutionalization of technological change especially research, development, innovation & diffusion—recently & increasingly a conscious emphasis on synergisms & serendipities

5. World-wide industrialization & modernization
6. Increasing capability for mass destruction
7. Increasing affluence & (recently) leisure
8. Population growth—now explosive but tapering off
9. Urbanization & recently suburbanization & "urban sprawl" —soon the growth of megalopolises
10. Recently & increasingly macro-environmental issues (e.g., constraints set by finite size of earth & various local & global reservoirs)
11. Decreasing importance of primary & (recently) secondary & tertiary occupations
12. Increasing literacy & education—recently the "knowledge industry" and increasing numbers & role of intellectuals
13. Future-oriented thinking, discussion & planning—recently some improvement in methodologies & tools—also some retrogression
14. Innovative & manipulative rationality increasingly applied to social, political & economic worlds as to shaping & exploiting the material world—increasing problem of ritualistic, incomplete, or pseudo rationality
15. Increasing universality of the multifold trend
16. Increasing tempo of change in all the above

Such sheets and lists offer summaries of Kahn's particular way of presenting and seeing (and, for that matter, selling) what he is doing. He pulls a mimeographed set of twenty-five sheets entitled "The Rising Sun." It is a fascinating collage of chronologies, trends, lists of social attitudes and emotions, graphs, vital statistics, import-export data, quotes, clippings, generalizations, examples, and possible futures all relating to Japan. He puts it simply, "If you study these charts for a day, you'll learn more about Japan than you could if you spent three or four months in a library studying the country."

Herman Kahn asserts that the Hudson Institute is widely misunderstood and almost impossible for an outsider to comprehend. He says, "I guess that there is almost nobody outside the system who has any good idea what we are, what the emphasis is and so on." Yet after stating more than once that Hudson is unfathomable to outsiders, he sees no inconsistency in his assessing the other think tanks in terms of capsule critiques. Most of the work of consulting firms is "worthless," the New York–RAND Institute is "a second-rate fiasco," the Brookings Institution "competent but dull," while the Stanford Research Institute is "exciting but not competent" and the Center for the Study of Democratic Institutions "pseudo-creative." He alleges, "No piece of contract research on urban problems is worth reading"—a statement that, when challenged, is rescinded to exclude a few items, including, of course, work that Hudson has done. He asserts that the think tank best serves areas of government where ". . . nutty, crazy, and unbelievably stupid ideas have been allowed to flourish."

His penchant for the dramatic statement, if backed up at all, is backed up with only one example and that one often doesn't measure up to the occasion. "The trouble with American education," he says typically, "is that we are not teaching work habits. That is proven when you pick up the telephone: no work habits." A member of the institute staff gives another example of Kahn's brand of overstatement: "He once saw an Eskimo fix an airplane, and every once in a while he drops this line about the mechanical ability of Eskimos, which he proves by telling about the airplane mechanic he once saw." Kahn may mention that there is no such thing as an automated factory in America, then interrupts himself a few moments later and says that there is one exception—automated oil refineries. If you mention that you have read of other kinds of automated factories, he then concedes that his information is probably out of date, and for all he knows there are more by now.

A term that gets a lot of play at Hudson is "mind-boggling" (as in: "We have this mind boggling plan for Welfare Island"), which is not at all an inept way to describe the institute itself. There is probably no other private group in America that can match Hudson on a man-to-man basis in grappling with issues of cosmic importance. Where else are heavy thinkers flitting from thermonuclear war to the millennium to reconfiguring continents, stopping along the way to add some thoughts on the problems of drug addiction or the future of youthful alienation?

Perhaps the key to Hudson's existence is that Herman Kahn has figured out that American government and industry will foot the bill for a place where unthinkable thoughts are not only thought but bound into neatly printed reports and where wild schemes can be hatched without embarrassment or too much fear of outside criti-

115

cism. The Hudson Institute, with its iconoclastic outlook and unbureaucratic ways, is the direct opposite of the sponsors who keep it
rolling. When a staff member responds to a leading question by saying that he really doesn't care what the inquiring "bourgeois journalist" thinks about him or what he's doing, it is clear that this is not
one of your organization men or standard bureaucrats speaking.

Despite Kahn's and Hudson's disdain for convention and their
outspoken approach to the world, they do not mask their enthusiasm
for the goals of the establishment, even while eschewing its solem-
nity, conformity, and methodology. The debate that swells around
Kahn as to whether he is a genius or a pitchman is academic to him.
It is clear that he is—and delights in being—both of these things.

What is most refreshing, finally, about Kahn and Hudson are its
candor and its ideas, which, if nothing else, are not for sale elsewhere.
When Herman Kahn told a Congressional committee a few years
ago, "If you want to keep your defense budget down, don't pay your
troops," he had to fill the void of silence after the pronouncement
by adding, "I'm not kidding." Kahn was just offering another alternative to cutting back on missiles and traditional weapons expenditures. The iconoclasm in such a statement comes in all shapes and
sizes on other issues: a nuclear war is winnable or unwinnable, build
a spare United States, and the like. If one takes the reasonable position that all the alternatives in a given situation should be examined
—no matter how apparently farfetched—then there is certain justification for a Hudson Institute.

However tempting, one cannot dismiss the institute as only an
educational idea bin operating off on a hill suspended above the
Hudson. The institute is plugged into the real world, into the war in
Vietnam, into the ABM project, into Portuguese Africa and into the
White House from time to time. Senior Fellows at Hudson plump
for new weapons systems and strategies with the zeal of the most
vested of interests in the military-industrial complex. In fact, in early
1970 Kahn was given an office in the Pentagon where he could sit
and help plot the Administration's strategy in winning acceptance
for new ABM deployments. Under the protection of rubber stamps
marked "Secret," Hudson has dwelt on such problems as counterinsurgency in Southeast Asia, new directions in military technology,
nuclear strategy, and new thoughts on America's role as peace-
keeper.

116

The future of the institute is bound up in exploring the future of mankind, and one of the most important aspects of that future is outlined in a discussion paper written by Kahn and senior fellow Anthony J. Wiener. It says, "It is clear that Western man now has Faustian powers, which are impossible to renounce. Realistically, the possibility must be faced that man's unremitting Faustian striving may ultimately remake both his inner and outer environment, to the point where he will be dehumanized or where his life on earth will be altered in some disastrous and irrevocable way. Already, awesome choices are before him. Suppose that in the future we can divert a hurricane. With this will come the responsibility of deciding where to send it."

The Hudson Institute exudes the same aura of Faustianism it raises: an insatiable striving for knowledge and power in an increasingly wider circle. As for the case of that hurricane, Hudson has raised the issue and will undoubtedly, before the time is upon us to decide where to send it, pose the alternatives.

2. *Machine and Man at Santa Monica*

(Italicized words indicate the response of the researcher)
GO ORBIT
PGM STARTED
ORBIT IS NOW OPERATING
PLEASE IDENTIFY YOURSELF, LAST NAME
    FIRST
NANCE, J. W.
WHAT IS YOUR STORAGE DEVICE TYPE? *2314*
WHAT IS YOUR STORAGE VOLUME NUMBER?
    3001
2314 VOL 3001 TO BE MINTED ON A4
PLEASE INSERT YOUR ID KEY
5527EA23
THE DATA BASE CONSISTS OF DATA EX-
    TRACTED FROM 8515 DOCUMENTS
IF AT ANY TIME YOU DESIRE TO TERMINATE
    A REQUEST, ENTER *ABORT*

ANY TIME INPUT IS REQUESTED, YOU MAY
CHANGE THE FORM OF DIALOGUE BY IN-
SERTING *LONG* OR *SHORT*
DO YOU DESIRE LONG FORM OF OPERATION?
Y/N *YES*
DO YOU DESIRE A DESCRIPTION OF YOUR DATA
BASE? Y/N *YES*
YOUR DATA BASE HAS THE FOLLOWING ELE-
MENTS. . . .

—Typical conversation between researcher and ORBIT (On-line Retrieval
of Bibliographic Information Time-
shared), an information system created
by the System Development Corporation

In April 1951 when Univac I, the first computer intended for nonmilitary use, was delivered to the United States Bureau of the Census, it was predicted that there was a market in the nation for several
dozen such computing machines to serve large corporations and government agencies. The prediction ranks as one of modern technology's most inaccurate projections. The computer population of the
United States is now close to 100,000, and few major corporations
and government agencies have fewer than several dozen of these
machines on the premises.

One such corporation that uses dozens of computers (over 200,
to be more accurate) and, more important, has had great impact on
their widespread introduction throughout government and industry
is the System Development Corporation. It is widely regarded as one
of the apostles of what computer people refer to as the "new environment"—euphemistic shorthand for all the concepts represented by the
dry but imposing terms of cybernation, such as information technology, the systems approach, data retrieval, systems sciences, simulation, information management, and automation.

The System Development Corporation is one of the world's leading computer software and systems firms. It produces no computers
or equipment but provides the human brain power—programs, ideas,
tests, designs, languages, and "abilities"—that bring those machines
to life. Since coming into being in 1956, SDC has handled more than
1,400 jobs for over fifty departments and agencies of the federal gov-

ernment. In addition, it has worked on scores of jobs for state and local governments and has been in the employ of over thirty major industrial firms. The growth of this think tank during the late 1950's and 1960's directly parallels the growth of computerization in American life during that period. It has been a catalyst in adapting the spaghettilike ganglia of the digital computer to virtually everything automatable from missile systems to billing for hospital care. It has been at the leading edge of cybernation and plans to stay there whether it be through further automation of the nation's defenses or new applications of computers in civil areas.

As befits a corporation in the go-go world of computers, SDC has had a fast-moving history. First created as a division of RAND, it has since gone through a rapid series of transformations that today make it one of the world's leading independent profit-making software and systems firms.

Its history goes back to the early 1950's when work started at RAND in the general area of the psychology of men working under stress. As RAND's interest in psychology grew, it became necessary to justify the work to its Air Force sponsor, so it was decided that Air Defense Direction Centers—the radar units that detect and control the interception of enemy air attacks—would be the subject of the studies and a replica of one of these centers was built as a RAND laboratory. RAND vice-president J. R. Goldstein describes what happened next: "We were using junior-college students for this work and we concentrated on developing their abilities to work with each other and face stress as a team. We encouraged them to come up with new techniques for handling the job on their own, and soon found they were improving vastly. General Fred Smith of the Air Defense Command was brought in to see our results, and he watched and concluded that these part-time men were doing much better than the regular men who handled such work for the military." It was soon decided that RAND would start a major program in training and training techniques; for this job the System Development Division was created in 1955. Concurrently, the Air Force decided to begin automating its air defense operations and called on the same division to begin working on the scheme. A year later that division, then three times the size of the rest of RAND, was felt to be too large and was spun off as the System Development Corporation—an independent think tank with Air Force sponsorship like RAND.

119

SDC grew rapidly as it took on a variety of computer-related and training jobs. In 1964 its relationship to the Air Force ended—partly as a result of SDC's desire to compete in an open market and partly because of Congressional pressure for more open competition in military markets. In 1969 SDC switched from a nonprofit to a profit-making corporation with major offices in eight states and sales of about $60 million a year. The fact that federal sponsorship had led to the creation of a profit-seeking company created both alarm and resentment among many of SDC's competitors, who felt its origin had given it an unfair advantage. Although it did not cite SDC by name, the General Accounting Office in 1969 said that it is "somewhat incongruous" of a government agency to provide fees to an outside organization to develop certain capabilities only to have the organization threaten to quit that agency. The GAO goes on to comment that competition by such an organization that has left government service would "appear to be inequitable" since the formerly supported group would have an unfair advantage over normal outfits required to build up their own capital and facilities—a potential advantage for any of the many federally supported think tanks.

The cluster of aircraft hangarlike buildings that constitutes SDC's corporate headquarters is located a mile or so from RAND in Santa Monica—although split from RAND and without formal ties to her, SDC remains in the same neighborhood. It is a big bustling place that invites the term "think factory" to describe it. The description escalates to that of "thought conglomerate" when one considers that it has major facilities in seven U.S. cities and offices with small staffs in over fifty communities in the U.S. and abroad.

Most of the work that SDC does is approached with a distinctive SDC style. Broadly, that approach is to look at each job as a system in which the primary considerations are the needs of the people who will use it. On the premise that even the most superior technological scheme will falter unless the people using it have taken part in its development, SDC has insisted that the designer, user, and operator of a new system all play a role in its preparation and introduction. SDC considers the training of the system's user a crucial part of the job, and, in most cases, the company plays the role of teacher. A final element in the approach is testing the system, often by means of simulation under the most difficult conditions. For example, its work on air defense systems has been traditionally associated with flexing those systems by simulating major air attacks. Beyond these particular characteristics, SDC adheres to the generally applied systems principles of bringing in a multidisciplinary team, of treating every system individually rather than taking a mass-production attitude, and of recognizing that each system must be built for its particular environment.

Despite SDC's close association with the computer, it does not hold that the computer is the solution to all the systems problems it grapples with and in many cases has suggested to its clients that a "manual system"—a scheme devoid of computers—is preferable.

Today SDC has two distinct sides to it, but the dominant one—comprising about 80 percent of its business—provides a strong automating arm for the military. This side of the company is closed-mouthed as it continually plugs away on mostly classified, highly technical jobs that put the brains in military systems.

SDC has performed nearly 1,000 military jobs, one of the first involving 500 specialists assembled to write over a quarter of a million computer instructions for the nation's air defense system—the largest computer programming job ever undertaken to that point. Its hundreds of millions of dollars in military work have had little to do with weapons themselves but rather with what ties the weapons and the men together, such as the remote radar stations and command posts—in short, the electronic glue of Cold War defense.

Air defense is one of SDC's major specialties. Its skills have been applied to both the major air defense systems for North America—SAGE (Semi-Automatic Ground Environment), the primary air defense system, and BUIC (Back-Up Interceptor Control), the second line of defense that fills in when all or part of SAGE is knocked out. SDC supplied most of the software for these systems, which, among other things, are automatically capable of maintaining an up-to-date picture of the air defense situation, interpreting data, and figuring out how to intercept incoming attacks. At the heart of the North American defense operation is the North American Air Defense Command Combat Operations Center, an operation buried a quarter of mile deep in Cheyenne Mountain, Colorado. This center, which SDC computerized and still services, handles information on such factors as attacking aircraft, missiles, hostile detonations, the status of U.S. and allied missiles and aircraft, and the status of communications. The underground command center is the place where possible air attacks

121

on North America are detected and its deterrents are dispatched. In the same vein, SDC has been a major contributor to the Strategic Air Command's Control System, which keeps information flowing on the nation's strategic aircraft, weather conditions, the location of enemy bases, and just about everything needed to conduct a war from the air.

SDC has worked for all elements of what is called the "intelligence community"—both a variety of military intelligence commands and the Central Intelligence Agency. For the Navy, for example, it designed the Space Surveillance System, which detects and records satellites flying over the United States.

Not all of its military accomplishments have been in designing and developing systems. One of its specialties is training. Its work in this area runs from actually teaching military computer programmers to preparing courses and manuals on such exotic subjects as electronic counter-countermeasures (ECCM), a form of electronic warfare in which an enemy's jamming and false electronic signals are countered by the United States. Another specialty of the house is preparing exercises and simulations. For example, SDC packages a line of war games for the military all of which simulate attacks on the United States to test the nation's defenses. While some of these exercises are small, local operations, others are major undertakings that test the entire defenses of North America. An SDC "package" for one of these major simulated attacks includes scenarios, pertinent maps and charts, films, tapes, messages, observers and evaluators, manuals, computer instructions, and communications needed to set up the simulation. Briefly, SDC establishes a state of alert with a realistic scenario and, according to its script, pumps into the problem all of the intelligence reports, enemy contacts and the like needed to test the nation's air defenses. When such exercises are over, the company evaluates the performance of the military complex under attack. This work is accompanied by affiliated studies by the corporation in such behavioral areas as stress and the psychology of decision-making. One classified study in this realm conducted for the Air Force, for example, studied emotional breakdown under stress—or as one SDC staff member described it, "What happens when a man falls apart in a nuclear situation, how do you tell he's cracking up and how do you know it's time to remove him?"

SDC has worked for just about every major element of the Department of Defense from the Joint Chiefs of Staff on down. Its role has been that of an agent for bringing in new technology—a designing, implementing, testing, and supporting force for automating the Cold War. Experience in this realm has been the basis for sDc's nonmilitary work. As claimed in one of its innumerable corporate brochures, "The foundation, the skills, the resources, the history and the future of sDc are intimately involved with America's national security. Our products are broadly significant and have stimulated change in many other segments of national life, but nearly all of them were created to support our national security." Although sDc is stressing its interest in civil work, it has no intention of forsaking its military mother lode of support.

Despite the fact that the nonmilitary side of sDc has borrowed heavily from the military experience, the two sides are not really complementary. One sDc researcher in urban studies confides that the two parts don't get along and freely offers the generalization that his side does all it can not to cooperate or be compromised ". . . by all that hostile crap they work with." Another young researcher, wearing one peace symbol around his neck and another made into a belt buckle, explains that there is an uncrossable wall between the two sectors of sDc and says that they are like two separate companies. Adding fuel to the fire, waggish military researchers have long explained that sDc stood for "Soviet Destruction Corporation." The gulf between the two sides of sDc is hardly unique in the world of think tanks. The clash between America's national priorities is sharply mirrored in this community as well.

Sheldon Arenberg is one of sDc's nonmilitary project leaders and an example of a thinker whose priorities have changed. Head of sDc's Public Service Research Group, he is personally in charge of three jobs: one in health, one in water pollution control, and a third on the allocation of equipment for law-enforcement purposes. Within the scheme of the giant company his relatively small projects are a fraction of a fraction of what is going on, yet they are symbolic of the nonmilitary side of sDc. An animated, outgoing man in his forties, Arenberg sums up his career as one that began in major missile projects, where he was, as he puts it, ". . . passed from one German scientist to another." "One day," he says, "I realized that what I was doing was all a form of intellectual masturbation. I had fallen in love with R&D as such and not with what I was doing or what it was

123

going to achieve. Like a lot of others of my generation, I had bought the whole thing about fearing war and annihilation so completely that fear became more important than love of peace."

Today, ". . . after a return to the synagogue and a demanding soul-search," Arenberg is intensely involved in these three projects, which he terms a switch from defense to offense—from, as he puts it, "the science of fear" to an attempt to make a positive assault on real problems. The work that most consumes his interest is a health project being carried out on the 4,500-square-mile San Xavier Reservation near Tucson, the home of 5,500 Papago Indians. The project he is advising is an experimental one called the Health Programs Systems Center. It was founded in 1966 to conduct health research and establish more effective means of delivering health services to the inhabitants of the reservation. The center is staffed by both Anglos and Papago and from its inception has actively involved the Papago community in its establishment of research priorities, plans, and staffing. Typical of its conscious attempt to be nonpaternalist and community-oriented was an early decision to include the reservation's "medicine men" or herbalists, diagnosticians, and curers in its program and get their approval for it. Today these men are actively involved in the program as consultants and agents referring patients to the program's M.D.s. Traditionally, these native practitioners have been excluded by outside health officers, with the understandable result that they have opposed their programs.

"Indian medicine is fifty years behind white medicine," Arenberg explains. "The average American Indian dies between the ages of fifty and fifty-two, which is far short of the white expectancy. This fact has been clouded by bureaucratic bull, meaningless indices and the like. When I first started working in this area people proudly told me that statistics show that Indians seldom die of heart attacks. Of course they don't—they don't live long enough."

Arenberg is working with the Papago center as a consultant applying technical tools and analyses to help it achieve better health services for the reservation. He points out that the basis for such work is not technical but in the uncovering of white prejudices and assumptions. "There are a lot of things we take for granted. In working with a health program, for example, you can't think of prescribing drugs unless you know that the patients have refrigerators to keep them in. Or using, as has been done, job absenteeism as an index for health.

Such an index may be fine for a Los Angeles suburb but not on an Indian reservation, where very sick men may work because they desperately need the money." He is so skeptical of the effects of earlier attempts at improving Indian health as to say, "Sometimes I think that things might be generally better today if we had taken all the money that has been pumped into these programs and divided it up among the Indians to provide their own services." The aspect of the Papago experiment that most appeals to Arenberg is that it belongs to the tribe and is not run from Washington. Although he is paid with federal funds, Arenberg considers himself an employee of the Papago.

One of the specific technical approaches that he has used is the application of computers to reservation health records. Each individual gets his own coded computerized health record that can be added and referred to quickly at any of the four health centers on the reservation. Coding is essential to insure privacy. "Simply," says Arenberg, "the computer keeps the individual from being lost in the system. He can go to any center and they'll have his record or, conversely, a doctor or specialist who might be at any of the four stations on any given day won't have to treat a man without knowing his history. The computer also gives us a handle on the health problems of the total population, a real chance to monitor the situation and find out, for example, where TB is cropping up and give us good clues as to why. It is also a tool for us to figure out how best to use our resources; perhaps we will find that nurses are not located in the best spots for maximum care and this will suggest better nurse placement."

Mathematical modeling is another technique that has been used among the Indians with surprising result. It has aided in cutting tuberculosis and trachoma (chronic inflammation of the eyes) by a half and inner-ear infection by a quarter. The trachoma control program on the reservation, which had been screening school children and then treating those children with the malady along with their families, was keeping incidence of trachoma at a level rate but was not cutting it. Then a mathematical model of the disease on the reservation was constructed to see if there was a better method of treatment. The model showed that trachoma could never be cut for two simple but previously unacknowledged reasons: The program was repeatedly treating the same segment of the population, and sources outside the reservation were contributing to the problem. A larger segment of the population was then treated, and a program was mounted to control the major source of outside infection— namely, infiltration from a nearby Navajo reservation. Although the first program was based on the advice of experts, the second program based on mathematics is bringing the incidence of trachoma down and will probably wipe it out almost entirely among the Papago.

Arenberg's other projects are also heavily based in mathematical modeling. One is an attempt to develop an economic and geographic model of the water resources in the region around Orange County in Southern California in order to aid a variety of groups in the area to get optimum use of the water without polluting it. Eventually it will serve as a tool for determining zoning, the best course for water-pollution abatement, location of sanitizing facilities, and predicting water quality as the population changes. Another model is being constructed for the Los Angeles sheriff's office to keep tabs on the police resources of the thirty or so police departments in Los Angeles County so that they can be most effectively marshaled during times of emergency.

While Arenberg has turned his back on military work *per se*, he is the first to admit that many of the computer and modeling techniques he and others in similar positions are employing were those initially developed for military and space projects. "After all," he says, "we're in a period right now when we've got to get the biggest bang for the buck in solving civilian problems, and one of the best ways to do it is to use some of that technology that's been paid for already."

While Arenberg's work is representative of a part of SDC's nonmilitary program, the variety of tasks it performs is considerable, among them:

Creation of a complex mathematical model used to simulate chemical reactions producing Los Angeles-type smog. Paid for by the National Air Pollution Control Administration, the model shows how smog is dispersed by wind and air currents, determines the chemical makeup of smog, and figures out which areas are actually being polluted and which are not.

A joint effort with the state of New York to develop a computer-based intelligence system. Once implemented, NYSIIS (New York State Identification and Intelligence System) will permit speedy, electronic information-sharing between the police and law-enforcement agencies in the state. It will provide for the storage and rapid retrieval of individual criminal records, fingerprints, mug shots, and the like. Similar contributions to the technology of law and order have been made for the Los Angeles Police Department, the California Youth and Adult Corrections Agency, the Customs Bureau, and the National Police Departments of Thailand and South Vietnam. (The Southeast Asian work was paid for by the Agency for International Development and in both cases sought to computerize crime records and statistics for those countries.)

For the Los Angeles Department of Airports, a study on the economic and technical feasibility of Skylounge—a futuristic scheme for speeding transportation between airport and downtown. It consists of mobile-bus-like "lounges" that would drive passengers and baggage to a central heliport where the lounges would be picked up by a crane helicopter and hauled to the airport.

The design and computer programming of an information system for the Washington, D.C., public schools. It assists administrators, teachers, and principals in processing records of attendance, supplies, personnel assignments, and other administrative items. Other educational information systems have been created for the Province of Quebec, Rockland County (New York), the state of New York, and California's Claremont College.

SDC also offers a great deal of advice on subjects ranging from computer software for industrial concerns to urban consulting. One interesting example of the latter is packaged disasters for cities—also another instance of how SDC borrows on its military experience for nonmilitary work. For a fee one can experience civil calamity by appointment at SDC's Emergency Operations Research Center—a 6,000-square-foot laboratory that simulates fires, earthquakes, nuclear attack, tidal waves, riots, hurricanes, and/or floods and trains those who might have to face such disasters by suggesting improvements in the way these dire situations are handled.

In a typical disaster simulation, a mayor from a Gulf Coast city might ask SDC to test his administration's ability to deal with a hurricane. Once an SDC team has set up a rough draft of the emergency scenario, members of the staff of the emergency center go to the city to get the information needed to make the simulation as realistic as possible. This data might include resources available to the police

127

and fire departments, medical facilities, and existing emergency procedures. When the scenario is put into final form, officials from the city come to the center in Santa Monica to run through their emergency. A large command room is set up with maps and displays indicating such factors as population concentration, the number of emergency vehicles available, and the extent of the disaster. So that the facts of the unfolding disaster can be transmitted into the command room, communications are set up including telephones, closed-circuit television, teletype, and radio. As the players act through the crisis, their behavior is watched and recorded. According to the scenario, for example, half an hour after the hurricane starts, officials are notified that a bridge has fallen into the local river. Confusion is introduced as three different accounts, with conflicting details, of the incident arrive at the center. Responses may be blocked by related simulated events, such as the stoppage of phone messages by a downed phone line. Real stress is achieved because the players never know what is coming next, save for the unexpected. The exercise is followed by an on-the-spot critique and later by a formal report evaluating the team's performance. More than forty cities have used the service, among them Denver, New Orleans, and Syracuse.

To illustrate the many directions open to SDC in a given area in the future, education is a good case in point. It has been heavily involved, to be sure, in those areas to be expected of a systems and software establishment. It has packaged instructions for teaching computer sciences to students, designed and developed computer information systems for a number of schools and colleges, offered schemes for computer-assisted instruction in which computers analyze student test results, and pioneered in computer-aided instruction in which students use computer consoles to learn in their courses. In addition to acting as teacher to a variety of clients—for example, it was hired by the U.S. Civil Service Commission to teach employees how to develop automatic data processing systems—SDC has participated in various on-the-job training programs, including one to place blind people as computer programmers. In this program, based on the assumption that blind people have certain compensating abilities that make them ideal for the remunerative field of programming, it has indeed been found that in general the blind have remarkable memories, an ability for intense concentration and strong analytical aptitude—all of which are ideal for the abstract art of programming. Their instruction at SDC goes from the elementary aspects of computers right up through participation in real, highly technical research programs.

Perhaps most interesting of SDC's work in education are some of its experimental educational schemes, such as the project with Syracuse University aimed at the development of a new program to educate teachers. It features the development of a five-year curriculum for education students, instructional modules to test the future teacher's grasp and comprehension of material, and individualized pacing—permitting the prospective teacher to proceed as slowly or as rapidly as he or she wishes.

Another educational experiment being developed at SDC is the design of an experimental school for the urban poor directed toward the ultimate goal of a "community school"—one that meets the special needs of the ghetto child but also becomes an important community resource. The theory behind the school is that by designing it as a small society it will meet the objectives of making the individual student an important participant, giving him a sense of place and belonging, and allowing him to have maximum latitude and responsibility for self-direction.

Such a community school would feature individual rooms in the building for each student—small, private spaces that the student can individualize to his own taste. Providing a piece of the school for the student to use and improve would be a great benefit to a child in a ghetto world where privacy is a luxury. Each student, moreover, would have the opportunity to work at a paying job at the school. These jobs would be varied in type, pay, hours, and skills required and, as closely as possible, would reflect the working society outside the classroom. Opportunity for employment would be visible, as would be the payoff for work well done—both in jobs and academically. Nor would it be "make-work" but rather the real work of operating the school itself in jobs like equipment repair, clerical work, and food preparation. The emphasis here would not be on vocational training, although that may be a benefit in some cases, but on showing students the opportunities for productive employment in the world at large. The rationale for this aspect of the school is that it would provide the students with money, be meaningfully related to academic progress, and offer firsthand experience within a productive society.

The school would also let the student choose the path of his academic program or career through the selection of curriculum units and would offer a continuous nongraded curriculum emphasizing mastery of skills rather than marks and grade levels. It is also being designed to make the student and his teacher work for the same rewards—for instance, a student's teacher would not grade him but an outside evaluator would be used, so that a more natural alliance would be built between teacher and student. The school would be functionally unified from preschool through the twelfth grade (although there would be no grades as such) to provide continuity, coordination, and unity for children of the same family. It would be open fifteen hours a day, twelve months a year, to make it a community center. The student would be required to attend school at least 180 days a year, but it would be open to him to use all year long. The school would further try to establish itself as a community center by offering such services as child care, community recreation, and courses for adults. Another novel feature of the school would be the presence of an ombudsman to handle grievances of teachers and students, especially those relating to bureaucratic aspects of the school. Teachers would be separated into three categories: practical professionals who would be primarily concerned with job training and job supervision; curriculum professionals, or the academic teachers; and evaluators, who would test and monitor progress. The rationale here is to divide the traditional roles of the teacher into three separate jobs, each of which to be filled by a person with particular aptitude in one of the three areas.

Robert Meeker, the prime researcher working on the school proposal, says that it aims at a full-scale reform of existing schools. He adds that none of the ideas is new in itself, but they have been tried before only on a piecemeal basis or have simply been suggested in research and never implemented. "It is based on the philosophy that a school should be a true microcommunity," he says—and intends to see it implemented.

The work, financed by the Ford Foundation, may be speeded by the federal government, which is expected in the near future to fund experimental schools on a wide basis. Meeker is the first to admit the difficulties that will be faced in implementing such a proposal. "It flies in the face of hundreds of regulations, from child labor laws to attendance laws to accreditation policies," he says, "but most large urban school systems, with some exceptions, are so desperate for improvement that we think they're willing to make some radical changes to improve things."

Meeker's project is not the only experimental approach being used with schools. Another undertaking, which Meeker points out is quite different from but not contradictory to his work since the problem is so large and complex that a blend of many new approaches will be required to solve it, is SDC's tutorial community project. It is a seven-year experiment being conducted in Pacoima, California, and is backed by the Ford Foundation. The main characteristic of this work at the Pacoima Elementary School, a predominantly Mexican-American and black school in the Los Angeles School District, is the central role of the student as tutor and helper—a role being made an integral part of the everyday school operation. Each student tutors those below him, aids in establishing objectives, participates in setting learning objectives and methods, and supports the teachers by correcting papers, keeping records of progress, and training other tutors. In addition to student tutors, parents and other members of the community are used to perform tutoring tasks. The project, which began in 1968, is being carefully introduced at the rate of a grade a year to allow for gradual implementation and time for revision of the plan, if necessary, as it goes along. Ralph J. Melarango, one of the co-directors of the project, comments: "What we propose is a radical change in education—a change to a genuine learning community in which students, teachers, administrators, and parents share responsibility, concern, and participation in improving learning for all." The long-term objective of the experiment is the development of a prototype tutorial school that could be used as a model across the nation. Though it will be a long while before the project can be fully evaluated, early reports indicate that students have taken to the idea and they are becoming effective teachers.

As an institution, SDC has distinctive characteristics. Its reputation is good, since it has kept clear of charges of excessive overrun and the malfunctions of so many military contractors.

At one juncture in its early history, SDC employed an estimated 90 percent of the nation's computer programmers. Though its corner on programmers ended some time ago, due in significant measure to SDC's success in ushering in the era of automation, one of SDC's marketing men says that he thinks of SDC as "the nation's prime university of systems." There is a lot of truth to the statement, for SDC has managed to stay on the leading edge of automation. In the future it will undoubtedly have a direct impact on many areas, including places that have thus far been untouched by the computer—for example, one job SDC is currently trying to get is that of creating an automated system to help Congress keep track of the vast quantities of information for which it is responsible.

While the System Development Corporation and the Hudson Institute are distinctly different in the kind of work they do and the way in which they do it, each is a logical extension of different aspects of RAND—Hudson of its work in addressing major policy issues and SDC of its long-established role as broker for new technology. Both were born as servants of the military and, though still quite dependent, are striving for fuller civilian status.

Just as these two think tanks illustrate the ever-widening market for the variety of research services first offered to the military by RAND, so do they also point out that, like RAND, other think tanks generally grope for solutions to problems while perched on ideological platforms. While Hudson's bent for forwarding iconoclastic ideas from a reactionary base is hard to miss, SDC's platform is subtler and less partisan. Through its contrasting campaigns to automate all defense and mount systematic social programs, SDC exhibits the technocrat's faith that the shortcomings of "the system" can be remedied by better attendant systems.

VII

THE MILITARY-
INTELLECTUAL
COMPLEX

---

1. Government Under Contract

> The DOD [Department of Defense] has been
> able to involve itself in research having only
> the remotest relevance to problems en-
> countered by the Armed Services—matters
> at no previous time nor anywhere else in the
> world deemed to lie within the province of
> the defense function—just because it has
> the money: it has more money than any
> other public agency.
>
> —Admiral Hyman G. Rickover in tes-
> timony before the Senate Foreign Re-
> lations Committee, 1968

It started innocently enough. An American professor who had
been born in Chile made two trips to his native land to get professors
there to join him in a study of Chilean society. One of those contacted on his second trip in April 1965 was a sociologist teaching at
Chile's Catholic University. The sociologist was shown a series of

133

working papers on the project and was told that it was being financed by the National Science Foundation. The papers made the Chilean professor suspicious because certain references had been erased from them, and there were other references which indicated that there might be political repercussions to the study in Chile. He wrote a letter expressing his doubts to the secretary-general of the University of Chile, who in turn became convinced that the study was "political in nature" and "constituted a grave threat against our sovereignty." The two men agreed to co-sign a letter of protest which appeared later in the *Latin American Review of Sociology* and, among other things, claimed that the study was actually sponsored by the U.S. military. They were right. The references that had been expunged from the working papers were to the U.S. Army. The National Science Foundation knew nothing about the study.

In short order, the Chilean press picked up the issue, the Chilean Chamber of Deputies announced that it would conduct a full investigation, and the United States Ambassador to Chile, who hadn't the foggiest idea of what was going on, cabled Washington to find out what had happened. The first U.S. news story on the fiasco appeared on June 25, 1965, in the Washington *Star* under the headline "ARMY–STATE DEPARTMENT FEUD BARED BY CHILE INCIDENT: DIPLOMATS SEE PENTAGON STUDY AS INVASION OF FOREIGN POLICY FIELD."

As revealed in a series of newspaper reports and Congressional investigations that followed the *Star* article, the facts were these: The Chilean study was part of a much larger Army study called Project Camelot, which was administered by the Special Operations Research Office (SORO), an Army think tank at American University in Washington, D.C. Camelot was a large research effort on the causes of revolution and insurgency in underdeveloped nations and geared to prescribing ways to cope with "potential instability" in specific nations.

The outcry over the Chilean venture brought about the cancellation of Project Camelot. Both Congress and President Johnson asserted their powers and insisted that future projects of the nature of Project Camelot must be first approved by the State Department. However, the Congressional consensus was that sponsorship of foreign-policy research by the military was valid to its mission.

Shortly after the Camelot furor died down, SORO changed its name to the Center for Research in Social Sciences (CRESS), and foreign studies by the Department of Defense continued to proliferate. Although Camelot as such was never started again, there were such efforts as Project Agile, a series of counterinsurgency studies of the size, cost, and scope of Camelot.

CRESS (nee SORO) was created in 1956 to support the Army's "third mission," which CRESS–SORO literature describes as ". . . all of the short-of-general war measures to cope with indirect aggression, subversion, and so-called wars of national liberation." The specific duty given to this think tank was to learn more about the peoples of emerging nations so that if and when the U.S. Army got involved in the activities of one of them there would be information on file on which to base strategic planning, military assistance, and psychological warfare. In addition, it was set up to serve as a service bureau or clearinghouse where military leaders could get quick cultural information. In 1967, for example, it prepared 392 responses to questions about such things as the "societal dynamics of Iran," draft laws in Latin America, and the economics of Thailand. One result of an Army request for information was a report entitled "Witchcraft, Sorcery, Magic and Other Psychological Phenomena and Their Implications on Military and Paramilitary Operations in the Congo," a report that was often cited in Congress as an example of provocative Pentagon research.

During the period from 1958 to 1966 it prepared a series of classified "area handbooks" for the Army that amount to guides to the conduct of psychological warfare in nations throughout the world. So highly classified that they are not available for Congressional scrutiny, the handbooks have been defended this way by Army R&D Chief Lieutenant General A. W. Betts: "We have a continuing need to build up a library of information that can be available to our military planners for any country in the world into which we might have to go."

CRESS managed the preparation of twenty-seven handbooks for such nations as Ghana, Iraq, Brazil, and Venezuela. Senator J. William Fulbright has been particularly critical of these handbooks as well as the Army's approach to foreign affairs in general. His general thesis is that the military should stick to military affairs and he has said, "All too many of these studies—under way and proposed— indicate that the Pentagon planners have not learned any lessons from Vietnam, but that they are busily engaged in blueprinting strategies where our military will play the key role in trying to maintain order in a disorderly world. I, for one, do not want the Senate to encourage the planning of more Vietnams."

Fulbright's comment may be a bit overstated. In truth, the handbooks are a product of Vietnam lessons in the sense that they attempt to prepare for other military encounters with more care—with an eye to not botching the war for the "hearts and minds" of, say, Ghanaians and Brazilians. Fulbright's general concern, however, would seem valid in that American military men and their hired analysts are busy conditioning themselves psychologically for Vietnam-like wars that today more than ever seem doubtful efforts for defending the United States.

Although the actual content of the area handbooks cannot be analyzed, their presence can be. They are just one example of the product line of the military think tanks. Granted that the product line is diverse—ranging from new equipment to new doctrine—the largest proportion of these products have the same over-all function: maintaining the military posture of readiness to go anywhere at a moment's notice, with the legitimacy of the excursion of subsidiary concern. For those who maintain that the U.S. military has a destiny to fulfill in Ghana or Norway or wherever, the think tanks must be a comfort. For those who maintain otherwise, CRESS and the other military think tanks are a threat.

As CRESS evolved, much of its intellectual attention focused on Vietnam, and the result was a series of studies used extensively in Army training ranging from the Green Berets training school to the Army War College. CRESS also found time to prepare "stability programs," conduct counterinsurgency research, and ready psychological warfare plans for nations in Europe, Africa, and Latin America.

Until 1969 CRESS was a part of the American University and enjoyed the status of "Federal Contract Research Center." But persistent student protest over its role in Vietnam and its work in preparing for war elsewhere resulted in its leaving campus. It was absorbed by the American Institutes for Research, a larger Pittsburgh-based think tank usually referred to by its disarming acronym AIR. This larger think tank is an independent, nonprofit operation specializing in the behavioral and social sciences with offices in Pittsburgh, Washington, Palo Alto, and Bangkok. Over the years it has conducted scores of behavioral and social studies for a variety of sponsors within the Department of Defense. Although AIR is receiving the funds that would have normally been given to CRESS, it is not on the official list of Federal Contract Research Centers.

As a Federal Contract Research Center, or FCRC, CRESS was one of about seventy-five institutions that receive all or almost all of their support from one sponsor in the government and one of a dozen such entities in the employ of the Defense Department. As a group of institutions these research adjuncts cost well over a billion dollars a year to support and in some years closer to a billion and a half. Although there is tremendous diversity among these think tanks— from mammoth research centers contracted for by the Atomic Energy Commission to the medium-sized RAND to tiny regional educational policy research centers operated by the Office of Education— the one factor uniting them is that each has a special, continuing, and trusted arrangement with a government sponsor. Of these contract centers, the most powerful, famous, and controversial are those belonging to the Department of Defense. As we have seen with RAND, SDC, and CRESS, they have been able to extend the power and influence of the Department of Defense.

In 1967 the Pentagon's "list" of FCRCS had twenty-one centers on it. As of this writing there are twelve still on the list. This paring down of the list reflected political pressure rather than the reality of the situation. CRESS, for example, is still paid for by the Army and is still part of its mental arsenal, but because of absorption by another think tank it is not on the list. SDC is off the list but still heavily subsidized by the Pentagon, and, in fact, there are well over 100 think tanks that get most or almost all of their money from the Department of Defense but are not on the list.

In 1968 the Hudson Institute was kicked off the list, although it continues to get Pentagon support. As elaborated in a letter from military research boss John S. Foster, Jr., to the House Committee on Armed Services, the reasons for the Hudson action were that: (1) It was not set up by the Department of Defense; (2) it does not have the intimacy of relationship with the Department of Defense that is characterized by continued privileged access to data; (3) it competes for government business with other think tanks (apparently not acceptable behavior for an FCRC); (4) it claims the right to work on commercial and non-U.S. projects without regard to conflicts of interest with work it is doing for the U.S. government; (5) it has as its goal reducing its Defense work to 50 percent of its work; and (6) to quote the letter directly, "Accepts no responsibility for conducting its affairs in a manner befitting an organization having quasi-public status." Besides showing that Kahn and Co. did not conform, even for their biggest client, the letter is the best operational definition of what an official military contract research center is. As a Department of Defense official puts it, "An FCRC is all the things that the Hudson Institute was faulted for not being."

The list is a fraud, an element of the cat-and-mouse game played between the military and the legislative branch. The game works like this. Congress wants the list to be kept under control because it generally views the military FCRCS as costly havens with too much freedom. It has limited the total spent on them to a relatively stable amount of about $250 million a year since 1966. Meanwhile the Pentagon has been busily working to "delist" centers with the result that those remaining on the list are getting more than—or at least as much money as—they always have. Thus there were twenty-one listed centers in 1966 and twelve by 1970, and in both years the amount given to the "list" was $257 million. The dropouts are then either funded from other parts of the gargantuan research budget or made integral parts of the Defense Department. For example, a Navy FCRC, the Hudson Laboratories, was absorbed by the Navy. The result of the game is that the Pentagon has its way while Congress holds the illusion of control. As transparent as the gambit appears, Congress has not figured out what is happening or, more likely, has chosen to look the other way.

Samuel E. Clements, assistant to John Foster, views the list as a "burden" to the Pentagon. "Congress looks at it as both a symbol of power and a symbol for an insidious group of insiders who are running the government. It has become a whipping boy." Clements then points out with unexpected frankness, "There are probably one hundred research groups that one could make a case for as candidates for the list."

A prime example of a Pentagon research adjunct that has been left off the list for political reasons but certainly belongs on it is the Logistics Management Institute. It was created by the Defense Department, works for nobody other than the Defense Department and, generally, is the essence of a contracted-for research adjunct. It is a small nonprofit corporation located in Washington and was founded

138

in 1961 with the authorization of Robert S. McNamara. It serves the Secretary of Defense in the role of consumer adviser, helping him decide what to buy, how to buy it, and how to take care of it once it has been bought. Since coming into being it has worked on over fifty separate studies ranging from developing new policies for negotiating contracts with industry to a massive study aimed at suggesting ways to improve food preparation and service in the Armed Forces. In the food study, for example, its recommendations ranged from that of establishing a "uniform ration" for all foods for all services to new designs for food-preparation equipment and utensils.

Its impact has been felt mainly in terms of new concepts and policies for the money men at the Pentagon. Among its contributions are "life cycle costing" and "value engineering." The former is a method for looking at and evaluating new equipment that calls for computing all of the costs of that equipment, including operation and maintenance, so that its total financial impact can be determined from the beginning. "Value engineering" is an incentive scheme used to motivate defense contractors to find effective ways to cut costs. The incentive boils down to giving the contractor part of the savings that he has made.

While most of Logistics Management Institute's work is concerned with such mundane items as warehouse procedures, policies on spare parts, and the scheduling of equipment overhauls, it has on occasion completed a study of interest to those outside the limited world of logistics policy. The most famous, or infamous, was a report released and promoted during Clark Clifford's reign as Secretary of Defense. It concluded that forty leading defense contractors, contrary to popular opinion, were not only not making large profits but were making less of a profit on their work than 3,500 companies with little or no defense work were making on nonmilitary commercial work. It claimed that defense profits averaged at seven percent while commercial profits were nine percent. "The LMI Report" was used extensively by those who wanted to prove that there was no profiteering going on; as could be expected, the report was attacked by those who believed that excessive profits were being made. The critics seemed to have more ammunition on their side. One of them, Senator William Proxmire, argued that the study relied on unverified, voluntary mail responses from the contractors and did not take into account such tangibles as large amounts of government-supplied

139

capital and government-owned equipment that had been put into the hands of private contractors. Proxmire showed that in 1967 there was $14.7 billion worth of government equipment in the plants of defense contractors. The study is a classic example of a research adjunct of the Pentagon coming up with a definition of "profit" suited to the needs of the era—i.e., that of turning back charges of excessive profits. During the same period, Professor Murray L. Weidenbaum of Washington University in St. Louis produced a similar study concluding that military contractors were taking home more than their nonmilitary corporate brethren. His definition of profit was different.

The LMI study is indicative of much of the research that the defense think tanks produce for their bosses, essentially researching arguments and rebuttals for military positions. The fact that the military think tanks normally shore up Defense Department positions with lengthy analyses is not that surprising; after all, they do work *for* the Pentagon. But what is surprising is that from time to time the arrangement gets so cozy that officials and trustees of these think tanks have felt the need to pay deference to independent thinking. In 1967, for example, Maxwell D. Taylor, then president of the Pentagon's Institute for Defense Analyses, issued an internal memo to his staff elaborating on this theme. It said, in part: "The indispensable virtues of IDA studies, in addition to high professional quality, must be integrity, independence and objectivity." The memo was prompted by the institute's trustees, who were becoming concerned by IDA's growing reputation as a skillful rubber stamp. The fact that some of the highest-paid scientific analysts in the nation's employ had to be instructed in the basic virtues of objective research is in itself an indictment.

Although there are more institutions like LMI that clearly rate a position on the official list, the list does serve two useful purposes: It identifies the most important military think tanks, and it presents a sample of the larger body of intellectual adjuncts created or conscripted for military service. While there are distinct similarities between some of those on the list—and they all hide to varying degrees behind their own walls of secrecy—it is worth examining them one at a time.

2. *The Armchair Generals*

> *Although most* RAC *work is done in the Washington, D.C. area, some research is conducted in other parts of the U.S. or at field offices in England, Germany, South Vietnam and Thailand. In any case, your assignment will allow a wide latitude for independent action.*
>
> —From a brochure used to recruit analysts for the Research Analysis Corporation

In the hierarchy of military think tanks none ranks higher than the Institute for Defense Analyses, or IDA. (Never say Ida, you are told by a staff member, because those at IDA think it sounds silly.) Located across an expanse of parking lots from the Pentagon, IDA does not advertise its existence. The ten-story, concrete-and-glass, paper-clip-Gothic high-rise that it fills carries no label save for a big sign for the Suburban National Bank located on the ground floor. In fact, most passers-by have no idea that the large building is anything other than a large bank. Inside, two uniformed guards stand at an elevator to make sure that all visitors have an escort. Even the lady who brings around the coffee wagon rates an armed guard. The woman at the front desk asks, "Will your visit be classified or unclassified?"

IDA's work is more analysis than research, and almost everything it does is secret. Its strength is its top-level senior scientists, and its forte is producing comprehensive reports and analyses in a minimum of time. It is an adjunct to the Office of the Secretary of Defense and has the clout and power of the highest levels at the Pentagon. "If we need the top six frogmen or aeronautical engineers in the nation, the Secretary of Defense will get them for us," says Christian J. Goll, who heads IDA's publications office and handles its extremely limited public relations. Unlike the more outgoing RAND, IDA is very quiet about itself. Its shyness is prompted by the fact that its work is intended for the nation's top strategists only. As an example of just how shy it is, Goll points out that IDA's annual report for 1969 was only half as thick as the previous edition because ". . . we've determined that we were giving out too much unclassified information, which could lead to conclusions about the classified work we're doing." Both reports are extremely vague, giving only the briefest description of its unclassified military efforts.

IDA's specialties are strategic and tactical studies, weapons evaluations, international studies, counterinsurgency planning, and economic analyses. It has completed several hundred studies for the Pentagon of which only a small handful are available to the public. Approximately three-quarters of its work is secret, and of the remaining quarter most carries the notation "for official use only" and is not for public consumption. With the exception of its nonmilitary work, journal articles by its staff members and some work in noncritical areas like civil defense and military manpower, it is difficult to detail its accomplishments, stances or findings. But there is enough information at least to indicate some of its major concerns.

Unlike most think tanks that do only long-range studies, IDA also does "quick response" work for the Secretary of Defense, the Joint Chiefs of Staff, and others. These jobs are mainly concerned with operations problems that must be solved quickly. Examples in this realm include working up suggestions on the detection of concealed weapons, a program prompted by the Federal Aviation Administration's need to combat air hijacking, and extensive work in resolving some of the problems associated with the M-16 rifle. Its longer studies have touched on most of the major concerns of those at the highest level of military planning. Among them: a report to President Nixon, delivered to him when he took office, on the international and domestic threats to national security he would face while in office; an exploration of "weather modification" for military purposes; a series of studies on the problems of re-establishing the U.S. government and economy after nuclear war; a variety of technical tasks associated with the ABM, and work on future alternatives open to the U.S. in its dealings with mainland China. The latter is just one of a number of IDA diplomatic studies one might expect to be under the control of the State Department or White House but which are actually being performed under Pentagon direction.

A unique entity within IDA is its Jason Division, composed of forty to forty-five outstanding university scientists and including several

Nobel laureates. The Jasons, as they are called, are generally professors with tenure at places like Princeton, the University of California, and MIT but spend much of their spare time, certain weekends and all of their summers thinking about warfare for the institute on a consulting basis. Each summer they and their families are whisked off to a remote resort where, under heavy security, they engage in intense group thinking on defense matters. Although the names of some of the members of Jason are known (such as Norman M. Kroll, who heads the Physics Department at the University of California at San Diego, and Edwin E. Salpeter, Professor of Physics and Nuclear Studies at Cornell), many are not. IDA's policy is to guard the list of Jason members.

The division concerns itself with the scientific aspects of major defense issues. Among the major items it has studied are ballistic missiles, submarine detection, anti-infiltration technology, tactics in Vietnam, nuclear weapons, and airborne mines. Little public detail has emerged from the Jasons' secret realm, but it is known that they have done extensive work attempting to resolve technical problems associated with the ABM, have contributed much thought to counter-infiltration technology in Vietnam (including work on the ill-fated "McNamara line" of electronic sensors), and had, at one point, according to a report appearing in *The Nation* in April 1968, prepared a study which looked at the possible use of tactical nuclear weapons in Southeast Asia. IDA's Goll sums up the work of the Jasons: "You can figure that any matter of great current concern to the Department of Defense will be the concern of the Jasons."

The institute has performed work on the civilian front that is not secret, work that IDA with Pentagon permission has contracted for with civilian agencies. Among the dozen or so jobs it has undertaken are planning work for the Urban Mass Transit Administration, design and development of a command center for emergencies and crises in the District of Columbia, a study of techniques that could lead to lower housing construction costs, and a variety of technical tasks for the U.S. Post Office geared to streamlining postal operations, including automatic cancelling equipment. Two of its civil studies resulted in conclusions clearly unwanted by their sponsors. A study of the SST paid for by the Federal Aviation Administration concluded that the development of the aircraft would have a negative impact on the U.S.'s balance of payments, while a 1967 report to the Office

143

of Economic Opportunity concluded that less than half the money (about 40 percent) funneled into the War on Poverty was directly benefiting the poor.

These two civil studies performed by IDA bring up an intriguing question: Are they objective, hard-hitting showpieces that bear no resemblance to the work done for the Pentagon or are they indicative of all IDA research? The question is, of course, unanswerable by anyone without a top-secret security clearance. The principle of secrecy for everything military operating here is one that has no place in an open, pluralistic society. If IDA is free to report on a failure of the War on Poverty, why can it not report on its findings about the conduct of the war in Vietnam? If IDA can come out and openly contradict the Department of Transportation and two Administrations on the effect of the SST on balance of payments, why can we not hear IDA's analysis of the ABM project? A common argument given in defense of military think tanks is that they are serving to enliven and sharpen debate. They may be, but only inside their own secret loops. Outside these loops the effect is to close debate on issues like ABM, policy toward China and nuclear war, and in doing so to make an open society less so. Undoubtedly there is some work, especially in new technology, that must be kept under wraps for security reasons, but keeping almost all military thought away from the public is arrogant and dangerous.

Another civil client of the institute is the Justice Department, which has pumped over half a million dollars into it for new ideas on combating crime. Most of IDA's specific suggestions have had to do with using computers, modern management techniques, systems analysis, and better communications to help deal with rising crime rates. IDA has also helped plan the recently established National Institute of Law Enforcement and Criminal Justice, a research group within the Department of Justice, has done much work on the feasibility and potential of nonlethal police weapons (thereby helping advance the acceptance of Chemical Mace as a standard police item), and has been working for several years on improving lie-detection techniques.

IDA has had a less than ideal relationship with Congress. Its secrecy has been one bone of contention. For instance, in 1964 it produced a study of the incidents at the Gulf of Tonkin that the Senate Committee on Foreign Relations was not allowed to see even though it persistently tried to get a copy. Committee Chairman Fulbright pointed out with considerable exasperation that the study was available to the institute's trustees, who were mostly university presidents, but not to the Senate, which had more than a passing interest in the events as they really occurred at the Gulf. Author Joseph C. Goulden reports in his book on the Tonkin affair, *Truth Is the First Casualty*, that the report was "reputed to be highly critical of the Pentagon's communications system" during the incident.

In 1966 the House Armed Services Committee took a look at the institute's operations and found, among other irregularities, that it had not obeyed Pentagon procurement regulations, had purchased computers without approval from its sponsors, was allowed an incredible amount of independence as to how it spent its money, was socking away a sizable percentage of its tax-free contract fees as what amounted to profits and was offering near utopian benefits to its employees. Prospective employees did well also. One man was given $25,200 from IDA to study in the Netherlands with the idea that he would come to work for IDA when he returned; however, he returned and chose to work elsewhere. Although the inquiry brought about some reforms, it did not prevent this nonprofit institution from stashing away its fees and profits. Like many Federal Contract Research Centers, the institute has a taxpayer-supplied kitty for supporting research that Congress does not authorize. Despite this, there has been no investigation of IDA since 1966 even though there are no lack of leads for starting such an investigation. IDA's 1969 annual report, for example, indicates an allocation of $835,000 for research it deemed important from its kitty of $2.9 million in "excess corporate funds." By any corporate standard that is a lot of cash to have lying around and much too much for a nonprofit defense group to have at a time when the Secretary of Defense boasts that defense expenses have been cut to the bare bone.

Although the technological and academic elite who work for IDA claim that their labors are in the public interest, they submit to regulations that prohibit them from trusting the public or the public's representatives in Congress with their thoughts. To give another example, a report made the rounds in 1969 stating that some of IDA's top analysts had determined that the Safeguard ABM was ill-conceived and, perhaps, even dangerous. Although it has worked as hard as any institution on evaluating ABM, IDA has never made a public

145

statement on its findings nor has it admitted to anything more than that it is ironing out some technical problems associated with the project. C. J. Goll of the institute sums up the policy on such information, "We have had many inquiries from the press about our ABM findings and all I can tell you is what I've told them. Every one of our divisions has worked on ABM and there are many individual opinions and findings on it. And that is really all that we can say."

The institute constitutes graphic evidence of how faceless men with a general disdain for Congress and without publicly scrutinized opinions have moved into the policy-making apparatus of government.

IDA was formed in 1956 at the request of Secretary of Defense Charles E. Wilson in an effort to attract and retain a permanent corps of civilians to aid the Weapons Systems Evaluation Group of the Joint Chiefs of Staff. The evaluation group needed help in arbitrating the costly, earth-shaking missile and weapons battles which brewed during Defense expansion in the 1950's—debates such as the Army's Jupiter vs. the Air Force's Thor, or the Air Force's Minuteman vs. the Navy's Polaris. A trusted and objective arbiter was needed to wade through the competing claims of the services and their contractors. Wilson asked the Massachusetts Institute of Technology to form such a group, and it agreed to do so but only if other universities helped form the corporation. The California Institute of Technology, the Case Institute of Technology, Stanford, Tulane, and MIT acted as co-founders and were later joined by the University of California, the University of Chicago, Columbia, the University of Illinois, the University of Michigan, Penn State, and Princeton. A $500,000 Ford Foundation grant got it into operation.

As the years progressed, IDA's sphere of influence broadened. It became adviser to the Secretary of Defense himself on the two most important elements of the Pentagon's technical programs: the Advanced Research Projects Agency and the Office of Director of Defense Research and Engineering. By the late 1960's it had grown to a corporation with five divisions, an annual budget of about $14 million, and a roster of about 600 employees.

In the fall of 1967 the Princeton chapter of the Students for a Democratic Society demanded that the university sever its ties with IDA. When the demand was rejected, a demonstration was mounted in front of the IDA Communications Research Center on the Princeton campus. Students at the University of Michigan followed the example of their counterparts at Princeton, and in the spring of 1968 university connection with IDA became one of the issues at stake in the eight-day student revolt that rocked Columbia University. These and other less serious rumblings elsewhere led the twelve universities involved with IDA to drop their institutional membership in it. Key individuals from those universities continue to participate in IDA's research program and sit on its board of trustees, but these academicians are there as individuals, not as official representatives of the schools. The fact is that the most secret of the major think tanks is still the one with the most impressive academic connections.

Another military think tank that has had its troubles and, like CRESS, has left a Washington, D.C., campus for quieter, less controversial ground is the Human Resources Research Office (usually referred to by its awkward abbreviation HUMRRO). It was established in 1951 by the Army at George Washington University to fill the need for research in "psychotechnology," or, to be more specific, research into training methods, GI motivation and morale, and psychological warfare. After HUMRRO severed relations with the university in 1969 it became a private, nonprofit corporation with home offices in Alexandria, Virginia. It is one of the largest behavioral research groups in the nation and employs about 230 people, mostly psychologists, who work at its main location as well as at five field locations on Army installations around the country.

There is a definite 1984-ish tinge to HUMRRO's work. Its scores of projects past and present have "work unit" code names like DESERT ROCK V, TREBLE, RAID, PROTECT, and STIR. The code words mask a variety of simple to esoteric concerns. DESERT ROCK V, for example, is one of a series of studies of the factors influencing the performance of troops exposed to an atomic shot. In this study it was determined that the better a man was indoctrinated before seeing a shot, the more self-confident he became and the more willing he is to volunteer for nuclear combat. TREBLE, on the other hand, is a survey of music as used in Communist propaganda, but its probably interesting results are not known because the study is classified. RAID is the code name for a series of inquiries for improving the effectiveness of small groups under stress; it has proven basic tenets for the Army, such as that a successful group is more cohesive than one that has experienced repeated failure. PROTECT studied the effect of gas masks

147

on troop performance and determined, among other things, that a
soldier's ability to communicate may be hampered up to 41 percent
by a mask. STIR examined delinquency in the Army and concluded
that being AWOL was more a function of personal background and
attitude than of the situations in which the Army puts a man.

In all, its research covers the broad behavioral side of warfare, including just about everything from helping the GI conquer his fear
of height to the elimination of flinching when firing a rifle to improving the psychological adjustment of the soldier to war. A recent
addition to its long list of concerns is that of developing "cultural
self-awareness" in the American fighting man. Called Project COPE,
this effort caused debate in the Senate in August 1969 when the subject of the proper research role of the Defense Department was
aired. The matter was brought to the attention of the Senate by
Senator Fulbright, who questioned the propriety, necessity, and cost
of teaching the American way of life to Americans. Although
HUMRRO does not cost as much to operate as most think tanks, its
annual budget has held steadily at the $3.5 million level in recent
years.

Much of its influence on the Army has been direct and easy to
trace. In this category are such "products" as the currently accepted
method for teaching the Army recruit how to aim and fire his rifle
(one HUMRRO innovation was replacing the bull's-eye target with
realistic man-shaped silhouettes that fall when hit), new rules and
procedures for GIs standing guard duty, instructions for teaching
night combat skills, the establishment of leadership training schools
for noncommissioned officers, ROTC course plans, training packages
for the development of Army technicians, and procedures for dealing
with problems encountered in counterinsurgency situations. It has
also produced a large variety of tangible items for the Army such as
classification tests, training manuals, course plans, electronic devices
for simulating battle conditions, and the literature of combat
(sample titles: "How Fast Can You Hit Him?" and "The Optimum
Kill Power of Man").

From a broader standpoint, HUMRRO's influence has been deep and
fundamental. It has been the major catalyst in changing traditional
training and task assignment procedures from those in effect during
World War II to new ones dictated by "the systems-orientation," or
training geared to the system that a man is to be a part of, whether

it be a "rifle system," a helicopter or a missile battery. The HUMRRO approach—and subsequently the Army's—is to look at men as integral parts of a weapons system with specific missions.

HUMRRO has given the Army new information on how to use its human equipment more efficiently. And the Army has been responsive. For instance, when HUMRRO found that single men adapt themselves more quickly to Army training the farther they are sent from their homes, the Army's training assignment procedures changed accordingly. Terms like "psychotechnology," "human engineering," "human quality control," "group performance," and "man/weapon" system dot HUMRRO literature. Such sterile, horrific terminology is more than mere jargon, though, the terms are valid descriptions of HUMRRO's brand of applied psychology and its mind-bending mission of getting the human weapon to work.

Undoubtedly the most important Army think tank is the Research Analysis Corporation (RAC) of McLean, Virginia—probably the closest to RAND of any think tank and often referred to as "the Army's RAND." Although it is slightly smaller than RAND, its work closely parallels that of the Santa Monica organization in that its major concerns are political studies, new weapons systems, applied technology, strategy and tactics, and new mathematical and management techniques. It has done less nonmilitary work than RAND, but, like RAND, is trying to get new assignments in that area.

An area in which RAC, again like RAND, has had a major impact is that of war games and military modeling. A copy of the RAC house organ, *The RACconteur*, claims that it has the greatest capability in war-gaming and military modeling "anywhere." Two of its most renowned products in this realm are a game called "Carmonette" and its "Automated Force Structure Model." Carmonette was developed in the late 1950's and has undergone continual refinement since then. It is a computerized game which tests new weapons and military innovations completely automatically. Or to put it another way, it fights battles by itself. Carmonette "players" feed it the characteristics of weapons and equipment that will be in the hands of two opposing battalions in the battle—such characteristics as time required to reload a rifle, tank speeds, and the kill probabilities of heavy guns. Once instructed, the computer then pits the two battalions in a ninety-minute battle and afterward tells the players each side's casualties and the extent of territorial advance or retreat. This game

149

has been used extensively to determine both the feasibility and the allocation of new equipment for Southeast Asia. One specific class of items tested by Carmonette was electronic night-vision aids. RAC's Automated Force Structure Model was created to help the Army quickly determine the most effective number and mixture of military units to contend with a given enemy force under given conditions. Simply, it is fed a problem and told what units and equipment are available, and it returns a suggestion as to which should be sent.

RAC is housed in a pentagonal structure in a research park outside of Washington. Its entranceway is a large aquariumlike globe that makes it look, quite literally, like a think *tank*. Although the Research Analysis Corporation did not come into existence until 1961, it traces its origins back to 1948, when the Army set up its Operations Research Office as part of Johns Hopkins University to evaluate the implications of the atomic bomb on Army operations. Between 1948 and 1961 the ORO conducted over 600 projects there and had great influence in diverse Army realms. To name a few, it worked up the plan by which Negroes were integrated into the Army, developed the tactical use of atomic weapons, mounted the Army's first psychological-warfare program, and was responsible for setting up a variety of operations research groups within the Army. The Operations Research Office of Johns Hopkins became the independent Research Analysis Corporation in 1961 primarily due to friction between ORO and the Army. Dr. Ellis Johnson, who headed ORO, felt that the Army was not giving his organization enough freedom in its selection and carrying out of research. He also maintained that the Army was imposing too much secrecy on ORO's work. This friction led to the Army's break with the university and the immediate creation of a new institution with a new organization and a new president. Because of the break, for several years the initials RAC were shorthand for "Relax and Cooperate" to many in the think-tank community.

In recent years much of RAC's work has concentrated on Southeast Asia. It has worked on problems ranging from alternative means of evacuating the wounded from Vietnam to the best places to use herbicides. In 1962 it opened offices in Bangkok and Saigon for "research" in those areas. A recent RAC recruiting brochure amplifies its definition of research by explaining that its office in Thailand is at the disposal of the U.S. and Royal Thai governments for the task of eliminating insurgency in that country.

In 1969 the Army reduced its official FCRC complement from four to two, and only RAC and HUMRRO survived the cut. Besides CRESS, the other unit dropped was one of the smallest contract research centers, the Army Mathematics Research Center at the University of Wisconsin. On August 24, 1970, that center was bombed with 1,700 pounds of nitrogen fertilizer soaked in fuel oil. The blast killed a researcher, injured three others, destroyed a wing of the building in which it was housed, and erased much of its research in progress. A letter intended for the media from the team of bombers stated, "On Monday morning, Aug. 24, revolutionary cadres of our organization conducted an attack on the Army Mathematics Research Center, a major US Army think tank. . . . The AMRC did the vital basic research necessary for the development of conventional and nuclear weapons, chemical weapons, small arms and bullets and much more. . . . The AMRC was a vital cog in the machinery of US imperialism. . . ." In truth, the center is one of the least important research entities on the Pentagon's roster. Its principal functions have been to do basic mathematics research, provide a facility for stimulating scientific contacts between military mathematicians and their civilian counterparts, and provide a training service in applied mathematics. Although it was removed from the list, it is still supported by the Army.

The branch of the Defense Department with the largest collection of contract research centers is the Air Force, with five. The RAND Corporation is one of those five but by no means the largest. The Lincoln Laboratory, managed by MIT, is larger than RAND, as are the Aerospace Corporation and the MITRE Corporation. The Lincoln Lab, created by the Air Force as a direct reaction to the first atomic explosion in the Soviet Union, is devoted to developing new means of nuclear defense. Among its major accomplishments are the Distant Early Warning (DEW) line created to forewarn the U.S. of attack and the design of an underground electronic system in Montana that monitors atomic explosions around the world.

Largest of all the military think tanks is the Aerospace Corporation of El Segundo, California. It gets about $75 million a year from the Air Force and employs over 3,000 people. Its concerns are exclusively technical, and its major role has been that of aiding the Air Force get its missile and space programs off the ground. Since it came into being in 1960, its roles have been those of problem-solver, engineer, and technical director to the Air Force, and it has been almost totally concerned with large weapons and space systems. Among the major jobs it has handled are the development of the Titan III missile booster, improvement of the Minuteman missile, development of a number of spacecraft and booster reliability programs, development of a number of military communications satellites, and a program called ABRES (for Advanced Ballistic Re-entry System Program), an ongoing effort to develop missiles that will successfully penetrate existing enemy defenses.

In 1965 Aerospace became the subject of hearings held by the Subcommittee for Special Investigations of the House Committee on Armed Services. These hearings provided ample evidence of both how a "nonprofit" corporation can take advantage of its status and how little control the government may choose to exert over its wards. During the course of the hearings a long list of abuses were compiled. To start with, Aerospace was charged with spending vast amounts on advertising and public relations which the investigators found to be "highly inappropriate" for an organization that was created for and by the government to do nothing but government work and that in its articles of incorporation stated that it would not engage in "propaganda or otherwise try to influence legislation." In four years it had spent over $1 million on its own public-relations staff, had retained a New York public-relations firm at $2,000 a month, and was running recruiting advertisements averaging over $200,000 a year which the subcommittee reasoned served to attract workers from other government jobs to Aerospace and its higher salaries. The corporation was also dabbling in real estate at taxpayer's expense; it had, for example, bought land in Florida for $261,304 without Air Force approval. Also on the list were findings of lax security procedures, constant refusal to account to the Air Force for its fee expenditures, and failure to obey certain contract stipulations, such as not expending $15.5 million in Pentagon payments for research but salting that money away, presumably to be used for a rainy day. The area in which it had really outdone itself, though, was that of personnel policies. These included unlimited sick leave, educational grants without any obligation to stay with the corporation, exorbitant relocation allowances (such as paying $3,133.03 to move an executive's boat from Massachusetts to California), subsidized meals for executives along with government-financed country-club memberships, "lavish entertainments," and, finally, to quote the subcommittee report, ". . . unusually high starting salaries, unusually sharp increases in pay after short periods of employment, very high salary scales for management-level personnel. . . ." The income for the president of Aerospace for 1964 was $91,730.77, a total that did not include such fringe benefits as company-paid life insurance and club memberships. The primary conclusion made by the investigating committee was that "Aerospace . . . continually violated government policy in its contract dealings with the Air Force, with resultant needless expenditures of millions of dollars of public funds." Although certain specific practices changed after the hearings, such as the retention of the New York public-relations firm, others did not. Salaries, for example, continued to rise until Congress finally stepped in and put a ceiling on them in 1969. Generally, the hearings had little effect on the corporation.

The MITRE Corporation is a large research and engineering firm in Bedford, Massachusetts, which bears much resemblance to the System Development Corporation. It came into being in 1958 as a spin-off from the Massachusetts Institute of Technology, which helped create it to take over MIT defense projects that were considered too big and not appropriate for an educational institution. Today it is a private corporation with no formal ties to MIT. Its name is both a reference to the verb "to mitre" (to match or fit together) and to the organization that created it. (It is sometimes waggishly maintained that MITRE stands for MIT REjects.)

Between half and three-quarters of MITRE's annual income is derived from the Air Force, for whom it conceives, develops, and helps implement advanced weapons, communications and computer systems. It employs over 2,000 people who work either in its large headquarters near Boston, its large suburban Washington complex or its twenty-four field offices scattered in locations ranging from Huntsville, Alabama, to Fuchu, Japan. Its military specialties include the development of systems for air defense, communications, and radar detection. It has handled over 100 jobs for the military, and its current work includes the development of new tactical communications satellites for the mid-1970's, an automated battle planning network, and development of AWACS (for Airborne Warning and Control System), an electronics-laden flying command post. MITRE's income for 1969 was the highest in its history—$40.3 million.

About 20 percent of its work is nonmilitary in nature, and, according to Charles Duke, the executive in charge of MITRE's planning office, the corporation is hoping to do more civil work in the future while continuing to serve the Defense Department. MITRE's greatest potential, in Duke's estimation, is as a designer and technical aide to those grappling with the problems of mass transportation, education, health care, pollution control, and law enforcement. It is developing some steady civilian clients such as the Commonwealth of Massachusetts, for which it is performing a variety of tasks that include the design of a statewide communications network for law enforcement, modernization for the Department of Public Health, and a study of court procedures aimed at streamlining the state's heavily burdened courts. MITRE would like to become the state's official think tank.

One of the most interesting areas that it is currently working in is the design and evaluation of futuristic mass-transportation vehicles for a variety of sections of the Department of Transportation. Its work ranges from nuts-and-bolts engineering studies for the experimental high-speed Metroliner and Turbotrain to the investigation (on paper) of relatively far-out mass transportation concepts, such as:

The tracked air-cushion vehicle, which is guided along a track, supported by an air cushion and propelled by an electric motor. Potentially able to go at between 150 and 300 miles per hour, it could be cheaper to build, easier to maintain, and smoother to ride than conventional trains.

"People movers," or continuous capacity belts, which would offer uninterrupted, continuously available seating on a moving belt. The belts would offer a short-haul, fifteen-to-twenty-five-mile-per-hour supplement to other forms of urban transportation.

Tube vehicle systems, which are powered by electricity and would be capable of speeds between 150 and 500 miles per hour. Several underground-tube ideas are being considered. One concept has the vehicle guided and supported electromagnetically in the tube; another calls for support and guidance from the tube wall; and a third would operate in a tube evacuated of air to reduce drag. As an intercity form of transportation, tubes would be an alternative to the train, car and plane. The tube idea faces a variety of hurdles, including the big one of high tunneling costs (although researchers at MIT, MITRE and elsewhere are looking into new ways to dig tunnels, including lasers, chemicals, flame jets, and fluids sprayed at high velocities).

"Dial-a-bus" systems, in which small buses would respond to telephone calls like taxis. Of all the futuristic systems this is probably the closest to actual experimentation. MITRE is working with several cities interested in testing the idea.

The support of this free and imaginative investigation of new concepts at MITRE (as well as at TRW Systems of Redondo Beach, California, and several other systems firms) is a recent development and for that reason too early to evaluate other than to suggest that a new framework for mass-transportation planning is emerging. It will be interesting to watch the future impact of MITRE in this area as some of these systems come into use. They will be far easier to evaluate than MITRE's missile systems, which it is hoped will never have to be tested.

Much smaller than either Aerospace or MITRE but no less important is Analytic Services Inc., or ANSER, a small specialized non-profit outfit. Located in suburban Washington in a leased building that looks like a dry-cleaning plant, it serves the Air Force's need for relatively quick, objective scientific data. Its strength is providing guidance for the development of advanced weapons systems on relatively short deadline. ANSER, aptly dubbed the Air Force's "short order" think tank by *Air Force/Space Digest*, works solely for the Air Force, which allocates about $1.5 million a year to keep it going.

Its work is classified for the most part, and many of the topics it is pursuing cannot even be identified for security reasons. Its main products are oral reports, consultation, and technical reports seldom publicly released. Its main characteristic is anonymity. In fact for much of ANSER's life, anonymity was a matter of policy. Papers authored by the ANSER staff were published as Air Force Air Staff documents, and its name was not mentioned in the reports. Outside of the annual request for ANSER funds and the fact that there was a building where ANSER people worked, there was little other evidence of its existence. The McNamara regime permitted ANSER to come out of hiding a bit and its byline started appearing on some documents.

The kind of questions that ANSER has fielded for the Air Force include such specific ones as what is the optimum rate for phasing out the B-47 aircraft, how should the Air Force best strengthen its strategic posture, what is the optimum composition of future strategic forces, and what are the potential military uses of space. Some of its contributions to military technology have included early studies leading to over-the-horizon radar now being developed for missile defense, contributions in the realm of intercontinental ballistic missile technology, and work on new aircraft materials, such as boron composite filaments, a material that promises application in radically lighter and stronger aircraft structure. It has worked on plans for such yet-to-fly aircraft and missile systems as the Advanced Manned Strategic Aircraft (or B-1), the AX tilt-wing transport, the F-X fighter, the SCRAMJET (or supersonic-combustion ramjet engine), and the advanced V/STOL (vertical-takeoff and short-takeoff-and-landing) aircraft.

During hearings before the House Committee on Appropriations on the 1970 Defense budget, both the obscurity and importance of ANSER were noted when Congressmen sought to find out what it was, what it did and why. The fact was that this key committee did not have any idea of what ANSER was, and after years of government support was finally discovering it. Some wondered whether the name ANSER was a misspelling of ANSWER. During the course of the discussion General Marvin McNickle, the Air Force's Chief of Staff for R&D, mentioned that ANSER was working on a study of the light intratheater aircraft, prompting the following conversation between the General and Representative William E. Minshall (R.–Ohio):

REP. MINSHALL: General, what is the concept formulation package for the light intratheater transport?

GEN. MCNICKLE: The concept formulation package contains the rationale of why we need and how we would use the airplane as well as the technical approach to be followed in developing it.

REP. MINSHALL: You say ANSER has been working on this for two years. What then have they come up with?

GEN. MCNICKLE: We have an almost finished package to submit to OSD [the Office of the Secretary of Defense]. I believe it will be finished in July.

REP. MINSHALL: This is a completely new aircraft proposal?

GEN. MCNICKLE: Yes, sir. It is expected to be a tilt-wing V/STOL airplane.

REP. MINSHALL: This is on paper?

GEN. MCNICKLE: Yes, sir, paper only.

REP. MINSHALL: In other words, this is just the camel's nose under the tent?

GEN. MCNICKLE: Not even that.

REP. MINSHALL: A whisker?

GEN. MCNICKLE: This is the initial paper effort to seek approval to come up with an airplane in a few years.

Besides showing how Congress sometimes ferrets out new and costly weapons programs under development, the exchange gives an indication of the role that a relatively small Air Force think tank plays in developing and justifying new military hardware.

Finally, the Navy has four FCRCS under its jurisdiction. Three are highly technical outfits really closer in function to laboratories than think tanks. Two of them share the name Applied Physics Laboratory and are located at Johns Hopkins and the University of Washington, and the third is the Ordnance Research Laboratory at Penn State. The fourth, the Center for Naval Analysis, is much broader in its concerns and plays a role analogous to those of RAC and RAND for the other services.

Although billions have been poured into the military contract research centers which represent an awesome extension of military power, Congress has only occasionally examined them or found reason to criticize them. In fact over the last decade the most persistent bone of contention has been over the relatively superficial matter of the salaries paid to civilian thinkers by the Department of Defense.

In 1969 the president of the Aerospace Corporation was getting over $90,000 a year, his two top deputies were making $66,000 and $65,000, and one had to go down to the sixth highest paid officer of the corporation to find somebody with a salary as low as that of Secretary of Defense Laird—$60,000 a year. Such salaries had been irritating Congressmen for some time. Senator Karl E. Mundt, for example, remarking on the fact that retired General Maxwell Taylor, who until recently headed IDA, was being paid $50,000 a year in addition to his military retirement pay, stated that the Pentagon think tanks represented ". . . a [costly] brain drain from civil service into 'private enterprise' paid for by the taxpayers." Finally, in 1969 an amendment was proposed, passed, and attached to the Defense appropriations bill for fiscal year 1970 which stipulated that think-tank salaries could not exceed $45,000 a year except when they were approved by the President of the United States or, in the case of MITRE and IDA, where the presidents were allowed $60,000. The amendment served to keep some salaries down, but in most cases the only "reform" accomplished was that the government paid only the first $45,000, with the difference or a large part of it coming from "corporate funds"—funds that can be easily traced back to management fees and other taxpayer-supplied funds. Of twenty executives getting over $45,000 in 1969, twelve were still getting over that amount in 1970. Hardest hit was the president of Aerospace, whose salary was rolled back by the White House to a paltry $70,000 a year.

Beyond the salary issue, two other major points have led Congressional critics to fault the arrangement between the Pentagon and its think tanks. One is their effect on the policy-making process, and the other is their preferred treatment as private institutions.

There is no questioning the fact that the studies and findings of these think tanks have had great influence on federal decision-making. As a result, anonymous analysts and scientists, with no direct responsibility to the electorate for their decisions, have supplemented the work of public servants and have been given some of the powers of government itself. While this point has been raised time and again in the abstract, it has never really been investigated by the nation's legislators, who themselves are confronted by a seemingly endless parade of new weapons, aircraft, systems, procurement policies and concepts from military planners. In reviewing the situation, Congress acts as if it does not know where the parade started. Individual items are seldom debated, let alone perceived, until they emerge as full-blown proposals or partially accomplished facts—for example, the recent spirited debates concerning C5-A, the F-111, ABM, the Cheyenne helicopter, and other costly items. It is obvious that by scrutinizing the military think tanks more closely, Congress could be ready to check or swiftly respond to the Pentagon's ability to come up with and defend costly new programs and policies.

In reality these think tanks have not just enabled the Pentagon to increase its arsenal of new ideas and new hardware but have served to extend the power of the Pentagon over Congress. Two examples, one real and one hypothetical, serve to illustrate this process. The ABM was researched exhaustively by the Pentagon and its research affiliates before the question of ABM deployment was brought to Congress. From 1956 to 1968 approximately $4.5 billion had been spent on ABM research. Once presented to Congress, entities like RAND, IDA, RAC, the Hudson Institute and others were used both overtly and covertly by the Pentagon and ABM supporters in Congress to supply testimony, memos and in briefings massive quantities endorsing the ABM on both technical and policy grounds. On the other hand, those who opposed ABM or were yet to be convinced of its worth had to rely on a "pick-up" team of analysts and scientists to supply contrasting opinions and evaluations. As mentioned earlier, it was during this period that Jerome B. Wiesner, former Kennedy Administration science adviser, stated that Congress needed an "anti-RAND"—a research body working for Congress that would provide analyses independent of military support.

A second and hypothetical example involves Thailand, a major subject for Pentagon-financed think-tank studies. A Defense Department bibliography on Thailand put out in 1968 lists 508 separate unclassified studies of that country, mostly produced by think tanks. RAC, the Stanford Research Institute, MITRE, SDC, the American Institutes for Research, Cornell Aeronautical Labs, to name some, have not only studied there but did at one time or now operate offices in Bangkok. Should a proposal or a decision be made for U.S. forces to intervene in Thailand, one can be assured that a large body of completed studies, policy recommendations, charts, and statistics would be produced overnight to justify the action. Just as in the case of the ABM example, those doubting or disapproving the action would have to start from scratch in mounting their factual rebuttal.

A final major point that critics have raised concerns the utopian corporate position given to the think tanks. The critics argue that the government supports them but exerts little control over them; they are neither restricted by the competitive constraints of the free marketplace (except when they decide to augment their fixed income by competing for a research contract) nor burdened with government and Civil Service regulations. Although in recent years Civil Service salaries have gone up and there has been some attempt to control FCRC salaries and benefits, think tanks generally offer more liberal compensation to their employees. It is an open secret that one reason that these institutions were created in the first place was to circumvent the salary and benefit structures of the Civil Service. The fact

159

that a RAND analyst flies first class when he travels by air or that he can be given a government-paid-for sabbatical and an analyst working for the government cannot do either has given rise to claims that think-tank employees are "overprivileged." It is often also argued that the FCRCS are given a decidedly unfair advantage in obtaining federal research work, which could otherwise be contracted for through competitive bidding, perhaps for less money. What is more, with the government paying the overhead, they are allowed to compete for nongovernment business. Typical of recent comments on this phenomenon are the remarks of Representative Charles S. Gubser (R.–Calif.) on RAND's agreement to contract with the stock exchanges. "What this amounts to is a subsidy to the New York Stock Exchange from the federal government—through the Air Force and RAND—which represents unfair competition to the many firms who sell these types of services."

Aside from the salary issue, Congressional criticism and other attempts at controlling the subsidized military think tanks have been generally sporadic and ineffective. Full-scale inquiries, such as the hearings on the Aerospace Corporation, have been few, and when they are held at all there is almost never any follow-up to determine if the abuses uncovered have been remedied. By far the most persistent critic has been Senator Fulbright, who has found fault with the government-aided think tanks mostly for their role in foreign-policy making and related work in the social sciences. The number of critics seems to be growing apace with general criticism of the military, although think-tank defenders still outnumber the detractors. The majority of those in Congress, however, either have no interest in the issue or do not understand it. In reading hearings and Congressional debates on the military think tanks, one encounters many examples of confusion over what they do and what they are. In fact, even Fulbright, who has made a point of educating himself about them, is sometimes confused when it comes down to details. In 1968 during hearings before the Senate Foreign Relations Committee, he said while looking at the list of Pentagon FCRCs, "I have a list of them here, but I cannot interpret some of the names. I have heard of some of them. IITRI-ECAC? I do not know what that is. Is it a company in this country?" The IITRI-ECAC that stumped Fulbright is a small FCRC contracted for by the Air Force and dropped from the list in 1970 (but still fully supported by the Air Force), called the Electromagnetic Compatibility Analysis Center (ECAC), run by the Illinois Institute of Technology Research Institute (IITRI).

Congressional criticism has been met with staunch defense by the Pentagon. Early in 1969 defense research chief John S. Foster told the House Committee on Armed Services, "We have received excellent services from these organizations, and we still do. Their services are, in fact, perhaps more critical today than ever before simply because, as defense problems grow more complex, we need as many experienced and objective analysts, designers, and managers as we can get." In general the Pentagon argues that its think tanks produce high-quality research, are free from conflict of interest, are intimately familiar with their sponsor's research needs, can respond quickly to the needs of the military, and have a highly effective capacity for interdisciplinary research. One point that bothers even the Pentagon, however, is that it has very little control over the future of these extraordinary institutions. Research boss Foster pointed out in House hearings in 1969 that he was concerned that some of the think tanks could be—and were being—readily lured out of defense work for new roles as domestic researchers with independent status. Anticipating the desire to work in other realms, the Pentagon's policy since early 1969 has been to allow them to accept as much as 20 percent outside nonmilitary work, but since RAND has already gone to 35 percent without so much as a slap on the wrist, the military is not strictly holding its think tanks to their quota nor is it probable that the Pentagon could actually make them adhere to it. The fact of the situation is that the think tanks that have been created, nurtured, and permanently supported by the Pentagon are legally quite free to go their own way if they decide to do so. Said Foster in 1969, "The choice, thus, is not entirely ours."

The fact that other think tanks could follow the lead of SDC in setting themselves up as independent entities has been in part responsible for experimentation entirely inside the military with groups with responsibilities like the think tanks. One Pentagon faction believes that future "policy research and technical aid groups" (i.e., think tanks) should be under stricter internal control.

In the past ten years there have been two important official examinations of the contract research centers. One was contained in a major survey of federal research by the Bureau of the Budget in 1962, and the second was conducted by the General Accounting Office in 1969. Both were critical of the government–FCRC relationship—mainly on the point of effective public accountability and organizational control—and both suggested that the alternative idea of government "institutes" or internal think tanks be considered. The "institute" concept advanced in both reports called for incorporating the most positive aspects of the contract research centers—such as some freedom in selection of projects, freedom from certain bureaucratic duties, and a certain flexibility of organization—while retaining over-all federal control. While both reports called for a broad investigation of the "institute" idea, no such study has yet been attempted. But several institutes such as those proposed in the studies have come into being in recent years and others are being considered. The Air Force, for instance, is seriously considering an internal, civilian-run think tank at Wright-Patterson Air Force Base in Ohio to help manage its big, expensive aircraft programs like the C-5A and F-111 efforts. The U.S. Army, however, has been the most active in this area, creating a string of institutes, the most interesting of them called the Institute for Land Combat.

3. At Play in the Wars of the Future

In assessing the threat which the U.S. Army may face in the future, we consider not only the current capabilities of potential enemies, but equally if not more important, we must visualize the significant advances they are likely to make. We know the Soviet's keen interest in achieving a world leadership position in technology, and we can expect their technological achievements to be reflected in their future military forces. We know that Communist China is far from idle in regard to its military posture. Whether or not direct ground combat confrontation between the United States and either of these major powers occurs, any other enemy the United States may face will most assuredly be supported by one or both.

> *The U.S. Army must be designed,*
> *equipped and trained with an inherent*
> *flexibility to meet the full spectrum of an*
> *enemy ground threat from an insurgency in*
> *an under-developed country to nuclear-*
> *supported ground assault across Western*
> *Europe.*
>
> —From a speech delivered by Lieu-
> tenant General George I. Forsythe to
> the National Security Industrial As-
> sociation, January 8, 1970

Having long ago fought the war to end all wars, the U.S. Army today maintains within its vast framework a group of 170 civilian analysts and military officers who are creating and "fighting" the wars to end all wars that may be fought in the 1990's. In addition, the staff of this outfit, the Institute for Land Combat, is picking the weapons that will orchestrate those wars. The institute is highly secretive about this pursuit and less than enthusiastic about publicity. Part of the reason for its shyness is no doubt the result of the military security surrounding its unique mission, but reasons other than "national security" may be involved as well. Says one of the many contacts that one must make before a visit to the institute can be arranged, "We're not too excited about certain Senators reading about the institute and misinterpreting what it does."

Getting into the institute, then, is something of a cloak-and-dagger operation. If the author's experience is typical, then the process begins with repeated requests for information that go unanswered. Then, if one is persistent enough, an invitation to be interviewed by the public-relations group at the Army's Combat Development Command at Fort Belvoir, Virginia, is extended. At this meeting the interloper's intentions are probed, and he may get permission to visit the institute—on the clear understanding that the Army does not like publicity for the institute. Notes one civilian PR man working for the Army, who, unlike others of his calling, derives a certain pride in reducing publicity, "*Life* magazine heard about the institute's war-game room and wanted to photograph it, but we had to turn them down."

Finally, when an "interview" is arranged with operating personnel,

163

it is quick, without substance, and canned. The meeting is conducted by several colonels and a civilian analyst working for the institute. Their greeting consists of setting ground rules: They are not to be quoted unless the quotes are cleared in writing. The "interview" is actually a quick series of slides narrated by the assembled panel. It lasts for less than an hour and does little more than serve to display the organization of the institute and state its mission in the most general terms. Such a process serves to create more questions than it answers, and the impulse to get a picture of this covert little corner of government and its activities becomes even more compelling. The picture has to be pieced together from interviews and documents other than those the Army officially volunteers.

The institute is located on the upper floors of the Hoffman Building, a privately owned office building entirely leased by the Pentagon that rises from a nondescript industrial area of Alexandria, Virginia. Like the inside of many other think tanks, inside it houses a drab series of offices but here are no kinky posters or other iconoclastic symbols that one finds in places like RAND and the Hudson Institute. Its spartan furnishings are set off by the conspicuous trappings of security. The rooms used for conferences and briefings look like big vaults, with combination locks on the doors, which are locked from the inside when meetings are in progress. The major color motif in the halls is provided by numerous large signs with red letters asserting that unescorted visitors will be stopped.

The institute is one of the research adjuncts of the Army's Combat Development Command, created in 1962 to cover the whole range of new ideas—whether it be equipment, a new organization, or new military doctrine—from their conception to their integration into Army routine. In all, the command has some thirty separate groups, departments, and institutes devoted to combat development. Of these thirty, seven are its think tanks or institutes. Besides the Institute of Land Combat, there are the Institutes of Advanced Studies, Combined Arms and Support, Special Studies, Nuclear Studies, Strategic and Stability Operations, and Systems Analysis. Unlike the Institute of Land Combat, which is looking at the broadest aspects of the future of combat, the others are future-oriented groups looking at specific aspects of warfare.

The Institute for Land Combat was created in April 1967 to act as a prime forecasting and long-range-planning center for the Army. It is the first group of its kind in that it has been given the job of taking an over-all view of the Army rather than, as had been sanctioned for earlier units, just one element of the service at a time. The idea for the institute emerged in 1966 when the Secretary of the Army was looking for a way to get a more unified approach to the planning of Army R&D. The most practical reason for its creation was to settle some of the chronic squabbles within the Army ranks such as the struggle between those who wanted more helicopters in the future and those with their hearts set on more tanks. The institute was commissioned to come up with an over-all plan for the Army of the future and instructed to use the other branches of the Army to create that plan.

The first edition of this mammoth plan is scheduled to be completed by May 1972. It will be entitled LCS-90, for Land Combat System–1990, and will be delivered to the nation's top military planners. LCS-90 will be produced as a series of individual studies and reviews are completed. These contributions are being made by both the institute and other Army groups. The final work will be an analysis of the alternative future armies possible by 1990 and will cover the period 1990–1995. When this plan is delivered, the institute will go into a second five-year cycle in which work will begin on another such plan that will probably cover the period from 1996 to the year 2000.

Basic to the study are investigations of the wars that may be going on in 1990, the roles the Army will be called on to play in that period, and the weapons and equipment that can be developed by 1990. This information is the raw material of LCS-90 and is contained in two preliminary works drably titled CSAT-90 (for Conflict Situations and Army Tasks–1990) and CPMO-90 (for Compendium of Plausible Materiel Options–1990). The former is primarily the product of Army Intelligence and the latter is mostly generated by a group within the Army Materiel Command. Although these two studies were nearly completed by 1970, they will be continually brought up to date through the later stages of the work. The next step in the process is the creation of Alternative Conceptual Designs, or ACAS, which will result in the creation of three concepts of the Army of the future, designated Armies A, B, and C. These three armies will be subjected to "preferential analysis," which is intended to show which can perform which tasks best and under what conditions. Finally, this analysis will be turned into a draft and subjected to intense review before LCS-90 emerges.

The institute has thus far identified almost 400 possible wars (385 to be more exact) for the year 1990 and about 600 new weapons and other pieces of equipment with which to handle those conflicts should they involve the United States Army. These 385 possible conflicts have been forecast by a twelve-man unit of Army Intelligence experts called the Intelligence Threat Analysis Group (ITAG). Of these future conflicts, ITAG has identified a total of 145 which could plausibly involve the United States. With so many possible conflicts potentially involving the Army, the list was reduced to samples that represent the extremes of climate, tactics, enemies, terrain, and weaponry. Among the possible 1990 wars being contemplated in detail:

A war in Yugoslavia with the U.S., Yugoslavia, and Italy pitted against the Soviet Union, Rumania, Bulgaria, and Hungary.

Conflict in northern Norway: the U.S. allied with Norway, West Germany, and Denmark against the U.S.S.R., East Germany, Poland, and Finland.

All-out war in Europe: NATO nations vs. the Warsaw Pact countries.

A desert war in North Africa between the U.S., Libya, Tunisia, Italy, and West Germany, and the United Arab Republic, the U.S.S.R., and Algeria.

An Asian conflict in Taiwan with the Republic of China, the U.S. the Philippines, and Japan fighting Communist China.

Finally, three internal conflicts involving the U.S. Army in the Congo, Bolivia, and the United States of America.

The Army defines this part of the work as the "range of plausible conditions and probable causes, areas and types of conflict." Also enumerated in this portion of the study are the Army "tasks" for 1990, which are eleven in number, many of them traditional ones, like defending the country and maintaining civil defense, while others are a projection into the 1990's of the role of world policeman that marks U.S. policy of the present and recent past—among them, international peace-keeping, operations to assist friendly nations, and the defending or restoring of the territorial integrity of friendly nations.

A companion study of the possible military hardware available during the period is based on a list of functional objectives for the year 1990. As defined by the institute, a functional objective is "A goal or aim or end result to be achieved by a land combat operation, the attainment of which may contribute to development of a larger whole or may stand on its own as a final accomplishment." In all, there are 165 functional objectives broken down into major areas of concern; for example, there are a dozen dealing with intelligence and nine relating to mobility. A few examples of such stated objectives are the abilities to:

Inflict casualties on enemy personnel and damage to enemy materiel in a ground and water environment by man portable and non-man portable means.

Detect, identify, and locate enemy forces, materiel barrier systems and installations with the capability of focusing on specific areas of interest.

Rapidly construct, maintain, and rehabilitate airfield facilities such as runways, taxi ways, parking aprons, and heliports.

Identify individuals who may develop undesirable behavior traits under stress.

The items of military hardware inspired by these objectives have come out of some forty-seven Army laboratories and research groups. The information was culled and brought together by the Advanced Materiel Concepts Agency, a study group composed of about 100 people primarily responsible for this part of the study. All of the approximately 600 items identified for 1990 are within the ken of present technology but do not yet exist. As one of the institute's colonels puts it, "These are mostly things that have to do with more horse-power, bigger firepower, or greater automation. It goes from some very far-out things that are quite big to things for the soldier to carry on his back." Examples are new tanks, stronger and more versatile helicopters, automated antitank rocket systems, devices to separate friend from foe on the battlefield, new systems to pinpoint the location of enemy troops, and items for military construction and logistics units. A specific example of the kind of item called for in study is a piece of construction equipment called a "High Power Pneumatic Actuated Water Jet," a tanklike affair that fires water to quarry and fragment rock into sizes usable for road bases and aircraft landing strips.

In the next step, now being taken, the three armies of the future will be created by three teams of military officers. The first two studies are used as guidelines along with some virtually sure predictions for the Army of the future—for instance, they are instructed that the manpower force will be either all-volunteer or nearly so and that there will be fewer U.S. military bases in Europe. With this instruction, they assume a smaller, more efficient and better motivated fighting force. Then each team is given a different image in which to create an army. Team A works on an "evolutionary" approach developing today's army into the future with no great increase in annual funding and no great change in direction. B is less conservative and prepares for traditional non-nuclear warfare with fewer constraints on expenditures. And finally C is formed with few financial or strategic arms limitations, such as nuclear arms.

Once these three armies have been created, a variety of techniques will be employed to rate them, including cost analysis, effectiveness studies, outside evaluation by other Army elements, and war-gaming. War-gaming, of primary importance in this effort, is conducted by the institute's War Games Division, which uses a recently completed $50,000 game facility that has been dubbed its "Battlefield Under Glass."

In the war-game room five large opaque projection screens on a monorail track depict battles in progress. The track allows the battles to be photographed for analysis later and also permits the screens to be rolled into a secure vault at night to protect the classified information stored on them. Around the main room are separate rooms for Red Army players, Blue Army players, and controllers (the war-game equivalent of umpires).

The role of games in LCS-90 is to select the strengths and weaknesses of the alternative armies in terms of their organization, weapons, and tactics as tested in the mock conflicts and to measure how Armies A, B, and C fare with different mixes of equipment. Gaming will also be used to test the effectiveness of each conceptual army in civil disturbance and civil disaster situations. One intriguing series of games still to be played will pit future American weapons against those of today, largely to determine if weapons the United States is now distributing to friendly powers can best our future weapons, should any of those friendly recipient nations turn hostile by 1990. As finally presented to the nation's military planners, LCS-90 will cite advantages and disadvantages of the three armies, including the impact of each on the American economy and resources, and propose a "Fourth Army" to be constructed from the best aspects of the other three.

Although the study will not be ready until 1972, there is little question that its major emphasis will be on much greater automation.

More specifically, the U.S. Army of the future will be directed to fit the concept of the automated battlefield—or, as it is sometimes called, "the porous battlefield." This concept has been described by various military leaders, including Army Chief of Staff General William C. Westmoreland, who gave a capsule description of it in a speech in October 1969:

> On the battlefield of the future, enemy forces will be located, tracked and targeted almost instantaneously through the use of data links, computer assisted intelligence evaluation, and automated fire control. With first round kill probabilities approaching certainty, and with surveillance devices that can continually track the enemy, the need for large forces to fix the opposition physically will be less important. . . .
>
> Hundreds of years were required to achieve the mobility of the armored division. A little over two decades later we had the airmobile division. With cooperative effort, no more than 10 years should separate us from the automated battlefield.

The Army has already begun the prodigious task of research for this battlefield. Thus far over $2 billion has been spent. Senator William Proxmire, who brought the matter of the electronic battlefield to the attention of Congress in July 1970, asserted that it could eventually cost $20 billion to develop—or, as he relates it to current fiascos, ". . . almost twice as much as we are spending on the ABM and four times as much as we have spent on the C5A." Proxmire also labeled the program ". . . a classic example of the Pentagon's 'foot-in-the-door' technique. Small sums spent for research and development are escalated into billions for new weapons systems which have never received a detailed and critical review by Congress as a whole." If this extensive package of electronic devices and instruments should be developed, it will become a major component of the Army of the future envisioned by the Institute for Land Combat.

This institute, its sister institutes and other policy research groups operating within the military framework are obviously working with the blessings of the highest echelon of government. Using the Institute for Land Combat as evidence, one concludes that the government has not hesitated to project the same interventionist policies that got the nation into Southeast Asia as the basic assumption in framing military policy for the coming decades. No one is evidently startled that Army Intelligence has been able to locate some 145 possible wars for the United States to become involved in, including both international and civil conflicts. Nor does it appear that Congress (which is supposedly entrusted with giving advice and consent on the future of American domestic and foreign policy) is aware or concerned that it is abdicating its role to the executive branch and, in this case, to entities like the Institute for Land Combat. And when legislators discover ideas, major weapons systems, and impending changes in policy that have been under development for some time they often express shock. Such centers as the Institute for Land Combat can be guaranteed to provide more "surprises."

In creating a systematic approach to the Army of the future, as one can be sure its supporters would argue, the institute is performing the necessary job of creating a more efficient Army. The grave doubts that are to be raised about such enterprising efforts have less to do with the notion of a more efficient Army than with the assumptions that are being projected into the future as the basis for planning that Army. The concentration of such power over shaping future Army policy and the threat that some of these prophesies could be self-fulfilling are scarcely academic considerations.

The institute has been charged with exploring the future of American conflict and has been told to assume that such conflict is the norm rather than something abnormal. It has brought no small degree of imagination to the task of normalizing war, witness the fact that 385 possible wars have been thought up as distinct possibilities. Most important, these men have been told to assume that the United States will have a role to play in many of these wars and must now be thinking how to win them. The danger in this is all too evident as the thin line between attitudes of preparing to defend ourselves and of *looking for conflict to prepare for* has long ago been crossed. It would seem, in short, that the major lesson the thousands of analysts in think tanks have learned from the Vietnam experience is that it has been inefficient rather than inherently wasteful and debilitating to all involved. Vietnam to them has become not a questionable enterprise so much as an imperfect product—one that must be improved on. To be preparing now for a possible war in northern Norway—or, for that matter, on the moon—in 1990 is to take an important step toward conditioning our policy-makers to gear up, literally and psychologically, for that prospect.

170

Perhaps the most indicting aspect of all of this is the fact that so many alert brains are being paid to think about war while so few, if any, are thinking about the normalization of peace or are gaming to avoid conflict in the 1990's or are pushing themselves to pose alternatives to keep the next generation out of war. As for the next generation, there is one crucial factor that did not entirely elude the civilian analysts at the Institute for Land Combat. At the end of the presentation on its operations one of them asked, "Have you heard of anyone doing good behavioral studies on the future of the thinking of American youth? We haven't taken a good look at the feelings of our young people, and we'd like to know if they're willing to fight our wars." Good point.

VIII

THE CEREBRAL SUPERMARKETS

---

1. From Cinnamon-Flavored Tooth Picks to Atomic-Tipped Warheads

Allow us to call your attention to the Chemical Laboratory which we have established at No. 103 Milk Street, Boston. . . . Mr. Griffin and Mr. Little have had several years' experience in the development of new chemical processes on the commercial scale and are prepared to undertake, either in their own laboratory or upon the spot, investigations for the improvement of processes and the perfection of products. Inventors and manufacturers engaged in developing new ideas can obtain from us full information upon any chemical points involved and feel sure that their communications will be considered Strictly Confidential.

—The first announcement, made in 1886, of services offered by a small laboratory later to become Arthur D. Little, Inc.

In 1939 a young inventor named Chester Carlson took an idea to the Battelle Memorial Institute of Columbus, Ohio, a research company. Carlson's invention was electrostatic printing. Battelle developed and refined it and then found a small company, the Haloid Company of Rochester, New York, to manufacture it. Within a few years Haloid had a product on the market, and in deference to the emerging importance of that product changed its name to the Xerox Corporation.

In 1940 another young inventor named Marvin Camras took an idea to another research institute, the Armour Research Foundation in Chicago. In a box he carried with him was the prototype of the modern magnetic tape recorder. Although the principle of magnetic recording was well established, he was the first to lick the problem of sound distortion on wire and tape. Camras joined the Armour Foundation (which later changed its name—infelicitously—to the Illinois Institute of Technology Research Institute) and with it worked on the device. Camras and others there patented over 300 recorder innovations that today serve as the basis for the tape-recorder industry.

Although fairly substantial institutions at the time these inventors knocked at their doors, Battelle and Armour both grew considerably in size and widened the scope of the things they do. In each case the inventions were major factors in their growth not only financially (through millions in fees and royalties) but in terms of letting others see dramatically what capable men in applied research were able to do. Of course, the inventors themselves got most of the credit, but American industry and government also took note of these institutes which had nurtured the inventions to full marketable fruition. After World War II the few existing applied-research groups in America were not only recognized as expeditors of new industrial ideas but as major contributors to wartime innovation. For example, during the same time that Battelle was refining Xerography it was also working on the first atomic bomb. No less than 400 members of its staff had worked on the Manhattan Project. Understandably, in the midst of the postwar boom new groups of applied researchers began forming, and those that were already in business before the war grew rapidly.

Places like Battelle and the Illinois Institute have emerged along with other applied-research institutes and corporations as the "jack-of-all trade" think tanks or, as this particular breed is sometimes

173

called, "brain banks." Unlike think tanks of the RAND variety, they contract for research with hundreds of sponsors and will perform a truly amazing variety of research and advisory tasks. These entities each boast of scores of specialties and count their completed jobs in the thousands. If, for example, you represented a small nation that wanted to hire someone to help it develop tourism, at least a dozen think tanks that could bid on the job and prove, with fancy brochures, that they have had experience in just this kind of work. Similarly, if you had money and announced that you wanted a tooth pick with a cinnamon flavor, an urban-renewal plan to submit for government funds, a computer program that would help discover new hybrid possibilities for corn, an analysis of the most advantageous place to erect a new church, a new industry for your region, electronic equipment to help locate avalanche victims in the snow, an analysis of a new weapon, a new use for an industrial waste, help in selecting a new college president, a report on why your company was not selling in a certain area, tests for a new cancer treatment, an investigation of why a fire broke out, a study of the economic impact of a new highway or the development of a new lubricant for an industrial process, you would probably find half a dozen bidders with some experience in each field.

Think tanks of this type fall into two major categories: profit-making corporations and "not-for-profit" institutes. Those in the first group are organized like normal American corporations and are responsible to their shareholders for making a profit, while those in the second group are allowed to, but not necessarily geared to, make a profit. Whatever profits accrue to the latter group must be plowed back into the institute for research and capital improvements. (A "not for profit" differs from a "nonprofit" in that it can routinely make profits to expand which nonprofits are not supposed to but oftimes do.) The not-for-profit institutes normally pay taxes on the fees they get from private sponsors but not on the work that the Internal Revenue Service defines as in the public interest (such as work for federal, state, and local governments and foundations). On either side of the profit motive there are about a score of major think tanks.

The three oldest not-for-profit groups were organized before World War II. They are the Mellon Institute (now part of the Carnegie Mellon University), formed in 1913; Battelle, formed in 1929; and

174

the Illinois Institute of Technology Research Institute (neé Armour), which started up in 1936. Riding the postwar industrial research boom and capitalizing on the government's new interest in such things as operations research and nuclear weapons development, new institutes started popping up all over the country. During the late 1940's the Stanford Research Institute (Menlo Park, California), the Midwest Research Institute (Kansas City, Missouri), the Southwest Research Institute (San Antonio, Texas), the Southern Institute (Birmingham, Alabama), the Cornell Aeronautical Laboratories (Buffalo, New York), and the Denver Research Institute were founded. Since then still others, such as the Research Triangle Institute (Research Triangle, North Carolina), the Gulf South Research Institute (Baton Rouge, Louisiana), the North Star Research Institute (Minneapolis), and the Syracuse University Research Corporation, have been created.

Each has its own strengths, weaknesses, and character. Spindletop Research, for example, is a small not-for-profit founded in 1961 and located in Lexington, Kentucky, which has done a large share of its work in its own backyard. Typical local projects have included conducting economic development surveys for the Appalachian region, helping the Commonwealth of Kentucky set up a state planning agency, studying and selecting the best location for a new junior college in Ashland, Kentucky, creating a computerized water information system for the state, preparing a feasibility study for a "new town" of Midland, Kentucky, and establishing a computer data center for keeping track of genetic information on the area's thoroughbred horses. Battelle, on the other hand, has emerged as a major international force in applied technology, with over 7,000 employees spread through six major installations in various parts of the U.K. Switzerland, and Germany. It has worked for clients in more than ninety countries.

Taken as a group, the not-for-profits bring in about $300 million a year, employ something like 15,000 people, and will research virtually anything researchable. They work for the federal government, foreign nations, corporations of every size, states, cities, individuals, and educational institutions. Their for-profit counterparts present much the same collective picture.

Among the leading for-profit research and consulting firms are Booze, Allen and Hamilton Inc., Arthur D. Little Inc., General

Electric's TEMPO group, the Planning Research Corporation, the Research Management Corporation, McKinsey and Co. Inc., Operations Research Inc., the Diebold Group, and the Auerbach Corporation. There is, as is true of the not-for-profit institutes, diversity within the group. TEMPO, for example, which was set up in 1956 in Santa Barbara, California, as part of the General Electric Corporation, started out doing primarily military analysis. Today it works for a variety of public clients—ranging from the government of Ireland to the governor of Maine—on a variety of policy problems. Among its major roles have been those of designer of military computer systems, long-range forecaster for the General Electric organization, aide-for-hire to a variety of city and state governments, and China-watcher for the federal government (it predicted in 1960 that the first Chinese nuclear explosion would occur between 1963 and 1965, probably in 1964; the explosion occurred in November 1964). TEMPO is small (about 300 employees) and serves mostly governments. Other for-profit outlets are much larger and do a much larger percentage of their work for industrial clients. Booze, Allen and Hamilton Inc., for example, annually takes on about 1,300 assignments for about 900 clients, the great majority of which are corporations. It typically addresses itself to relatively short studies of corporate problems—should a company merge, or how should a company diversify in the future—and has a reputation as a "business healer."

Two jack-of-all-trade think tanks that are big and represent the breed at its most diverse are the for-profit Arthur D. Little Inc. of Cambridge, Massachusetts, and the not-for-profit Stanford Research Institute of Menlo Park, California. Arthur D. Little is the older of the two and got its start in the last century when an MIT dropout determined that the Yankee merchants in Boston's harbor district were willing to pay to have molasses and other products analyzed by experts to see how good they were before they bought them.

176

2. 75,000 Little Problems

Q: What don't you do here?
A: Nothing that I can think of.

—From an interview with Dr. Howard
O. McMahon, president of Arthur D.
Little, Inc.

In 1921 Arthur Dehon Little, co-founder and head of Arthur D. Little Inc., decided to make a personal contribution to American philosophy by debunking one tenet of conventional wisdom that he felt condoned lack of imagination. The tenet: "You can't make a silk purse out of a sow's ear."

First, 100 pounds of sow's ears were purchased from a Chicago packing company. The ears were then reduced to a glue something like the viscous liquid that comes from the silkworm. Then Little's scientists dispersed it in water, forcing it to jell with small amounts of acetone. Chrome alum was added to speed the setting process. This mixture was then filtered under pressure through an apparatus with sixteen small holes about $\frac{1}{1000}$ of an inch in diameter. The threads which emerged were then plunged into a hardening solution of acetone and formaldehyde. After the fibers dried they became brittle and dull, but when they were subsequently bathed in a solution of glycerine and dyed they became soft and smooth to the touch. A hand loom was used to weave the threads into a silky fabric, which was then sewn into a purse. Today the purse is on display in the Smithsonian Institution in Washington, and the firm that Little founded is, as it was in his day, a vital force in research and problem-solving.

Little himself, considered by many to be the father of American industrial research, left the Massachusetts Institute of Technology in 1886 at the age of twenty-two to work for a paper company in Rhode Island as a chemist. A year later he and another young chemist named Roger B. Griffin decided to go into business for themselves. They opened a laboratory on Milk Street in Boston and announced that they would undertake chemical analyses and conduct investigations for the improvement of processes and the perfection of products. Most of their early business was chemical analysis of products like molasses, sugar and nitrate which came into Boston harbor. In 1893 Little's friend and partner Griffin was killed in a laboratory accident. In the course of a fat-extraction operation a flask of volatile solvent broke and sprayed him with flaming vapor. After nearly deciding to close down the laboratory, Little chose to carry on alone.

The 1890's saw a boom in new industrial processes and innovations which insured that the small laboratory would have a role to play in serving American industry. Little himself went to Europe and returned with information on artificial silks (later to be called acetates and rayons) and nitrocellulose which he introduced to America. Before his death in 1935 he had built his laboratory into a multifaceted industrial research firm of over eighty employees. In his lifetime he and his growing staff had, among other achievements, helped General Motors create a research department, steered the chemical industry from coal to petrochemicals as a source of organic chemicals, discovered the process of making alcohol from wood waste, aided modernization of the engineering departments of MIT, and introduced dozens of innovations in the paper industry.

ADL has continued to grow as a leading industrial research firm, but it carries on many functions outside this basic area now, including consulting, medical research, national economic development planning, and policy research. A profit-making corporation, it has never allowed itself to be dominated by one client in peacetime. Approximately a quarter of its work is done for the federal government, the other three-quarters divided more or less evenly in three broad categories: businesses and other private institutions, including colleges and trade associations; domestic American governments smaller than the federal government; and foreign governments and industries. Its work is almost equally divided between technical work and what its officers term "soft" work, which includes management studies, economic development work, and educational projects.

Although there are notable exceptions from time to time, it specializes in projects that are modest in size and take less than a year to complete. According to one executive, the average bill for a non-federal job is about $25,000, while federal projects on the average run longer and cost more. Its annual revenue in recent years has averaged about $40 million. It has a dozen branch offices located throughout the U. S. and overseas, but most of its work is conducted at its Cambridge headquarters, located on what it calls Acorn Park (in honor of the unofficial company motto, "Scatter acorns that oaks may grow"). The buildings are austere but pleasant monuments to glass and cinder block (even the walls of the offices of its top executives are painted cinder block). Bright colors predominate inside, and the complex has something of the aura of a Hollywood back lot, replete with props and constant activity. Its front lobby is neatly strewn with samples of tangible end products of ADL research—things like a Chiffon margarine tub, welding equipment, a pack of Lark cigarettes (for which ADL developed the filter), and a replica of a small sensing device which ADL built for NASA to leave on the moon. At any moment, one is likely to see two sheep being herded into a laboratory for wool experiments, men walking between buildings carrying hugh sheets of colorful plastic, or a group of young Africans moving through the halls in traditional garb. There are tanks for testing life jackets, machines spinning fabrics, experimental kitchens, and one of the world's largest collections of bottled aromas (known as ADL's "odor library"). As if there was not already enough exotica around, two-story-high tropical plants fill open stairwells in various wings of the buildings. Some of the sights are more subtle and have to be pointed out. An innocuous-looking tube running out of the window on one floor into a window on the floor below is part of an apparatus that regularly produces kilo batches of tetrohydrocannibonal, or THC, the active ingredient in marijuana. The synthesizers of the laboratory "pot" found that they needed a downward force for good production, and rather than drill a hole in the floor they opted to pump it out through the window.

During the course of an average year ADL gets about 30,000 inquiries, from which many of its jobs come. Since its founding it has worked on more than 75,000 problems for clients and in recent years can boast that among its corporate clients have been more than 400 of the firms listed in the annual *Fortune* magazine list of the 500 largest corporations in America.

A project at ADL is called a "case," and for each case a leader is appointed who becomes fully responsible for its completion. The case system is unique in that a relatively junior man who is given a case to lead is free to move through the staff of any department to line up the team that he needs to get his work done. The team may be composed of his seniors up to and including the president or chairman of the board. Normally a man is working on more than one case at a time, so it is not uncommon for the Case A team to include the leader of the Case B team, on which the Case A leader is also working.

There is no prevalent methodology to ADL's work other than its system of cases, usually tackled by interdisciplinary teams. Computers play important roles in certain jobs, but generally terms and concepts like systems analysis and program budgeting are used sparingly. Unlike at many think tanks, there is a distinct bias against jargon and "think-tankese," and its reports tend to be clearly written and detailed.

Its structure is remarkably flexible. The managing partner of ADL's New York office, Robert Graff, points out that he was recently elected to that post by his co-workers. Although the major officers of the corporation function as such, they are the first to point out that ADL's structure is "organic"—that is, one which resists permanent operating structure and possesses a minimum of hierarchical authority. It has only nineteen vice-presidents, which sounds like a lot until one realizes that its closest competitor in the problem-solving field, Booze, Allen and Hamilton, Inc., has about 180. Communications between individuals is direct, and there is no need to see somebody else's boss before involving him in a case. Nobody is *assigned* to do anything; rather, people are asked if they want to lead a case or if they will participate in one. Obviously, one does not say no very often. Paradoxically, this rejection of bureaucratic pattern is one characteristic of a company that numbers among its specialties helping others with their bureaucratic tangles.

This brings up the question of what functions are left to its executives. Its president, Howard McMahon, a Canadian scientist who was a member of the MIT faculty before coming to ADL, says, "The job of the people running this place is to foster an environment in which teams can be formed and in which meaningful and creative tasks can be performed." McMahon points out that managing such an environment often means not making up a lot of rules and policies. In reality, McMahon and others who run the firm do have functions. They make the final decisions on which cases will be taken, generally watch over the quality of work being done, help drum up desired clients, work on cases, and set the future direction of the company.

McMahon believes that part of the key to the firm's ability to get things done is its flexibility and its lack of a predisposed approach to problem-solving. McMahon is a specialist himself, having spent most of his professional career working in cryogenics, the physics of extremely low temperatures, but is skeptical of specialists as problem-solvers. He believes that too often research firms rush in specialists where generalists are called for. He says, "We've handled cases in medical administration where we don't have a doctor on the team because it was apparent to us that the people called for were those with behavioral and managerial and not medical backgrounds. On the other hand, we wouldn't consider taking on a case in advanced electronics technology without men who are experts in solid-state electronics. In many research institutions there is a skepticism about generalists. The difference here is that we're skeptical of specialists because they're the ones who probably got whatever it is that we're trying to unscramble all loused up in the first place. Urban transportation, for example, has been in the hands of experts for years and look where it's gotten us." He adds somewhat gleefully that one of the functions of management at ADL is to keep things out of "the paralyzing grip of experts."

The company's chief generalist is General James M. Gavin (U.S. Army, retired), who serves as its board chairman and chief executive officer. He is very prominent in ADL's activities and one of its most active researchers. Like Arthur D. Little before him, he is very much the guiding spirit of the company today.

Gavin, who was orphaned before the age of two, enlisted in the Army when he turned seventeen. After scoring high on a competitive examination, he was admitted to West Point and received his commission. During World War II he was an early advocate of a large paratroop force and before the war was over led four major parachute assaults into Europe and planned the airborne invasion for D-Day. As the wartime commander of the 82nd Airborne he became the youngest division commander in the Army since the Civil War. In 1954 he was elevated to the job of Army Chief of Plans and Research and Development; however, he retired from that job and the Army in 1958 in protest over the military's inflexible devotion to the policy of massive nuclear retaliation. On retirement he joined Arthur D. Little and became its president two years later. Save for

181

two years during which he served as President Kennedy's Ambassador to France, he has been there ever since. In 1968 there was a flurry of interest in him as a possible antiwar candidate for the Presidency.

Gavin's professional career has been characterized by innovation and outspokenness. Paradoxically, while he is generally credited with the "air cavalry" concept of an Army-in-helicopters that has been applied so broadly in Vietnam, he is also credited with being one of the earliest critics of U.S. involvement in Southeast Asia. He counseled President Kennedy against intervention in Laos, and in 1965, when the escalation of the war in Vietnam was getting into full swing, he publicly opposed broadening the war. It was Gavin who first called for "enclaves" or protected defensive areas that could be maintained with few U.S. troops while a negotiated settlement was being sought.

As chairman of the board of the company Gavin exerts considerable influence over his domain, and as many in it point out, ADL has very much become an extension of Gavin's thoughts and principles. His name evokes ready testimonials from his employees—not unlike the esteem with which his paratroopers held him during the war (it has been said that his troops would have jumped with him anywhere).

During Gavin's reign the company has grown considerably, moved from its old "Research Palace," a large building on the banks of the Charles River, into its sprawling complex on the other side of Cambridge and become a public corporation with public stockholders. It has de-emphasized military work and consciously plotted a course to become less dependent on the federal government for research support. Federal work accounts for a stable quarter of its work, and the staff is quick to point out with pride that its largest 1970 military contract is not a weapons project but a study of the future of military hospitals. Gavin's touch is also seen in other ways. In the early 1960's, before it was fashionable, he ordered his people to start finding black analysts to fill key slots, and he has made ADL one of the few think tanks where it is not a rarity to find women by-lining research reports or filling nonsecretarial staff jobs.

Gavin is a trim, balding man who dresses in a manner that evokes the word "natty." He is notably soft-spoken and not at all the stereotyped retired general who has become the captain of industry. "One of the things we are striving for here," he says, "is the ability to set our own priorities. One of the ways we address this task is searching for problems before they become obvious." He says that ADL never knows if it is right when it makes its picks, but some of them work out. One that did was ADL's decision in the early 1960's to get involved in the area of health-care management, which it felt would become a greater problem as the decade wore on.

The ADL philosophy as elaborated by Gavin is one in which the individual is "terribly important." He notes with satisfaction that there are no organization charts, no staff limousines, and no demand that a man be oozing with corporate loyalty. "Our style is to offer people this big place and then tell them to get involved—if they do they stay on. This calls for looking for a certain type of person who is innovative, has integrity and is genuinely curious. In general, we're interested in the kind of person who identifies more with himself than the type who needs a corporation to identify with."

Gavin outlines his job as that of keeping tabs on ADL's finances, hiring new people, expanding the company into new realms, and making its major decisions. He also functions as its chief trouble-shooter. "Many times we have to give our clients bad news by telling them what they don't want to hear, and often they find it difficult to accept this. Sometimes I have to step in and help them understand. Not too long ago a major West Coast aerospace firm bought out a small company with a new industrial process. We were brought in to help them evaluate the move. Our team determined that they had made a mistake and told them so. The company was mad at the report we gave them and I had to go out and convince them that they had indeed made a major mistake."

Gavin is also one of his company's chief idea men. It is an open secret that on a recent trip to Moscow he made overtures to the Soviet government offering to work for them in a research or consulting capacity. If such an arrangement were to emerge it would, of course, swell ADL's coffers, but it would also function to test Gavin's stated belief that American business can be a major factor in warming relations between the two nations. The move might also serve to strain the company's relations with the U.S. government. Even during a relatively short interview his penchant for expressing and testing new ideas is apparent. At one point in a conversation he started talking seemingly spontaneously about the problems of the United Nations and its future as a peacemaker and noted that one flaw inhibiting its effectiveness is that it possesses no modern means of

183

rapid communications, while the military and national communications systems of member states are excellent. "It's as if the police aren't allowed to have radios and only the criminals are," he says. Gavin's conviction that the UN is stacking the deck against itself in this vital area has led to involvement as personal adviser to the organization on communications.

Gavin's aides point out that he does more than just come up with ideas; he follows them through as well. For example, thinking about the problems of the hot urban summers of the mid-1960's, he decided that sports might produce a minor but helpful pressure valve, and for openers he urged all of the Ivy League colleges to open their athletic facilities for the summer. The colleges put one condition on cooperating with the suggestion that they be given a federal grant for the insurance they would have to buy to cover major lawsuits that might result from athletic injuries. Gavin fought for the grant and even took the request personally to President Johnson, who turned it down.

ADL's bread and butter is its traditional work for industry—generally an extension of the functions established under Little himself. Most of ADL's work for industry is technical and concerned with processes, engineering, services, and new products. Its specialties include analytical chemistry, plastics, textiles, electronics, and applied optics.

One of its specialties in the technical realm is that of "food and flavor." This interest can be traced back to a day in 1926 when Arthur Little read an article about the manufacture of monosodium glutamate in Japan and how it was being applied to food. His fascination prompted him to add a kitchen to his laboratories. Today ADL approaches food-and-flavor cases with a broad collection of tools and techniques, many of which are of its own innovation. It brags of one of the world's largest odor reference libraries, a collection of thousands of scents which is consulted when aromas are being created or modified in food work. An ADL technique developed in the 1940's is the "Flavor Profile Method," a quantitative approach to characterizing and duplicating flavors. It details the order and intensity of each element of a flavor so exactly that the flavor can be duplicated. This method is not only used by ADL in food development but is also taught, for a fee, to its clients so that they can improve their own flavor research. There are tasters to complement technical analysis. One staff member points out that ADL tasters are "swallowers, not spitters." He explains that in the world of flavor there is a deep division of opinion on how best to taste a product. ADL has opted for swallowing, instead of tasting and then spitting, because it contends that part of the test of anything is associated with how it feels going down.

Strangely, there is probably no area in which clients are less likely to let others know about the work that ADL has done for them than in this one; thus, most of its work in this area cannot be named. Among the products that can be identified as having been developed by ADL are Howard Johnson's Ho Jo Cola, Ocean Spray cranberry sauce, Quaker Oats' Cap'n Crunch breakfast cereal, and Chiffon margarine. Another large job was developing the flavors, processing techniques, and prototype equipment for Dunkin' Donuts. Recently it has been working with the United Distillers of Ireland to open new markets for their products and as part of this work has developed a line of "softer" Irish whiskies. It also serves as a consultant to Anheuser-Busch, working to double-check the quality of Budweiser beer. Among its major anonymous tasks it has developed new "soft" whiskies for several major U.S. liquor companies, worked with a number of major California vineyards to improve existing wines and develop new ones, and invented new soft drinks. During the flap over cyclamates, it worked for several major soft-drink bottlers to find sweeteners that could be substituted for the banned substance.

In other areas as well, ADL's end product is often a new product or process. For example, under contract from the Owens-Illinois Glass Company it developed the first successful process to manufacture fiberglass, and for American Airlines it developed the first computer reservation system for air passengers. A recent example of a product development job is the work ADL has been doing for the Riegel Textile Company, the largest supplier of cloth diapers in America. The company came to ADL to see if it could develop a material that would have wet strength but dissolve when flushed down a toilet. After considering a host of possible formulas for such a material, ADL came up with paperlike sheets made from microscopic, ribbonlike rayon filaments that held together when 80 percent wet but fell apart when soaked in water. The fabric was developed and its production started in Sweden. With the diaper development nearly completed, Riegel and ADL began working to apply the same fabric to the development of a flushable sanitary napkin. Under the brand name Flite, the napkin was test-marketed in two states in 1970, and the diaper was scheduled for release in late 1971.

Still another fairly recent example of an ADL development started when Liggett and Myers came to them for basic research on the effects of cigarettes on human beings with the intent of finding some innovation that would cut down on the harmful effects of smoking. It was discovered that a filter composed of certain inhibiting agents (such as acrolean and hydrogen cyanide) makes smoke less irritating, so these agents were incorporated in a new filter marketed as the Lark "activated charcoal filter."

Some of ADL's most interesting industrial work involves not new products and processes but investigations. One area of expertise that ADL has established is that of checking out innovations to see if they are, indeed, innovations. Arthur Little himself ran several spectacular hoaxes to the ground for clients. One that had already attracted $500,000 in backing was billed as a spectacular new source of electricity produced by the oxidation of carbon electrodes. The inventor of the scheme had ingeniously connected his apparatus to regular power lines—a fact that Little's investigators discovered before most of the $500,000 had been spent. More recently it has debunked, among others, a scheme for extracting gold from low-grade ore by radiation and a process for producing antifreeze at unheard-of low production costs. The antifreeze hoax was unmasked even as plans to build a multimillion-dollar production plant were being firmed up. As in the electricity hoax, the antifreeze inventor's pilot operation was being supplied with already manufactured antifreeze from hidden drums.

ADL also commonly collects fees for performing what amounts to industrial detective work for clients. Typical detective jobs have included work for a photo lab to find out why it was having small explosions (an explosive compound was being formed as silver compounds and ammonia mixed) and for a chemical plant to determine why workers were being overcome by a strange unidentifiable odor (a lacquer from the plant was draining into a culvert under the building and, when mixed with organic wastes in the culvert, produced a substance called isovaleraderhyde, which has hypnotic, sleep-producing effects on human beings). In the same vein, ADL sells the service of checking for hazards that may produce accidents in the future, such as testing out a new laboratory or examining factory equipment.

It has also played the role of detective for the government from time to time. It worked with NASA to help determine the causes of malfunction on Apollo 13 and has worked for the Coast Guard to determine why fires have broken out aboard merchant ships. Recently, the Post Office found that its Mailsters, those strongly touted three-wheeled, gas-powered vehicles used on urban and suburban mail routes, were producing a number of accidents and fatalities. Before it went ahead with its plan to buy 25,000 more of the vehicles the Post Office wanted to know why they were so accident-prone. ADL's report on the subject not only showed that the three-wheelers were inherently more dangerous than their four-wheeled counterparts but actually cost more to operate. The Post Office quietly canceled the whole program.

Only a very small percentage of ADL's $10 million a year in fees from the federal government is for such detective work. Its work for Uncle Sam is as diverse as its work for other client groups. In 1970, for example, it was helping the Department of Transportation plan the future of mass intercity transportation, working with the Department of Housing and Urban Development on low-cost housing technology, and working for the Army to develop more effective antimalarial drugs.

Its military work in the last few years has amounted to about 10 percent of its total effort, with only a small percent of that work being classified. One major classified project that it accepted was a million-dollar research effort for the Army that ran from 1965 to 1969 to develop incapacitating chemical-warfare agents. Internally, this contract was quite controversial, although there were those who defended it, reasoning that incapacitating agents do not kill and are therefore preferable as subjects for investigating to lethal gases or those that render permanent damage. Other military projects it has worked on in recent years include antisubmarine-warfare technology for the Army and designing military transport systems for the Air Force.

During both world wars the company found itself virtually conscripted for military research. But by far its most important military contribution came in the mid-1930's when the Navy contracted with it to review a number of technical problems it was having. One of them, the inability to provide fresh water in submarines, was one that ADL felt it could solve. As incredible as it seems today, in that era the Navy did not have any money for the development of new equipment, so ADL proceeded with the development of the compression still, a device for economically extracting fresh water from salt water. The company financed the project itself in the hope that it could recoup its investment later by selling production licenses for it. The development was successful, and the stills were being installed in submarines at the time Pearl Harbor was attacked. The still has been credited with enabling submarine forces to conduct long patrols and operate in hostile areas, a capability previously lacking.

One of the potentially significant jobs it is doing for the government today is as a prime researcher in a program aimed at the treatment of cancer through drugs. As part of what is called the cancer chemotherapy program, ADL is one of several contractors who as a group are attempting to unlock the secrets of cancer by exploring virtually any substance or methodology which might have an effect on the disease. ADL maintains a large laboratory for experimentation with various cancer treatments on animals. The process involves a great deal of trial and error, so that it has thus far worked with hundreds of chemicals and techniques for administering them. One of their current efforts in this program involves bathing the brain in anticancer drugs as a possible treatment. Work in this area has included the design of an apparatus to pump the drugs into a monkey's brain and recording the effects of the drugs on its behavior.

Another important drug research program under way at ADL, this one for the National Institute for Mental Health, finds the company researching marijuana. Much of the work thus far has been to synthesize the active ingredients in major quantities before moving on to an examination of the chemical structure of the drug in an attempt to determine what organs it affects and how. John Crider, who is in charge of public relations for the technical divisions of ADL, says that in the future the company wants to start looking into the possible therapeutic uses of the drug. He says, "Our research has begun to suggest to our people that marijuana may have medicinal uses one of which may be that of an effective analgesic for the suppression of pain."

One of the areas in which ADL has had its greatest impact is in helping other nations develop economically. The company's first study of a geographic area outside the United States started in 1916 when the Canadian Pacific Railroad asked it to survey the natural resources of Canada with an eye to developing new industry. The job led to the creation of Arthur D. Little Ltd. of Canada and in time 165 separate studies of Canadian resources used in the industrial development of Canada during the earlier part of this century. This first job made ADL an international operation; since then it has worked in more than eighty-five nations, from Argentina to Zambia, and it has completed hundreds of jobs to become an international force in its own right.

ADL has helped India develop its defense industry, Iran its port operations, Chile its chemical industry, Mexico its small industries, Colombia its export industries, Greece its food-processing industry, New Zealand its paper and lumber industry, Surinam its police forces, Ireland its national airline, Zambia its transportation system, and Holland its long-range plan for the decentralization of population and industry. It has also worked with a dozen nations to make tourism more profitable. Clients in this area have ranged from the Galapagos Islands to the Commerce Department's United States Travel Service, for which it helped work up a program to attract foreign visitors to the U.S.

Two of the largest international development projects on the ADL drawing boards in 1970 were a major study of the transportation and economic development potentials of seven Southeast Asian nations and a project to help the Brazilian state of Minas Gerais develop industrially. In the former case, the Asian Development Bank has put ADL in charge of framing the alternatives for developing the area in coming decades. The end product of the study will be a report on the transportation possibilities of the area and their impact on its economics. It will also deliver a computer model that the bank will use to see how more than 100 possible transportation developments —some as visionary as building a canal across Thailand—will influence the economies of the nations involved. The study, to cost about $2.5 million, has involved over 100 ADL analysts; ADL, in turn, has hired consulting groups from Denmark, the Philippines, Australia, Japan, and elsewhere in the U.S. to help with the work. The Brazilian case in Minas Gerais is described as an "action program." About twenty-five ADL staff members have taken on the job of, as one of them puts it, ". . . helping Brazil's fifth largest state jump into the twentieth century." Among the functions it is performing are identifying the most promising industries for development, finding and involving outside investors, and planning the state's future role in research and training. ADL's partner in advising the state is a consulting and engineering firm from Rio de Janeiro.

One of the longest and most influential roles ADL has played in a geographic area outside the continental United States was as chief consultant to Puerto Rico, a relationship that lasted almost twenty years, after which the island's government felt the process of industrialization had moved to the point where it no longer needed outside help. The island's governor first asked ADL to size up the industrial possibilities of Puerto Rico in 1942. Its first bit of advice, rendered that same year, was to build a bottle factory so that it could take advantage of wartime whiskey shortages and get its rum to market. The company helped get the plant into operation, and it proved extremely successful. Thereafter, ADL was Puerto Rico's adviser. It helped the island launch many other industries, lobbied in Congress to get tax incentives for mainland U.S. companies moving to the island, promoted Puerto Rico among investors in the U.S., started a major campaign to popularize its rum (after working on its flavor), and wrote the island's ten-year industrial development plan that was in force during the 1950's. It undertook technical research on such projects as making frozen pineapple concentrate and extracting cloth from pineapple fiber and turned its findings over to the island government. It also performed many minor but important tasks, such as tracking down new industrial processes and helping Puerto Rican students get into American technical schools. Within the first ten years of the relationship between Puerto Rico and ADL some 320 new industrial plants were established on the island. The company played a crucial role in changing Puerto Rico from a predominantly agricultural to a predominantly industrial area.

The final quarter of ADL's work is for localities on the American mainland. To cite just a few of the typical jobs it tackles for state and local governments, it has helped the state of Montana establish its priorities for the future of public education, is helping the state of North Carolina frame a new training program for police, is currently working for the city of Cambridge, Massachusetts, training its police in community-relations work, helped New Hampshire set up a new tobacco taxation program, worked with the city of Portland, Maine, to set up a vocational high school, and, for the state of Washington, set up a plan for the development of community colleges that was later adopted by the legislature.

One of the larger and more interesting jobs it has accepted in recent years ran from 1967 to 1969 when the city of East Cleveland, Ohio, hired ADL to help it develop a truly racially integrated community, to preserve its environment and standards of service, and build the community leadership necessary to support the first two objectives, regardless of the city's racial composition. A twenty-four-member ADL team was assembled to draw up a long-range set of suggestions for the community as well as to present immediate ideas for action.

East Cleveland, a city of 40,000 people, lies on the outskirts of Cleveland, and in 1967, when it came to ADL, its population, once almost all white, was fast approaching the point of becoming half white and half black. An enlightened city government knew that the community was undergoing profound change and felt that it needed help in unifying and maintaining itself as a quality community no matter what its racial composition. ADL's "action" proposals came fast and ranged from organizing an Easter-egg roll to protesting against a freeway project that threatened to cut off an area of the city. It helped the city tighten its housing-code enforcement process, got park concerts started, initiated a summer day camp, worked with the town's leaders on a fair housing law, helped start an employment office in City Hall, designed a logotype for the city to help give positive community identity (the emblem, a stylized rendering of the letters E.C., with an arrow running through them, now appears on everything from street signs to checkbooks), and aided East Cleveland in getting community-renewal funds from Washington. Some of its "action" was an admitted flop. People never did get interested in having a town meeting, as ADL had suggested, and its plan to achieve community identity by painting all utility poles orange was met with integrated outrage from the community.

ADL's long-term suggestions were contained in a 1,500-page report developed with the city. The report called for government reorganization, a revitalized city recreation program, a new plan for public financing, an urban design plan, and the creation of the East Cleveland Development Corporation, which would serve to develop housing and businesses in the city. The East Cleveland "case" was closed with the delivery of the report, and nobody has yet made any claim about the ultimate success or failure of ADL's work. As William Claggett, who heads the company's Urban Affairs Group, puts it, "We'll probably never know how successful we were because there are so many other factors to consider, like the general tone of race relations in America in the next few years. But the city was pleased and we worked to do the best we could." Although it is far too early to evaluate, it would appear that ADL's impact will prove to be positive in that it acted as a catalyst in bringing new ideas to the thinking of a city. An indication that the city has responded to ADL's intervention is that the final 1,500-page report listing recommendations for the city was co-authored by ADL and the city government. In short, some of the thoughts of ADL have become those of the city, and there is little chance that the master plan will gather dust on the shelf.

Although Claggett did not work on the East Cleveland team, he has handled many urban cases himself since coming to ADL in 1962 as a young Harvard-educated urban planner with experience working on community renewal programs in the Midwest. A case typical of those he has worked on was one in Kansas City, which in the late 1960's brought in ADL to help it find a location for and develop a new community junior college. Claggett says that the atmosphere created by those interested in the school was "highly charged" when ADL entered and got more so before it was over. "The location of the campus had become a very significant and divisive community issue," he says. "The blacks and Puerto Ricans felt that it should be downtown, and they were opposed by a large group in the community, predominantly white, which felt it had to be located in the suburbs."

The case involved much more than merely finding a location for the college, but that became the most challenging aspect of it. The results of Claggett's study in Kansas City led him to the conclusion that the best location would be downtown. His determination was predictably controversial. At one point he was confronted by 200 angry white students who told him pointedly that the location of the school was none of his business. As he explains it, his job was to get a site selected without tearing the community apart. To compromise factions in the community, he helped establish a twenty-eight-member committee representing every community opinion group from the suburban PTA's to CORE. Finally, this group was able to agree on a location directly identified with neither the suburban whites nor the inner-city ghetto blacks: downtown, adjacent to a cluster of insurance-company buildings on a bluff overlooking the river. Says Claggett, "In a sense both sides won. The whites did not have to enter the ghetto, and the blacks did not have to leave downtown for the suburbs."

A final example of an ADL case involving a domestic problem was a job performed for two hospitals in Burlington, Vermont. The city's two hospitals were faced with problems that could be solved only by a merger, but each felt it had a lot to lose by such a step. According to Homer Hogedorn, who specializes in health-care cases at ADL, "The hospitals contacted us by writing us a letter that began, 'Dear Dr. Little.' They told us they were interested in merging and, basically, they needed help but didn't know what kind of help."

The team assembled to investigate found a considerable number of problems. Says Hogedorn, "One hospital was Catholic and generally reputed to be a comfortable, homey place to go and get well, while the other was Protestant, had some of the most up-to-date equipment and prided itself on its ability to treat the very sick. The hospitals were very different in people's minds, and each was afraid of the other. On the other hand, they both realized that neither was big enough or strong enough to do the things it wanted to do. Neither could really afford nor justify the purchase of new $100,000 pieces of equipment but both needed the use of them."

Hogedorn says the techniques the team used in serving as a catalyst for the merger were straightforward. For one, the team acted as what he calls a "water carrier"—that is, taking the gripes, rumors, and concerns of one element of the community and bringing it to the other. "The doctors were very worried about certain aspects of the merger and were becoming more and more alarmed. We interviewed them and recorded these concerns, then took them to the board that was trying to accomplish the merger so that it could address itself to the doctors' concerns. Similarly, some rumors broke out, such as the one held by some Protestants in the community that the nursing nuns at the Catholic hospital were going to leave with the merger and leave everybody in the lurch," says Hogedorn, "and we ran them to the ground." Another element was a public-relations program in which the community was kept informed by rumor-free dispatches on what was happening. The most important element, though, was the preparation of a financial analysis by ADL which

Hogedorn claims was instrumental in proving that each side had so much to gain that it would be a mistake not to merge. Backing up this financial analysis was the ADL contention that the resulting combined medical center could better serve the community and, if handled properly, could emphasize the most positive attributes of each hospital. The upshot was that forces in the community began to jell in support of the merger and, in time, the combined medical center was approved. Hogedorn says that the team never told the two institutions that they had to merge but, rather, consistently attempted to clarify the issues surrounding the merger so that an informed decision could be made.

Tucked into ADL's work for its four more or less equal client groups are dozens of small cases that display one of the most fascinating aspects of the firm—that is the unpredictable places where one can find its people at work. The American Baseball League, for example, has used ADL for the last fifteen years to conduct periodic studies of the economic picture in professional baseball. ADL has worked, too, for the U.S. Olympic Committee to determine new ways of insuring future American Olympic strength. Eight theological seminaries—both Protestant and Catholic—in the San Francisco Bay area felt that they were running up unnecessary operating and capital expenditures and came to ADL for help. A research effort was mounted to figure out which courses could be made ecumenical to eliminate duplication. To solve the problem, a computer program was put together to coordinate the course offerings of all eight institutions. When the Swiss-based Organization of Petroleum Exporting Countries, an association of oil-rich but less developed nations such as Algeria and Venezuela, decided that its members needed help in negotiating leases with giant international companies, it came to ADL. (Satisfied with ADL's work in its behalf, the government of Algeria has since been using it for a variety of jobs, including the complete reorganization of the nation's telephone system.) Recent examples of people coming to ADL for out-of-the-ordinary help include the artichoke growers of Brittany, who wanted overseas markets for their product explored; the government of Bolivia, which needed help in preparing for negotiations for joining the emerging Andean Common Market; and the backers of a new North Carolina ski resort, who wanted ideas for attracting skiers.

ADL's greatest assets are those members of its staff who are its ac-

194

complished generalists, those with rich but mixed credentials who revel in the fact that in this era of greater and greater specialization they are not specialists. These are the analysts who are able to put together teams, ferret out diverse cases, and find solutions. They are not the typical ADL men, nor would they be typical anywhere else.

Some of these generalists are actually specialists to begin with but can roam through cases of great diversity within that specialty. A good example is Dr. Thomas Davis, a research physician and physiologist. A large, rugged-looking man in his fifties who was born in the Cook Islands of a Welsh father and a Polynesian mother, he was educated in New Zealand and returned to the Cook Islands as a physician and later the head of the Cook Islands Health Service. When appointed to the job, he let it be known that he would not enforce the law then in effect on the islands that prohibited medicine men from practicing. He purposely gained the friendship of the witch doctors and with them developed a policy whereby they would refer physical cases to him and he, in turn, would turn over certain psychological cases to them—for example, those who felt that illness was a punishment for being bad. He also gave them paramedical duties and with them set up mosquito control and tuberculosis prevention programs. Accepting a post at the Harvard School of Public Health in 1952, he sailed with his family on his own small boat from Wellington, New Zealand, across the Pacific to Peru and then on through the Panama Canal to Boston. Shortly before joining the ADL staff in 1963 he served with NASA as Medical Monitor for Project Mercury and as Chief of Environmental Medicine for the Air Force. Co-author with his wife of several books on their experiences, he is an admittedly fanatical sailor and races motorcycles.

Davis, who normally works on ten or twelve cases at any given time, talked in late 1970 about two of his cases that serve to demonstrate his versatility. One case, supported by the U.S. Coast Guard, concerns the stability and buoyancy of the human body. The purpose of the work is to create design criteria for life jackets. One of the goals of his research is to determine how a jacket might be able to serve as insurance that an unconscious person would be rotated into a face-up position so that he or she will not drown while floating face down. One of the most surprising findings of his research thus far is that, for reasons that have not yet become clear, males and females have critically different buoyancy characteristics. In the female 55 percent of buoyancy is below the waist and in the male 55 percent is above the waist—a finding that may lead to the creation of different life jackets for males and females.

Another of his concerns is chemical pollution in water and its impact on health for the federal government. In this case, his job is that of setting down some of the major questions that must be answered to insure that Americans are being protected from their water supplies. "We're at a very serious stage in this country where we know that there are a lot of chemicals getting into our water but we know very little about them. We know, for example, that people with cancer have a higher level of pesticides in their systems than those who do not. It could be that the cancer has changed people's metabolism so that they retain more pesticides, or it could be that the pesticides contributed to the cancer. This is the kind of thing we don't know and have to find out quickly."

In contrast to Davis, whose varied concerns are in the hard sciences, Robert J. Fahey is typical of the ADL analyst whose career has led him into interesting crannies and corners of the "soft" sciences. He is in his late thirties and has worked for ADL for the last thirteen years. A graudate of the MIT School of Industrial Management, he has worked for clients as diverse as an international oil company, a computer manufacturer, American Airlines, NBC News, the players of the National Football League, and several religious orders. He is a tall, trim man, as at home talking about the problems of the mutual-fund industry as about the role of religion in the Middle Ages. If Fahey has a specialty, it is that of the internal organization of institutions and helping institutions find their organizational purpose.

Of the scores of cases he has worked on, two serve to exhibit the diversity of tasks encountered as an ADL analyst. The first case had its origins in the Second Vatican Council, which called upon all religious orders in the Church to re-evaluate their work and renew their structure. As a result two regional Provinces or large geographic districts of the Jesuit order asked ADL, along with several other consulting firms, to submit proposals for a study of the options open to them in the next decade. Initially, ADL chose not to bid on the study because it felt it would have an arm's-length formulation by outsiders and would in all probability get filed away. The result of ADL's rejection was that the Jesuits agreed with the Little prognosis and hired ADL to help design and structure their own planning process.

Fahey explained how the planning procedure emerged. First, the ADL team opened discussions with members of the order, playing the role of skeptical outsiders and asking tough questions on the worth and future of the order. This step was taken to raise basic questions about the order within the order. Then a planning process was designed jointly by the ADL team and members of the order. The process as it evolved had five steps. In the first, members of the order working alone or in small groups assumed the roles of their superiors and created their own plans for the coming decade. Unique to this step was the fact that each man was given detailed information on the order's finances and manpower so that he could plan realistically. This kind of information had never before been given to the rank and file. In the second stage, a congress of elected representatives examined the many proposals that had been turned in and determined their feasibility. Next, task forces of members at each ministry were assigned the job of examining and pulling out the best proposals that had come back from the congress. In the next to last step, the congress made its choice from among the goals and, finally, the goals decided upon were given to the Superior for the Province to decide upon. As Fahey explains, "The fifth step in one of the Provinces amounted to little more than the announcement of the decisions that had already been made by its members." He adds, "The development of this procedure has a certain nice irony to it which is that the process is not too much unlike that employed by St. Ignatius of Loyola when he and his original band of Jesuits first started in Paris before moving around the world. His method of planning was simply to use the gradually emerging consensus of followers. Ignatius would then give that consensus back to them in the form of firm decisions. This 'new' procedure for decision-making isn't really new as it goes against the trend to centralization that has cropped up in the order over the centuries."

The impact of the procedure, according to Fahey, has been to help the order gravitate toward new social goals and to allow the whole community to participate in framing those new goals. In all, Fahey and others at ADL have performed similar tasks for establishing goal procedures for fifteen other religious communities within the Catholic Church, including groups of Dominicans and Sisters of St. Joseph. Seven of the ten Jesuit Provinces in the U.S. have used ADL for this purpose. In addition, the United Church of Christ came to ADL for

197

help in setting up procedures for ordering its future goals.

Another of Fahey's cases began when the National Football League Players Association (NFLPA) came to ADL for help. The association, which serves some of the functions of a trade union for professional football players, wanted ADL to help it with its office organization to find ways in which it could better communicate with its members. After a series of meetings with the association, the company suggested it could best serve the NFLPA if it were allowed to take a more fundamental look at the economics of football and the players' share of football profits. As Fahey explains, "The association wanted to become a more effective agent for the player, and it was mutually decided that a new office organization was not what was needed, at least not at first."

ADL's work began with an exploration of the economics of pro football. It was quickly learned that although players' salaries had gone up in recent years, the players were actually getting a diminishing percentage of the profits from the game. Next on the agenda was a survey of the players themselves that set out to determine what they wanted in terms of compensation and what functions they felt the NFLPA should fill. Out of these two surveys Fahey and the others working with him derived what he terms a "simple strategy" for bargaining with the club owners. The new strategy simply called for bargaining from a knowledgeable base rather than using the traditional strategy of simply asking for a raise. ADL supplied the association with a large package of data which the players then used to deal with the clubs in their 1967 negotiations. Included were such items as which clubs were high payers and which were low, how each player's compensation compared with that of other players in the same field position as well as to others on his team and others in the league with comparable seniority. The net result of the work was the strengthening of the association and the creation of a new and much stronger bargaining position based on the principle that the player deserved a share of the profits commensurate with the booming prosperity of the game. The markedly different tone, temper, and results of the 1967 sessions and those that have followed reveal the impact that the new view of bargaining has had on the players.

A final example of a member of the ADL staff whose range of case work is wide is Robert Graff, mentioned earlier as the managing partner of ADL's New York office. In 1970 he was a member of the team working for the Brazilian state of Minas Gerais and team leader of a series of studies for the state of Connecticut. Graff, a dapper, middle-aged man, has spent most of his professional life making films. He produced both documentaries for television and made feature films (his last was *Young Cassidy*, a film biography of Sean O'Casey; his son was one of the producers of the film *Joe*). Graff gets unabashedly excited about case work at ADL and speaks in terms of its nonfinancial rewards, which he lumps under the term "psychic income" or the general excitement that comes with problem-solving work.

According to Graff a great deal of satisfaction can come from leading cases in which the discovery of a new technique or innovation not only helps the study but can be used by the client to improve his competency. One such case was a 1969 study for the Connecticut Research Commission to explore the role new technology could play in the state's future housing plans. Among several aspects to the study were a survey of how houses get built in the state and of the latest technological innovations in housing and how they might be applied in Connecticut. One stipulation in the contract called for ADL to look into consumer preferences, especially among the poor. For this part of the study a variety of traditional means for determining preferences were used, but an additional one was added. A box containing pieces of a house was given to a variety of respondents —many of them poor, black, or Puerto Rican—and they were told to design the house they most wanted to live in. As Graff explains, "I think we were able to get a new appreciation of what was most important to people. We found, for example, that to the poor we tested, the most wanted room was a dining room, and in using the device as means of getting people talking about where they would put their house and what they wanted nearby we learned a lot more." Two of those lessons were that services and operations—garbage collection, adequate schools, playgrounds, and the like—were seen as more important than the actual housing itself, and, second, respondents felt that mixing of persons of different social, economic, family, and racial characteristics was critical to the success of new housing developments. Those participating strongly felt that "category" housing, such as that for mothers receiving aid to dependent children, reinforces the poverty cycle and becomes subject to derogatory stereotyping in the community.

Though ADL rejects routinized approaches to problem-solving in favor of all methodologies and though it works to keep its concerns diverse, it does have a direction and sense of cohesion. It works to balance its list of clients and the realms in which it operates. By doing a little bit of everything, it has kept itself open to the kind of diverse innovative work that its staff admittedly craves. There is an appealing egotism to the place. It does the work it wants to and, the federal government notwithstanding, sets its own priorities and picks its own clients. As a result there is little of the division that is felt at other think tanks between the war workers and the social workers.

On the other hand, there is a self-righteousness to the place. True, ADL attempts, in many of its cases, to be socially useful, but others are highly dubious in their social utility. Soft whiskies, Lark filters, flushable sanitary napkins, and some of the other gimmicks that come through ADL's portals are not only of questionable social utility but are problem-generating in themselves. After all, easier-to-swallow liquor facilitates getting drunk, the filter adds to the illusion that the ill effects of smoking can be mitigated, and the flushable napkins and diapers that are to be flushed down toilets around the nation can by definition do nothing to help the problems of water pollution and probably will add to them. Similarly, while it is true that many nations desperately need to be developed industrially, it is questionable whether ADL contributed a great deal to human progress in helping India develop a defense industry to better enable it to come out on top of its chronic crisis with Pakistan.

Although ADL, like all groups that sell advisory services, is prone to speak of its many successes, it is far from infallible. Many of its product developments simply do not work out, it occasionally promises too much in a study and must cancel it, and from time to time it gives bad advice—all items which neither ADL nor its clients are likely to brag about.

One recent flub is the still somewhat confusing situation surrounding an industrial development project in the Canadian province of Manitoba. ADL has worked for the provincial government since 1956 as adviser on economic development. Their early recommendations led to the creation of a development board called the Manitoba Development Fund (MDF), which, in turn, has used ADL to help attract and develop industry. A major project begun in 1966 involved helping the MDF develop a paper-products complex at The Pas, a small city in northern Manitoba. As the project moved along its estimated costs and expenditures escalated rapidly. An earlier estimate of $85 million crept quickly to $135 million—a matter of no small public concern since two-thirds of the funds were being supplied by the public. Since ADL was keeping track of the project's expenditures, it was thrown into the midst of the controversy.

ADL was faulted on two counts. First, it was maintained that the original figure of $85 million was a good one and that ADL had, by revising its estimates, allowed the project to overrun to the benefit of the companies building the complex. Second, ADL along with its client, the MDF, were censured for keeping many of MDF's papers in the U. S. with ADL. This situation prompted the staid *Financial Post* of Toronto to remark, "An office in another country is a highly inappropriate location for the vital records of a provincial government board." While the exact causes of the overrun have not yet been made public by the official body studying the situation, ADL was clearly a contributor to the mess. An ADL spokesman said in 1971, "We believe that we calculated the costs as higher than they should have been and this allowed the mills to cost too much. It is still not clear, however, how much we overestimated." While there is no evidence of actual wrongdoing on the part of ADL, it apparently made costly miscalculations that have harmed its client.

In contrast to ADL's over-all research direction there are other think tanks of the jack-of-all-trade variety that show less cohesion and are the research equivalents of the oriental bazaar where a corporate roof is provided for a variety of problem-solving stalls.

3. Research à Go-Go

This nation occupies six percent of the land area of the world, has seven percent of the world's population, but now possesses 67 percent of the world's wealth. . . . Research must be the heart, the foundation, the life blood of our present defense economy if we are to maintain this position.

—Jesse Hobson, first president of the Stanford Research Institute, in 1951

Faced with a novel problem, the governor of Alaska contacted the Stanford Research Institute in August 1969 to see if it could help him. The state was coming into a fortune as a result of selling leases to petroleum companies for the oil-rich North Slope area of Alaska. The down payment from the companies was $900 million, and by the mid-1970's the annual royalties would amount to about $500 million. His problem, albeit an envious one, was that the state did not have a clear idea of how best to spend its sudden wealth.

After being contacted by the governor's office, three SRI analysts went to Alaska and held discussions with its Secretary of State, its State Planning Office, and other key officials. The state and the institute agreed to a study of the state's needs, to be accompanied by planning guidelines for its future. The governor wanted a sound study and he wanted it quickly, as he and his administration could incorporate its suggestions into the legislative program to be proposed for the next year. The deadline set for the study was fifteen weeks.

Francis Greehan, an SRI specialist in problems of state governments, was put in charge. He staked out a large office area in SRI's main building, put in extra phones, assembled what was to become the largest library on Alaska outside of Alaska, and put together a team of thirty-six. Says Greehan, "We have the largest group of economists in the free world at SRI, and we started picking from that group first." The group was predictably heavy on economists but well salted with specialists in such areas as tourist development, public health, fishing, and air transportation. Members of the team were assigned alone or in pairs to twenty-four basic topics considered essential to planning the future of the state. For the fifteen weeks of the study many of the researchers dashed around Alaska talking to game wardens, state officials, citizens' groups, bankers, and just about anyone whom they wanted to talk to or who wanted to talk with them. Back at SRI, they studied such factors as Alaska's laws, history, finances, and industrial statistics. Toward the end of the project each of the twenty-four topics was addressed and discussed in a working paper ranging from twenty-five to 100 pages in length. The working papers were then shown to the governor for his suggestions, and from these comments and the papers themselves, the leaders of the team started mapping out a series of proposals.

What finally emerged was an eighty-eight-page document entitled "Planning Guidelines for the State of Alaska." It is devoted to five major issues (industrial development, transportation, community development, individual development, and public finance) and contains scores of specific recommendations, including expansion of the university system, replenishment of the state's abused salmon stocks, better education for Alaska's Eskimo and Indian population, new air services, an alcoholic rehabilitation program, the training of paramedics for remote villages, development of a tourist industry, a new emphasis on agriculture, fluoridation of water supplies, the setting of new tax policies, and the establishment of new planning responsibilities for the state government. The final report pays particular attention to preserving the state's natural environment and elevating the status of and opportunities for its Eskimo and Indian citizens.

Greehan sums up the final outcome: "The governor used our study as the basis for his 1970 legislative program. He proposed that almost all of our recommendations be implemented, and the legislature agreed to most of the programs he proposed." The bill for the study was $180,000.

The Alaskan study is a good example of what a big think tank like SRI is capable of doing. A clearly defined problem was posed for a quick solution. SRI was able to respond with a team of talented people who gave their undivided attention to the problem. It will, of course, be years before the impact of the study can be assessed. There is little question, however, that the study was important, and many of the ideas kicked around by SRI's economists in the fall of 1969 are now legislative programs helping shape the future of the state.

The Alaska study, the charge for which constituted about one thirty-thousandth of SRI's 1969 income, illustrates the responsibilities that SRI is routinely given. As with ADL, its "products" range from major programs with international significance to making minor, but amusing, determinations. It helped determine, for instance, the location of Disneyland, invented those futuristic-looking, computer-readable letters and numbers that appear on everybody's checks along with the equipment needed to read them, worked with the government of India to help establish its network of small industries, invented the homing system now standard in Army aircraft and helicopters, helped Puerto Rico develop tourism, and invented "pressureless printing," an electrostatic process that has allowed printing on rough or uncommon surfaces. Among the 800 or so projects going on during 1970 were the development of a land-reform program for

Vietnam, an investigation of the sonic boom effects from the SST, work on a prototype artificial heart, cancer and leprosy research, and the development of a new laser device to detect and photograph invisible smog and air pollutants.

The concept of an institute at Stanford University was first advanced in 1939 but was shelved because of the war. In 1945 the idea became popular again, and in 1946 the Stanford Research Institute came into being as a wholly owned subsidiary of Stanford University. It opened at a fortuitous time. In 1946 R&D was concentrated on the East Coast. Although it seems strange now when California is liberally dotted with research institutions, in 1946 the eleven westernmost states had fewer industrial research outfits among them than the state of Connecticut. It was felt that a major West Coast research institution was needed to help the region develop economically. Besides revenue from the university, it got early financial and contract support from Pacific industry. The strength of SRI as a Pacific institution is probably no better illustrated than by what is referred to at the institute as "the million-dollar luncheon." In 1950 SRI was booming with new contracts and, though it was making a steady profit, it wanted money to expand its facilities. To get funds it held a luncheon for leading West Coast executives at the Fairmont Hotel in San Francisco where RCA board chairman David Sarnoff gave a speech asking everyone to do all he could for SRI. As a result, many companies chipped in a tax-deductible $15,000 to become "SRI Associates," a sort of booster club of industries working to help SRI grow. A little more than a year after the luncheon over a million dollars had come in from new Associates.

Since SRI was founded it has been paid over half a billion dollars to do research for others. Today it takes in about $60 million a year in revenues, and its total staff numbers around 3,000. Its headquarters in Menlo Park cover much of the eighty-acre estate on which it is located. Up front are its modern headquarters building and its new international building. As one moves back on the estate the buildings begin to look like the drabber side of an Army post. In fact, some of the buildings were part of a sprawling one-story military hospital used to receive the wounded from the Pacific during World War II. Off the main research estate are laboratories and offices scattered over the adjacent area, several sites in remote areas of northern California, where it does explosives and ordnance research, a site across

San Francisco Bay, where it houses its large collection of sea mammals, and a major environmental laboratory, opened in 1970 near the University of California at Irvine. There are also branch offices in major U.S. cities as well as Zurich, Tokyo, Stockholm, Sydney, and, until recently, Bangkok.

It has a reputation among others in the think-tank world as an outfit that is highly competitive, puts few controls on what its individual researchers do, and is capable of both very good and not so good research. The reputation is apparently deserved since its own executives make no bones about its hands-off policy on research projects and its interest in profits. One top executive who chose to talk on the subject for nonattribution says, "Management, of course, has to approve every project that comes in, but it is extremely rare that a project is turned down." Since it issues no annual report on its finances, there is a paucity of public data on its profit picture, but its people note with pride that there has been only one year in its nearly twenty-five-year history as a not-for-profit that it has not made a profit. Its president, Charles A. Anderson, points out, "We're as competitive as any profit-making enterprise and as sensitive to the needs of the marketplace. If we don't make a profit, management is not doing its job." An oft-heard remark here is that it is not SRI's job to set priorities; rather, it is SRI's responsibility to accept the priorities set by the nation. Ironically this not-for-profit institution, established "to aid and supplement scientific research at Stanford," has become more interested in money than internal moral direction or priority setting. It is, as several officials point out, not in business to crusade.

SRI's corporate attitude toward the world is typified by Weldon "Hoot" Gibson, its executive vice-president and president of SRI International. Gibson joined the institute when it opened in 1946 and as its most senior executive is referred to there as "Mr. SRI." A forceful speaker who seldom speaks in nondeclarative sentences, he asserts that no other organization has the abilities of SRI in economic development research and refers to competitors in the field as "crusaders" who make political and moral judgments when deciding whether to take a job.

Gibson says SRI imposes few strictures on the question of whether or not to take a job. "We're not crusaders and choose not to stand in judgment of others. The main thing we're interested in is rational problems to work with." He illustrates his point by stating that SRI works for both the Arabs and the Israelis and that it has done work for South Africa. He adds, "Now the students at Stanford have accused me of being an economic imperialist. I meet that charge head on—I am one and I try to be a good one. We're not in business to make moral judgments. Now the Swedes have a Socialist government, and we do a lot of work there and we don't make any moral judgments against them, just as we don't make them against South Africa." Apparently Gibson is fond of bragging about SRI's lack of moral discrimination. He is quoted in James Ridgeway's book *The Closed Corporation* as saying, "Would we develop a more destructive atomic weapon? Yes, if there were a need for it and a contract was there. We don't have any crusades." Ridgeway also attributes to Gibson the comment that SRI would not research gambling or vice because it would be counter to SRI's public image. (For the record: *Saturday Review* reported in 1967 that SRI had worked for Harrah's Club in Reno to determine the best schedules for buses bringing gamblers to the club.)

Examples of the mercenary mentality are not hard to find in many think tanks, but few display it as willingly or as openly as do those who run SRI. Although its officers persistently declare that it has no ideology, it does. By swelling its own coffers and making SRI bigger by working for just about anyone on anything, it says all research is good save for that which might hurt its image.

Though there are similarities in much of the work that SRI and ADL perform, SRI's character is distinctly different. While ADL attempts to set its own priorities and keep its programs balanced, SRI's priorities and balances are those of the highest bidder. Also unlike ADL, little control is exerted over the quality of work and on those things which impinge on its reputation, with the result that it is regularly cited for good work as well as laxity and lack of ethical direction. Some years back, for example, the General Accounting Office accused SRI of trying to defraud the government out of $250,000 by charging it for depreciation on buildings it had given Stanford. And in 1969 a report that it had prepared for an oil firm defending restrictive oil import quotas was cited by Senator Proxmire as being marked by invalid assumptions, loaded conclusions, and at least one major error in mathematics—an error of 44 percent in favor of the position they were defending. Proxmire said on the occasion, "Quite obviously, the jingle of the cash register has lulled SRI into forgetting fundamental principles of academic honesty, scholarly research, and objectivity." Similarly, the Federal Communications Commission regularly contracts with SRI for studies costing hundreds of thousands of dollars that have been regularly held up by the communications trade press as statements of the obvious that contribute little that is new. In a 1968 interview Raymond Spence, then Deputy Chief Engineer of the FCC, mentioned that an SRI study of radio frequency allocation policy was ". . . something that you and I could have put together in a few weekends working in a good library." SRI has carved out a niche for itself doing at best mediocre research for the FCC, which keeps coming back for more.

What many find most disturbing about SRI is that it was formed as a regional institute, presumably to be of some social and technical use to the West Coast, and has become much more dependent on the federal government for support than on local municipal and industrial sources. In recent years Washington has supplied it with about 75 percent of its income, and though it has never been on the list of Federal Contract Research Centers, it is actually one of the largest military think tanks. In 1969, for example, its military income was $24.8 million, which was close to half its income and more than RAND and the Hudson Institute combined got from military sources that year. Its military specialties are many, but prominent among them are just those that most antagonize Americans who oppose the war and decry recent directions in military technology—chemical and biological warfare, studies in support of ABM systems, new explosives technology, counterinsurgency research, and secret civilian participation in counterinsurgency operations abroad. In 1969, for instance, SRI's bill to the government for research and operations in Thailand alone ran to $2.9 million. The work conducted by its Bangkok office has ranged from research into Thai culture to activities clearly transcending any definition of academic research, such as the testing of electronic ambush aids and reconnaissance. Stanley Karnow of the Washington *Post* described in a 1969 report from Bangkok just how far one SRI researcher got from research. Karnow revealed that an SRI man working on a $280,000 study of guerrilla detection systems had fallen in with exiled Laotian General Phoumi Nosavan and was aiding him in his plans to take over Laos. Although the U.S. finally condemned this free-lance coup adviser, the story illustrates the freedom of action that "researchers" are given in war zones. SRI's general involvement in Southeast Asia has been eager, well rewarded, and clearly in wholehearted support of the Pentagon.

There had been rumblings about the institute's war work on the Stanford campus for several years, but campus demonstrations did not begin in earnest until April 1969. One laboratory was occupied for nine days, picket lines appeared, and pamphlets and broadsides detailing the institute's involvements came out with regularity. At stake were five demands put forward by a group of students and faculty and rejected by the university's trustees. Their demands were: (1) an end to chemical and biological warfare research; (2) to bring SRI under closer university control and establish guidelines for socially acceptable research; (3) an end to counterinsurgency research; (4) an end to classified research; and (5) an end to research in support of wars in Southeast Asia.

Early in 1970 the trustees of the university announced that they had relinquished control and ownership of SRI and were selling it to SRI's directors for the bargain price of $25 million. It was also announced by SRI that it would end all research in chemical and biological warfare—not too great a concession actually since the government was at that time ending support of such research. The result of the events of 1969 was that the dissidents had achieved one demand, but, more important, the university had made an end run by cutting free its controversial ward and thereby washing its hands of any attempt to control it. The legal annulment did not affect the professional ties between the institute and the university since many professors from the university still moonlight as SRI researchers.

SRI can be viewed as a collection of many smaller think tanks and R&D institutions rather than a single large institute. One finds relatively autonomous entities within the organization, including SRI International, an Office of Education Federal Contract Research Center (see Chapter XI), a body of thinkers who see the world in a radically different manner from Gibson and other institute executives; a research lab that has been seeking a use for tallow for meat renderers since 1949; several long-established ordnance research units; a civil-defense research group, which has been working for the Office of Civil Defense for almost twenty years; and a small RAND-like operations research unit that works for the Army. The group that tends and works with SRI's collection of seals, sea lions, and other sea mammals has been working for some time to unlock the secret of their ability to communicate and perceive underwater. This is part of SRI's bioengineering program, largely underwritten by the Navy to get clues from these animals it hopes will lead to innovations in such underwater equipment as sonar. Still another group is working to find new applications of laser technology to real problems ranging from their use as precise cutting tools in eye surgery to their utility as an instrument for counting plankton in sea water.

The think tank doing some of SRI's most interesting work is its information sciences and engineering group. Two of its projects illustrate the degree of sophistication the group has achieved. One is the construction and development of a robot; the other involves a search to find out what man can accomplish when he "lives" with computers.

Both of these projects are mainly supported by the Advanced Research Projects Agency (ARPA), a special research contracting adjunct to the Secretary of Defense, created in 1958. Its specialty is officially termed "advanced" research that does not fit into the research programs of the individual services. As stated by Pentagon research director John Foster, its primary mission is to insure the U.S. against "technological surprise." The kind of research it stirs up interest in and then pays for includes ideas like the natural environment as a weapon (can small explosions kick off volcanos, or can weather be modified to keep a nation parched?), small flying machines and backpack rockets for propelling individual foot soldiers, behavioral research on potential enemies, and exotic metals and materials that may have potential in new weapons. ARPA also has the funds and flexibility to kick off quick pet research projects for the Secretary of Defense, such as designing new river patrol craft for the Thai Navy and work on laser-directed bombs for Vietnam. ARPA is, as might be expected, a big supporter of the not-for-profit research institutes.

"Shaky" sat in the middle of a large room and was being worked on by its keepers the day it was shown to this visitor. A member of SRI's public-relations staff casually tossed off the line, "It's too bad he's down today; it's really something to watch him in action." The "he" and the "him" in the sentence rolled out naturally, not in jest. The fact that the hunk of electronic equipment known as Shaky rates a masculine pronoun is unnerving but not as unnerving as finding out what he/it does.

It sits on four wheels and is abstractly human—something that a sculptor working with cast-off industrial equipment might title "Man in the Age of Cybernation." Where its head and eyes should be is a television camera and several range-finding devices. Cables wrap around its neck like a heavy scarf, and atop the device is a shield that strangely resembles a beret. Protruding from its thin electronic body are wires that help it sense its environment.

The conception of Shaky occurred at SRI in 1963, and ever since researchers have been building and refining it. By 1970 it was mature enough to respond to a variety of commands and to find a way to carry them out. Sitting at a keyboard in a nearby room, for instance, a technician can type out the instruction "LOCATE THE CUBE AND PUSH IT OFF THE PLATFORM." At this point Shaky will take off to scan his surroundings for the cube. Once it locates the cube Shaky may determine that it is too high for it to reach. It will then move around until it locates a small ramp that it nudges over to the platform. It next moves back, builds up speed, runs up the ramp and knocks over the cube. This task completed, it is then ready to take on a new job, such as moving three objects to a certain point on the floor.

The main concern of the twenty-five or so researchers who work on and with Shaky is its brain, a remarkably versatile computer. Working in a field they call artificial intelligence, the researchers are trying to show that such a computer can not only compute but think. The computer has been instructed by being given basic criteria for making conclusions and decisions, a capacity which, coupled with the ability to see—actually to detect geometric shapes through its camera that are then translated into simple geometric propositions in its computer—enables Shaky to perform. At present the team working with Shaky is helping it solve one problem based on the solution to another problem—i.e., getting it to think by analogy. Shaky, who already knew how to push a wedge and cube, had to put these two abilities together to learn to push the wedge to a point where it could reach the cube and to push it over.

For an object that was conceived in 1963, it has matured rapidly. It understands over 100 verbal commands, which it translates into formulae. It can find its way around its quarters even when its human associates place obstacles in its path, and it is regularly let loose in its quarters for the sole purpose of "understanding" more about its environment. Its developers believe that in the not too distant future it will be able to recognize the human beings who work with it. It is completely within the realm of possibility that by the time it is ten or fifteen years of age it will be better able to perform certain cerebral tasks than human beings conceived in 1963. For one, it will most certainly have a better memory.

Nearby, twenty-eight people work in SRI's Human Augmentation Research Center. The center is contained in a large central room with small offices around its edges. The people who work there refer to themselves as an "on-line community." It is a very quiet community where the members sit in front of computer consoles and look into video screens. In appearance many members of the community contrast with the straight crew-cut and slim-jim tie image of the rest of the institution. Zapata mustaches, long hair and denim shirts give the impression of a certain hipness in the air.

James Norton, one of the straighter-looking members, explains that the main purpose of the center is to get men closer to computers, to learn more about them and to use them as an extension of man's intelligence. The community works to make this man/machine interface as natural as possible. Norton, for instance, points out a not very extraordinary-looking chair designed under commission from the center by designer Herman Miller to make working at a computer console most comfortable and natural.

The most intriguing aspect of the community is that its accumulated knowledge, reports, and paperwork are all in the system. Contract information, individual research projects being conducted by its members, administrative data, and the like are all stored in the computers.

One innovation to come out of the center's research is a small device aptly called "a mouse" because that is what it looks like. The mouse is cupped in the hand of a man sitting in front of a video screen and moved across a plane surface in front of the console to pinpoint information on the screen. If, for example, the mouse is pushed forward, a blip on the screen moves upward. By putting the blip on a key word on the screen the operator is telling the computer that he wants to enter the files at that point, and by pushing a button on the mouse's body the file's contents appear on the screen. When the mouse is moved again to the part of that file he wants and the button is pushed again the desired information appears on the screen. Norton, who uses the mouse with amazing dexterity, plows

211

through charts and files in seconds, using the mouse to find the exact information he is looking for.

During my visit the community was working on what Norton called a "super-document" of its experiences, findings, and operations to date. There were no typewriters clacking and the piles of paper that one associates with a massive report were missing. The report, as Norton signified, was "in there," indicating the console, and to prove it he located it and projected its outline on the screen. He moved the mouse and called up a chapter outline and then with another move called up an element of that chapter which for lack of a better term could be considered a page. He then put on a display of editorial dexterity with the mouse and console keyboard as his blue pencil. He rearranged paragraphs, moved commas, added phrases, and excised others.

sri's computer community is not isolated. It is in the process of plugging into a network where other such communities are working on other aspects of human augmentation. Together, all of the participants in what is called the ARPA network represent the emergence of the most important attempt in the nation to discover the outer limits of man's ability to extend his thinking through computers.

The network now being hooked up will eventually be tied to a score of research units across the nation. RAND, SDC, MIT's Lincoln Lab, UCLA, ARPA itself, Harvard, and the Bell Telephone Laboratories are some of the institutions tying in. Once in operation, it will link some 1,500 researchers and consoles and more than thirty computers. The emerging network has more than one unique aspect to it. For one, for the first time it will allow computers of different size, vintage, manufacture, language, and complexity to borrow from one another, assign one another jobs, and, generally, interact. IBM 360s, Sigma 7s, PDP 10s Univac 1108s, and other cybernetic families will begin working together. It will also serve as an experiment in determining how far a man can extend himself via access to some of the most sophisticated computers and computer programs in the nation. A researcher at sri, for example, will be able to browse through the work of a cohort at Harvard to see if he has a formula for solving a particular problem, or for an hour or so he might want to plug into a University of Illinois computer with particular abilities.

The Stanford Center has a key role to play in the network—that of librarian, cataloguing the network's documentation. The sri setup will permit users to search for key words to help them solve problems, browse through sources, and update the master file with the latest information.

As intriguing as these two projects are, they cannot be viewed as mere research curiosities. Though both certainly have nonmilitary applications, they are not being funded by the Pentagon for these reasons. The computer community and the network, as ARPA has clearly stated, are being funded to advance the technology of "command and control"—essentially the immediate control of weapons and forces. The reason for funding a robot is less apparent. The stated justification is to enable man to have a greater comprehension of the ability of machines when properly harnessed. Such a generality can easily be extended to specifics. The "automated battlefield" cited in the previous chapter will probably be a reality before Shaky's descendants can discriminate accurately between friend and foe. But as one comprehends what the machine has been taught in a few years, one can envision that a machine built a generation from now could be taught to be an extremely effective and adaptable fighter in an advanced automated fighting unit.

Finally, there is still another way of looking at these projects. At this point, they are extremely sophisticated toys, military baubles to be played with in the sanctity of a tax-free preserve at the public's expense. As cybernetic playthings they offer a strange contrast to the nation outside of SRI in which services decline, hostility builds, and cities rot.

As a group, the "cerebral supermarkets" defy generalization save for the obvious one that among them they do practically anything for anyone. Individually these powerhouses of applied research show distinct differences as they determine to what ends they will apply their research know-how. Some, like ADL, have chosen their own course, while those of the SRI variety have opted, like Hessian soldiers, to tie their abilities to the aspirations of the highest bidders.

IX

URBAN THINK TANKS

---

1. Technological Setback

> ... the nation's response to the crisis of
> the cities has been perilously inadequate.
>
> —Report of the Urban Coalition,
> "One Year Later"

To begin with, the nation had not done its domestic homework. It quickly became apparent as the 1960's wore on how little was actually known about the problem. While Pentagon planners and space experts had all sorts of sophisticated data at their fingertips, there was genuine ignorance of the real social problems. In 1969 former Presidential Assistant Joseph A. Califano, Jr., testified to this point before a Senate Labor Subcommittee. Califano stated that it took the Johnson Administration almost two years to find out who the seven million people were who were on welfare in America. It was the first study of welfare recipients ever conducted. It also took two years to come up with the determination, finally made in 1967, that twenty-six million new housing units would have to be constructed in the next decade. Califano also noted that when the Watts ghetto erupted in 1965 the government had to send a team of twenty into the area to find out who lived there and under what conditions. He summed up the situation this way: "The disturbing truth is that the basis of recommendations by an American Cabinet officer on whether to begin, eliminate or expand vast social programs more nearly resembles the intuitive judgment of a benevolent tribal chief in remote Africa than the elaborate, sophisticated data with which the Secretary of Defense supports a major new weapons system." It was obvious that the tedious business of collecting data had just begun.

A major lesson began to be learned soon thereafter: that massive, direct transfers of techniques from military and space systems to domestic social problems did not work. Many early attempts to apply high technology and systems engineering to the nonmilitary world had been decided flops. A case in point and one of the most ambitious attempts was launched by the consulting firm of Schriever, McKee Associates of Rosslyn, Virginia. The firm was founded and is headed by retired general Bernard A. Schriever, former chief of the Air Force Systems Command, who as the developer of the Atlas, Titan, Thor, and Minuteman missiles is considered to be one of the ablest practitioners of the art of systems engineering. In 1967 Schriever began putting together a consortium of major American companies to mount a multidisciplinary attack on urban problems. The consortium was called Urban Systems Associates Inc. (or USA Inc.) and it included Lockheed and Northrup from the aerospace world, Emerson Electric, Control Data, and Raytheon from the electronics area, the architectural engineering firm of Ralph M. Parsons, and American Cement.

For almost two years the consortium tried to get off the ground, trying to cultivate a major client for a massive urban-development project—preferably in housing. But USA Inc. did not fare well. An official of the consortium reported in August 1968 that the group was having trouble determining who its clients should be, making the distinction between technological and sociological problems, and in cultivating a market. Although they had discussed a major San Francisco urban-development program and a regional development and water-resources program for the state of Arizona, none of the serious discussions between USA and potential clients was leading to anything solid.

General Schriever admitted defeat, and USA Inc. was shelved. He frankly addressed the reasons for the failure by admitting the limitations of the consortium's approach. Said Schriever: "Though the need for a systematic approach to urban development exists, unfortunately its application today is extremely difficult. The key problem is that social and psychological phenomena cannot be rigorously posed in mathematical terms as can physical phenomena. It is not feasible to define on an analytic basis the consequence of urban development strategies. It is also unfortunate that empirical approaches cannot be used due to the lack of a meaningful data base." Another reason was the potential clients themselves. Among the shortcomings: government is fragmented, local governments have not defined their needs, their tradition is to react to crises rather than plan to prevent them, local officials cannot think beyond their term of office, and few mayors or governors comprehend the systems approach.

An analogous illustration of the optimistic contention that existing technology held the solutions to domestic problems can be seen in the nation's desire to curb crime. In February 1967 the Presidential Commission on Law Enforcement and Criminal Justice began releasing reports on crime and possible solutions to the problem. One volume—prepared for the most part by the Institute for Defense Analyses—offered scores of suggestions for bringing modern technology and systems thinking to bear on the criminal justice system. Other volumes covered additional aspects of the problem, and, in all, over 200 recommendations for curbing crime were made. During the same year the President asked for and received $50 million for research and pilot programs in crime prevention; he would boost the figure to $300 million the next year.

Three years later the big war on crime looked like a skirmish in which nothing much had happened other than that the problem had become bigger. Of the more than 200 specific recommendations put forth by the commission, only a handful had been implemented. Money had been spent, but as critics noted it had been parceled out in such small doles across the nation that the over-all effect was as if an eye dropper had been emptied down a well. Many grants for important projects had been so watered down by the time they trickled to the local level that they had become meaningless gestures —for example, the city of Evansville, Indiana, was given $112 for a drug-abuse education program and $89 for drug-detection equipment, while grants for programs elsewhere were as low as $75. In most cases, there was little chance for anything innovative. Beneficiary police departments could do little more than contract for a study or buy a few extra pieces of equipment. Despite lack of success, it is now predicted that federal subsidies for crime prevention will reach a billion dollars a year in the next few years. A study of anticrime funds by the National League of Cities published in 1970 cited a number of factors in describing the failure, among them failure of the program to recognize that urban crime needs more attention than rural crime; lack of coordination at both the state and federal level; a proliferation of paperwork, red tape, and delays in getting funds to areas that need them; limited participation by local officials; duplication in study areas and grants with too great an emphasis on "studies" of subjects that have already been studied; and high administrative costs.

It had become painfully obvious that the technologist was going to have to come up with new approaches if he were actually to help solve the problems.

One more major problem—and the one that may be the hardest to remedy—arrived with the many outfits that began to make fast bucks on the funds coming out of Washington for problem-solving. It would be hard to say who was more at fault—the giver or the receiver—but it is easy to say who was losing out as an observer reviews a social measure like the War on Poverty. Much of the criticism directed against that war—for a variety of motives, from liberal outrage to conservative penny-pinching—was aimed at the funds eaten up by high-priced consultants and corporations that entered and profited from the war. Examples abound:

In 1965 and 1966 alone, the Office of Economic Opportunity spent over $12 million on evaluation contracts—it was not only a lot of money for evaluation of infant programs but the results were sad. Says one ex-OEO official, "The money was handed out with little care to people who didn't know what they were doing and, to be honest, we didn't know what to tell them to do."

Federal employees left government to put up their shingles as poverty consultants and land huge contracts to evaluate antipoverty efforts. For example, one outfit, Leo Kramer Inc., headed by ex-OEO employee Leo Kramer, picked up seven contracts from OEO worth $1.9 million in 1967 and 1968. Six of the seven contracts to Kramer during that period were awarded on a sole-source basis; that is, without any other competition. William Kelley, former director of the Job Corps, now serves as contracting officer for a firm that has received over $25 million to provide "logistical services" to OEO.

Among too many gold-plated studies of questionable value, one outfit (National Analysts of Philadelphia) picked up $39,000 to study the letters sent in response to a government-sponsored rock-'n'-roll show on TV, while the Hudson Institute got $74,932 for a general treatise on poverty in America—a study rapped for its vagueness.

Typical of the skepticism that grew out of federal efforts at domestic problem-solving are the comments of James A. Kalish, a Washington consultant who wrote of urban contractors in the November 1969 issue of *The Washington Monthly* this way: "An urban problems industry could be—indeed, should be—the public's technical arm in this endeavor. When such an industry takes advantages of the government's need of it (by double-talking, by flimflamming, by feathering its own nest—which is what the urban problems industry does fairly consistently today) it does more than fail to solve urban problems; it actively impedes their solution." In short, a major impediment facing domestic problem-solving is the hustler.

Finally, a very considerable factor hindering a meaningful assault on urban issues today is the shortage of funding. Initial failure, politics, lack of specified goals, and the costs of the Vietnam war share the blame, but the fact remains that money was and is not being conscientiously applied to the problems in large, consistent doses.

For the scientific-technical community this last factor poses a severe problem on two fronts. On one hand, a war-weary nation is demanding and causing cutbacks in military and space spending, which can be expected to erode still further after the end of the Vietnam war. On the other hand, money and action in the domestic problem area is in short supply, many once promising federal programs are not moving, and local governments are either broke or headed in that direction. Nonetheless, a considerable number of research institutions plan to devote at least part of their future to domestic problems because they believe that there will be funds in this area eventually. More and more institutions are signaling their readiness to get going with these problems. In 1969 the Urban Institute, a new urban think tank, reported what it termed to be a trend

218

of "phenomenal" growth. It found that while in the 1950's there were only about two dozen university-based urban research centers, by 1967 there were about eighty of them—and by late 1969 the total had jumped to nearly 200. This campus trend is just as evident elsewhere: Old institutions have been turning part of their attention to new internal, civil, urban, and environmental matters as quickly as new institutions are being created for problem-solving in these areas. This shift in emphasis is especially dramatic at institutions with a strong military heritage. Defense contractors, think tanks, and R&D firms have been creating new divisions to apply their skills to domestic matters. Elsewhere, consulting firms, architectural firms, and scientific groups are among others shifting at least some of their emphasis.

To be sure, the reason for much of this shifting is tied to survival. There are other reasons as well. Federally supported military think tanks offer a good case in point. Survival is certainly a prime factor, for they have already felt the bite of a leveling off of Defense spending—likely to continue leveling, if not actually turning into a major drop. Even the military recognizes the problem as it tries to keep its institutions solvent. A letter circulated by Secretary of Defense Laird in 1969, for example, offered the civilian agencies of government the analytical services of the Institute for Defense Analyses (for an appropriate fee).

For the military-oriented think tanks there are other reasons for the shift beyond survival, including the oft-stated and well-publicized one that they believe that they can and should turn their brains to critical domestic problems. S. J. Deitchman, director of the IDA's newly formed Office of Civil Programs, points to four reasons for the general shift in military think-tank emphasis: "First, I think there is a general lack of continued interest in Vietnam and war. People think we've done an awful lot in this area—it's time to move onto something else. Second, I think there's a shift going on in the nation which will result in more money going into civil programs. Third, the think tanks are getting new, younger people who don't want to do defense work and, finally, more pioneering is going on in the new civil areas, and this is where bright young people want to be." William Schneider, Jr., a Hudson Institute economist, says simply, "We've been heavily involved in war research and a lot of people around here either got bored or disillusioned with it and are now moving into new areas." An official of the MITRE Corporation says his company's move into new areas has both a corporate and individual rationale. On one hand, the new direction ". . . justifies our self-image as a problem-solver and our position as a national resource." On the individual level, he adds, it opens new horizons for employees whose skills threaten to atrophy after working on one military system after another. He notes that civil problems also allow the specialist more freedom to publish and be known as an expert because his work is not stamped secret.

While there is a promising aspect to this shift—namely, that it will create a sizable base of technological experts who could spearhead a much better and more systematic attack on civil problems—there is an aspect to the shift that encourages skepticism. The constant theme that the military-oriented think tanks hit upon in making their pitch for urban problem-solving work is that they have the techniques and brains needed for the job. One must logically wonder where all these thinkers were when the urban problems were first getting out of control and why they have waited till now, when further military cutbacks threaten, to assert themselves as the saviors of the cities.

As the older groups shift to varying degrees, there are also new think tanks emerging created specifically to come to grips with the basic problems of analysis, policy research, and training for the cities. Unlike the first rash of politicians, marketeers, and PR men who came to the fore promising quick answers to the problems, these new groups generally come on with a certain modesty born of concern over additional problems created by so many unfulfilled promises. They offer no promises of quick problem-solving swoops and panaceas and view the Apollo program as a relatively easy challenge in contrast to the one that now must be faced. As a group, they emphasize concerted long-term aid in the form of research, application of research, new tools, and better analysis and evaluation of problems and programs. They see problems as urgent but also see that urgency as reason for not going off without fully understanding the problems they are trying to attack. Still generalizing, one finds that they usually steer clear of the ammunition of the first assault on the problem—press releases, optimistic pronouncements, gimmicks, slogans, and flashy reports—but instead rely more on constant study along with consultation and communication with those who have to make problem-solving decisions.

Some of these groups have been around for a while, but most are new. One example of an older group is the University of Wisconsin's Institute for Research on Poverty, a $1-million-a-year think tank created in 1966 and sponsored by OEO that is emerging as a strong force in the profound thinking beginning to be devoted to America's poor. Its multidisciplinary team of twenty-five experts is concentrating much of its work on reforming welfare systems. A major architect of "negative income" proposals, it is conducting the nation's only major experiment on the concept—a three-year study with 1,000 families under family assistance in New Jersey. It is also conducting smaller rural experiments in welfare programs and basic research on other welfare alternatives. Its major impact will be felt if and when welfare reform programs go into effect.

Probably the most important of the new think tanks, though, is one created by a consortium of government agencies. From the first there was little question as to the image in which it would be created: It would be the RAND of domestic urban policy research.

2. *Think Tank for the Cities*

Until the early 1960's, the comfortable assumption of many was that if we directed more public resources to particular problems we could readily solve them. Now we are finding—as we look at black-white tensions, or alienation, or maldistribution of income —that this is not necessarily true. For some decades we have been providing the money and manpower to deal with the problems, for instance, of education and transportation. We put these inputs, figuratively, into a little box, representing our society and its processes—trusting that the results would pop out the other side. Well, they did not. The outputs have been less than we expected. The disappointment and the puzzlement over where to turn is a great deal of

221

what confrontations, citizen participation, black power, and the rest of the things that most people regard as the crisis of the cities is all about. We recognize now that we need new understanding.

—William Gorham, president of the Urban Institute

A recurring theme that one hears at the Urban Institute is that not only have many wrong answers been given in response to the problems plaguing the cities but too often not even the right questions have been posed. The job that the sizable corps of analysts working at the institute have envisioned for themselves is framing better questions to yield better answers. What kind of questions are they asking?

Are there any federal social problems that have been successful? And, for that matter, why don't the legislators and bureaucrats who have authorized them know which programs have helped and which have not?

Are the cities as broke as they say they are or are there still local sources of money to be tapped?

To what extent are federal policies making problems worse—for example, does the government foster major population shifts from South to North and from rural areas to the cities?

Isn't there some way to get away from just saying things are bad and instead coming up with the means to measure how bad and find if things are actually getting better or worse?

Applying broad-gauged analysis of this sort to the cities is not a new idea. In fact, it has been discussed for years, but very little has actually been done. The Urban Institute itself had a typically long bureaucratic birth. Its conception can be traced to ideas advanced first during the Kennedy and then during the Johnson Administration as various agencies and Presidential task forces, recognizing the problems they were having with domestic issues, discussed the possibility of creating policy research entities (or, as they were often referred to, "urban RAND's") to help them in their respective areas. The general idea appealed to President Johnson, who mentioned the possible creation of an "Institute for Urban Development" in several speeches on urban policy. Encouraged by Johnson's remarks, various agencies petitioned him for their own policy research institute. Johnson then put together a group of distinguished incorporators (including several ex-Cabinet members and then Secretary of Defense McNamara) to work on the idea. The incorporators decided that one such institute should be started but that, unlike RAND, it should avoid being embraced by any one agency of government. Rather, their plan called for an independent nonprofit think tank supported on a contract basis by a variety of civilian agencies and, to whatever extent possible, by private foundations. It got started in April 1968 with its main financial support coming from the Department of Housing and Urban Development, the Department of Health, Education and Welfare, the Office of Economic Opportunity, the Department of Labor, and the Ford Foundation.

Closely identified with the Johnson Administration, the brand-new Urban Institute (so named in lieu of the Institute for Urban Development, probably because of the unfortunate acronym IUD) was soon faced with a new Administration. "The first reaction by Nixon's people was extreme skepticism," says one ranking institute official, "but the 'enemy camp' image wore off as we proved to them that our interest in problem-solving was nonpartisan."

Today the Urban Institute is the largest and fastest-growing think tank dedicated strictly to domestic problems. The staff has rapidly grown to about 160 and will pass 250 before 1973. The plan, says Joseph Lewis, who directs the institute's Urban Governance Programs, is ". . . to find the most effective size in the next few years and level off at that point, but that level will probably be quite substantial." He adds that RAND leveled off when it found that 500 professionals were most effective for them. The institute is located in downtown Washington, where it occupies several floors of a new high-rise office building.

The institute as it exists today has mapped out a mammoth territory for itself. Its interests cover the spectrum of urban problems. Today the institute is relatively unknown outside of official circles and those closely involved with urban problems.

The president of the institute, William Gorham, is one of the systems "whiz kids" brought to the Pentagon from RAND by McNamara. He went on to become an Assistant Secretary of Health, Education and Welfare and has been with the institute from its beginning. Now in his late thirties, Gorham is a scholarly looking man with a casual but no-nonsense manner of speaking about his job and the Urban Institute. He is not at all defensive about the fact that his group is not famous; he explains that it is just not that kind of organization, nor does it want to be. There have been significant developments at the institute in its first years, according to Gorham, but they are not the kind of things that make headlines. He says paradoxically: "Our importance lies to some extent in remaining seemingly unimportant." There are two fundamental reasons for this. The complexity of urban problems is such that they do not lend themselves to splashy announcements of progress but rather to concerted, relatively undramatic and incremental advances. And, second, the institute has chosen to work quietly but closely with those who can make the decisions to solve urban problems. As he says, the job of the institute can be best performed by a private, rather than public, advocate of change.

As an example of the kind of perception that the institute has evolved, Gorham cites the idea of "existing stock" in housing. The institute's study of housing revealed that the federal policy of looking at new construction as the sole answer to the nation's housing crisis contained a basic fallacy: They were forgetting the simple fact that significant advances would never be made unless existing housing (or stock) was safeguarded from steady deterioration, abandonment, and demolition. Concern with conserving and reclaiming housing as a major emphasis was seen as a major oversight in federal housing strategy. A series of papers to the policy-makers from the institute emphasizing this point, says Gorham, caused federal housing officials to take notice of this aspect of the housing crisis, and now they are amending their policies. Although the concept seems, and indeed is, a simple one, it was in fact being overlooked by the housing officials in government. The situation is indicative of other errors of omission made in government planning and underscores the fact that sometimes think tanks have their greatest impact when catching such oversights. Gorham explains that locating and detecting the importance of this kind of error—and performing the sometimes difficult job of convincing officials that it is, indeed, a serious oversight—is the kind of function that has to be performed by groups like the Urban Institute in helping to arrive at better policies and goals. The job of telling the Emperor about his new clothes has become a think-tank role performed with tables, analyses, and statistics. While think tanks are sometimes faulted for issuing reports with obvious conclusions, in cases like that of "existing stock" the obvious is essential. Ironically, a newspaper editorial or a private citizen writing to his government pointing out that housing goals will never be met because too many houses are falling apart would probably have no impact. When the same conclusion is repackaged as the concept of "existing stock" and formally presented as a well-documented think-tank analysis, the bureaucrats take heed. In the realm of housing policy this straightforward Urban Institute report may well have touched off a change as fundamental as the one that occurred in defense thinking after RAND's strategic-bases study.

The tasks the institute has been performing in the process of attempting to set up proposed welfare reform and income maintenance programs provides another good example of its early goals. It has worked with Congress, the Bureau of the Budget, the White House, HEW and the Department of Labor as an adviser on new welfare legislation. Says Gorham, "We've provided the estimates for all the proposals and counterproposals for welfare reform, trying to keep everyone abreast of what each program will cost." In this particular case, a computer is at the heart of the guidance supplied to policymakers. Each new welfare package proposal is fed into a computer model for the purpose of determining the long-term costs of the package, its meaning to people in various income groups, and how it compares to the present welfare package and other proposals.

Gorham lists as another function the role the institute is now playing as a general resource for the great variety of people who need help in urban matters. This concept of serving as resource goes far beyond being a consultant to the high-ranking urban czars and includes aid to many others—local officials, academicians, civil-rights leaders, to name a few—who must be party to the solutions. "Part of this," says Gorham, "boils down to the simple fact that there is now a place to call for help, information and advice where there was none before."

Typical of the kind of advice sought was a recent request from Fort Worth, Texas, for information on allowing policemen to take their patrol cars home with them. The city was thinking about the idea because it was felt that perhaps such a practice might have an effect on law enforcement not only because of the increased visibility of police cars as a deterrent to crime and hazardous driving but because it makes police more quickly available in emergencies. The institute responded by sending an analyst to Indianapolis, which is experimenting with the idea. Then a complete analysis of the pros and cons was prepared, including analysis of police morale, operating costs, maintenance costs, and effect on crime. (It was found, for example, that in Indianapolis the incidence of crimes committed outdoors has gone down since the practice was adopted there.) Finally, the analysis was sent to Fort Worth, and though it did not make a final recommendation, it gave all the data and listed all the potential costs and benefits deemed necessary for a well-informed decision. After studying the report, Fort Worth officials decided against the plan, reasoning that its added costs, especially that of having a patrol car out of operation for part of a 24-hour period, outweighed its benefits. (The mayor of Indianapolis, on the other hand, cited the same report as justification for his costly but effective program.)

Another important service that Gorham cites is the institute's ability to help the federal government evaluate its innumerable programs to determine what works, what doesn't, what difference it makes, and under what conditions. Evaluation has long been acknowledged as one of the weakest links in attempting to solve urban problems. In fact, some agencies have actually done no evaluation and so have little idea of what difference was really made by a program. And those that have evaluated their programs haven't done much better, according to Joseph Wholey, head of the institute's evaluation group. As he puts it, "Most evaluation programs weren't done well and consequently millions of dollars have been wasted." Wholey's group conducted a year-long study of evaluation procedures in fifteen programs administered by major agencies and concluded that none was satisfactory. An example of one of the major problems uncovered by the study is that millions are being spent each year on noncomparable, unrelated evaluations of individual projects that Wholey argues are worthless for program planning on either the national or local level. The value of such evaluation, he adds, is nothing more than to satisfy the demand for paper marked "evaluation." His suggestion to remedy this is simply to do comparable evaluations of groups of projects dealing with the same problem, such as using the same measures and methodologies to compare the results of educating black children of low-income families living in big-city ghettos under a variety of education programs. The study group has come up with over 100 similar suggestions and is now working with such groups as the Department of Labor, OEO, HEW, HUD, and the Model Cities program to develop better evaluation procedures. Wholey points out that the institute plans to extend its evaluative aid to others; for example, teaching community groups to assess local schools and programs against others so they can be better prepared to make their officials accountable for local conditions. The stress on evaluation at the institute is based on its belief that part of the urban problem stems from a failure to think about separate parts of the urban problem, partly caused in the first place by the nation's failure to figure out which of its myriad social programs work and which do not.

Gorham sees the challenges faced by his group as far greater than those initially faced by his alma mater, RAND. He explains, "RAND worked on a lot easier problems—military and strictly technical matters are relatively simple compared to the terrain we are trying to cover here, which is practically unlimited and much more complex. They grew up serving one constituency, the Air Force, while we are already serving many. RAND has been quite effective in instituting ways of defining and achieving goals in the military realm, but in the social realm one has a much greater problem getting people to agree on the goals you want to reach, let alone finding ways to achieve them." He does believe, nonetheless, that the institute will be able to make definite contributions toward improving domestic policies. "I believe," he says, "that our major contributions will be in the areas of new methods for choosing programs, substantive information for assessing programs, and the creation of tools for social policy analysis."

Besides acting as a consultant to agencies of government, the Urban Institute is involved in a variety of specific projects aimed at a particular aspect of the urban problem. These projects fall under the institute's research and experimentation program, designed to answer the need for specific information in urban matters. It is not tied to any specific approach, but rather is tailored to fill gaps in essential areas. Where there is ignorance of a problem, it conducts

227

basic research, and where basic information exists, it attempts to facilitate application of this information. Just as there is no special approach to its research program, there is similarly no preferred technique for conducting research. It would be impossible to cover the scores of projects under way at the institute, but a representative sampling might well start with its attempt to create urban indicators —an example of one effort to create a new tool for policy analysis.

On the assumption that the nation needs objective nontechnical ways to measure the quality of urban life, several researchers at the institute are working on a long-term project toward that end. It is their contention that a set of urban quality indicators can replace hearsay, intuition, and isolated bits of personal information as the major basis for citizen and official decision-making. The indicators also aim to replace government's traditional means of perceiving the quality of life in cities. As Martin V. Jones, one of the researchers, points out, "Our interest in measuring the quality of urban life is a revolt against the present method of looking at everything from the standpoint of dollars—many officials now know little about cities socially except for how much is being spent for this or that." Michael J. Flax, another researcher, adds, "Most of our decisions today are being made in a vacuum—we simply lack even the crudest comparisons between conditions relative to different cities and have little idea of whether things are getting better or worse."

The researchers call their first study a "Model T" version of what they hope urban indicators will be in the future and admit that what they have thus far is really just a crude beginning. This first work is a comparison of social variables in eighteen major American cities over a two-year period. Although only one indicator was used for each of many areas studied—for example, narcotics addiction was used to indicate social disorganization—many indicators will be used to determine each quality area in later studies. The initial study showed the researchers for the first time how cities compared with each other and with themselves for the two years investigated. For the first time, for example, a profile of Washington, D.C., was available that was capable of giving quick, meaningful indices of where that city stands in answer to the question "Is Washington's quality of life improving or deteriorating?" The following report was produced based on a comparison of 1968 vs. 1967:

228

Direction of Change	Quality Area	Indicator
Apparent improvement	Income Level Poverty Health Mental Health Community Concern	Per Capita Income Low-income Households Infant Mortality Rate Suicide Rate United Fund Contributions
Little or No Change	Education Citizen-Participation	Draft Rejection Rate Presidential Voting Rate *
Apparent Deterioration	Unemployment Housing Air Pollution Traffic Safety Racial Equality Social Disintegration Public Order	Percent Unemployed Cost of Housing Air Pollution Index Traffic Death Rate Nonwhite/White Unemployment Narcotics Addiction Rate Robbery Rate

* In the case of Presidential voting the 1964 rates were contrasted with the 1968 rates.

Or to give another example, a fix on Washington's standing relative to eighteen major metropolitan areas yielded the following ratings, with the lower numerical rankings representing more favorable conditions:

2nd—Poverty
4th—Unemployment, Racial Equality
5th—Mental Health
7th—Health, Traffic Safety
8th—Air Pollution
10th—Income Level, Housing
13th—Social Disintegration
14th—Community Concern
16th—Public Order
18th—Education, Citizen Participation

Although the report is admittedly crude, Flax points out that even crude indicators are better than the void that now exists in the field. This void can be illustrated by comparing the paucity of urban figures to a situation in which a doctor would have to try to treat a patient without knowing his pulse, temperature, and nervous response. The research team, working on a similar study on a comparison of the quality of life between cities and their suburbs, is charting many more indicators to describe quality areas—for example, they are looking at eight variables that, together, could indicate the quality of education. Indicators will be collected and tabulated on a continual and broader basis eventually to provide substantial data on urban trends.

An example of the institute's approach to a very specific problem is the "beat commander" program being carried out by its Public Order and Safety Group. It is aimed at making better use of police manpower to control crime and improve police-community relations. A pilot project based on the institute's concept is now being tested in Detroit. According to Peter B. Bloch, a young lawyer on the staff who is directing the project, the pilot experiment involves the creation of small permanent units of seven policemen under the control of a "beat commander." The unit—unlike traditional police precinct operations—is permanently responsible for a small area of a city equivalent to an eighth the size of a normal precinct. The idea is to determine whether small groups of police working continually in the same small area will foster greater responsibility, efficiency, and community confidence. The teams are encouraged to develop unconventional techniques in handling day-to-day problems—for example, members of the team are made available for complaints and assistance for part of the week. New roles for the police are also being encouraged, such as referring a jobless youngster to a job-training program instead of ignoring him, or getting a narcotics addict into a Methadone treatment center instead of booking him and/or ignoring him. It is also hoped that the unit will develop new programs spontaneously, such as starting community improvement efforts in cooperation with church and civic groups. The presumption at the beginning of the program was that it would enable the police to get a new appreciation of the over-all problems of the neighborhood and thereby better serve the public. At the same time, it would serve to overcome the mistrust and ill will held toward the police by many inner-city residents.

230

Experimentation began in May 1970, and to evaluate its first five months in operation the institute retained a veteran police sergeant and a black law student. Although their viewpoints regarding the police were admittedly quite different, the two men voluntarily decided to produce a joint report. They agreed that the program held considerable promise, and both criticized the police and the institute for moving too slowly in expanding the experiment. Certain data backed up their conclusions:

The crime rate went up in the area, paradoxically—a looked-for mark of success, since a rising crime rate may be interpreted as a new willingness to report crimes not previously reported.

The two judges observed better job attitudes on the part of the police in the area, citing as one measure of this estimate the fact that sick leave taken in the experimental area was one third that taken in the precinct as a whole.

The police were able to give quicker service because the time spent responding to the average call within the area was about half that of the average for the city.

Finally, to quote their report, "Surprisingly enough, there has been no opposition to the program, even among the youth. And even more surprising have been the instances in which citizens voluntarily produced supporting evidence for Beat Commander personnel who have been accused of improper conduct by arrestees."

While experimentation continues in the original area, it is currently being expanded to ten new high-crime beats in the city. The institute will monitor these ten areas closely by interviewing their residents before, during, and after experimental periods in order to see if the frequency of victimization from crime, incidence of graft, fear of crime, and level of citizen respect for the police have changed. Meanwhile, New York announced in early 1971 that it would begin a similar experiment with the institute, and according to those at the institute, at least a half dozen other cities are expected to see if the program works for them. Says Peter Bloch, "There are many theories about crime control and police effectiveness. This is one of the few attempts to measure objectively the relative merits of different forms of police organization."

One of the least academic aspects of the institute's work is its Urban Fellows program, which brings in action-oriented civil-rights leaders from the community to form the nucleus of the institute's Urban Analysis Group. These leaders are each enlisted for a year to engage in study and planning in order to develop improved programs for black inner-city residents. Lacy Streeter, a black who has been involved in community programs in both North Carolina and the District of Columbia, is one of the Fellows. Some of the specific projects that he and the other Fellows are involved in include black political participation and its outcome for the community, black economic development, political organization in the inner city, and an identification of the human and financial resources in the black community. Streeter is particularly interested in the area of black economic development and points to some of the issues involved: "First, we're taking an over-all look at the subject, funding levels required and community enthusiasm for development. We are also looking at models and strategies that we can use to bring development programs about. And we're giving a lot of attention to resources for the community from both federal and state sources and intracommunity sources."

Streeter says that much of what he and the other Fellows are looking into has to do with resources that exist but have not been tapped. "There are resources within the black community that have never been marshaled," he says. "We're trying to quantify and identify these items and see how much power there is in the community." He cites the fact that black communities have sororities, lodges, fraternities, and clubs that have never been looked at for what they are: potential resources. They are also trying to pinpoint the potential accessibility of federal funds. He says, "Most black leaders need information on where federal money is, what kinds of programs are conducive to federal funding and how to cut red tape in getting it." He adds that there is often a disastrous lag between the start of a new federal program and its recognition in the black community. "Often," he points out, "people get excited about a program at just about the same time that Washington has committed all the funds." For this reason one of the specific projects that the Fellows are working on is a handbook for community leaders that will try to eliminate this discrepancy as well as give aid on such items as preparing proposals to the government for community projects and improving their chances of acceptance.

While the Urban Fellows are a research entity in themselves, they also serve as advisors to the research program of the rest of the institute and especially as monitors for projects which will have an impact on the inner city. As Streeter puts it, "One of our major functions is to keep this place from becoming an ivory tower."

One of the broader inquiries being undertaken by the institute is aimed at finding new sources of revenue for the cities and exploring the use of fiscal power as a tool for urban reform. The inquiry is being mounted to examine revenue sources from both inside and outside the city—especially user charges and property taxes.

Regarding user charges, the contention is that city services, like water, solid-waste disposal and sewerage have not been priced to assure rational use of services and also bring in reasonable financial return to the cities. All services are being investigated to see if they can be more equitably priced both to control resources and bring in more money. An example of the kind of question the institute is asking is why in so many cases is an industry that disposes large amounts of wastes and detergents charged no more for waste disposal than an industry that is relatively clean. Or: Are present pricing policies on such services as mass transit, sewers, and roads actually encouraging urban sprawl and conspiring so that the inner city is subsidizing the suburbs?

On a second front, erratic, unfair, archaic, and self-defeating tax situations are being attacked by the institute, since property taxes in many localities are rated a major contributor to creating slums, and an effort is being made to single out models for cities and states to use. Landlords who improve housing are often punished with higher taxes while slumlords get the benefits of low taxes and rising land values. In fact, in some cases the tax structure is kindest to those who board up their buildings and let them rot or to those who hoard vacant land.

Other approaches to the financial issue involve questioning certain sacred cows, such as low-tax industrial enclaves in bankrupt urban settings, as well as looking for novel sources of money. In the latter case, for example, several researchers are exploring the means by which unemployment trust funds and state and local retirement funds could be induced to finance the construction of public facilities. This inquiry into urban finances is significant, if for no other reason than that it creates machinery to test whether the cities are getting all the financial aid they can.

The institute is not without its critics. It is being watched closely by other think tanks where there is considerable skepticism as to its value thus far. Most of the criticism, however, is based on the institute's comparative meager output of research reports. Those who work at the institute recognize their susceptibility to the doctrine of "publish or perish," but argue that more reports are not what is going to solve urban problems. In fact, many at the institute are particularly skeptical of adding more paper to the problem. Joseph Lewis, who heads the programs examining urban governments, says, "We are very concerned about the gap that exists between new knowledge and its practical application. With all the urban research that has been paid for, it is almost impossible for a man in local government trying to grapple with a problem to point to one piece of research that has really helped him." He adds, "The job that really has to be done is not more articles in scholarly journals but the transmission of ideas, sound advice, and comprehensive analysis."

"The institute's approach," says Walter Rybeck, who is in charge of its publications and communications program, "is geared to both reports and less formal vehicles of communication." He points out that there will be more reports as the institute makes legitimate findings, but rather than rushing out jargon-laden papers of little consequence, it will concentrate on practical items of use to those facing urban problems on a continuing basis. Meetings and personal contact with decision-makers are some of the "less formal" vehicles of importance to the institute. For example, Rybeck cites as typical meetings with a variety of groups, including Congressmen, to discuss welfare programs; black community leaders, on civil-rights strategy; bankers, to look at new means of financing community projects; and the sponsors of the first Earth Day, to help brainstorm strategies for keeping the environmental movement going.

The Urban Institute is not only the first major urban application of the RAND-like advisory role but it is the first multiagency think tank. When the initial commitment of $5 million from its sponsors for its first three-year period of development runs out, it now has assurances from those agencies of continued funding. It is now also being supported by more agencies than when it started—another indication that it is finding its niche.

Thus far there is little question that the institute is performing a necessary function as an analyst and communicator of ideas. Admittedly some of its findings seem obvious—such as telling the government that its housing policies have neglected "existing stock" or firmly pointing out that evaluation of social problems is generally inadequate, but they are crucial points that need to be made by those with access to the highest levels of government. Should the institute be able to develop in the direction it plans, it will be providing not only remedial findings for federal policy but new programs, analytical tools, and ideas. If it can come up with new plans for financing the nation's impoverished cities, that one function alone will more than justify its existence.

In the future, the institute foresees closer ties to the cities themselves. For starters it is already working with a dozen cities in the application of modern management and budgeting techniques. In addition, Gorham and others at the institute are encouraging individual cities to develop their own capabilities for analysis and research, or, in other words, create small think tanks of their own. The first such group and the one that is being watched most closely by those, including people at the Urban Institute, who think that such groups are needed at the city and state level is a cooperative effort between the city of New York and the RAND Corporation.

3. *Urban RAND*

The City should make an annual determination of the minimum rents needed to cover the full costs of providing well-maintained housing. . . . Rent controls should be revised to allow rent increases up to the appropriate minimum rent. . . .

Families unable to afford these minimum rents should be granted rent assistance adequate to their needs. . . .

Code enforcement should be reformed to insure faster and more effective prosecution of housing code violations, particularly in the case of violations affecting health and safety. . . .

The City's legal and administrative ability to acquire clear title to buildings . . .

235

*should be strengthened so that such build-
ings can be acquired at an earlier stage of
deterioration than is now the case.*

*On an experimental basis, the City should
assist community groups in acquiring rental
housing for nonprofit or cooperative management.*

—Summary of proposals for confront-
ing the rental housing crisis in New
York City in February 1970 by the
New York–RAND Institute

Both the most ambitious and most important program that has
been undertaken by any of the predominantly military think tanks
toward resolving urban problems is the work the RAND Corporation is
doing with the city of New York. Discussion between RAND and the
city was initiated in late 1967 when Mayor John V. Lindsay and his
then Director of the Budget Frederick Hayes asked if the RAND Corporation could give the city some sorely needed analytical aid. Out
of several months of meetings between members of the RAND staff
and members of the mayor's staff came four contracts for work in the
areas of health, housing, fire protection, and police operations. In
January 1968 RAND opened a special-project office on Madison Avenue. Other studies—in welfare administration, budget analysis for
the Economic Development Administration, and water-pollution research—were initiated during the years as plans progressed for the
creation of a permanent nonprofit Project RAND for the city, to be
administered and staffed by RAND and governed by a board jointly
selected by RAND and the city.

The New York–RAND Institute came into being in April 1969 as a
center for urban analysis and research entirely devoted to the problems of New York City. As stated in its Certificate of Incorporation,
the job of the institute is "To conduct programs of scientific research
and study, and to provide reports and recommendations relevant to
the operations, planning and administration of the City of New
York." Funded mainly by the city, the institute's budget is currently
running to about $2.5 million a year. Besides fees it receives from the
city, the RAND Corporation provides about $150,000 a year. In addi-
tion, the institute received some federal money, including a $360,000
grant from the Department of Housing and Urban Development and

a $900,000 three-year grant from the Ford Foundation. Its staff currently is about seventy-five people, of whom approximately fifty are professionals drawn from such areas as mathematics, engineering, law, medicine, economics, and operations research.

Creation of the institute was an unprecedented departure for both a city and a think tank. New York became the first American city with its own permanent think tank, while RAND created an entity that moved the company in an entirely new direction. Facetiously, and no doubt with a certain amount of envy, the departure was labeled "RAND's Second Coming" or "New Incarnation" by others in the field of military analysis.

Peter L. Szanton, a native New Yorker who heads the institute and has been with it from the beginning, says that the enterprise got off to a "bruising start." RAND, he explains, had little experience in doing work for a single city on a substantial basis, while the city had no experience with the kind of analysis that RAND was bringing to it. Since then, he says, "We haven't failed and we have contributed to the city in a variety of areas. We're not going to save the city single-handedly, but we'll get in there and help as best we can. The concept has succeeded thus far if for no other reason than that we have found ways to save the city money."

As stated by Szanton, the objective of the institute can be put simply: "To improve the efficiency of the city's government and by means of those improvements not only save money but improve the quality of life." He believes that the most important factor going for it is that it will take a fresh look at everything it considers and not be bound by old ideas, including, he is quick to point out, those tied to traditional military systems analysis and analysts. He explains, "Of our total employees only about seven come from Santa Monica, with most of the rest being freshly recruited New Yorkers." He adds, "Most urban systems proposals you hear about these days offer little more than a shifting of employees from military or space systems to urban problems." The average institute professional is in his late twenties, makes a shade under $20,000 a year, and was picked from approximately fifty applicants.

Szanton himself is a forty-year-old, good-looking lawyer who graduated from Harvard Law School in 1958. After a clerkship and a short stint with a private law firm, he entered the government by serving subsequent stints on the Policy Planning Staff for International Security Affairs in the office of the Secretary of Defense, in the Bureau of the Budget, and as a part of a Federal Task Force on Government Reorganization. In the parlance of the early 1960's he was, like the Urban Institute's Gorham, one of the "whiz kids" brought in by the Kennedy Administration. Today, he is optimistic about the institute and feels that four factors will act to minimize its chance of failure. First, the institute has approached the city with calculated modesty if not humility. Second, in Szanton's words, "We are willing to work first on the more immediate and operational problems with the idea that we will gradually build up to the grand system for approaching problems." His third point: "We are not going off into a corner to do research, but are doing everything jointly with city officials." Finally, he points to the factor of luck: "The city has been sophisticated in its dealings with us. We were lucky to find a client that's a good consumer of what we have to offer."

But he is the first to admit that considerable skepticism existed as work began for the city, much of it resulting from New York's experience with other outside consultants. One of the reasons the city wanted to work toward a long-term relationship with RAND was the hit-and-run variety of research that had typified much of its earlier use of outside analysts. As in other cities, earlier consultants had produced fat, jargonized, and generally impractical reports, which told the city (in new language) what it already knew, or turned out a public report severely criticizing the people who had commissioned it. What was more, because of the nature of such contracts, the advisers inevitably left when a report was completed. For a city like New York —which, according to the New York *Times*, spent an unprecedented $75 million for outside consultants in 1969—such unsatisfactory arrangements can be quite expensive. Mayor Lindsay pointed out how the RAND relationship would differ when he announced the establishment of the institute: "A common failing of consultive relationships is that the consultant has little interest in implementing the programs it has helped to develop. This is often fatal when it turns out that the hardest part of the implementation is retaining the character of the original idea in the actual program. Compared to previous experiences, we see a welcome willingness on the part of RAND to leave model-building long enough to assist in the application of their new systems in a real agency in a real city." In the same March 1969 announcement, Lindsay noted another general reason for bringing in

238

RAND: "New York City, like all other American cities today, is long on problems, long on politicians, and long on critics. It is short on problem-solvers. It is short on talented people who will go beyond a recital of the mess we're in and devote themselves to finding solutions. In RAND we have people who will roll up their sleeves with us, who will help figure out the right questions to ask, who will frame and evaluate the alternatives for decision."

RAND's approach to the problems of the city has been to focus on the more pressing, short-term problems first, with more ambitious overview and total systems work slated for later. Szanton sees four progressive phases of involvement. The starting point is to look at and aid in the solution of specific problems for city agencies. "This is something we will always be doing," Szanton says. The second phase comes with viewing these problems in a larger framework of the total problems of the city. In the next phase the institute is on top of these linkages between specific problems and devises solutions to larger problems. "For example," he says, "a linkage between a housing and a fire problem can be made as we discover that one percent of the buildings in the city account for thirty to forty percent of the fires. This is the kind of thing that prompts strong, unequivocal recommendations." The final phase—one which Szanton sees as six to ten years away—occurs when the institute has the ability and knowledge to "model" the city as a whole, to view and analyze it as a large-scale system. He says that the final integrated phase is a mammoth intellectual task, a long way from completion.

The work of the institute (and its predecessor, the New York–RAND Project Office) is beginning to have a detectable impact on the city. While no single major change can yet be attributed to the institute, some significant new ideas, experiments, and procedures can be cited. One of the earliest areas of RAND involvement in the city was in the area of fire protection. One project sought to explore the old idea that fires are mathematically random in nature and, for this reason, are not predictable. The institute took the records of over a million past alarms, analyzed the factors surrounding them, such as time, weather, location, type of building, and population characteristics, and incorporated the data into a detailed mathematical model. The model has been used, successfully, to establish what had always been thought to be impossible: relatively accurate predictions of the occurrence of fires and false alarms. Besides being a tool for Fire Department planners in positioning men and equipment, the model shows promise as a crude urban barometer or early warning system. The number of fires and false alarms in a community has been shown to be closely related to other social and economic factors in the neighborhood, such as deterioration in housing, juvenile delinquency, and a high rate of migration in and out of the neighborhood, and so weekly analysis of alarm data may serve as a signal of community improvement or further deterioration.

This model and others of varying degrees of sophistication have already had an impact on departmental practices. For instance, modeling showed that alarm rates in the city between 3 P.M. and 1 A.M. were twice as high as those for the rest of the day. It further showed that minor events—such as rubbish fires and false alarms—were highest during this period. While these incidents did not require a full response on the part of the Fire Department, it was standard policy to send out three engines, a pumper and two ladders to each alarm. The institute's analysis showed that this policy was tying up too much equipment during peak periods when alarms were likely to be minor or false, so that other alarms got much less than the standard response. Furthermore, when additional equipment was needed, it was hard to find. The institute suggested an adaptive response policy that involved varying the number of men and equipment dispatched, depending on the likelihood of given types of alarms, hazards, and time of day. This suggestion was made after institute analysis showed that during the peak periods of the day the adaptive response policy would actually give full response to major fires faster than the old policy. This strategy, along with another to add to the size of the force during peak periods, became department policy in late 1969. Then, quite unexpectedly, the institute discovered that the old rule about dispatching the unit closest to an incident was questionable since units have widely different workloads. The institute has since helped the department introduce new procedures for determining the most effective unit to call in response to an alarm.

Another role that the institute has played is in searching for and introducing new technology to fire protection. One of its most dramatic discoveries is "slippery water"—water spiked with minute quantities of a cheap, nontoxic chemical, a long-chain polymer, that reduces water turbulence, thereby making it flow faster and farther. In May 1969 a public display of "slippery water" at the Fire Department's training center on Welfare Island showed that an ounce of the chemical added to 200 gallons of water increased the flow of the water from the hose by 60 percent and allowed the water to travel twice the old distance. "Slippery water" offers more power for conventional hoses and opens the option of using smaller hoses for greater speed and maneuverability. The city has decided that by 1975 all equipment will be outfitted with the chemical mixing chambers needed to use "slippery water," and the Fire Department has estimated that when all its pumpers are so equipped an increase in departmental efficiency will be gained that otherwise would cost $15 million a year to achieve.

Another technological innovation being investigated by the institute is the possible use of sensitive, reliable "ionization" detectors as the basis for an early-warning and detection system for fires. Though such a warning system has been long thought to be too costly and technologically difficult, the institute has examined a system that includes the detection of fires and the automatic transmission of alarms that is both technologically feasible and not overly expensive. Although several detectors would be required for each building, they would cost only about twelve dollars apiece per year. This concept is undergoing further investigation by the institute and the Fire Department.

Still another way in which the institute has had an impact on the city's fire-protection operations is in the area of communications. Some of the changes effected have been small—such as recommendations for new equipment and improvement in radio-frequency allocations for the department's radio network —while others have been much more significant. One of the most interesting changes has been new procedures for dispatching fire-fighting units. Early in the RAND work it was decided that a critical aspect of fire protection was the dispatching centers linking alarms to fire-fighting units. A researcher was assigned to the Brooklyn Communications Office, the city's busiest, where night after night he observed the operations. The researcher, Arthur Swersey, returned after weeks of observation to construct a model of dispatching operations. Swersey's model not only showed that there were serious bottlenecks in the system but that the system was close to breaking down. By simulating the operations of the center it was found that two previous suggestions for improvement—increasing the number of dispatchers and using high-speed

241

computers—would have very little positive effect on the system. The change that was suggested by the model grew out of its determination that the critical bottleneck was occurring not at the point where the alarms came in but at the point where decisions were made as to how to respond to the alarms. The institute recommended dividing operations at the decision point, and the department accepted it and put it into operation in July 1969. At peak periods the change has enabled the Brooklyn center to reduce response time from eleven minutes to two. This and other communications changes at the Brooklyn installation are now being used as guidelines for improving other dispatching centers.

Future work in fire protection will include focusing on detection and warning systems and deeper analysis of the causes—both technological and sociological—of fire. It will also assist the department in developing a computer-based management, information, and control system.

Work during the same period for the New York Police Department and other law-enforcement agencies, such as the Department of Corrections and the Mayor's Criminal Justice Coordinating Council, has concentrated on operating policies. The institute's contributions in this realm have run from on-the-spot advice on improving communications procedures to long studies leading to suggestions of new ways of assigning patrol strength and allotting that strength to precincts. It has contributed to new procedures, including one credited with reducing from eight to two hours the average amount of time spent by the arresting officer in booking a suspect. In this case, after long study, the institute concluded that streamlined procedures, along with a change in the place of booking from the precinct to the divisional headquarters, would significantly cut booking time. It is estimated that the time saved in booking now is equivalent to adding 440 additional patrolmen to the force. The institute has reviewed all aspects of police force deployment, has addressed the problem of recruiting and retaining minority-group members for the force, determined the optimal number of emergency operators to have on hand at various hours of the day, and worked to alleviate delay in police response to calls. A RAND analysis of calls and radio-car deployment was instrumental in getting a "fourth platoon" experiment going to add to the existing three eight-hour "platoons" or shifts. As a result of trends spotted in the analysis, in late 1969 an added platoon was placed in the Bronx from the hours of 6 P.M. to 2 A.M. In its first six-month period of operation arrest rates rose more than 40 percent over the preceding six months. Because of that experiment, a "fourth platoon" now operates throughout the city.

A more recent area of institute involvement is health care. It is working to develop a major new program that will establish 20 to 30 new Community Mental Health Centers beyond the five now in operation—an achievement that would reverse the present situation where therapists and doctors spend a surprisingly small percentage of their time with patients, less than half of a doctor's time in most cases. The institute is working to solve this problem by redefining the functions of various employees of mental-health centers. It is also looking into the legal problems involved in creating community health services tailored to the need of a specific community—such as city-run free clinics in areas like the East Village, where emphasis would be placed on dealing with drugs and venereal-disease problems. Other health work is geared to appraising and working toward better out-patient services, describing and quantifying the demand for services by the seriously mentally ill, and looking into specific health threats.

Results of its inquiries into specific health problems have led to direct action. A study of lead poisoning showing its widespread threat to children led to an expansion of the city's lead-poisoning program. An inquiry into the problem of venereal diseases revealed that while the city was effectively locating and fighting syphilis, it was neglecting its program to deal with a growing gonorrhea problem—a finding that has affected city plans to expand its VD-control programs. Other institute findings beg for action. An analysis of alcoholism in the city concluded that the vast majority of alcoholics come from neighborhoods where there are few treatment facilities. Its work on drugs is just beginning but will concentrate on what aspects of drug use should be prevented and what programs for dealing with addicts actually show the most promise.

Similarly broad in scope has been the institute's exhaustive series of analyses of the economics of housing in the city. Its work on programs to reverse the deterioration of housing has already led to the conclusion that existing rent-control laws have contributed to the deterioration because they prevented rents from reflecting the long-run cost of providing housing. Some of its recommendations in this

243

area have already been reflected in changes in rent-control regulations, while others are being considered. Prior to 1970, for example, increases in controlled rents were tied to apartment turnover; now they are tied to owner costs and improvements as a result of one RAND recommendation. An extensive set of RAND-generated housing-code reforms are being considered and experimented with by the city. It has also embarked on a series of detailed analyses of publicly assisted housing. One such analysis of housing geared to middle-income families with children showed that it was in fact benefiting people without children who had incomes that by most criteria would be categorized as upper rather than middle. Proposals for changing the entrance rules for such projects have been submitted to the city's Housing and Development Administration.

The institute is also working with city agencies on specific problems in the areas of welfare, water pollution, economic development, migration of municipal resources. Although it has done little work in such areas as transportation, air pollution, education, and waste disposal, it plans to involve itself increasingly in these subjects. Besides its work under contract with city agencies, a portion of its efforts is self-sponsored—that is, paid for either with Ford Foundation grant money or from its own retained earnings. This self-supported program serves as a middle ground for work the institute thinks may later interest the city or is valuable but for some reason has been dropped by its original sponsor. An institute-sponsored effort to develop a mathematical model of Jamaica Bay for use in investigating alternative means of water-pollution control has recently attracted the sponsorship of the Environmental Protection Administration. On the other hand, some work that was dropped by the Police Department is continuing under institute sponsorship. (Work for the police was a matter of some controversy from the beginning and was, according to sources at the institute, dropped for the same reason that it was controversial in the first place: the threat of civilians without official status becoming heavily involved in police operations and departmental power blocs.)

In every area of inquiry, new alternatives are being looked at, including some that have received little previous attention. After finding, for example, that despite the tightness in the housing market an increasingly large number of structurally sound buildings were being abandoned or closed because their owners considered them unprofitable, the institute started investigating city-assisted ownership of certain types of buildings by nonprofit or cooperative groups. It is investigating the not-so-obvious and reaching surprising conclusions, such as that certain forms of welfare, like aid to families with dependent children, increase with a general rise in employment rather than with a rise in unemployment. One hypothesis to explain this seeming paradox is that upsurges in the job market for low-income males has been concentrated in the suburbs, causing heads of households to leave the city temporarily to take suburban jobs—and thus contributing to family instability, which in turn requires welfare services. The institute's belief is that uncovering and understanding such not-so-obvious relationships is essential to urban reform.

A large part of the justification for the institute is that it will be able to help the city out of its deepening economic crisis. The cost of running New York is rising 15 percent a year, while revenues are growing at only 6 percent a year. This differential portends further deterioration of services on the way to bankruptcy. The institute is there to buck that trend. In order to succeed it must save money while improving services—a prodigious feat by any standard. An innovation like "slippery water" is looked upon as an example of a step in the right direction because it both improves a service and is an improvement that will ultimately save money. In the future, the institute will examine many of the city's services and institutions with an economical eye toward controversial steps like handing a private contractor a basic municipal service (snow removal, say, or certain health services), or charging city residents and businesses a user fee for certain services (for waste disposal, say, or consumption of large amounts of water).

A major program to help solve the city's economic ills has involved the institute in the city's budget. It is beginning to apply the planning, programming and budgeting system (PBS) that RAND applied to various federal operations in the 1960's to New York City of the 1970's. The system, like so many of the management concepts developed for Washington by the think tanks, is firmly rooted in common sense. As applied to the city, it requires that each year an agency state its long-range objectives (usually five years), identify alternatives for meeting its objectives, explain why they are choosing specific programs, and what they hope to accomplish over the years and at what cost. In short, it requires urban bureaucrats to think about and plan for the future while looking at present alternatives. To give a more concrete example, one element of RAND's planning, programming and budgeting system is looking at "life-cycle costing" (think-tankese for figuring out how much a program will cost over its lifetime) which reduces the likelihood of making commitments to programs with small initial outlays that will grow to such an extent that they cannot be afforded in later years. As reasonable as this sounds, it stands in direct contrast to the urban *status quo*: the departments just submitting an annual budget to get by for another year without being forced to think about the long-term implications of expenditures. The institute is helping the city develop the capacity to do such analysis on its own.

New York, like most cities, has general objectives for its economic development, and full employment for all of its inhabitants is one of them. Major areas of RAND's investigation in this field include: migration in and out of the city, income as it relates to New York's labor force, and employment as it relates to welfare policy and wage policies. The institute work will hit hard at things as they are. It has found, for example, that in recent years the city has been losing low- and middle-income jobs and gaining in the high-income bracket. The institute seeks to learn how city policies may be contributing to this trend.

The New York–RAND Institute has not made a lot of noise outside the corridors of the New York bureaucracy and has, in Szanton's words, ". . . been very shy about publicity." This shyness is attested to by the fact that most New Yorkers have never heard of the institute. Nonetheless, for those who manage cities or hope to give aid to cities it is being watched with great interest, just as for others in the think-tank business it is an experiment that may be tried elsewhere. Szanton says, "Our purpose is not to be a prototype, but it is inevitable that others will observe us to determine the style, scale, and size of other operations which will emerge. We cannot dodge the fact that our success or failure will and should provide lessons for the rest of the nation." Other alliances are already emerging that could deepen in the years or months ahead. RAND, which has performed a good deal of work for other cities, is seeking another relationship like the one it has with New York. MITRE is involved in a variety of analytical chores for the state of Massachusetts, Los Angeles is getting aid from a small group called the Los Angeles Technical

Services Corporation, TEMPO, the Battelle Memorial Institute, the Stanford Research Institute, the Institute for Defense Analyses, and others have current contracts with cities and states which, according to their officers, could—and they hope will—lead to more permanent arrangements.

Dedication, honesty, and good work by RAND—coupled with the city's ability to listen—can eventually produce a basic justification for such think tanks: improvement of the quality of urban life in America. The challenges facing the institute cannot be minimized. Improving things at all in New York is no small trick for a relatively limited group with a tight budget. The problem is compounded by the question of trust. One researcher sums up the dilemma in this area: "The police are extremely leery of us, while some of the students we've worked with at first think we're here to help the police bring in helicopters to control the ghetto."

Another immediate challenge is survival itself. By March 1971 the institute was in the awkward position of not having been paid since the previous July, and it had no prospects of getting its money. The reason was a battle between Mayor Lindsay and City Controller Abraham D. Beame over the use of consultants. Beame was upset with Lindsay's ever-increasing use of consultants and further had uncovered what appeared to be conflicts of interest in several contracts (although none involved RAND); he demanded new procedures for handling such contracts. Lindsay would not budge on his right to hire consultants, and Beame was holding up all consulting fees. The standoff was such that the Mayor had not even presented the institute's bill to the city, knowing that it would be held up. Luckily, there was enough in the kitty in Santa Monica to keep the New York operation going, but this form of support could not go on indefinitely. Should the institute survive this particular crisis there are other real political pitfalls ahead. A new Mayor could easily give the institute the kiss of death by simply not supporting it, a possibility not at all out of the question since the institute is looked upon as Lindsay's baby.

While the institute is working with a real city in trying to come to grips with very real problems, other groups are working with theoretical cities toward the same end. One such group is Environmetrics Inc. of Washington, D.C.

4. Computer Cities

Your city is approximately 133 square miles in area with a population of about 1.03 million. The surrounding county area (which encompasses 492 square miles) has a population of about 513,000 persons.

Big City's downtown core, bisected by a bay inlet, is a concentration of commercial and industrial activity nearly a hundred years old.

Until 1945, the downtown area was the focus of employment as well as residential and cultural activities. With its relatively slow population growth, it easily provided room for residential development close to downtown.

—Typical introduction to a city given to the players of City Model, a game developed and played by Environmetrics, Inc., Washington, D.C.

It would have been hard to predict still more problems for the already problem-ridden city, but they hit and all at once. A severe confidence gap was splitting the citizenry from its nearly new administration. For one, a promised "State of the City" report from the city council was long overdue, and a coalition of citizens' groups had marched on the council chambers to demand a verbal report. Blunders on the part of officials prompted the group to walk out. The final straw came when the chairman of the city council stated that he felt one of the most needed changes for the city was to bring whites back into the city from the suburbs—not exactly the thing to say to a group yelling about runaway rents, rats, and overcrowding.

On the heels of the walkout came these disclosures from the city government: A promised school-construction program was not going to start on time; due to what the administration termed "computer error," city employees had been vastly overpaid, and taxes would have to be increased again even though the city realized the fact that personal debt among its residents was at an all-time high. The administration then did the only thing it felt was right in these circumstances: It offered itself up to a "special election." After a long series of meetings between officials and citizen groups, it was decided that the election would be bypassed and the two groups would continue talking, stop generalizing and see if, in the year ahead, the severe problems could be unscrambled by both groups working together.

All these events transpired during one round of a game called City Model, played regularly at a small nonprofit research outfit called Environmetrics. Walking onto the tastefully appointed floor in a Washington office building where it is located, one may pick up the incongruous odor of a gymnasium. The rigors of the game itself are the reason, for it is likely that somewhere between twenty to 100 tense people are off in the game room participating in an advanced round and sincerely struggling with the decay of an urban complex.

Environmetrics has one major function: creating and refining games that can be used to simulate problems on a metropolitan scale. The games are cities—compressed in time and space with the aid of a computer—that are meant to be played with by people who actually grapple with the problems of real cities. Put another way: It creates cities to be loaned out for education and experimentation. Environmetrics' "product" is experience offered through a neutral tool. Peter House, the company's thirty-three-year-old president, makes the point of neutrality clearly: "We don't represent a school of thought or a theory. Rather we're here to build replicas of reality. Our principle is employing intellectual honesty in building these models so that others can better understand reality. When we design a city we check our egos at the door and work to make them as free from bias as we can humanly make them. The models are neutral—like hammers, they can be used to build or break things."

City Model is the most advanced game in the Environmetrics stable. It was preceded by games called Region I, Region II, and City I. The models have been played by a wide range of people in government, business, and education, including such diverse individuals and groups as the editor of a local underground newspaper, former Agriculture Secretary Orville Freeman, a high-school class, the top administrators of the Philadelphia public-school system, a group of young scholars studying at the White House, officials of the corporation that is developing the "new town" of Columbia, Maryland, and leaders of the black community in Washington, D.C.

A typical game begins as each participant is given a role to play. One may be a key individual, such as the mayor, head of the board of education, a suburban commissioner, or be picked to represent a bloc of citizens or a group of private interests, such as landlords. The players are then given a city from the repertoire of possible cities in the model. The city can vary in size and form of government, depending on the problems to be dealt with—for instance, a city with the general demographic, geographic, and governmental characteristics of Savannah, Georgia, can be set up on demand. Each player is given a detailed over-all briefing about the city he and the others will be working with. The game goes on to describe neighborhoods in both the city and the suburbs, the form of government, recent political issues and current problems. In general, it describes a growing, sprawling, and generally healthy suburban situation and a city that is beset with such problems as a deteriorating school system and high unemployment. The city that is usually played with bears considerable resemblance to Baltimore, Maryland.

In addition, each player is given very detailed information on his own role in the game. The mayor of Big City might find, among other things, that his city's total debt is $479 million, while his suburban counterpart, the county chairman, finds that the burden of suburban debt is only $58 million. Each player representing a social group is advised where his people stand in income, debt, level of education, taxation, welfare, recreation time, and the like. Similarly, each player who controls buildings is given information on their location, value, and inhabitants. All of this data is provided by a computer print-out. Each player is also given computer-generated maps of the metropolitan area which display in detail the condition of neighborhoods, building ownership, bus routes, locations of schools and factories, and other similar data that quickly orients one to the patterns of the city and its surroundings.

The game is played in several game rooms. The main room is large and well lighted, with all accessories in black. In the center is a pit containing a scale model of the city. Around the pit is the "bargaining rail," a plush upholstered circular bar around which the players meet to wheel and deal like traders at the pit of a commodities exchange. The social and economic sectors of the community work out in the main room. To the side of the main room are a series of offices where the powers of urban and suburban government operate. In addition there is a long conference room for the city council and offices for heads of such departments as education and planning and zoning.

The game is divided into rounds, each representing a year in the life of the city, that last for half a day apiece. The first round, or year, begins as the three major participating groups—social, economic, and government—begin to make decisions to effect change. Each player has a list of actions at his disposal. A social decision-maker, for example, can call a strike or a boycott, vote in elections that are called periodically, or reallocate the time that his people spend in various activities (such as politics or recreation). There are no rules as such, so that coalitions may be formed, seemingly irrational decisions may be made, or political doctrines imposed. A social decision-maker representing a large bloc of unemployed may, if he so chooses, decide to do nothing, work to get new jobs in his area, or latch onto a radical plan that might take any shape from forcing his unemployed charges into the wealthier suburbs—where, presumably, there are more jobs —to collectivizing his neighborhood. Everybody has the ability to change things in his sector by writing out instructions on a slip of paper that is copied on a teletype and fed to the computer. Shortly after the end of each round, the computer "works out" all the instructions fed to it, and before the beginning of the "next year" new packages of information come back from the computer showing the players how their sector of the city has fared for the year. As a result of all the actions taken, any given player invariably finds changes in the sector of the city under his charge. Even if he does nothing, the actions of others will have an impact in his realm. To illustrate, a social decision-maker who sits back and lets taxes and rents be raised by others finds that his people's debts are much higher and, presumably, so is their dissatisfaction.

Invariably the results of the first year's play provide surprises. A social decision-maker who might have decided that his people will spend more time in trying to better themselves through adult education finds that his well-meaning plan lacked one realistic dimension: He had not lobbied with the board of education for expanding adult-education programs, so there was no room in the existing small programs to accommodate the sudden onrush of new students. The computer picks up this discrepancy and tells the social decision-maker that not only have his people wasted time trying to get into education programs that were not there but that their level of dissatisfaction with the city has increased. In another such example, a well-meaning mayor makes a decision to provide free bus transportation, which he thinks will help the residents of the inner city. He is told by the computer that his eager do-gooding has not been carefully thought out because he had forgotten to amend bus routes to serve the inner city, where few routes ran, and all that he really did was to improve the lot of the bus-riding suburban commuter by giving him a free ride. Then there is the kind of case in which a landlord comes to an agreement with a citizens' coalition to turn tenements into cooperative apartments, only to find that his grand plan has been checked by the existence of strict zoning laws which a city administration had just put into the computer as a means of preventing further slum deterioration. In this case, the computer served as a check on two well-intentioned but uncoordinated actions. Still another case in this vein is that of the administration that boosts welfare payments without coordinating that boost with suburban welfare packages so that its action brings about a large migration of suburban poor into the city, compounding problems of city debt, unemployment, and overcrowded housing.

As the rounds progress, elections are held, new and sometimes unlikely coalitions are formed, new projects in housing and education are kicked off, and, in a real sense, the actions and institutions of a city are simulated. Since there are virtually no rules, anything may happen: newspapers and radio stations are formed to boost or oppose candidates, walkouts are staged, bribes are offered, lobbies are established, and policies are created. New institutions are a definite possibility. If, as one group did, it is decided that it would be interesting to determine the impact on the economy of a Disneyland in one of the city's large parks, the computer will dutifully create such an institution.

There is nothing to prevent experimentation. One group created a Marxian coalition of the people and the government who then struggled against and smashed the capitalists who controlled housing. Often these experiments provide the most interesting lessons. Another group banded together to create a "new town" but failed because it tried to move too quickly and, as the computer dispassionately indicated, the players had used up all the investment capital in the urban area. Still another group playing the same game established a Model Cities type of program in one of the most problem-ridden areas of the metropolis. Thanks to cooperation offered by other elements in the city, they succeeded in wiping out unemployment in the Model Cities area, but by not keeping track of resources, they caused unemployment figures to creep up in all the other areas of the city. In another game the players chose to assess the effect of a major shake-up in transportation patterns and its impact on jobs. The computer was instructed to destroy a tunnel that ran under the bay inlet bisecting the city; as a result, unemployment rose immediately, revenues went down, and, later, entirely new employment patterns emerged. And in one recent game a social decision-maker who was unable to improve the condition of his people through government or the economic sector instructed the computer to destroy two major factories and compute the economic effect on the city. His action attracted immediate and continuing attention as the rest of the city became aware of the unemployment and small depression he had caused.

Such experimentation, however, is not practiced in most games as players grapple with such mundane items as taxation, rent control, the city budget, bus routes, improving schools, zoning restrictions, and launching new public-housing programs. Typically, as the rounds progress, players become more and more aware of the dynamics of their city. Large public-works programs have scant effect the first year or two, save for increasing taxes; there are few if any simple solutions and the suburbs are, like it or not, a major factor in the life of the city. Keeping the players honest and often frustrated, the computer in round after round tracks human decisions, registers taxes, recomputes the city budget, monitors migration to and from the suburbs, assesses land values, measures the impact of boycotts and strikes, enters changes in the law, and spends money. There is no typical end to the game. After five or six "years" of intense play—depending on who is playing and how they play—the city may be in shambles, a little better off, or on its way to vast improvement. It has happened in some games, for example, that the city is greatly improved but the suburbs are in a state of deterioration. Or after players have introduced bribery and corruption the city is no better off after a long series of rounds but is involved in a major reform movement. Similarly, there is no typical response by the players who have participated in the City Model. To many, the game is a significant educational experience. Some are bothered by their failure in trying to save the city. Others see it as little more than an amusing diversion. A number find it mind-jarring and feel that they would have to play again before they can comment on it.

The author played the game for three hectic days with a diverse group including a physicist, playing the game as part of a self-administered program to become an urban problem-solver; a curious electronics-company executive, interested in the computer aspects of gaming; and a nun, who was there to get a clearer appreciation of the urban dilemma. In three ten-hour sessions the players had taken a problem-beset city and, first, made things worse and then seemed to be on the track of making them better. The staff felt that the group had generally played well but had been too self-conscious about their roles at first. Beyond that, the staff left it up to the players to evaluate.

The young physicist was extremely skeptical, insisting, "If telling us that running a city is a very tough job is the purpose of the game, you're belaboring the obvious." Others argued that that lesson, driven home graphically, was enough. The electronics executive, who had had an extremely difficult time as the city's manager, admitted that he had approached the game confident of his administrative skills and left it with that confidence shaken. In rebutting the physicist he said that he had abstractly known that running a city was tough but he had now obtained an appreciation of how tough. He suggested that if more executives could play the game, a new and more constructive mood would develop in the business community, which today glibly insists that problems of the cities can be solved by better management and a few new programs. The nun came out of the game convinced that its value went beyond illustrating how tough the problems were but presented a rare opportunity to experiment with new ideas. Like others, she felt that the first game was a fine warm-up, but it would have to be played again before she could really start experimenting. All agreed that the game had been demanding, frustratingly real, and confidence-shattering.

Environmetrics' president Peter House sees two major uses for the games. "They are laboratories in which researchers and urban planners can test their theories without having to try them in real cities on real people," he says, adding, "It's cheaper then renting a real city." Second, the models can be used by students from high school on up to learn to deal with urban problems in a unique manner. House points out that planners, policy-makers, educators, and students of urban planning all face the very real problems of the city but have only specialized academic studies to guide them in their attempts at problem-solving. He believes that games and simulations fall in the middle, offering a totally new approach to coming to grips with the problems.

As an educational tool the games throw open many possibilities. On a general level, they give the student the chance to see the complexity of the problems. House says, "We don't teach anything—we just let students play and teach themselves. The student who thinks he can really remedy a problem with a new law and then sit back and expect it to work will find that things don't operate that easily." Several school courses have used the games already, and the National Science Foundation has given the company a grant to get the game into more universities. Environmetrics is developing a scheme whereby many high schools and colleges will be able to play the City Model remotely via teletypes tied to the central computer.

Another aspect of the games is that it can help educate a man for a specific task. House says, "A Harvard Ph.D. who is going to Cleveland as a planner can play a version of the game that most closely approximates the situation in Cleveland, giving him 'experience' before he goes on the job."

House, who works with his shoes off, paces as he talks and spins off ideas about cities and models with computerlike rapidity. He got into the field of computer modeling after a stint at the Department of Agriculture as a tax expert and then having taken his doctorate in public administration from Cornell. He feels his young firm has passed its early tests by coming up with realistic models that have gained wide recognition for verisimilitude. His plans for the future are ambitious. A new game, Metropolitan Model, is being financed by the U.S. Office of Education and will be much more complex than City Model as it adds such variables as joint public and private land use, more public institutions, and even soil type. Still another new game, Regional Model, to be a complex model of a multicounty area, is be-

255

ing prepared with backing from the Department of Agriculture. A major long-range concept under development is that of "modular modeling," which would permit the simulation of virtually any urban or environmental situation. The system would have models at five levels—national, regional, metropolitan, central city, and neighborhood. At each of these levels there would be modules or sections representing the economic, political, physical, and social aspects of that level. While work was proceeding at any one level—say, the central city—the other levels would operate on their own, automatically, directed by the computer. In other words, the players or experimenters, just as in real life, would operate with uncontrollable factors— with such things as weather, national economic trends, and federal and state actions provided by the computer—as well as with controllable factors initiated by the players at their own level. Players would be affecting and being affected by a model of the entire nation. Once these individual models are designed and integrated, the result will be the Environmental Model, which would theoretically allow for every sort of playing possibility—a national ecological decision could be traced through the physical modules on different levels of society just as a neighborhood rent strike could be traced to its effect on the county economic module.

Work is beginning on the modular concept, but House says that due to the challenges of putting it together, including both technical problems and the immense job of collecting and assimilating data, it will probably take between five and ten years before the scheme can be realized and tested. Once it is developed, he feels it will offer dramatic new methods for urban problem-solving. One that he mentions is that of "action-oriented studies," where specific policy decisions can be sought and then tested before being put into action. For instance, a city trying to resolve the question of how to deliver a mass-transit system to benefit the maximum number of citizens would send its planners to the model to test rapidly a large variety of alternative schemes, routes, and mixes of types of transportation. The plans could be tested in a few days for their impact on the city and the region over a period of years. House is also hopeful that such work will help to frame a general urban systems theory to aid scholars, researchers, and theorists in understanding the dynamics of the national environment. Such a general theory would consist of subtheories in specific areas—for example, a theory in mass transportation would be derived from handling a number of cases like the one mentioned above.

Such use of sophisticated electronic games for nonmilitary use is not new, nor is Environmetrics' idea of creating urban games an exclusive one. At present there are something on the order of forty to fifty games and simulations in some form of development that attempt to come to grips with one or another aspect of the urban dilemma. Urban simulation and gaming are new arts just beginning to come into their own. Whether they will have a strong positive impact on the urban situation remains to be seen. Peter House, for one, believes that they can be as effective as people want them to be. They will be useful to those who sincerely want to help, nothing more than expensive playthings to those who are indifferent.

House's point is driven home when one looks at less theoretical models with more immediate application to the planner or official with a problem. Here it is most obvious that the models are effective only when a definite solution is sought and its seekers are willing to apply it. Researchers at the System Development Corporation are working on models aimed at solutions in single areas. This group of models operates on the basic assumption that many problems are solved by the proper allocation of resources—whether it be the best place to locate firehouses, how to deal fairly with political reapportionment, where to situate a new airport, or achievement of racial integration of a school system. A team at SDC, led by V. V. Almindinger, has developed a series of such models geared to using factual information from the 1970 Census as their data base.

The integration model serves as a good illustration of how these models work only when a community is sincerely interested in solving a problem. In the prototype model the town of Turners Falls, Massachusetts, and its four schools are used to show how the model can test integration plans to determine which will minimize cost, disruption, distance traveled to school by children, and busing. The computer keeps tabs on many variables—such as the number of seats filled, racial balance, and mean time spent traveling to school by pupils—as different plans are tested. At one point in a demonstration of the model the following situation existed in the four schools:

	Number of whites	Number of blacks	Mean distance to school in minutes
School 1	100	6	8.4
School 2	53	118	9.2
School 3	451	29	11.2
School 4	88	79	17.0

The computer was instructed to see if a plan would work in which no school could be more than 75 percent white without appreciably increasing the mean distance to school in minutes or overcrowding any school. In a few seconds the computer plan came back with this result:

	Number of whites	Number of blacks	Mean distance to school in minutes
School 1	100	57	10.6
School 2	64	53	9.6
School 3	360	28	9.8
School 4	88	53	18.5

In this case, the schools are closer to being integrated and the time spent getting to school has, on the average, gone up only .7 of a minute; however, because of the constraints put on the model (not to overcrowd and not to add much time to school), the third school is more than 75 percent white and some students have not been placed. This particular plan is imperfect, and more plans need to be tried. Plan after plan can be imposed on the computer as variables are manipulated—for example, new bus routes can be mapped out and tested in order to produce fuller integration and reduce the time to get to school. The advantage of the model is not that it is going to hit upon an optimum plan right away but that many plans can be quickly tested and compared.

As with the other two approaches to urban problems—a policy analysis group for federal social programs and a think tank in the service of a single city—the efforts of those working on gaming and simulation at Environmetrics and elsewhere are still in the pioneering stages. All three of these methods rely heavily on techniques, such as modeling and program budgeting, originally developed for analysis in other areas. By the very nature of the complex problems they are attacking, the urban challenge is unquestionably the most difficult one posed yet for the think-tank concept—and certainly the most important in determining the future of that concept. Equally unquestionably, there is no area in American life today where advances in science and technology are so poorly geared to reality. A battle for priorities is in full swing in America, a fact that has not been missed by those in science, technology, and academia. Only the future will tell whether they can effectively serve as the bridge between those with the knowledge needed to solve these enormous problems and those with the power to do so.

X

CENTERS TO
ALL SIDES

---

1. Public Think Tanks

> *The "establishment" and the "dissidents"*
> *have found a common ground. They both*
> *want clean air, clean water, more open*
> *spaces and less noise. At a "think tank"*
> *session at Arlie House in the Virginia*
> *countryside near Warrenton 100 students*
> *from colleges across the country—with*
> *funds provided by the federal government—*
> *spent the weekend trying to figure out the*
> *best way to foment a revolution for a better*
> *environment.*

> —From an article entitled "Think
> Tank Spans Establishment–Dissident
> Gap," by Roberta Hornig, the Wash-
> ington *Star*, October 26, 1969

Yehezkel Dror, an Israeli policy research expert and a student of
the think-tank phenomenon, has offered three predictions on the future of think tanks:

1. Greater think-tank redundancy—more and more of them in
general and more and more of them working in any given area of
policy.

2. Think tanks emerging as educational institutes for training

policy professionals and policy scientists.

3. The establishment in the United States of a Constitutional basis for think tanks working directly for the public.

His first prediction seems safe, since proposals for new think tanks abound and new ones pop up with regularity. So, too, does the second: There is much evidence of major think tanks teaching their arts both in their own institutions and through universities. The third prediction, however, is more questionable. Dror admits that he is speculating on the basis of the premise that future issues will become harder and harder to solve as they grow more complex. From this he concludes that the government will eventually have to create public think tanks that report directly to the people. One can seriously question such a conclusion since public think tanks would, of course, be expensive to create and, once functioning, would be a thorn in the side of government if they were truly public.

Part of the prediction, however, makes sense and is already coming true, for there is a definite trend toward public (but nongovernmental) think tanks. Today there are a score of institutions that fit the description of "public think tank" and serve at least a percentage of the public. Though they span an ideological range almost as diverse as the nation itself, they have certain traits in common. They operate without being dependent on federal money and in most cases reject it as a matter of principle. Their finished work is usually never proprietary in the industrial sense and never has the secret stamp of an agency affixed to it. As a class, they try to influence decisions, not in the vested role of contractor but from outside. They are not primarily action groups or lobbies, though they sometimes move in those directions; they are mainly intellectual bases for grappling with issues. Their usual form of financing is foundation grants, bequests, gifts, sales of their publications, and public solicitations.

As free outsiders not dependent on those they advise for support, these think tanks are in a unique position. Unlike the "captive" adjuncts to government like RAND, they do not get into the closed-door meetings where policy is made and are restricted in this form of influence. Since they are not for hire and nobody's captive they are in a superior position to make trenchant public criticism and open the major policy-making debates to a larger audience. It is on this ability to make policy debates lively, to the point, and public that the "public" think tanks must be judged.

Probably the best known of the "public" think tanks is the Center for the Study of Democratic Institutions. To the "straight" think-tank world represented by RAND, the Stanford Research Institute, and IDA, the Center is the place singled out as an example of the diversity of the think-tank world. As expressed by a public-relations man for the Stanford Research Institute, a fairly typical attitude is "Don't call us a think tank—we've got more to do than think. We produce. I'll tell you what a think tank is—it's that place down in Santa Barbara. Those guys are paid to think. That's all they have to do: think."

2. The Center: Dialogue on a Hill

The Center for the Study of Democratic Institutions is not a think tank hired to do the planning that public agencies or private business cannot or will not do for themselves. Neither is it a refuge for scholars who want to get away from it all to do their research and write their books.

It is an organized group, rather than a collection of individuals. It is an organization of men who are free of any obligation except to join in the effort to understand the subjects they have selected to study.

It is a community, and, since its members are trying to think together, it may be called, at least in potentiality, an intellectual community.

Its talk is oriented to action. It talks about what ought to be done. The Center Fellows come to the conference table in their capacity as citizens. The talk is about the common good. . . .

The truth about the Center for the Study of Democratic Institutions is that it is not a very good Center, but it is the only one there is.

—Robert Hutchins, founder of the Center for the Study of Democratic Institutions

If a Hollywood director was "casting" a think tank, he would undoubtedly pick the Center for the Study of Democratic Institutions. Located on a secluded estate overlooking Santa Barbara, California, it is housed in a large, white-stucco building in a mixed Spanish/Greek style which has been appropriately dubbed "El Parthenon." Inside it is cool, quiet, and enormous. The impression it produces is one of a serene anachronism, like an Ole Miss fraternity house poised above and removed from the oil slick, booming skid row, Chicano labor problems, and twice-burned bank that scar the city below. The impression is invalid. There is ferment here, too—though mostly verbal—and it's far from serene. An anachronism? Only if one rejects the premise that democratic institutions are worth preserving, reforming, and improving.

The center is a completely independent entity where five days a week for the last decade and probably for a long time to come basic issues confronting the nation and humanity in general are debated, discussed, disputed, dissected, and—when it achieves its goal—clarified. It is not, as its Fellows point out, an action group but a place where plans of action are weighed and passed on to those willing to listen. Its particular form of madness is that it is trying to change the world with words.

What is its bias? Generally, the political stripe is liberal, strongly reform-oriented, and democratic (with both a small and a large "d"), although individuals at the center protest against such labels. "Ideologically," says Harry Ashmore, the dapper president of the center who has long been active in Democratic politics, "the only constant institutional bias we have is in favor of Constitutional democracy. For years that belief has brought us condemnation from the Right; now the Left is coming at us too." Frank Kelly, an ex-newsman who was once a speech writer for President Harry Truman and is now vice-president of the center, elaborates on the theme: "The Left accuses us of not acting and the Right suspects us of being too action-oriented. Quite a few people refuse to believe we do what we say we do." The controversy that swells around the center is real. It has been accused of being Rightist, Leftist, Communist, Papist, atheist, and just about everything else one can imagine. Typical of the Right's attacks is that by Red-baiting Representative John Rarick of Louisiana, who calls it ". . . an outfit loaded with Communists." The late Senator Everett Dirksen blamed the "strange mood" of the

263

country on such organizations as the center. On the other side, Ashmore reports that students who have been brought to the center in recent years have opened discussions by damning it as "senile," "irrelevant," and "handmaiden to the Establishment." During a recent dialogue with students at the center, one of the fellows asserted, "I have news for you. There isn't going to be a revolution." Countered a student, "This is a lot like going to my grandfather's house."

Of course, the center's members don't look for such accusations but accept them as an occupational hazard of the role they have chosen to assume at the center. This role creates something of a paradox as, on the one hand, the center tries to educate, communicate with and be respected by the world outside, and, on the other, tries to play the role of the little boy in the fable who attempts to tell the Emperor the truth about his new clothes. According to Ashmore, the center attempts to be "an early warning system" for society. He explains, "We're trying to raise major issues before they come over the horizon, trying to clarify them and then present them to others. It's a megalomaniacal task, but it's the one we've chosen for ourselves: We're trying to tackle what everyone else is not doing." He adds, when asked about the center's critics, "By trying to be at the leading edge of issues we're bound to be unpopular to many."

To illustrate what he means by an issue that is coming over the horizon, Ashmore cites a student critic of the center who recently labeled it a cop-out by asserting that its members were more interested in the sea bottom than in Watts. Ashmore explains that the role the center has set for itself calls for paying attention to both but that the sea bottom at this point in history offers compelling reasons for the center's attention while Watts is the concern of many other groups and, frankly, is an issue which they feel they have less ability to affect. Man's inevitable push to exploit the seas, on the other hand, is seen as a more important issue for the center to pursue because it may be brought under control before getting out of control. "We see this as the type of subject that truly reflects our real capacity," says Ashmore, who points out that when the center first brought up the issue of peaceful uses of the high seas and the sea bed two years ago, it was generally dismissed as neither relevant nor realistic. The original center work in the area, conducted by Elisabeth Mann Borgese, long-time Fellow of the center and the daughter of author Thomas Mann, suggested a model for an international statute for peaceful uses of the seas. Among other things, the legal suggestions and discussions made by Borgese led to an international conference at the center in January 1970 on arms control and disarmament on and under the world's oceans. In the summer of 1970, at the invitation of the government of Malta, a *"Pacem in Maribus"* convocation, with leaders from around the world, was held on that island to explore the peaceful uses of the seas.

Another current indication of the center's desire to supply an early warning on issues is its deep interest in the biological revolution, especially progress in genetic experimentation and genetic engineering. One proposal generated by the center is that the nation might do well to consider a Constitutional amendment guaranteeing "environmental right." This proposal would not only give one the right to a pollution-free environment but also to such biological rights as freedom from genetic manipulation and psychosurgery.

The center has recently issued its "Model Constitution" for the United States, a project seeking to gear the Constitution to present conditions, policies, and problems. The Constitution proposed in 1970 was its thirty-fifth draft, a result of the constant revision to which the project was subjected. Among the provisions of the final version are Presidential election every nine years, with the limit of one term per President; two Vice Presidents, who would be alloted a greater share of the President's administrative load; and the end of the present Supreme Court, to be replaced by a series of specialized Supreme Courts, such as one to handle just matters relating to taxation. In general the new plan opts for greater federal power and lessens the powers of the states. Rexford G. Tugwell, the Senior Fellow in charge of the project, explains its rationale for rewriting the document: "Who would have said in 1787 that welfare, control of the economic cycle, regulation of business or national public works, and the control of pollution would ever be objects of governmental policy? No one, of course—and no provision was made for such things. The present Constitution is silent about them. It was not made resilient or accommodative. It was, in fact, made not to be." The project aimed at presenting a well-thought-out and viable challenge to the central document of American government. The center does not expect its Constitution to be adopted or to find broad official or popular acceptance; it was meant, rather, to provoke new ideas about the Constitution. Once released, it was attacked from many sides for many reasons and hotly debated among Congressmen—which is what the center had hoped for.

Ashmore gives a historical example of a subject that the center has been investigating and talking about for years but is only now becoming generally recognized as a legitimate issue. He says, "When we first started talking about the legal constraints that would have to be placed on science seven or eight years ago, it was thought of as heresy in the scientific community. Now it's popular—even for scientists—to talk about the runaway state of science and what must be done about it." Ashmore adds that this is a good example of the early-warning concept at work. Frank Kelly gives two examples of other warnings given by the center that have had an impact on American life. He points to the work that author Michael Harrington did as a consultant to the center on the subject of blacklisting of entertainers for political reasons. While Harrington was working on the project he became impressed with the terrible conditions under which out-of-work actors were living. This got him interested in the subject of poverty, which he went on to investigate and write about in his book *The Other America*. The book is a bitter portrait of American poverty and is generally credited with having convinced President John F. Kennedy to begin his war on poverty. In 1967 Harrington told the New York *Times*, "There would have been no book without the intellectual atmosphere and advice of the center." Still another center study entitled *Cybernation: The Silent Conquest*, a 1962 work that took an unflinching and horrific view of the future of automation, created much discussion that resulted in the appointment of a Presidential commission to look into the subject.

Past concerns of the center have been broad, important, all-encompassing. So, too, are the areas of concern outlined for the future. Frank Kelly, in a recent issue of *The Center Newsletter*, a bulletin for the center's members and friends, lists the current thoughts of center members on what their goals are:

> We must find ways to make our political process work more effectively than it ever has before.
> We must strive to bring science into Constitutional structure.
> We must change education to clear the way for man's endless search for what it means to exercise the enormous powers of the human being.

266

We must consider the possibilities of a new Constitution for the United States—and a Constitution for the world.

We must explore all the possibilities of communicating with one another across all the barriers of ideologies and cultures.

This statement of major present and future concerns is embellished by Ashmore, who comments on trends taking the center in new directions. For one, the substantive concerns of the center are becoming more international. He says that more and more the center is coming to believe that issues confronting the United States cannot be isolated from international issues—for example, problems of environment. Therefore, the center's level of concern will increasingly be with issues of internationalization. Among the specific international subjects outlined for the future by Robert Hutchins are ". . . issues of world development, multinational corporations, conglomerate mergers, control of science and technology, the role of the professions, the meaning of modern federalism, and the future of the city." Another departure cited by Ashmore will be establishing a dialogue between the center and American radicals. He adds that there has always been an emphasis at the center on establishing dialogue with outsiders—perhaps the most important is the attempt to join the United States and the Communist world in dialogue—and that increasing dialogue with native radicals is a natural extension of this pattern.

The ground rules established for this broad enterprise are simple. Nobody tells those at the center what to do, although they are open to suggestion from everywhere. They take no contracts, accept no federal money and are beholden to no foundation (save for the Fund for the Republic, which, in fact, is the center in that it is the legal and financial entity with its major program being the center itself). Contributions from individuals are its major source of income. Says Ashmore, "We can function only if we stay independent. Although it's been tempting, we've spent a lot of time turning down proposals and funds for projects. If we were to accept them, we'd set up a vested interest in certain problems and lose our ability to attack the ones we see as most important." On the other hand, the center does not exclude ideas from the outside; in fact, on many occasions visitors and letters from the outside have prompted topics for consideration.

As for the senior Fellows, junior Fellows, visiting Fellows, and consultants who take part in the center's daily routine, rules are practically nonexistent, save for their main obligation to participate in the center's dialogues on the major issues of the day.

Dialogue is the core of the center's activity, both its major technique and product, because from these dialogues come its ideas, communications, and calls to action. The setting for the dialogues is a large airy room in the center of the building, dominated by an enormous green-covered rectangular table. Each morning at 11 A.M. or thereabouts Robert Hutchins bangs on a school bell and the Fellows come out of their offices to enter that day's session. Usually the dialogue lasts several hours, starting with a paper or presentation by one of the Fellows and moving on to general discussion. Almost any topic is likely to be scheduled—strikes by public employees, the fate of the American small town, the future of desegregation, avoidance of nuclear war. Usually the dialogue leader is Hutchins, who ruminates on the difficulty of dialogue this way: "This is harder than you might think. Though 'dialogue' has become a tired word in the American vocabulary, a candid exchange of ideas and a willingness to learn from one another seems to be harder to obtain in our country than in any other in the West. . . . Americans like to make speeches, but, as the bland head-nodding on television panel shows suggests, they prefer to talk past one another. . . ." Others there agree that achieving the desired quality of dialogue is difficult, and as a result many of the daily meetings fall far short of the goal.

For the center's members the rest of the working day is spent primarily in matters relating to the dialogue. Papers are prepared, thoughts ordered on the next day's topic, research is done, and thoughts generated from the dialogue are readied for transmission to the outside world if it is thought they merit it.

Although internal dialogue is the core of the center's activity, it does not form a closed loop. Formal convocations and symposia are held at the center to focus a larger body of thinkers on an issue, and others are encouraged to participate in its "open table"—an invitation that has been taken up by those ranging from local high-school students to internationally known scholars. Sometimes this option is taken by noteworthy individuals. For instance, in 1967 the center received and accepted a request from Judge Warren Burger, now Chief Justice of the United States, to put together a meeting at the center on the subject of challenges to the American legal system.

Similarly a request from an international association of broadcasters brought about a center conference on the role of communications in the development of a world civilization. Each year the Center receives hundreds of visitors from all over the world, some who come from pure curiosity, some to discuss a specific issue.

At its most dramatic, the center's dialogue escalates to the level of international convocation, such as the recent *"Pacem in Maribus"* meeting in Malta. The other two major international meetings were *"Pacem in Terris"* I and II, held respectively in 1965 in New York and 1967 in Geneva. Both were inspired by Pope John XXIII's encyclical *Pacem in Terris,* and both sought "to examine the requirements of peace." At the first meeting some 2,500 people from around the world gathered to try to formulate a commonly acceptable definition of coexistence. The center feels that this convocation offered a revival of the dialogue of peace—and, incidentally, was a major factor leading to Pope Paul's decision to visit and address the United Nations on world peace. The 1967 peace convocation further explored coexistence and specifically focused on five major topics: threats to coexistence, the case of Vietnam, the case of Germany, Interdependence, and "Beyond Coexistence." More than seventy nations were represented at the meeting, although the U.S.S.R., North Vietnam, Communist China, and the United States, for a variety of reasons, chose not to send officials. Russia and the United States cited the existence of ongoing crises as their reasons for not attending. The meeting was held on the eve of the Six-Day War and during a time of particular crisis in Vietnam. Although nobody claims that the *"Pacem in Terris"* convocations accomplished any miracles for the cause of peace, they did offer certain by-products. For instance, the second meeting provided a common ground for East and West Germany to initiate a previously nonexistent dialogue. It also served as a forum where delegates from more than seventy nations reached a consensus on eleven major points concerning peace. They were:

1. The United Nations must be strengthened and made more independent.
2. Membership in the United Nations must be made universal.
3. The war in Vietnam is at best a mistake.
4. Southeast Asia must be neutralized.

5. The Cold War must be ended.

6. Racial discrimination is intolerable.

7. The developing nations must be assisted, and aid to them should be multilateral.

8. The terms of trade are intolerable for the developing countries; the ratio of industrial prices to those of primary products must receive the most earnest, explicit, and immediate attention.

9. No military solutions are adequate for the present day.

10. No national solutions are adequate for the present day.

11. Coexistence is a necessary but not sufficient condition of human life. Survival is not, perhaps, an ignoble aim, but it is not a noble one either. We must move onward and upward from coexistence to what Pope John called the universal common good. This is an aim worthy of humanity. It will require the organization of the world for continuous peaceful change and the revision of the status quo without war.

At both meetings the object was to convene citizens of the world —not necessarily but preferably with the blessings of their governments—in the cause of peace, an objective that is still very much at the heart of the center's program. The Fellows of the center believe that bringing the world's people together to discuss peace is the first step toward achieving it.

Although the peace-generating role that the center has set for itself has been, at best, a limited success, it has been doggedly persistent in its attempts. It has tried again and again to engage the Communist Chinese in dialogue, although each attempt has met with failure. This persistence has aroused suspicion and even hostility from certain official groups, including the U.S. State Department, but it has also gained the center supporters from around the world. For example, Silviu Brucan, former Rumanian Ambassador to the United States and a Visiting Fellow at the center, feels that the center is an effective international force. Asked why he sought to come and work at the center, he says, "Very few institutions in the United States or in the world have succeeded in gaining the trust of people of different viewpoints the way this one has."

International dialogues are by no means the only method the center employs to get its messages across. As proof, Frank Kelly, who besides being vice-president of the center is also the director of its education program, cites these statistics: Over seven million copies of its 200 books, papers, and pamphlets have been distributed, and somewhere between 2,000 and 3,000 educational institutions use the center's extensive series of tapes of its dialogues (a sampling of recent tape titles include "The Rich Pay a Fine, the Poor Go to Jail: A Sociology of the Law," "The Jury: Safeguard or Anachronism?" "The Role of the Jury in Political Crimes," and "Surveillance and the Future of Privacy"). In addition, circulation of the bi-monthly *Center Magazine* is now over 100,000. Kelly also points out that the center has been encouraging the readers of its publications to take the information it distributes and use it for ". . . forming small centers in people's homes." He says that this is one way in which those reading center literature can use it to prepare themselves to take effective political action.

The people who populate this think tank are, as a group, scholars with the optimism to be convinced that their communications with the outside world and their daily dialogues can indeed make a difference. As individuals, they are a mixed lot. At the top are its senior Fellows. Harry Ashmore, a journalist, who with his paper the *Arkansas Gazette* won two Pulitzer Prizes and who later went on to head the Encyclopaedia Britannica, is the chief operating officer of the center and one of its senior Fellows. Robert Hutchins, author Harvey Wheeler (co-author of the novel *Fail-Safe*), philosopher-physicist John Wilkinson, New Deal "brain truster" and former governor of Puerto Rico Rexford Tugwell, former New York *Times* religion editor and current editor of *The Center Magazine* John Cogley, and Elisabeth Mann Borgese round out the list of senior Fellows. They are complemented by a half dozen or so visiting Fellows who are invited to the center for various lengths of time and about the same number of junior Fellows, who are mostly between the ages of twenty and thirty. Then there are the associates and consultants, who are the equivalent of its part-time help—an impressive list of about twenty-five that has included such notables as biologist Paul Ehrlich, educator Clark Kerr and writer Milton Mayer. Finally, there is the center's administrative staff, which maintains its education programs and turns out its tapes, periodicals, and books.

The senior Fellow is Robert M. Hutchins, now chairman of the center's parent Fund for the Republic and the man who conceived and founded the center. Though now over seventy, he is still unquestionably its leader. In 1929 he became president of the University of Chicago, a job he got four years after graduating from law school and held for twenty-two years. In 1951 he became a director of the Ford Foundation and three years later moved over to the Ford-backed Fund for the Republic as president. The Fund was established as an entity to defend and advance the principles of the Declaration of Independence, Bill of Rights, and Constitution. Hutchins later described the early days of the Fund as ". . . a small island of sanity in a McCarthyite world." The idea for a permanent center grew out of a Hutchins-inspired Basic Issues program, established in 1957 to look at and advance the basic concepts of democracy. Two years later that program was institutionalized as the center with the Fund for the Republic becoming its corporate entity. It has long since ceased being supported by the Ford Foundation—or, as Hutchins has put it, it is now a "wholly disowned subsidiary of the Ford Foundation."

To start the center, Hutchins put together a small group of scholars from a variety of disciplines to hold frequent discussions on the subjects of civil rights, civil liberties, and democratic institutions. In time the center grew to as many as eighteen full-time senior Fellows who studied, wrote about, and discussed major national and international problems on a nine-to-five basis. In 1969, on the center's tenth anniversary, Hutchins decided to change the course of the center. His term for the shake-up was "refounding," a process that involved demoting senior Fellows, albeit democratically, and pruning their number to seven. The process of elimination worked like this: Hutchins, the first of the seven, picked another fellow to stay; then those two elected another, making three; those three elected another; and so on, until there were seven. Physicist Linus Pauling, the late Bishop James A. Pike, educator and classicist Stringfellow Barr, and sociologist John R. Seeley were among the senior Fellows who were asked to leave. In addition, four members of the inner circle were moved onto the administrative staff, a step that meant that they were still at the center but were no longer principal participants in the daily dialogue.

The creation of the new regime was not accomplished without controversy. Most of the Fellows who were dropped expressed disappointment and at least one, Seeley, declined public comment on the coup but was reported to have put the matter of his dismissal in the hands of his lawyers. Some surmises by outsiders held that a number of the more activist members had lost out, although those who remain debate the contention. An article in *The Nation* by Santa Barbara newsman Robert H. Sollen stated, ". . . a generalization—which has notable exceptions—can be made about those who have been dropped. They are the activists, the humanists, the involved." Sollen then went on to elaborate on the activist records of the Fellows who had been dropped. Frank Kelly, one of those moved out of the senior circle as a result of the election, answered Sollen in a letter. He maintained that Sollen gave a "distorted impression," pointing out that those remaining were similarly active, humane, and involved.

Those remaining also point out that the suggestion to prune democratically had been agreed to by all the senior Fellows present at the time of the vote. There is general agreement by the survivors that there were valid reasons for the shake-up—among them that there were some Fellows spending less and less time at the center (for example, Linus Pauling had been on leave for two years doing research) and that the center needed new direction. The survivors add that as a result the center is better off for it.

Now past its first decade, the center seems determined to survive for some time. Its recent history of shoestring financing is over, for at least, a while since it has been the recipient of several large bequests, including one of over $5 million from the late inventor of Xerography, Chester Carlson, and paid circulation for *The Center Magazine* has leaped spectacularly in the last two years due to an intense direct-mail advertising campaign.

Hutchins' plan for a financially stable and "refounded" center calls for the addition of new senior Fellows (probably five to seven) who will be picked carefully over the next few years. The major occupation, as it has always been, will be thinking—either aloud in discussion or privately—about present and future problems. The question that must be asked of this particular think tank is: Is all of this relevant? Can these thinkers perched on a hilltop really make a difference with their dialogues and learned papers or is it all a futile exercise? It is a question that those at the center do not hesitate to ask themselves—and one for which they have no standard answer.

Dean Kenneth S. Tollett, a visiting Fellow on leave from the law school at Texas Southern College, says, "I see elements in society making the center more essential than it has ever been before. Because many are equating dissent with treason, because of certain actions by Congress and the Administration and because of widespread attacks on the Supreme Court for what, I think, was its finest hour, the center is as important today as the Fund for the Republic was in the 1950's." He also cites the center's role in attempting to find world peace. "This place is interested in peace and there are, of course, good reasons to be pessimistic about any small group or any group for that matter having a positive effect in this area. But the center thinks that it is worth looking beyond this pessimism just on the chance that something can be done. The center is Utopian; I think there must be Utopians to see what can be. Let me put it this way—work is going on here on a model Constitution which will probably be impossible to implement when it is completed. But it is being worked on and it will enable us all to see the existing one anew, to evaluate it and think how it could be improved."

Frank Kelly sees the center as "a halfway house between an academy and the real world." Kelly, who has been with the center since its founding in 1959, assesses the relevance of the center this way: "We are not an action group as such. There are thousands of action groups, but not very many that think about courses of action. That's what we do and that's how we contribute."

Ashmore says that if the center can help clarify issues, then it is doing its job and is relevant. He cites two recent attempts at clarification—one on the international front and the other locally. The center sponsored a meeting in Mexico City in 1969 to which national-development experts were invited from all over Latin America. Ashmore says, "This meeting showed us that unless these men are in the United States conferring with our government, they never get to see each other and discuss their mutual problems. It was the first time that they were ever convened without being overseen by officials of the U.S. government. The meeting was held to examine the failure of U.S. aid to Latin America, the Latin view of the Americas and their view of what must be done to improve things. Their conclusions were much different from those inherent in U.S. policy in these areas." In this case, Ashmore asserts, the clarification fostered by the center was in providing a platform for a side of South American development that is not heard in North America. His second example is a more personal one—the ongoing dialogue that he has held with young people who visit the center. "The kids tell me that they've located the enemy in the Establishment," he says, "and they really believe that it is this Establishment that is creating all the problems besetting us. I tell them that it's really worse than they think, that there is no Establishment." Ashmore thinks that they've set up a straw man, that the so-called Establishment did not plan the problems nor can it get them under control. He says, "New York City is breaking down. You can't convince me that there's an Establishment and that it has control of the situation or that it can get the situation under control. Perhaps, if there were an Establishment, then it could possibly handle the problem." He adds that the students he faces refuse to believe his contention that rather than an Establishment at the top, a vacuum exists that has to be filled. "In order to have a revolution, you have to find the enemy, and I don't think they've found theirs," says Ashmore.

The center's particular form of megalomania is an accompaniment of its own style: fierce independence, chronic optimism, and iconoclasm. Its singular dedication to clarification of existing issues and to the attempt to give early warning to those issues that will crop up in the future is a task of ever-increasing difficulty. If dialogue—rather than war or revolution—ever becomes the vehicle by which the nation and the world cope with present issues and face future ones, then the center will have made an impact.

One of the most difficult tasks that the center must face in the future is gaining the intellectual respect of and rapport with young America—especially its more activist and radical elements. This gap is a source of concern to the Fellows and justifiably so. A good example of the attitude on the outer wing of the Left toward the center is expressed by Marcus Raskin, author, radical intellectual, and one of those indicted in the celebrated Boston antidraft conspiracy case. Raskin thinks that the center has had a positive impact and has done good work, but he can readily tick off what he regards as its four most persistent shortcomings: (1) it has succeeded over the years in isolating itself from the young; (2) it looks at society institutionally in its attempts at reform, a view that denies the possibility that some of our institutions may not be worth saving; (3) it has turned away from putting ideas into actual practice, instead existing in a world that is composed only of ideas; and (4) it has overemphasized dialogue and dialogic thought without analyzing the actual situations as they exist in the United States and the world, or, to put it more simply, the center's members have talked themselves away from reality.

Considering the armies of critics the center has attracted—on both the Right and the Left—Raskin's raps are mild. Unlike other critics, Raskin not only poses an alternative to the center and its philosophy but himself operates an alternative think tank that has had a direct influence on the creation of allied alternative groups. He is co-director of Washington's Institute for Policy Studies, the farthest one can travel to the Left on the think-tank continuum.

3. The Institutes: the Movement's Establishment

> If this were 1773, and the city were Boston, the Institute would be holding a seminar on British imperialism. There would be tables and charts to show the injustice of the tax on tea. Probably somebody from the Governor's office would be invited. Then independent of the Institute, six or seven of the fellows would go out and dump a shipload of tea into Boston Harbor.
>
> —Karl Hess, Fellow of the Institute for Policy Studies, quoted in *The Washingtonian* magazine

The Institute for Policy Studies is attempting to lay the groundwork for the new society that will replace the present collapsing one. It not only has dedicated itself to ushering in the new society by inquiry and experimentation but is also doing what it can to hasten the demise of the present one.

To accomplish this, the institute has as its tangible resources an old but airy brick townhouse on New Hampshire Avenue in Washington, a modest annual budget approaching $400,000 and a staff of fifty full-time and part-time scholars and activists. It is led by Raskin and co-director Richard J. Barnet, ex-bureaucrat, author, and, with Raskin, one of the institute's founders. On its roster of Fellows and part-time Associate Fellows are such well-known individuals as an-archist-author Paul Goodman, journalist I. F. Stone, "radical his-torian" Arthur Waskow, sncc leader Ivanhoe Donaldson, University of Chicago professor Hans J. Morgenthau, and radical journalist Andrew Kopkind. Tying these resources together is a philosophy that dictates the institute's plan of study and experimentation.

"Existential pragmatism" is the term that Raskin uses to sum up its operating philosophy. As he explains it, this way of thinking dic-tates the need to perceive present irrationality—accomplished via the institute's studies of existing policies and institutions—and then to move beyond that to experimentation with alternatives to present policies and institutions. Raskin's intellectual premise is that to develop social theory one must be involved in social experimentation and action. Firmly aimed at the concept of change, it also dictates that social theorizing must be closely identified with those who are powerless and oppressed.

The institute has been in operation since 1963 when a small group of academicians and frustrated civil servants established it as an independent research organization to explore social, economic, and military issues without the benefit of government sponsorship. Since then it has involved itself in the widest range of societal concerns—from the abm to neighborhood government, from women's liberation to communes, from the performance of TV stations to the effects of technology on society. The impact of its work has been felt mostly on the political Left, both new and old, and that impact has been considerable. For instance, besides being involved in the Boston conspiracy case, Raskin and several other Fellows were members of the Committee to Defend the Conspiracy, a group which was organized to come to the aid of the "Chicago 8." Also, Raskin founded the New Party in 1968, a group that stands for the dis-mantling of the military establishment, arms control and disarma-ment at all levels, including police and civilians and a hands-off policy for the United States in foreign insurgencies. Though he has been superseded as its chairman by co-directors Dick Gregory and the president of Antioch College, James P. Dixon, he is still closely associated with the concept and is working to develop the New

Party as one of his projects at the institute. Raskin is well suited to his many roles. He is young, serious, and insightful, and has a dry sense of humor and irony. Physically, he has the rumpled look of an overworked college professor rather than that of, as he was charged, a conspirator.

Raskin is not alone in his involvement. Perhaps the most visible of the institute's Fellows is Arthur Waskow, an outspoken roly-poly scholar/activist who seems never to miss a major demonstration or political event. Among other things, the ubiquitous Waskow has played a crucial role in setting up a center to assist the victims of the Washington, D.C., riots of 1968, in starting the more leftish than liberal Federal Employees for a Democratic Society (FEDS) and another group called Jews for Urban Justice, in planning demonstrations at the 1968 Democratic Convention and the Counter-Inauguration, or the demonstrations surrounding President Nixon's inauguration. Waskow is generally credited with (or blamed for, depending on one's convictions) coining the term "creative disorder" and is one of the major advocates of such a policy. Writing in *New University Thought* in 1968, he said it meant ". . . to simply keep experimenting and to discover at what point one is neither smashed nor ignored, but creates enough change to move the society." At the institute, Waskow currently lists as his areas of study the politics of the District of Columbia, the future (he is working on a book on the subject of the year 1999), the New Left, and radical Jewish organizing.

Institute Fellows have been active in virtually every issue of concern to young activists. Raskin claims, "The institute has had a profound effect on the Movement. It's hard to pin down where our influence can really be felt, but our existence has mattered." He explains that one way in which the institute counts is that it is not only chronicling what is wrong but is also attempting through social experimentation to give young activists some possible answers to the question that is often asked of them: What do you propose to erect in the place of the institutions of present society?

Though not as great, it has also had an influence on the existing system. The institute's work in starting community-development corporations and its investigations of community control of health facilities, for example, are concepts that have subsequently been adopted and backed respectively by the OEO and the Public Health

Service. Many of its prominent members are alumni of the Establishment themselves, a status giving them added credibility in official and academic circles. Raskin is a good case in point. Now in his mid-thirties, he began his multifaceted professional life as legislative consultant to a group of twelve liberal Congressmen in the late 1950's. During that period he helped put together legislation on such items as the foundation of the Arms Control and Disarmament Agency and reorganization of the Department of Defense. He served on President Kennedy's National Security Council as a special adviser on disarmament and was a member of the U.S. delegation to the Geneva talks on disarmament in 1962. Between 1963 and 1965 he was an education adviser to the Bureau of the Budget, a member of the Presidential Panel on Educational Research and Development, and a consultant to the White House Office of Science and Technology. He dropped all federal affiliations in 1965 because of his objections to the war and what he terms "the militarization of universities." Co-Director Richard Barnet worked for both the State Department and the Arms Control and Disarmament Agency before joining Raskin and others to form the institute. Other examples include Karl Hess, a current Fellow who was one of Barry Goldwater's speech writers during the 1964 campaign, and Leonard Rodberg, who was, like Barnet, an official of the Arms Control and Disarmament Agency.

Not only are many of the institute Fellows products of established institutions, but some still participate in or initiate selected Establishment activities. Perhaps the most interesting example of an institute associate working inside the system concurrently with being a member of the renegade think tank is a thirty-six-year-old economist named Richard F. Kaufman. He serves as staff director of the Joint Congressional Economic Committee, which is looking into defense expenditures. As a Congressional staff man, he has functioned as a leading figure in the ongoing attack against excessive Department of Defense spending. He has been an important investigator in dredging up information for Senator William Proxmire, which the Senator has used in his continuing attacks on waste in the military. Kaufman's research was crucial to Proxmire's exposé of the waste in the Air Force's C5A jet-transport development. In his role as an institute Fellow he has been involved in a project called the Congressional Seminar on Military Procurement, which ran from 1968 through

1970. It began when Kaufman contacted Congressional offices asking to speak to whoever works on military spending and then, after getting to the man in charge, asking him if he would be interested in meeting on the subject of improper procurement practices, defense spending, and its influence on the economy and the need for reform. His calls netted thirty-five Congressional aides who met in regular seminars over the two-year period. At its conclusion, the nucleus of those who had attended the seminar formed an informal Congressional Review Committee to keep an eye on defense spending. Such seminars are not uncommon at the institute, with gatherings being held for such groups as Members of Congress for Peace Through Law, the Council for a Livable World, and the Mobilization Committee to End the War.

Seminars are just one form of institute project. The work is organized into studies, seminars, courses, and experiments, scheduled annually to cover the next September-to-June academic year. Each full-time Fellow leads seminars, writes, lectures and leads or works on several experiments and studies. For instance, Frank Smith, a former SNCC leader now working at the institute, was listed for 1969–70 as working on studies of the food industry and consumer protection and organizing efforts to set up co-ops in the black community. Each year the institute embarks on about twenty major projects to be started and often completed during the academic year. Some result in reports or books, others are series of meetings such as Kaufman's seminar, and others are experiments. A sampling of the almost forty studies and experiments going on in the 1969–71 academic years includes: an analysis of the Defense budget by several former Pentagon systems analysts working at the institute; a three-volume study of the origins of the Indochina war, being put together by seven institute-supported authors; a Reconversion Study Group, intended as a national program for professors and students to study ways to transfer local economies from a military-industrial base to a base suited to civilian needs (one of the planned areas for conversion from the concerns of war to those of peace is the area around Stanford University, which would include pacifying the Stanford Research Institute); the implementation of cooperative food stores in the Washington ghetto and participation in the development of the Peoples' Appalachian Research Collective, a nonprofit research group located in Morgantown, West Virginia ("Our purpose," says

280

a publication of the collective, "is to engage in an active analysis of the political economy of Appalachia which will confront the region's colonizers by contributing to people's movements for a democratic society").

An experimental project headed by Raskin that got off the ground in January 1970 is called the Washington Mini-School Corporation, one of several school projects being developed by the institute, including a school for dropouts scheduled to go into operation in 1971. Raskin describes the rationale for the Mini-School: "It is based on the assumption that people are born with impulses for political and social action that society screens out through the educational process. The school idea grew from the opposite premise of present schools, which is that children should learn by understanding the social, economic, and political institutions of society."

In the new school, children will start learning *away* from the classroom in such places as the courts, TV studios, museums, hospitals, and newspaper offices. It assumes that with guidance from teachers, students can learn such basic skills as reading and mathematics while learning about social institutions. The planned atmosphere of the school is one in which individualized work, non-authoritarian teacher-student relations, and encouragement of student questioning and decision-making are featured. According to a proposal prepared for interested parties, it differs from other experimental schools in that "A primary goal of the Mini-School has been to focus the fertile imagination of elementary school children on the task of creating alternative institutions for society."

The first experimentation with the idea began under Raskin's direction in the District of Columbia in early 1970. It had the blessings of D.C. school officials and was conducted after school for four months. Its student body was twenty-three racially mixed fifth- and sixth-graders from the Shepherd School, a public elementary school in the northwest section of Washington. During the experimental period, the students worked with architects, doctors, Congressmen, and an art museum, to name a few of the outsiders. For instance, eight afternoons were spent at the Corcoran Gallery of Art in Washington, where the children observed, painted, drew, and asked questions of the gallery's curator about why, among other things, the museum was not designed for children to enjoy. The experiment proved to the institute's satisfaction that children are

281

responsive to this type of education. Two bits of evidence leading to this conclusion were that although attendance was not required, the pupils kept coming in full force, and, unexpectedly, it was found that students were voluntarily tutoring one another during the afternoon sessions. Full-time operation of a Mini-School for forty students began in late 1970.

Another unique institute project is its studies of the American communications industry, particularly television broadcasting. The work is being conducted in three stages: first, an examination of present license holders to see if they are acting in the public interest; second, helping community groups work toward denying license renewals to stations not responsive to community needs; and, finally, putting forward new ideas for innovative and responsive programming and framing a model National Communications Act. In late 1969 the institute produced a 336-page report entitled "Television Today: the End of Communication and the Death of Community," which contained a study of the performance of television stations in the District of Columbia, Maryland, Virginia, and West Virginia as well as the institute's thoughts on public ownership of the airways in contrast to present "ownership" by the Federal Communications Commission, Congress, and the networks. In this vein the report said, "It is time to call a halt to the rapacious plundering of our mental life, unloosed by the Federal Communications Commission and Congress." Its investigation of stations resulted in a ranking based on such variables as extent and nature of black employment, programming content, and the feelings of the community it serves as revealed in surveys. The report came up with general complaints of poor performance against certain stations, suggested investigations of others, and in one case, Washington's ABC-affiliate WMAL-TV, suggested that its future request for license renewal be rejected. Based on its criteria, it determined that stations in towns like Weston, West Virginia, Bristol, Virginia, and Petersburg, Virginia, were outperforming their big-city counterparts in Baltimore and Washington. Subsequent to the issuance of the report, the institute has been working with several community groups to deny the aforementioned WMAL-TV its license on the basis that it does not serve Washington's large black community.

Beyond such major projects, the academic year at the institute is characterized by lectures, impromptu seminars on current events, short-term projects, and a "core" course. The core course is a series of classes held for area students and institute associates which covers such areas as methodology, the urban crisis, and the world revolution. Under the heading of methodology in 1969–70, the subjects taught included systems analysis, social invention in reconstruction, scientific methodology in analyzing social problems, and futurism— in short, a blend of traditional and institute-inspired inquiries into policy research.

The institute draws its support from a number of sources. Financing has come from the Ford Foundation, the Stern Family Fund, the National Board of Missions of the Presbyterian Church, the Field Foundation, the Milbank Foundation, and numerous individuals. Funds also come from royalties and fees for the dozens of books and hundreds of articles that have been produced by its senior staff, which turns over its fees and royalties to the institute. Full-time Fellows are paid between $10,000 and $20,000 for the academic year. Commenting on the institute's ability to stay solvent, Raskin says, "Over the years our people have made a lot of contacts with people with money. They've learned the essential art of hustling money for projects without picking up the strings that could inhibit the outcome of our work."

Understandably, the institute does not sit too well with many elements of official Washington. Twice it has been examined by the Internal Revenue Service—in 1967, after Raskin's indictment in the antidraft case, its expenditures were audited, and in 1970 a seven-month investigation was conducted to see if its activities could be construed as an attempt to influence legislation and thus to qualify it as a lobby. The institute had no trouble with the first investigation, while, as of this writing, the outcome of the second inquiry has not been made public. Senator Strom Thurmond has been one of the institute's most persistent critics. "By giving a tax exemption to an organization like the Institute for Policy Studies, our government is allowing tax exemption to support revolution," the Senator from South Carolina said in 1967. In October 1969 on the floor of the Senate he characterized it as an "elite" trying to make changes without reference to the desires of the American people, and he singled out the institute for participation ". . . in the recent attack on the Administration's military procurement authorization bill"— which, to Thurmond's thinking, is the closest thing going to pure treason. Others, too, have found specific aspects of the institute's activities to be upsetting. Senator Paul Fannin of Arizona was quite disgruntled in 1969 when he learned through an article in *Barron's* that Arthur Waskow was being used as a consultant to the Justice Department-underwritten Center for the Administration of Justice at American University. Fannin fumed, "Personally, I think that we can bear an investigation into the circumstances that allow U.S. taxpayers' money to be used in payment of consultant fees to a man who had led demonstrations demanding community control of the police. . . ." Raskin and others at the institute refuse to be rattled by their critics, and, though not eager to lose its tax privileges, Raskin vows, "I can't imagine that there is any kind of pressure that will cause the institute to roll over and die." One of the main reasons for such fortitude, in his view, is the character of its Fellows, to whom he ascribes the collective qualities of ". . . brilliance, integrity, and bravery." As for the institute's detractors, Raskin says: "We refuse to take them too seriously because if we were responsible for all of the things they claim we are, then we would be the most important institution in America."

Not content with what it has stirred up thus far, the institute plans a network of similar think tanks around the nation. Three satellite institutes have been franchised and are now operating, and Raskin predicts confidently that still more are on their way. There are three criteria for these new institutes. First, it is necessary for one or more apostolic institute Fellows to get interested enough in an area of the country to go there and organize an institute. Second, a "critical mass" of scholars is needed—which means that the area must have a nucleus of bright, alternatives-seeking intellectuals who want to become institutionalized outside a university structure. Finally, it requires a geographic area where institutelike analysis and application of programmatic change promises to make a difference, just as the federal government and the urban problems of Washington provide ample raw material for the Institute for Policy Studies.

Largest and most important of the new satellite institutes is the Cambridge Institute. It has a large agenda of projects focusing on such items as worker control of industry, community control of neighborhoods, and the creation of new towns. Although like the Institute for Policy Studies in many ways, it has its own unique aspects. Founded in February 1969 by Gar Alperovitz, who had been the legislative assistant to Senator Gaylord Nelson and wrote the controversial book on Cold War tactics, *Atomic Diplomacy*, and Christopher Jencks, the young protégé of David Riesman and Associate Professor at the Harvard Graduate School of Education, it has quickly grown to a staff of twenty-five housed in an old red wooden building on Boylston Street in Cambridge, a stone's throw from Harvard Square. As at the Institute for Policy Studies, where Alperovitz and Jencks were Fellows, its work is organized into research and action projects. Its goal is changing society in fundamental ways.

One of the distinctive aspects of the Cambridge Institute is that the institute itself is one of its projects. John Case, a young man who is one of its five co-directors, a recent Harvard graduate, founder of the *New England Free Press*, and a former Fulbright scholar, points out that the institute is an experiment in the innovation possible in an American institution—in this case a research institution. What they are aiming for is an experimental egalitarian "counterinstitution." Everyone there, Ph.D. and dropout alike, is called a Fellow, and all the Fellows participate in determining the agenda of the institute, electing its directors, running its day-to-day affairs, and making all major decisions (made in community assembly). Everybody shares in the dull and dirty jobs that have to be done, so nobody is working in a subordinate role more than part of the time. Direct appeals are required for major menial jobs—"Painters of the World Unite!" says a typical bulletin-board item put up by one of the directors. Salaries do not vary greatly and are based on "collectively defined need" rather than an individual's "market value." Hiring is determined by all the Fellows working on a project rather than by the project leader.

The institute's major activities, or, as they are called there, "central projects," are long-term efforts all aimed at offering alternatives to present domestic institutions. Projects already undertaken by institute task forces include:

Workers' management—a long-term study of strategies to create industrial structures where workers manage themselves. The institute feels that the development of worker control is needed so that labor can transcend the need for collective bargaining, so that government can develop workable forms of decentralization, and so that workers can participate in industrial democracy, or the management of their own affairs.

Transportation and regional development—an examination of

285

ways to extend current battles against superhighways as well as demands for new kinds of land-use planning and transportation planning in the Boston area.

Urban family study—a Boston-based inquiry into the desires and needs of the white working and lower classes. As stated in an institute publication, "The intent of the project is to uncover ways in which urban working-class families can more actively participate in American social and political life and effect social change."

Each project is organized into a task force composed of an assortment of Fellows and "friends of the institute." The groups meet weekly to coordinate their research activities. As with Establishment think tanks, the emphasis is on the multidisciplinary approach. For example, its New City Project includes those with expertise in such areas as economics, architecture, education, systems analysis, theology, and social work. In each case, the plan calls for extending the work of the task force into actual practice, and in this respect its members emphasize that it goes beyond the normal concept of a think tank. The New City group will inevitably produce reports, but it also plans to set up a new city. What is envisioned is an experimental community with broad citizen participation in planning and combined government and community control over services and industry in the city. The task force working on the new city began in September 1969 with broad representation from the institute and participation by members of the faculties of Harvard, MIT, Brandeis, and Goddard College. Since then it has been divided into two separate task forces: one preparing a theoretical prospectus for the city, the other looking for a location and financing.

Another central project of the institute is its information exchange on community-development groups. Community-development corporations—simply, a democratically controlled corporation owned by residents which owns property on behalf of the community—are of paramount concern to the institute since they are thought to portend a democratic vehicle for social change in American life. The institute has held meetings with members of over fifty such corporations from around the world to find out how they set up their groups and what problems they have encountered. Profiles of these fifty groups are being collected for what promises to be the first of many handbooks for emerging community-development corporations.

Institutionally the Cambridge Institute itself is branching out. It

286

has under its wing two smaller institutes called the Center for Community Economic Development and the Center for the Study of Public Policy. Both manage federally funded projects for the institute and seem, frankly, to be a hypocritical dodge—separate entities to accept the federal money which the parent group rejects as a matter of principle. The Center for Community Economic Development is a research and assistance group for community-development projects, while the other center is primarily concerned with education. One project for which the Center for the Study of Public Policy has achieved national attention is a study of tuition vouchers in education. Led by co-founder Christopher Jencks, the study recommended a large experiment in which urban parents would be given vouchers for each of their children, most of them equal to the amount the system presently spends educating each child and special, more valuable vouchers for children who are harder to educate, such as retarded children. Vouchers could be used at the school of the parents' choice whether the school be across the street, across town, or public, parochial, or private. The schools would cash the vouchers in for funds. The plan would start in the slums and, according to Jencks's theory, force local schools to improve or close for lack of students. Understandably the idea has been attacked. The NAACP sees it as a device that will perpetuate segregation, and both the American Federation of Teachers and the National Education Association list among their objections to the plan the feeling that it might lead to gimmickry on the part of schools that were trying to attract students. Other objections include opinions that it would destroy the present public-school system and serve to isolate the children involved. Despite such objections, the Office of Economic Opportunity, which had sponsored Jencks's work, announced in 1970 that it would experiment with it, perhaps as early as 1971. Jencks views the idea as an alternative to the present situation in which the state dictates most educational decisions for students and their parents.

In addition to these centers, Cambridge Institute members have been instrumental in forming still other organizations. For example, a member of the transportation task force has founded the "Free Wheel Movement," a unit fighting for alternatives to the extension of highways and automobile transportation. Another close affiliate of the institute is the newly established Graduate School of Social Change, formed in conjunction with Goddard College in Vermont.

The unique graduate school is geared to action projects and research directed to social change.

While the central projects at Cambridge are handled by task forces, there are smaller, usually individual, projects. One Fellow, for example, is forming a group that will give free consultation to companies heavily involved with the military to convert to nonmilitary work. "Advocacy planning" is a service that Fellows provide to community groups. Broadly defined, it is simply free professional assistance. For instance, one of the co-directors of the institute, James Morey, a teacher who has worked for both RAND and MITRE, is aiding the Roxbury Action Program (RAP) in locating funds for financing rehabilitations and cooperative ownership of the housing in the Highland Park area of Roxbury, a predominantly black section of the city.

Financially the institute has a broad base of support. It got its initial push with money from the Institute for Policy Studies but now depends mostly on contributions from individuals and philanthropic and religious groups, including the American Jewish Committee, Carnegie Corporation, Rockefeller Family Fund, National Council of Churches, and the ubiquitous Ford Foundation.

The other two institutes spun off from the Institute for Policy Studies are the Institute for Southern Studies, established in Atlanta in June 1970 and co-directed by black legislator Julian Bond and Institute for Policy Studies Fellow Sue Thrasher, and the San Francisco-based Bay Area Institute, which began in 1969. Each of them has its own general focus. The Institute for Southern Studies is concentrating on the economic and political structure of the South, with particular attention being paid to the region's priorities and the possibilities for reversing and re-establishing them. The major projects slated for its first years of operation include an examination of the impact of defense spending on the South, a study of the current state of the black movement in the South, a critique of regional poverty programs with an emphasis on the role that poverty programs play as a political patronage system, and an oral-history project aimed at filling in the gaps in the history books by presenting the histories of Southern people such as the East Kentucky coal miner. There are about a dozen Fellows at the Southern Institute, which will be operating on an annual budget of about $150,000 a year. The size of the Bay Area Institute is about the same and, again, its focus is regional.

Its two major concerns are the ecology of the western United States and the power of that region in the entire Pacific region of the world. Its work in ecology will concentrate on documenting present ecological perils and on offering models and plans for dealing with them. As for the role of the American West, it will investigate the force of capital, technology, and the tools of war in the Pacific. Still another institute is being considered for Toronto in the future.

The emergence of these affiliated institutes provides dramatic evidence of how far the think tank has moved from its genesis as an aid to military and industrial policy-making. The institutes have become the RANDS and SRIS of antimilitary and generally anti-*status quo* analysis. The point can be made, as it was to the author in an informal conversation with a RAND official, that these institutes cannot be considered think tanks because of their activist roles. But it is difficult to accept RAND's deep involvement in developing weapons systems, conducting the war in Vietnam, and the like as anything less than activism, albeit of another stripe than what is being worn by the institutes.

These institutes are by no means the only public think tanks to emerge in the last few years. For example, there is the recently established Institute of the Black World in Atlanta, which *Ebony* magazine recently called the first think tank for black scholars. Operating out of a house that was once occupied by W. E. B. DuBois, it plans to undertake intellectual work that defines and directs the American black population.

Another recent entry is a think tank created by consumer advocate Ralph Nader which, though new, is already active and raising bureaucratic and corporate hackles.

4. *The Uninvited Consultants*

> *In a disturbingly real sense, air pollution is a new way of looking at an old American problem: concentrated and irresponsible corporate power. "Clean air buffs" who fail to recognize this fact of economic and polit-*

ical life had best begin organizing nature walks or collecting butterflies. Throughout this book, the Task Force has illustrated how the public's hope for clean air has been frustrated by corporate deceit and collusion, by the exercise of undue influence with government officials, by secrecy and the supression of technology, by the use of dilatory legal maneuvers, by special government concessions, by high powered lobbying in Congress and administrative agencies and—in ultimate contempt for the people—by turning a deaf ear to pleas for responsible corporate citizenship. . . .

In 1970, for the first time, Americans rallied around the cause of preserving our environment. But their enormous enthusiasm had yet to find direction or true leadership. The two men with the greatest opportunity to chart new passages—Richard Nixon and Edmund Muskie—dusted off old maps, and are now attempting, each in his own way, to steer the same course which has brought us to our present peril.

—Excerpts from the concluding chapter of the Task Force on Air Pollution Report (published commercially under the title *The Vanishing Air*), a joint production of the Center for the Study of Responsive Law and its summer help, known popularly as "Nader's Raiders"

Government agencies and major corporations are both fond of having themselves studied—a fact that is attested to by the scores of $100,000-and-up consultant studies around. In the summer of 1969 six such studies of major proportions were undertaken by 110 students, selected from hundreds of applicants, for the unheard-of total cost of about $100,000. While most of those studied never thought of these students as consultants but rather as a venal horde ordered down upon them, that is the function they performed, though in no case were they invited, as is normal in consulting arrangements.

"Nader's Raiders," as they have been called, are, of course, the creation of their namesake and leader, Ralph Nader. They are also one aspect of an *ad hoc* "consulting" operation conducted from two floors of offices above an office-supply store in Washington. The drab offices are the home of the Center for the Study of Responsive Law, a crucial part of Ralph Nader's growing consumer organization. Not too long ago it would have been correct to look at Nader as the lone crusader; today there is a substantial and ever-growing Nader organization, a consumer conglomerate. Besides the center, which is essentially its research arm, a recently established "public interest" law firm serves as the action arm of the organization, pursuing in court the issues uncovered by other elements in the program. Nader also has a small operation working strictly on the issue of automobile safety and keeping up the pressure on the issues first raised in his hard-hitting critique *Unsafe at Any Speed*. Finally there is the facet of his organization that those around him refer to as his "amorphous and largely secret network"—Nader's followers from all over the nation on whom he and his lieutenants can call to ferret out special information.

The Raiders are the most famous aspect of the center's operations. When they started in the summer of 1968 Nader explained the rationale behind the operation: "Students have long come to Washington to work *in* federal agencies for the summer. My idea is to have them come down and work *on* the agencies: to come down and study relentlessly on a daily basis what an agency is doing. This has never been done before." The first group assembled was assigned to two agencies: the Federal Trade Commission and the Food and Drug Administration. For that summer there were seven Raiders in all. In 1969 the Raiders returned, grown now to more than 100, from all over the country, bearing varied credentials. More than a score were women, a half dozen were engineering students, and several were medical students. Under the direction of Robert Fellmuth, Harvard law student and veteran of the first summer, the number of targets increased. Teams were assigned to the Interstate Commerce Commission, the Food and Drug Administration, safety agencies of the Department of Health, Education and Welfare, the health and safety activities of the Labor Department, the Department of the Interior, and the influential Washington law firm of Covington and Burling.

The major product of the first summer's work was a stinging 185-page critique of the Federal Trade Commission. Strong documented charges made against the commission led to the recommendation by the Raiders that FTC Chairman Paul Rand Dixon should resign. A typical charge in the report stated that the commission was masking its varied failures with secrecy, misrepresentation, and "collusion with business interests." The FTC report received plenty of news coverage, touched off charges and countercharges, and precipitated a Presidential study of the FTC. The Presidential study, conducted by the American Bar Association, not only came up with similarly stinging charges but cited the Raiders' report with approval.

Other major studies stemming from the joint efforts of the center and the Raiders have been *The Chemical Feast*, a study of food protection and the Food and Drug Administration, *The Task Force Report on Air Pollution*, and *Surface Transportation, the Public Interest and the Interstate Commerce Commission*—all blistering indictments of the federal apparatus as it affects single areas of consumer interest.

There was unprecedented interest in the summer group for 1970; over 3,500 applied for slightly fewer than 200 slots on fifteen teams. For the first time teams were deployed across the nation and not restricted to Washington. Among the items targeted for investigation: the impact of Maine's paper and pulp industry on the state; the problems associated with the pollution of the Savannah River; the impact of the First National City Bank of New York on the community; the abuse of land in California; think tanks and their relationship with the government; the power of E. I. duPont de Nemours Company in the state of Delaware; the self-policing mechanisms of hospitals and in the medical profession; the effectiveness of the Justice Department's Antitrust Division; and the quality of care provided by private nursing homes. In addition, follow-up studies were scheduled to determine what changes had occurred at agencies studied by previous teams.

A typical team of the Raiders' class of '70 is a group that operated out of a cluttered second-floor walk-up above an insurance office in Savannah, Georgia. It called itself "The Savannah River Project" and was directed by Jim Fallows, a twenty-two-year-old Nader protégé who sandwiched in his term as a Raider between his graduation from Harvard and the beginning of a Rhodes scholarship. The team consisted of ten young people, male and female, with a variety of specialties, among them law, engineering, political science, history, and sociology. Each was given $600 to cover the summer's expenses. Their concern was the polluted river and its relationship to the city of Savannah, its industry, its politics, and its economy. Each team member focused on one aspect of the situation—for example, the role of industry in pollution of the river, the role of the state of Georgia in water-pollution abatement, and the economic impact of pollution on individuals, such as fishermen. The result of the team's labors was a report on Savannah and its river called *The Water Lords*, which appeared in 1971.

While the Raiders account for much of the center's investigative momentum, they are "summer help" to the much smaller permanent staff of the center. It is this permanent group that whips into shape mountains of data provided by the summer groups, keeps year-round pressure on the federal bureaucracy and target industries, and sets the direction and tone for investigation. Besides conducting its own studies and tying together the work of the Raiders, the center is a source of raw material for the lawyers at the new law firm. It is also a locale for managing long-range consumer projects, one of which is a "citizens' handbook," now being compiled for publication in 1972, that will outline ways in which a citizen can participate in government proceedings to secure his rights. The center—exclusive of the Raiders—costs about $200,000 a year to operate. The money comes from such sources as the publication of studies, individual contributions, and foundation support. One of its largest bequests thus far was a "no strings attached" grant of $100,000 from Gordon Sherman, the Midas Muffler king.

The center is short on formal organization and bureaucratic trappings. Its director, Theodore Jacobs, a tall, outgoing attorney who was a classmate of Nader's at Princeton and Harvard Law School, explains, "After what Ralph has seen in government, it is understandable that he is wary of setting up his own top-heavy bureaucracy." While it shies away from "overorganization" and organizational formality, it is quite formal about accuracy. Jacobs and others at the center emphasize that one of the reasons that Nader has moved to the prominence and respect that he now enjoys is that he never lets up on double-checking his facts before using them. If there is a secret to the study technique of the center, it is intensive, investigative reporting backed up by thorough review and documentation. John Schulz, an alumnus of the Raiders who worked on the FTC report and is now teaching law, explains a technique common to Nader's study teams both permanent and temporary as he relates how his group operated: "Typically a member would do his homework on an area of the commission's activities by reading public documents. Then meetings would be arranged on an off-the-record basis with people who were in a position to know about that area of the FTC's operation. Finally, an interview would be set up with the FTC officials in the particular area of interest. In the interview a response which was not in line with what had been learned in the off-the-record interviews would be pressed and the responses recorded." He points out that the pursuit of facts in dispute between outside sources and the FTC yielded some of the team's best leads. After such leads are discovered they are nailed down by follow-up interviews and further examination of documents.

Although Nader is clearly in charge of the center, his lieutenants are definitely individualists with their own styles and habits. One of them, John Esposito, who specializes in investigating pollution for the center, actually smokes cigarettes—a condition Nader never tires of trying to cure. Their main similarity to Nader is not in their personalities but in their thoroughness in pursuing subjects and their devotion to the ever-broadening cause of consumerism. One of the eight permanent consultants to the center is James S. Turner, whose concerns and activities are typical. An Annapolis graduate and ex-Navy officer, he is a young lawyer and like Nader in one striking respect: He is constantly on the go and seems to have a dozen things on the griddle at once. Like the other consultants who have specialties—such as pollution, agriculture, transportation, and health—he generally concentrates on one area of food and health.

His work began in 1968 when, as a participant in one of the first summer groups, he and two others began looking into the functioning of the Food and Drug Administration, especially the role of the FDA in food protection. A second team worked on the issue under Turner's direction during the summer of 1969. Their efforts produced the study entitled *The Chemical Feast*, authored by Turner and published in 1970. In all, he used nineteen assistants who helped him collect over 10,000 documents and conduct over 500 interviews on the subject of the FDA and food protection.

The final report is a well-documented and authoritative exposé highlighting such specific abuses as the FDA's failure to enforce food regulations, inadequate food labeling and testing, misleading advertising, and the inadequacy of research into nutrition and food health. Turner and his associates detail their charges of deception and bureaucratic failure in case after case; the evidence clearly supports Nader's claim in his introduction to the report: "In a word, the Food and Drug Administration has been an official sponsor of processing and marketing practices that transformed the defrauding of consumers into a competitive advantage—a kind of reverse competition (deceptive packaging alone costs consumers billions a year)."

Unlike traditional consultants who finish long-range studies and run, Turner considers his work merely a "first step" rather than a closed case. He sees it as a guidebook for consumers, a source of litigation, a starting point for new inquiries, and a document for concerned legislators that tells them what Turner has in his files for their use or can testify about to help reform food regulations. Turner has consulted with a substantial number of interested people and committees on Capitol Hill about issues brought up in the report and has already initiated six lawsuits based on discoveries made in his work. The legal action ranges from filing a suit under the Federal Freedom of Information Act to force the FDA to release its "classified" information on the safety of monosodium glutamate to challenging a list of food additives which the FDA has not tested but has permitted to be used under the assumption that they are "generally recognized as safe"—a description that Turner believes is not warranted. Now Turner is starting new studies, including Raider-assisted investigations of supermarket practices such as pricing policies, date coding, grade labeling, and deceptive promotional gimmicks; national policies on milk and meat prices; and food that is marketed for children, including the effect of food companies on children's diets and food preferences. As a guide for consumers, *The Chemical Feast* offers many specific bits of information that should make the wary consumer more so. For example, it shows how the manufacturers of Gatorade have avoided federal nonalcoholic-beverage standards by not calling it a beverage but rather "a thirst quencher," or how Coca-Cola has fought long and hard to keep from putting on its bottles the fact that caffeine is an ingredient, or how Lipton's beef stroganoff mix is primarily made of soy beans, not meat, or how widely water is used to dilute bottled orange juice that is sold as pure.

Turner is convinced, as are the others at the center, that investigations like theirs are of little value unless they are followed up with action. Thus, every consultant at the center has the equivalent of one and a half lawyers from the law firm working with them to follow through on the abuses they uncover.

The chairman of the board, founder, inspiration, and guide for the center is, of course, Nader himself. The center is part of Nader's plan to transform his unique one-man crusade into a swarm of gadflies who share his concern for consumer rights. To him, the center is both a training ground for "public interest" specialists and a permanent research program conducted for the American consumer.

"Household word" is not a term to be used with abandon. It is safe to say, however, that Nader has become just that. He is better known than the vast majority of U.S. Senators and is unquestionably the most famous of all Washington lobbyists or lawyers. In the period since Nader first came into national prominence with his critique of automobile safety, he has discovered and effectively played the role of the outspoken advocate of consumerism in the nation. To the dismay of old-line lobbyists, Nader has beaten them at their own game, only he has chosen the general rather than the vested interest in his advocacy. He has carved out a niche for himself in Washington, yet is neither salaried, appointed, elected, nor employed by any client or organization. Although Nader attracts money, which he pumps into his organization, he has limited his own income. He lives in an eighty-dollar-a-month furnished room on 19th Street in Washington near DuPont Circle and wears ready-made suits.

He is bound to no predetermined issues—thus the ever-increasing assortment of topics he and his allies have become involved in since he began exploring the safety of automobiles. In conversation he moves quickly from area to area, just as he does in public. An hour spent with Nader is likely to be one in which he touches on such diverse subjects as pollution, the role of the elderly in America, nursing homes, pipeline safety, transportation safety, law schools, law firms, food, medicine, and the effects of noise. As he launches into each subject he brings up facts and statistics with dazzling facility. In discussing secrecy in government, for example, he makes his point by carefully but quickly citing court cases, specific dates of actions, quotes from officials and memos, and lawsuits that he and his allies are bringing. From time to time somebody predicts that this proclivity to attack many subjects at once will result in his spreading himself too thin and subsequently cause him to flounder as he zeroes in on an issue on which he can neither substantiate his charges nor muster any public indignation. Though conceivable, such an error is not probable. Two traits those close to Nader most often ascribe to him are his thoroughness and his uncanny sense of timing.

Judged in terms of what was a short time ago a one-man operation, he has been phenomenally successful, something that even his enemies glumly concede. His power has grown apace with diversification. Despite periodic predictions by his detractors or skeptics that his influence will soon wane, it shows no signs of doing so. He has achieved in a few years the kind of momentum that politicians dream of but seldom attain even after years on the hustings.

A key to Nader's success is that people want to hear what he has to say—and he obliges them. In 1966 when the furor and interest over *Unsafe at Any Speed* was still high, he mentioned in an interview in the *Saturday Review* that the auto issue had been so successful because Americans are ". . . starving for acts of the individual in a conflict situation outside the sports arena." Many conflicts later, his colleague Turner ascribes much of Nader's success to his "depolarizing influence." Explains Turner, "He has decided to act on the universal complaints. He has something to say to the hard-hats and the students whose heads they bang—and they both listen!"

One of the most important parts of his constituency has been students and young people because he has long realized that they are the most likely apostles for consumerism. Over the last five or so years he has been in almost constant communication with students. He has found time to advise students who contact him, is one of the most sought-after speakers on the college lecture circuit, and has given "short" courses in consumerism, including a two-week course at his alma mater, Princeton. His delivery and content are as strong on campus as they are in the Congressional hearing room. He told a student group in Michigan in 1968 that the United States ". . . will see consumer demonstrations some day that will make civil-rights demonstrations look small by comparison." Nader says that he likes to address students because he feels their energies can be channeled into public-service investigation. For years he has found time to advise and tutor individual students interested in consumer investigation.

If one chooses to call Nader's consumerism a movement, it is a movement of unique power. Nader's success offers an outstanding example as the exception to the rule. In this complex era it is easy to say that no man can really have an effect on the system—to change institutions or make the government more responsive. Nader's name in itself is a rebuttal to such generalizations.

Contrary to many portraits of the man that have described him as a dour, one-dimensional character, he is a personable, enormously energetic, wide-ranging young man. At the person-to-person level he is friendly, relaxed, courteous, and devoid of his public cynicism. His most striking characteristic is his sincerity. His view of the future is bleak. He contends that we will all be hearing more and more about the "environmental assault on our physiology." The assault of the future will include not only those forms of pollutions and hazards already catalogued by Nader and his allies but also "many, many more." All these concerns merge in one theme stated by Nader: "We are heading pell-mell into a period when we may endanger the very survival of the species on the planet by our reckless and boundless development of new technology and processes."

He envisions crises of increasing magnitude. The thalidomide tragedy, he asserts, is the precursor of the larger crises that may be upon us in a few decades, when, for example, man may be confronted with the fact that he has seriously diminished his own supply of oxygen. It is Nader's belief that people can and will be alerted to these dangers. He adds, "I think this is something which will some day be the core of a very substantial reform movement in this country."

Nader's center is not the only study/action group of its kind. Others are cropping up at an amazing rate, all of them, to varying degrees, inspired or aided by Nader. In Washington alone there are the Citizens Advocate Center, the Center for Law and Public Policy, the Urban Law Institute, the Washington Research Project, the Public Law Education Institute, the Project on Corporate Responsibility, and a cluster of single-purpose consumer groups working out of the George Washington University Law School. All of these groups are to some extent functioning in the same general areas of interest as Nader and his staff. The Citizens Advocate Center of

Washington, for example, is a new group that describes itself as "A privately funded watchdog on federal programs which affect the poor." It has produced two major studies: one on hunger in the U.S., the other on the government's treatment of the Indian. The groups working out of George Washington University generally use Nader's team approach to issues of public interest. Collectively these groups have been dubbed "Banzhaf's Bandits" after their leader, a consumer-oriented law professor named John Banzhaf—thus setting up a cordial "Raiders"–"Bandits" rivalry. (The Bandits are given to naming their units with tricky titles that fall naturally into descriptive acronyms; for examples there is ASH (for Action on Smoking and Health), SOUP (for Students Opposing Unfair Practices, which started by going after Campbell Soup for its practice of adding marbles to the soup shown in its TV advertisements to make it look thicker), and GASP (for Greater Washington Alliance to Stop Pollution). A new group closely associated with Nader is called the Project on Corporate Responsibility, a group of young Washington lawyers who launched themselves into national prominence with their "Campaign GM." The effort, which was strongly supported by Nader, sought (1) to amend the corporate charter of the giant automaker so that it would not undertake any activity inconsistent with the public interest and (2) to make room on the GM Board for three representatives of the public. Although it did not achieve its goals, the drive did draw attention to the cause of reforming the automobile industry. More recently, it has taken on the nation's corporate farmers for their treatment of migratory workers.

As these examples illustrate, a class of institutions—born of the complexity of modern issues and sustained by affluence—has emerged in America to play the role of gadflies to the Establishment. As with any class, there are different species. Some of these institutional gadflies, like Nader's Center and other consumer groups, bite hard hoping to reform. When that doesn't work they try to pester and drive the more incorrigible elements of the Establishment out of existence, stampeded like so many insect-crazed cattle off a cliff. There is, however, another species that is more friendly to things as they are. They can sting, too, but they do so rarely and then only to drive the Establishment in a particular direction rather than to harm the beast.

5. Free Advisers and Their Advice

[Brookings] *publications cause something of a stir in the world. Newspapers print summaries of them on their front pages. Economists, editorial writers and some politicians cite them much as Fundamentalist preachers draw upon Holy Writ. Although the emotional appeal of these books is nil, their statements have caused many highly placed or otherwise prominent persons to yell bloody murder.*

—New York *Times*, March 20, 1938

A number of think tanks specialize in an old commodity: free advice. Taken as a group, they are close to government, public in the sense that their research is available to whoever wants to read it, and all have the stated objective of clarifying issues. They advise on foreign policy, military matters, economics and domestic problems and demand little in return. That is not to say that they are never rewarded. Their advice is almost always listened to and sometimes heeded. And the men who think for them often find that they are in a prime position to be picked for jobs within government just as high-echelon office holders find them good places to retire to when their tenure is up. They are much closer to the political and social Establishment than any of the public think tanks discussed thus far.

Oldest and most venerable of these groups is the Brookings Institution. Incorporated in its present form in 1927, it merged the Institute for Government Research (founded in 1916 and generally acknowledged to be the first private group devoted to analysis of public policy issues at the national level), the Institute of Economics (founded in 1922 to study economic problems), and the Robert Brookings Graduate School of Economics and Government.

Over the years its influence on government has been significant. Although it works directly for the government only on special occasions (and then only on the condition that the work will be un-

300

classified and publishable), its studies are often more carefully considered than those made by federally supported groups. Historically, it helped create and define the federal budgetary process, formulate war-debt policies, and reform-tariff policies in the 1920's. During the Hoover Administration it was primarily responsible for convincing the nation that a plan to create a St. Lawrence seaway was too expensive, thereby helping to scuttle the proposal. Brookings was a constant and influential critic of various aspects of the New Deal, and during World War II its analysts helped to create and manage a variety of wartime agencies. After the war it served as the principal architect of the Marshall Plan.

In more recent years the Institution has presented each incoming national Administration with a written summary of the major problems and issues thought to face it. Theodore Sorensen, in his book *Kennedy*, said of Brookings' written "agenda" given the Kennedy Administration: ". . . it deserves a large share of the credit for history's smoothest transfer of power between opposing parties." Brookings staff members served on a variety of task forces establishing New Frontier programs. Other assists for the Kennedy Administration ranged from helping it set up the research program for the Space Agency to free consultation on economic policy. Similarly, it was active in helping to mold Great Society programs during the Johnson Administration. Said Johnson at a celebration marking the fiftieth anniversary of Brookings in 1966, "You are a national institution, so important to, at least, the Executive branch—and I think the Congress and the country—that if you did not exist we would have to ask someone to create you."

Today, after fifty years of building a solid reputation for telling the government what to do, it is still doing just that. For example, just as it had done for past Presidents, it gave President Nixon a memorandum upon his election (published nationally under the title *Agenda for the Nation*), which told him politely what in their opinion were the problems facing him and what he would have to do to contend with them. Financed by a $175,000 grant from the Ford Foundation, the 620-page report contained papers by eighteen experts from various parts of the political spectrum, writing on foreign and domestic problems, among them Henry A. Kissinger, Clark Kerr, Charles L. Schultz, and Edwin O. Reischauer, whose views and recommendations were treated as major news by the press.

Though it was certainly not accepted as a blueprint for Nixon policies, it was studied by the incoming Administration.

Brookings has been called a university without students, where learned men do research; a well-heeled publishing house because it produces about twenty-five books a year under its own imprint; a graduate school for federal officials because it conducts conferences and seminars on public problems for interested officials; a government in limbo because of the number of ex-high-echelon appointees in its ranks and its role in supplying and lending its people to government—and as the single most important outside economic consultant to federal fiscal policy-makers. All of these characterizations are valid.

Its resident staff is composed of about 160 people, augmented by the brain power of about eighty-five scholars from around the country who are associated with its research programs. At any given moment Brookings is working on about 100 research projects, which are likely to range from specific and rather technical studies of monetary and fiscal matters (e.g., "Price Policies of the French National Railways" and "The Economics of Copyright") to major critiques intended to have an impact on governmental programs and policies. An illustration of the latter is a work produced by Brookings in March 1970 entitled *Setting National Priorities: The 1971 Budget.* It is a team-produced analysis of President Nixon's fiscal 1971 budget which examines the alternatives that faced the Administration in putting it together. Says Edward K. Hamilton, Brookings' young vice-president who worked on the study, "It's an advocacy document meant to give people a knowledge of the alternatives that the government faced and of the ones it took so that they can be better advocates of change." Hamilton adds that this analysis will probably become an annual reaction to the federal budget. He hopes that one of the long-range impacts of this analysis will be to prevent what he terms "horror stories" or things that are obviously wrong but which nobody has been able or willing to remedy. For example, one of the many items cited is "impacted aid," or the program, originated during the Korean war, under which the government agreed to provide financial assistance to school districts with a large number of students whose parents are federal employees. Brookings' analysis shows that this particular program produces a variety of inequities, such as the fact that very wealthy bedroom suburbs of Washington,

D.C., are receiving substantial aid for the "burden" imposed on their schools by parents who work in Washington. This is just one of a number of such boondoggles cited. Another aspect of the report is the revelation of what Hamilton calls "budgetary gimmicks," such as the process by which Congress keeps doubling the values of new public-works programs while it shows on paper that it has cut the budget—a trick accomplished through starting mammoth long-term projects by appropriating small amounts while cutting back slightly on costly ongoing programs.

Located on Massachusetts Avenue in Washington close to the center of government, the Brookings Institution's "urban campus" is composed of a large imposing stone office building, an annex and a conference center. It is a nonpartisan, independent organization in the unique position of being free of government supervision but a major participant in government policy-making. Although it has been accused from time to time of being a partisan of the Right or the Left, such charges are usually based on single studies and never seem to stick. But other think tanks in the business of dispensing free advice have acquired labels that stick.

Three think tanks that have been lumped together under the term the "Cold War think tanks" are the University of Pennsylvania's Foreign Policy Research Institute, Stanford's Hoover Institution on War, Revolution and Peace, and Georgetown University's Center for Strategic and International Studies.

Smallest of the three is the Pennsylvania Foreign Policy Research Institute. Established in 1955 as a nonprofit organization that counts among its purposes the examination of long-range problems of U.S. foreign policy and suggestions of guidelines for United States foreign policy and programs. Most of its support comes from private corporations and foundations, though it has received some contracts from the Department of Defense to investigate military strategy. Its studies have consistently dealt with Cold War strategy, and it has unfailingly served as an advocate of aggressive defense policies.

Oldest and largest of the three is the Hoover Institution, which traces its origins to the era when Herbert Hoover headed the American Relief Administration, an agency directing relief centers in Europe after World War I. Hoover found that there was a paucity of economic, social, and political data in the United States on Europe. In 1919 he pledged $50,000 to Stanford University to begin to fill the void by collecting information on the Great War. Over the years the Hoover gift was parlayed into one of the nation's top libraries on international affairs. In the late 1950's, at Hoover's insistence, the institution took a new tact: more concentrated research on communism. As Hoover stated in 1959, "The purpose of this institution must be, by its research and publications, to demonstrate the evils of the doctrines of Karl Marx. . . ." The institution became strongly partisan in the 1960's, plugging the hard-line internationally and conservatism domestically (in 1967 the *Wall Street Journal* called it "a haven for Goldwater men"). Recently the Hoover Institution has shown signs of becoming more moderate, less partisan, and more diverse.

Today the institution runs on a relatively large annual budget of nearly $2 million a year, most of it from individuals and private foundations, with a small amount from federal contracts. Its activities range from a broad scholarly research program with about 125 projects proceeding at any given time to the newly inaugurated program of giving "Peace Fellowships" to young scholars of all nationalities. Its million-volume library, which takes up much of the space in the 285-foot Hoover tower rising above the Stanford campus, is one of the best of its kind in the world and is frequently consulted by various branches of the federal government.

Though still strongly concerned with communism and Cold War strategy, it is also doing a substantially increased amount of work on such topics as peaceful change, arms control, domestic American problems, and nonstrategic studies of areas of the world. In 1969 it sponsored a major conference on Peaceful Change in Modern Society, and its literature now carries the motto "To Promote Peace."

Probably the most influential of the three is the Center for Strategic and International Studies. Besides sharing concerns with the other two Cold War think tanks, it practices considerable interchange with them in terms of staff, directors, and academic cooperation.

CSIS is an odd mixture of characteristics. It is affiliated with a major university, yet as was pointed out in an article about it in *Hoya*, the Georgetown student newspaper, ". . . [it] is less familiar to most students than the terrain of the Sea of Tranquility. Few have heard of it, and, among those few, misconceptions abound." It refuses to do any classified research, yet it classifies its list of contributors (who kick in almost half a million a year) as strictly confidential. Its reputation is deservedly conservative, and it has tended to be hard-line and militaristic in its outlook, yet it is conscientiously trying to refute that image. It categorically refuses federal money as a matter of principle, yet it takes enough money from oil interests to be thought of as a research arm of the petroleum industry.

At its beginning in 1962 it was, according to one staff member, ". . . heavily involved in Cold War politics just like the nation itself was." Its founders were Admiral Arleigh Burke, Chief of Naval Operations from 1955 to 1961 and now head of CSIS; Reverend James B. Horigan of the Georgetown faculty; and David Abshire, who until recently was its executive director and is now Assistant Secretary of State for Congressional Relations. Its birth was aided both financially and administratively by the American Enterprise Institute for Public Policy Research, a politically and economically conservative research foundation and lobby founded in 1943 and dedicated to ". . . the maintenance of the system of free enterprise." CSIS severed its ties with the group in 1966.

Nobody at CSIS denies its conservative heritage or the fact that there are conservatives on its staff and well salted throughout its advisory board. Nor do they claim that Admiral Burke has rejected the hard-line views for which he is known. But they do claim that its political vistas have broadened considerably since its early days. Jon Vondracek, CSIS's young enthusiastic director of communications who covered military affairs for *Time* before taking his present job, says, "The center has a substantial base and background in conservatism, but never extremism. We like to think of ourselves generally as moderate—close to the vital center."

Most of the earlier studies completed by CSIS generally contain both recommendations and conclusions that support the assessment that its goal was to throw all of its intellectual weight behind winning the Cold War. Its major concerns through the mid-1960's were such things as Soviet nuclear strategy, the strategic implications of East-West trade, the Soviet technological challenge, Cold War strategies, and China. Things have changed somewhat. CSIS still does strategic studies, but the scope of its work, the range of opinions appearing in its studies, and the divergence of opinion of the people it taps to work with it have all opened up. Vondracek says that CSIS cannot be categorized as having a single point of view or even that it tends in that direction any more. "Intellectual brokerage house" is what he calls it because of its stated position that the examination of policy issues must be directed to the full range of assumptions and alternatives. He adds that they are not in the business of reconciling the divergent views they solicit but rather presenting them clearly in the belief that such clarification is the most useful way of solving policy problems.

Recent activities bear out the conclusion that CSIS is a diverse and, in sum, moderate—though conservative—force in generating thoughts in the international area. For example, its frequent seminars, convened to examine the major issues of U.S. foreign policy, have been structured to make sure all sides are represented, as in several instances when Marcus Raskin and Richard Barnet of the Institute for Policy Studies were participants. Its studies also seek to dispel its partisan past. To illustrate, one notably unhawkish conclusion of a 1969 study of U.S.–Japanese relations states, "The United States should welcome Japanese efforts to open further contacts with the Chinese Peoples' Republic . . . the United States should not press the Japanese to avoid trade in strategic items with Communist China." In just about all of its studies, along with the majority's conclusions, there are inevitably dissenting conclusions made by panelists who are given equal space to take the majority to task. In a report in which the majority advocated that the United States maintain military pressure in the Persian Gulf, a Harvard professor on the panel wrote a scathing rebuttal.

There is no specific research plan as such at CSIS; rather, the primary work for its staff of thirty is putting together studies, panels, reports, and books on international policy issues that it thinks have not been properly or adequately examined. Work in progress in 1970 included such international concerns as the role of the U.S. in the Western Pacific, the key issues in Brazil's future, Canadian foreign policy, outlook for the future of the Indian Ocean area, and a report on the Suez Canal.

While it does not carry the clout of Brookings in government, CSIS is nonetheless influential. All of its reports are offered to Congressmen, and 250 to 300 legislators consistently respond to new studies by asking for copies. Sometimes its influence is felt directly. A 1967 report about the Panama Canal treaty in which the majority of its contributing panelists urged a speed-up in U.S.–Panama negotiations for a new treaty was cited extensively in Congressional debate on the issue. Its 1969 report entitled *Soviet Sea Power* carefully explored the strengths and weaknesses of Russian maritime capabilities. One source who has worked for CSIS on several projects says that the Soviet sea-power study shows the difference between the old and the new center: "In the old days it would have been a study of Soviet strength, but now it's both strengths and weaknesses." Among the large number of copies sold was a batch bought for distribution by the White House. Its report on the *Economic Impact of the Vietnam War* has been broadly quoted on its judgment of how badly the government misjudged the inflationary impact of the war. A 1966 study of American intervention in the Dominican Republic, which concluded that the U.S. did what it was obliged to do in the circumstances, was widely read by those in government, including President Johnson, and was cited as a document to support continued U.S. intervention in Latin America. A 1969 inquiry into the implications of British withdrawal from the Persian Gulf by 1971 was reportedly a significant factor in causing the Wilson government in Britain to review its decision.

Since it takes no federal money and does not reveal the sources of the approximately $500,000 a year it needs to conduct its program, the question of who its benefactors are is not without interest. Its position is that it does not indicate sources of support because it is competing for funds with other study groups. Despite the secrecy, some facts are known. About forty supporters kick in each year. Defense industries contribute less than 5 percent, according to Senator Claiborne Pell, who sits on CSIS's advisory board. The bulk of its money comes from foundations, such as the W. H. Donner Fund and the Eli Lilly Endowment, and private companies ranging from a major brokerage house to oil companies. The substantial stake of oil companies and oil-supported foundations in CSIS is noteworthy: At least ten oil companies, including Esso, Occidental Petroleum, and Gulf, regularly contribute, and it is known that the oil firms have made grants to support studies of the Middle East and other oil-rich areas of the world. Frank N. Ikard, head of the American Petroleum Institute, the oil industry's prime lobby in Washington, sits on its board along with other petroleum partisans. To a significant extent, CSIS has become a center for policy research for the oil interests. This is not to say that it is shading the results of its studies to coincide with the views of the oil companies but, rather, that the oil interests are contributing to the till so that studies of areas of the world they are interested in are made. Former Executive Director Abshire told an interviewer from the Georgetown student newspaper that the control and direction of all studies are completely in csis's hands, and he noted, ". . . the value to corporations would drop if there were an attempt to shape the research." According to Vondracek, in the future csis is planning to change its policy toward new grants and, in line with its new image, will make the names of its supporters public.

The ideological span separating think tanks that profess to be working for the public is wide. From a variety of bases—Socialist experimentation to fervent antisocialism, to name just one span— they are all attempting to cope with what they believe are the major problems of American society. They all evince the same faith in dialogue, study, and experimentation as Robert Hutchins' Center for the Study of Democratic Institutions. The fact that csis regularly bats around ideas with thinkers from the Institute for Policy Studies or that Hutchins' Center unilaterally embarks on peace conferences or that Nader is using his center to harness the vitality of students to attain uncompromising reform all point to a broad dialogue with an idealized public. Because they are appealing to the public and trying to sway policy-makers, they are, in the broadest sense of the word, lobbyists. They attempt to cajole the public and its government through studies, reports, and experiments. As lobbies, they are an improvement over the traditional variety since their appeals are public and based on scholarship rather than the behind-the-scenes dictates of vested private interests. To be sure, these centers raise many new ideas and alternatives—whether it be a new Constitution or continued aggressive military policies—that could well produce more problems than they solve, so it is important for those on the receiving end of their brain production to listen well and critically. Regrettably, it is often hard to hear them.

As a force in opening policy debates to the public they have failed in one critical area. Save for Nader's group, which is both a product and a beneficiary of Nader's ability to generate sparks, none is a truly dynamic public force. Brookings has restrained itself to the point of dullness. The three so-called Cold War think tanks are all but unknown on their own campuses. Outside circles where its authors are quoted in teach-ins, the Institute for Policy Studies is, thus far, seldom mentioned. The Center for the Study of Democratic Institutions appears to be trying harder but still can claim only a limited constituency. Nader, on the other hand, has been able to give policy issues a sense of immediate and pressing importance. He has opted for the dynamic over the academic. A contrast of more than symbolic importance is that while most of these centers close down or slow down for the summer in the grand academic style, that is when Nader is deploying his largest force.

XI

PROSPECTING THE FUTURE

---

1. The Futurists

> *The SDS Weathermen and the Federal Government both offer the promise of a better future, but I'm afraid that neither has given much thought to what they mean.*
>
> —U.S. Office of Education official (who chose to offer the opinion anonymously)
>
> *My interest is in the future, because I'm going to spend the rest of my life there.*
>
> —Charles Kettering, American inventor

Runaway technology and man's historical unwillingness to look at the long-term impact of his discoveries are two factors often cited by those trying to explain our present predicament. These same two factors are also credited with inspiring a new kind of research that is gaining ground throughout the world. It is a form of policy research variously called futures research, prognostics, prospection, forecasting, futurecasting, futurism, futurology, and futuristics. The premise be-

310

hind it is that the future is too important to be left to chance.

Although its practitioners differ sharply on methods and have yet to agree on a name for their pursuit, they do agree on basics and can present a common front when it comes to their tenets. They believe that the future can and must be explored. Unlike the crystal gazers and Sunday-supplement prophets, they don't think the future can be predicted exactly because there are too many unknowns. But they do believe that we are creating our own future. They argue that, like it or not, we are now in effect creating it with our decisions, discoveries, actions, and inactions. Since we are creating the future, they contend, we are in a position to determine at least part of it. By looking at what possible alternative futures can or should be, the futurists feel that they can give the rest of us the perception to make better decisions about the future we want rather than one that engulfs us because of our own haphazard actions. Specifically, the futurist believes that he can have an impact where expenditures of time, money, energy, and thought can conspire to cause some events and prevent others. They agree that some aspects of all futures are beyond our control.

While this view of the future is by no means new to man, the very existence of a loose international confederation of thinkers who have—or claim—an ability to grapple with the future constitutes a new and unique intellectual direction. Though the concerted study of the future got its first major push only in the 1960's, it already possesses its own leaders, journals, schools of thought, associations, institutions, and jargon—in fact, all the accouterments of a full-fledged intellectual movement. Largest of the futures associations is the World Futures Society, formed in 1966 in Washington to serve as a clearinghouse for long-range planners and forecasters. Its president and founder, Edward S. Cornish, now claims more than 6,000 members in forty-five countries. Groups of futurists have been forming in other countries: Japan, Denmark, France, Italy, West Germany, and Sweden now have at least one futures society apiece. Two major international conferences on futures research have been held—one in Oslo in 1967, another in Kyoto in 1970. Other conferences have been held to explore the future of a single topic, such as the meeting held recently in Amsterdam on the urban environment predicted for the year 2000. Futurists also keep in touch through their journals, such as *The Futurist, Technological Forecasting,* and *Futures.* Futures

311

studies are being conducted by a number of governments, commissions, and universities, and more than eighty American colleges and universities now offer courses in exploring the future. In addition, there are several companies and schools specializing in teaching forecasting to people in industry and government—among them, the Technological Forecasting Institute of New York and an Alexandria, Virginia, firm with the intriguing name of Synergistic Cybernetics Inc.

The current popularity of futures research can be traced to a diverse group. First, the movement owes much—like it or not—to American military research in think tanks. Researchers at the RAND Corporation, who developed a method for forecasting called Delphi, made popular the idea that objective methods for exploring the future were possible. Scenario-writing (or scripts for the future) of the Herman Kahn–Hudson Institute school offered the notion that people would read —and pay for—speculation on the future. Kahn's work prompted both positive and negative reaction, but in either case it got people thinking about the future. Long-range studies of weapons technology, mathematical models of the future, alternative developments, and the like showed that new techniques for researching the future were available. In addition, such oft-told stories as RAND's predicting the first Soviet space launch or TEMPO's picking the year of the first Chinese atomic detonation helped give credence to the idea that intelligent men studying future events can come up with valid conclusions.

Not to be overlooked is the influence of the serious science-fiction writers like Jules Verne, H. G. Wells, Arthur C. Clarke, Robert A. Heinlein, Isaac Asimov, and the novels of Utopia and anti-Utopia. These creative individuals, not constrained by the discipline of normal scientific and academic writing, have cast about in the future, sometimes with amazing prognostic results. The fact that in 1945 Arthur Clarke perfectly described the communications satellite, thirteen years before it had been developed, is one of many examples that credit the imaginative use of scientific knowledge in foretelling future inventions. Similarly, works like George Orwell's 1984 and Aldous Huxley's Brave New World showed that well-constructed visions of the future, based on pervasive social trends in society, can provide powerful images of alternative futures that must be avoided.

Finally there is the influence of the pioneering works on futures that, taken as a whole, outline the necessity and feasibility of futures research. John McHale's *Future of the Future*, Gerald Feinberg's *The Prometheus Project*, Bertrand de Jouvenel's *Art of Conjecture*, and Dennis Gabor's *Inventing the Future* laid the philosophical basis for futurism. Then there are the "how to" books that give the methodology of futures research, such as Ralph Lenz's *Technological Forecasting*, Marvin Cetron's *Technological Forecasting: A Practical Approach*, and Robert U. Ayers' *Technological Forecasting and Long-Range Planning*. This last group of books is not for the layman with a casual interest in futurism; they are rigorous technical discussions of the variety of forecasting techniques.

It is no surprise, then, that there are many approaches to the future among those who now study it. At one extreme are those who project the future that may, should or conceivably could be—projections based in large measure on private visions and troubled speculations, as Huxley projected his *Brave New World*. Then there are those who rely on traditional means of study—for example, General Electric's Business Environment Section has conducted several long-range studies of the future of values and the business environment in which its "technique" consisted of surveying about 100 scholars, mostly social scientists, for their opinions. On the other hand, there are those who use a precise methodology and call their approach "technological forecasting"—a term that has become a misnomer. It was given because the first subjects of these forecasts were mostly technological, but they have long since been expanded to include social, political, and economic events. In general, technological forecasting is the name given to a variety of techniques that attempt to monitor trends and events likely to develop in the future, determine their implications, and suggest controls over those developments.

The most famous and popular of these techniques is the RAND development called Delphi. Invented at RAND almost twenty years ago, it is now being used by scores of corporations, universities, and government agencies to probe the timetable of the future.

Delphi is based on the simple premise that in making a forecast "X" heads are better than one. Its method of forecasting is to use a set of procedures for forming a group judgment on speculative subjects. Typically, a group of twenty to sixty experts are asked to make a forecast, anonymously, in response to a specific question. For example, "By what date will we have full control over the forces of gravity?" "When will we be able to grow new organs and limbs by means of biochemical stimulation?" "How long will it be before we can make direct information 'recordings' on the brain?" Though not always addressed to developments as far out in the future, such questions are usually asked in large batches to force experts to think about both near- and far-term events at the same time. The first estimates are tallied and the resulting opinions are fed back to the experts, who then respond again after reflecting on the first-round thoughts of the other experts. In this second interrogation, the experts are asked to support their original answers or to change them if they prefer. The process of interrogation is repeated for several more rounds so that something close to a consensus can be formed. In the process, one of two outcomes is possible: Either the consensus is sharpened from round to round or the reasons why such a sharpening cannot be achieved are documented. The key to the technique is that all of the panelists remain anonymous and separated throughout the polling, which is usually conducted through the mail, in order to keep the experts from being embarrassed about changing their minds after reading and reflecting on other opinions. This process also serves to prevent the emergence of strong personalities who might dominate the group.

The results of a Delphi panel's labor typically include: (1) a modified list of developments, refined by the respondents to include those they feel are most important; (2) estimates of when these developments are likely to happen; (3) estimates of the probability that the developments will occur during this period; (4) estimates of the consequences of these developments should they occur; (5) evaluations of the desirability of these consequences; (6) description and evaluation of policy alternatives that might be considered to enhance the likelihood of those events thought most desirable and to decrease the likelihood of those felt to be undesirable; and (7) reasons for extreme opinions at each step in the process. For example, the bulk of a large Delphi panel assembled by RAND to look into the major areas of scientific breakthrough, population growth, automation, space progress, probability and prevention of war, and future weapons systems predicted, among many other developments, the ability to stimulate new organs and limbs by 2007, the direct recording of information on the brain by 2600, and control over gravity by the year 2050. In virtually any panel there are, of course, dissenters who foresee these events as occurring considerably earlier, later, or never. In the case of this large study, eighty-two experts were employed, including both members of the RAND staff and prominent outsiders such as Arthur Clarke, Isaac Asimov, and Bertrand de Jouvenel. The study, conducted with four sequential questionnaires spaced about two months apart, showed, as have other such studies, that as questions about specific events were repeated over the rounds, the opinions of the experts were in increasing agreement.

Not all Delphi studies are aimed at broad views of the future. Many solicit judgments on more immediate matters. In this regard, it is interesting to note that one of the first tests of Delphi was an attempt to forecast the number of automobile fatalities over a holiday weekend—a forecast that was within a few of being right. A very specific Delphi study conducted by RAND for the Air Force in the 1950's sought the consensus of a group of experts on how many A-bombs an enemy would require to destroy the American munitions industry. In this case, the extreme estimates shifted over five rounds from fifty to 5,000 bombs to 167 to 360 bombs in the last. The final median, and the answer given to the Air Force, was that it would take 225 A-bombs to wipe out the American arms industry.

Norman C. Dalkey, RAND Senior Scientist and co-inventor (with Olaf Helmer) of the Delphi technique, has been working on its refinement since the early 1950's. Over thirty major experiments have been conducted with Delphi at RAND, the most recent aimed at showing not only that it is a convenient way to elicit and refine group judgments but that it is also accurate. Dalkey has conducted controlled experiments using nonexperts, usually students, to come up with answers to obscure facts of the type that are to be found in almanacs but that few people know, such as how many telephones there are in South Africa, how many votes John F. Kennedy got in Texas in 1960, and how many women Marines there were at the end of World War II.* These experiments were performed with two groups, one using carefully controlled Delphi procedures in which the respondents were polled anonymously and the other using a looser technique in which students met face to face after each round. It was shown that the students using the Delphi technique came

---

* The answers: 1,333,600 telephones in South Africa, 1,167,567 Kennedy votes in Texas, and 23,145 women Marines.

closer to the right answer and, furthermore, that the Delphi group came closer to the correct answers on each successive round.

Delphi's appeal is that it produces an emerging group consensus among experts and thereby produces a better response than is obtainable from a single expert or a traditional discussion or conference in which persuasion, vanity, and the bandwagon effect of majority opinion come into play. Nothing magic is claimed for Delphi, nor is it billed as a producer of "the truth"; its advocates see it simply as one of the most promising crystal balls available to those who need a framework for future planning, action, and analysis. Dalkey explains his rationale for the technique: "It was developed because we felt that a large amount of advice from the expert community was not solely based on well-developed theories and data but tended to be a summary of personal experience. Delphi forces experts to consider and reconsider the basis for their opinions because in each round they are confronted with the other experts and must either muster support for their original prediction or change it." He looks at Delphi as a move in the direction of what he terms "opinion technology" and feels that in the long run Delphi and other forecasting techniques will have a great impact on government and industry because they will allow us to be more realistic in setting goals and calculating the probabilities for reaching those goals. He explains, "Until now politicians have had virtually no restrictions on policies or ambitions except for elections and the policy process itself. Delphi hints at a new and meaningful control that says, 'Is this objective possible?' If a politician says we will accomplish something in twenty years, we can ask him to subject that goal to the controlled consensus of experts."

To illustrate Delphi's potential use as a tool in determining group goals, he has used the process to question values. One set of experiments sought a consensus on what factors are most important to happiness. In this particular case he found that a group of UCLA graduate students and career government employees were in close agreement on what constituted happiness. The average panel involved in the happiness study ranked factors in the following clusters:

1. Love, affection, sex
2. Self-respect
3. Security and peace of mind

316

4. Challenge
5. Social acceptance and being needed
6. Achievement and prestige
7. Comfort and leisure

The fact that groups can come to agreement among themselves—and, as this experiment suggests, seemingly quite different groups may not be as far apart as suspected—shows that Delphi may be important as a means of determining desired societal goals.

Delphi is now coming into widespread use in industry to determine new markets, possible new products for the future, and pitfalls to development. It is being used in government and universities to explore subjects as diverse as future political alliances, possible war-prevention techniques, the future of air travel, and medical developments over the next thirty years. The Japanese Federal Science and Technology Agency is embarking on one of the most grandiose efforts in forecasting yet by using 4,000 experts to project Japanese technology over the next thirty years. *Business Week* reports that hundreds of U.S. corporations have expressed an interest in Delphi, some of them already deeply involved, like TRW Inc., which has fourteen Delphi panels at work on a variety of issues. TRW's work has thus far resulted in 400 predictions of technical events to occur before 1985 that are now being used to plan that company's technological programs. TRW's experiences in the coming years will no doubt provide interesting conclusions on the viability of the Delphi technique for corporate planning. The military has commissioned a large number of Delphi studies and, to a lesser extent, so have other agencies of government. RAND reports that copies of its Delphi studies are the literature most requested by visiting Soviet scientists.

The technique is being modified, tested, retested, and refined by other forecasters—a process that can be followed in the various forecasting and technical journals. Among the factors being explored: Can the time-consuming polling processes be automated? What is the best definition of expert as it relates to the technique? What is the optimum number of experts to have on a panel? How can one insure that mavericks and experts who don't accept conventional wisdom are included in a panel? If, as Dalkey and others claim, Delphi is not just another fad but the beginning of a new technology of opinion and analysis, the process will undoubtedly require refine-

317

ment and answers will have to be found to these and other questions.

Among other forecasting techniques now receiving attention are trend extrapolation, the construction of "relevance trees," morphological analysis, and mathematical modeling. Trend extrapolation is probably the most common form of forecasting because it is the easiest to perform. A graph in which data is plotted is extrapolated into the future, yielding a line or curve indicating the future trend. A simple case would be extrapolating the rise of a certain air pollutant into the future to predict what will happen if it is not controlled. Relevance trees are, as the term suggests, graphic presentations of the future that when drawn look like trees. They are created as coherent outlines identifying all the potential events, discoveries, threats, opportunities, short cuts, and alternative routes along the trail leading to a major objective. Should the goal be the better preservation of food nutrients, as one tree constructed by the Battelle Memorial Institute graphs, some of the positive junctures on the road to that goal include packages with smaller oxygen volume, quicker turnover of foods in stores, and the development of oxygen-absorbing chemicals. Closely related is morphological analysis, which also breaks up a given goal into all the parameters. Unlike the relevance tree, it is usually employed for specific technical goals such as new inventions or products. The result is an elaborate check list of those technological occurrences that can help lead to that product. Finally there are the mathematical models that process the forecasts, facts and assumptions fed into them. This data is sorted quickly to provide answers to specific questions about the future. Such elaborate computer-driven models are widely used by the military to handle technological questions. Specific military systems such as PATTERN (for Planning Assistance Through Technical Evaluation of Relevance Numbers) and QUEST (Quantitative Utility Estimates for Science and Technology) are operating models yielding predictive data.

It is far too early to determine the impact of the futurists and their techniques on the nation or whether that impact will be positive or negative. The least that can be said, however, is that their basic premise appears valid. We cannot be blind to the future we are creating and the developments heading our way if we expect to improve things. If the futurists prepare us for what's coming, then they will assume an increasingly critical role in man's development. But it is important to grasp that futures research could produce a runaway technology of its own, capable of generating its own problems. Futurists argue that they are creating new tools for policy-makers to use in comprehending and analyzing decisions, but as with other tools, they can be used or misused or backfire. If futurism is not kept in perspective, it can in itself become a diversion from pressing current needs and make their solutions seem less imperative. Critic Alessandro Silj summed up his attack on the luxury of living in the future in an article entitled "Down with the Year 2000": "It is as if you were trying to swim away from a shipwreck and the same time were being distracted by someone talking to you about all the ships that will be built in the future—about all their likely (or unlikely) shapes and colors."

It may prove increasingly difficult, furthermore, to avoid imposing today's values on future generations as the notion of inventing the future becomes more of a reality. Pressing today's goals, ambitions, and standards on the future may lead to—or indeed help foster—as yet undetermined ills. Jules Verne's images of gleaming modern technology in a clearly Victorian atmosphere come to mind as illustrative of such a pitfall.

There is the distinct possibility, of course, that the futurists may be making grave errors that could only mislead. Perhaps futurists will be led astray by forecasts that rely too heavily on technology and economics and not enough on human values; or, perhaps, they will miss a great and important technological or economic trend. Such a possibility is illustrated by one of the first attempts to look into the future of the nation, a 1929 report by President Hoover entitled "The President's Panel on Recent Social Trends." It was a significant attempt to forecast events and was quite accurate, save for overlooking one central fact: The nation had begun moving into a long and massive depression.

No matter how altruistic and democratic the motives of the futurists may be, they are vulnerable to the charge that a manipulative elite is administering the future—and further entrenching divisions within society. And of course there is also the chance that a genuine manipulative or demonic elite of futurists could emerge to mesmerize the rest of us. Put to strictly parochial use, the ability to create the future could certainly be used to perpetuate the wishes and impulses of one group. Much forecasting work has been conducted by the military and therefore offers a good example: The creation of a future with heavy emphasis on military hardware would obviously move us toward an even more militaristic society. Such imbalance would create a strong military posture at the expense of pressing civilian needs such as, say education.

Finally, and perhaps most important, there is the very real danger of self-fulfilling and self-negating prophecies—a danger that cannot be understated. If a future estimate of world politics casts Finland in the role of possible enemy in 1990, as the Institute for Land Combat has done, and policy is shaped to defend against that possibility, the forecast itself may help to convert that possibility into reality. Properly used, of course, this or any forecast would be employed to prevent hostilities, but a process, once set in motion, may not submit readily to our control. Indeed knowledgeable forecasts of new technologies open up a variety of possibilities. If it is predicted that "contraceptive warfare"—war in which chemicals are used as weapons to prevent reproduction—is a possibility as one futurist think tank has argued, doesn't the prediction spur that possibility? Similarly, prediction of a more violent society or of economic setbacks may psychologically encourage such social conditions. On the other hand, there are self-negating prophecies, such as in the hypothetical case where a quick cancer breakthrough is so convincingly predicted that as a result young researchers pick other diseases to work on—thereby holding off the cancer breakthrough.

Most futurists argue that they are trying to avoid such perils by acting responsibly. What most worries futurists, though, is that their pursuit may end up as an intellectual fad. But in fact virtually all think tanks aim some of their work at specific aspects of the future and are either using existing forms of forecasting or developing new ones. RAND's Dalkey estimates that there must be 400 independent research groups in America doing some form of futures research. In recent years, however, new think tanks and research units have been created—both inside and outside governments—for the single purpose of inventing futures. Some, like the British Government's Committee on the Next Thirty Years, the recently formed Berlin Center for Futures Research, and the American Academy of Arts and Sciences' Commission on the Year 2000, look to the future of society as a whole. Others try to isolate possible futures in a specific category, such as the Ford Foundation-financed Resources for the Future Inc., which looks at the future of raw materials and natural resources, and the U.S. Army's institutes, considering the future of land war. Of all the new groups, the most ambitious start has been made by an institute that does not limit itself to one aspect of the future. Located in a suite of offices above a small shopping mall on drab Main Street of Middletown, Connecticut, the Institute for the Future is the only major nonprofit corporation in America exclusively dedicated to making its living from systematic interdisciplinary studies of the future.

2. *The Oracle in Connecticut*

Solution of the foreign-body rejection problem will have greatly improved the process of organ transplantation, and to meet the need for natural transplantable organs, "parts" banks will have encouraged black markets, although the importance of these markets will have been diminished by legislative regulation of transplantations within the hospital-physician community and by the development of artificial organs, including, for example, implantable artificial hearts with power sources capable of lasting five years. Research will be continuing into the use of tissue-compatible animals to provide yet another source of medicine from repair to replacement, a development accompanied by the rise of new industries, technologies and classes of medical personnel.

Several other biological technologies will have significantly affected the world of 1985. Contraceptive drugs will have been developed which will lower fertility rates, being mass-administered as aerosols or as additions to water supplies or staples (as iodine is added to table salt). Societal acceptance of this practice will result from extensive public education about the consequences of overpopulation. But this development will

321

have led to the possibility of a new form of warfare: surreptitious contraception. Research and development projects will have been implemented to create an anticontraceptive pill and detection system. The drug will form only one more addition to the arsenal of biological and chemical weapons.

—Excerpt from a scenario of the technological world of 1985 prepared by the Institute for the Future from the results of a Delphi panel—part of a study of the future conducted for the state of Connecticut, prepared September 1969

The self-described realm of involvement for the Institute for the Future is the period stretching from five to fifty years into the future. Its purpose in this realm is to assess the long-range impact of today's decisions, to forecast socio-economic trends and their future implications, to warn of significant departures from existing trends, and to develop and refine forecasting techniques.

It brings to this ambitious endeavor the ideal think-tank pedigree: strong lines to the RAND Corporation; a "blue ribbon" board of educational, industrial, and foundation notables; and an impressive list of U.S. and international analysts who serve as its advisers, including Herman Kahn, French economist Bertrand de Jouvenel, and Dennis Gabor, the British physicist who is recognized as the father of holography, the infant field of three-dimensional laser photography. Several senior RAND members who were joined by other futures-oriented scholars and scientists launched the enterprise in 1968 with money from RAND and several major foundations, including a $52,000 Ford grant. The rationale for the institute as outlined by its organizing committee was that although many institutions were looking at some aspect of the future, none planned to explore the wide spectrum of societal problems and their long-term implications. The strategy was that the institute would work on contract but that each contract would fit together into a larger, balanced program for futures exploration.

Like that of other futurist groups, the philosophy of the institute is based on the concept that it is possible and desirable to intervene now to give direction to the future. This premise is clearly stated in the Organizing Committee's original prospectus, published in May 1966:

> The idea for the Institute . . . arises from a change in attitude toward the future. The fatalistic view that it is unforeseeable and inevitable is being abandoned. It is being recognized that there are a multitude of possible futures and that appropriate intervention can make a difference in their probabilities. This raises the exploration of the future, and the search for ways to influence its direction, to activities of great social responsibility.

> The responsibility is not just an academic one, and to discharge it more than perfunctorily we must cease to be mere spectators in our own on-going history, and participate with determination in molding the future. It will take wisdom, courage and sensitivity to human values to shape a better world. Now is the time to commit ourselves fully to the problems of the future of our society. The proposed Institute would constitute a key step in getting on with this urgent task.

An important distinction is made, however, when it comes to its research: It will steer clear of policy formulation, and, rather than make decisions, it will display the alternatives open to the policymaker. To its credit, the institute has given itself guidelines to prevent thoughts of a conspiratorial, covert, or manipulative role in advising planners. It does not undertake any studies that will result solely in proprietary publications. That is, every project—no matter who sponsors it—leads to publications that are available to all. It will also stay away from military research although its senior Fellows are definitely interested in working on such subjects as the prevention and limitation of war through nonmilitary means. It will take only contracts that impose a minimum of intellectual constraints on its researchers; for example, it will not permit its sponsors to have control over the study design, nor will it accept contracts or grants to investigate subjects that are very narrowly defined or otherwise ill-suited to exploration through the techniques of futures research.

While they have no commitment to any given forecasting technique, there is strong identification with two techniques whose inventors are key members of the staff. Olaf Helmer, president of the institute, was the co-founder of Delphi at RAND with Dalkey (who is an institute consultant). Theodore J. Gordon, vice-president and senior Fellow of the institute, is most closely associated with "cross-impact analysis"—a technique being developed at the institute.

In general, Delphi is the organizing principle behind most of the institute's studies used primarily to generate forecasts, while the cross-impact technique is a means of specifying the relationships between forecasts. Most of the institute's work is an experimental mix of old and new techniques—from library research and interviewing to gaming and cross-impact matrixing. A good example of how they work is contained in one of the institute staff's largest jobs thus far, the development of long-range forecasting methods for the state of Connecticut. The work sought not only to identify issues of substance for the state between now and the year 2000 but also to give the state an insight into systematic methods for performing its own forecasting.

The study began with the convening of three Delphi panels, one each on technological developments, social developments, and potential opportunities in Connecticut. The social and technological surveys looked at society as a whole, while the third focused on the state. An example of the expectations of the panel looking for societal developments is this summary of their collective thoughts on urbanization:

> The panel expected a gradual abandonment of the concept of the city as a discrete and definable entity as metropolitan areas merge into a growing metropolis. In this context, two possibilities were foreseen for municipal government in urban areas: some of its responsibilities would remain subject to neighborhood control but under the strong influence of state standards (e.g., education, police), while other services would gradually be assumed by regional and metropolitan government. The panel expected that during this time the balance of political power would increasingly favor the more densely populated areas within the states. Though the panel was rather hopeful about our increased ability to carry out effective, responsive and visionary central planning and large-scale urban development, there was strong disagreement as to the likelihood of a major redirection of

resources from military and space programs to urban programs. . . .

As a whole, most respondents did expect that increasing government support would eventually result in converting city cores into more stable residential areas. . . .

The majority of respondents foresaw continuing disorder and disequilibrium as well as an increase in the alienation and impersonality of urban life. . . . Efforts at integration were generally expected to be increasingly successful toward the latter part of the century.

The revolt of today's youth against institutions that deny individual participation was interpreted as possibly leading to the creation of new political institutions. . . .

Most respondents agreed that urban elementary education will be decentralized at a moderate rate and that primary and secondary education may, in the 70's, experience some confusion and regression resulting from a continuing power struggle over its control. The institution of the communiversity was envisioned as one possibility for improving community life and providing cultural enrichment for the aged and unemployed; however, this was not expected to occur before 1980.

Among the sample predictions made for the state by the Connecticut opportunities panel were these:

FORECASTS (Education)

—Needed changes in the educational system will occur after a general worsening of conditions and a traumatic experience in the schools.

—Changes in the educational system will not emanate exclusively from within the schools, but will involve politicians, lay leaders and boards of education.

—Improvement in the economic status of teachers will occur only after productivity (the student-to-teacher ratio) has been improved. This will be accomplished either by greater use of automated teaching machines or non-certified teaching assistants.

—The role of the educational system will change from passive response to present situations to anticipation of future environments.

—Higher education will become a continuous process with fre-

quent periods of training and employment interspersed.
—Financing the educational system will become more central-
ized with a greater share coming from state and federal sources.
FORECASTS (Leisure)
—Unsatisfying leisure time will be a serious problem in Connecticut, especially for the poor, the aged, and those with below-
average education.
—The inability to establish individual goal structures applicable
to leisure time will result in serious psychological disturbances.

Each of these sets of specific forecasts for the state is accompanied
with sets of "Opportunities," or action areas with possible amelio-
rating impact on the state in that particular area. Leisure, for example, is the subject of seven opportunities ranging from redirecting
the educational process toward greater free choice in activities to the
creation of new recreation facilities. The forecasts generated by the
Delphi panels were then used to play a simulation game in which
state officials and academicians dealt with the long-term developments to gain an appreciation for the decision-making process that
lies ahead.

In addition, the Connecticut projections were subjected to the
new process of cross-impact analysis. Geared to pick up where Delphi
leaves off and involving the use of a set of mathematical maneuvers
performed by a computer, these maneuvers boil down to a mathematical representation of the interaction between events that are too
complex for quick human computation. The system recognizes that
events forecast by experts will change as other events leading up to
them change. The assumption is that an event will (1) enhance the
likelihood, (2) decrease the likelihood, or (3) be unrelated to the
likelihood of other events occurring. Such judgments as to relationships, the strength of those relationships, and their impact on the timing of events are human judgments. This form of analysis attempts to
keep track of these judgments in relationship to each other by computing and recomputing new estimates of probabilities of events
occurring as other events change. For example, if reliable one-month
weather reports and limited weather control were improved, then
there would be an increase in the numerical probability of eliminating
crop damage from adverse weather. Such judgments can be incorporated into matrices in which the impact of each event is assessed

in relation to every other event in that matrix. A computer can work with a large number of these events to give information on the probability of a complex series of events occurring by a given date. The computer becomes necessary because it is able to compute all possible relationships—relating 100 events to one another, for example, works out to the computation of 29,700 probabilities. This form of analysis amounts to a speedy way of determining the effect of any one event on other forecasted events.

In the Connecticut study, research into this type of analysis helped produce a package of information for the state, including:

- A list of scientific developments for the next thirty years.
- A description of current societal trends along with the expected direction of these trends and new trends.
- A list of probable issues facing Connecticut between now and the year 2000.
- An indication of the alternative policies the state may take in the next twenty years and their effects.
- Illustration of the potential effect of certain action on the quality of life within the state.

Foreseen in these studies are major technological events—among them, personality-modifying drugs, chemical control over heredity, sophisticated robots capable of a variety of jobs, computers with IQs over 150, much greater control over aging, and the possibility of mass-administered contraceptive drugs—that will be outside the control of Connecticut but will, nonetheless, be part of its problems. For example, the Delphi panel sees the strong possibility that science will produce techniques for choosing the sex of one's children by 1980—an event with wide implications for any governing body that must contend with the resulting problems. For example, certain imbalances might result as lower-income families chose mostly male children on the assumption that they would later be able to bring higher earnings to the family. Likewise, small wireless telephones carried on one's person (probable by 1990) will require new regulations to protect individuals from constant intrusion, just as the widespread use of thermonuclear power plants (probable by the 1980's) will require a new ability to deal with the problem of thermal pollution.

Besides making long-range predictions, the study sought to suggest areas of action for the state to take in heading off problems of a broad societal nature as well as listing possible consequences of those actions. For example, the study group foresees two general trends in the realm of "law and order":

• Society will initiate action against people creating civil disorder without waiting for complaint. Individual examples of this type of action will curb mass uncivil behavior.

• There will be an increase in the use of techniques which encroach on the rights of the individual; for example, wiretapping, bugging, preventive detention, and so on.

In the face of these predictions the panel asks the state to consider the following list of actions and possible results:

Suggested Action Areas	Possible Impacts
Initiate a legal reform program to liberalize statutes on matters that are not threats to society; for example, abortion, nonharmful drugs, and protest meetings.	Reduction in some causes of civil unrest and over-all easing of law-enforcement problems.
Provide a mechanism for assuring commitment to adequate money and resources to fulfill the intent of new and existing laws.	Greater assurance that laws will be enforced as originally intended.
Increase educational requirements for all personnel in the legal system, including judges, lawyers, police, and others.	More effective law-enforcement mechanisms.
Reform the penal system to emphasize treatment rather than punishment.	Consistent with societal intents at reduced cost.

On a more parochial level, the over-all study looked at the state itself to identify future problems—for instance, a coming crisis in middle-income housing—as well as to make specific forecasts for the state—for example, the lowering of the voting age, the introduction of a state income tax, and the emergence of a more socially and politically powerful group of poor people.

In all, the six reports to the state constitute an attempt to give Connecticut's officials an insight into the world they will be facing and time to consider the options open to them. One of the most valuable results of the Connecticut study was the creation of its list of "Candidate State Actions," steps that can be taken to prevent or mitigate future difficulties. Though primarily suggested for use in the simulation game, they exemplify the kind of thinking forecasting can generate. Examples of the nearly 100 candidate actions:

Implement community development on a regional basis.
Establish an ombudsman's office.
Institute a statewide government data management system.
Enact statewide flood controls.
Rezone to decentralize urban areas.
Reform building codes to accept technological innovation.
Place zoning controls at the state level.
Enforce health and safety standards in housing vigorously.
Establish new communities in rural areas.
Build a bridge to Long Island.
Construct a floating airport in Long Island Sound.
Charge a toll for personal cars entering urban centers.
Remove all highway and bridge tolls.
Offer welfare bonuses for family planning.
Offer bonuses to welfare recipients who become self-supporting.
Subsidize integrated suburban housing.
Provide low-cost business loans for welfare recipients.
Initiate penal-system reforms.
Teach birth control in the public high schools.
Enact and enforce antipollution standards for water, air and
    noise.
Limit prices charged to ghetto residents.
Improve educational requirements for police.
Require registration of firearms.
Discourage use of "heroic" medical measures in futile cases.
Make drug use a noncriminal act.
Provide free medical insurance for all.
Offer adult educational retraining.
Extend the educational period.

Institute high-school work-study programs.
Offer compensatory payment for scholastic achievement.
Raise salaries of teachers.
Provide free college for all students.
Legalize homosexuality.
Legalize abortions.
Provide wildlife reserves.

Completed in 1970, the study has been widely circulated both in the state and to officials in state governments throughout the country. Connecticut indicated it was pleased with its unique study, and Georgia is planning to have the institute perform a similar study.

Another major study completed by the institute is a projection of the future of employee benefits in the nation over the next fifteen years. Sponsored by du Pont, the study sought to outline some of the changes in employee benefits that might be expected as well as to identify the developments likely to prove crucial in shaping those trends.

The analysis began with a Delphi study of the future of benefits using eighteen experts in such fields as education, labor, corporate structure, finance, and demography. The Delphi results were synthesized along with three other factual studies—a picture of current benefit patterns, an examination of welfare and labor regulations throughout the world, and employer-employee relations in various countries.

Results of the study appear in three data-crammed reports but they are rendered most graphically in their scenario form—in this case a report on national benefit patterns in the year 1985. Briefly, it is a world where employee benefits have merged with compensation and welfare. Security is a major factor, and the "rugged" individualists who prefer cash to guarantees against hard times have all but vanished. Employers now dispense half of their payroll in benefits—a situation prompted by such forces as organized labor, automation, and the past pressure of militant minority groups. The dollar is worth 58 percent of the 1968 dollar because of inflation, in part the cause of "cost-of-living" pension plans in which the retiree is guaranteed a way of life rather than an amount of money. More women and minority-group members are in the labor force, and proportionately more workers are white-collar. Workers get more vacation, and the average work week is now down to about thirty-five hours. Employers offer more leisure-oriented benefits and educational programs. Subsidized housing and company cars are offered to many more than in the past. Employee counseling services are generally available on everything from taxes to retirement plans. Automated record keeping enables companies to offer the worker benefit programs of great diversity, so he can tailor his benefits to meet his particular needs. Psychiatric and dental costs have been added to medical plans, and pension plans can be transferred between jobs. Union membership has not increased substantially, but unions remain a potent force in bringing new benefits. Employee benefits now cost over $100 billion a year and have a great impact on society.

Other works completed by the institute range from a look at the future environment for education in America to an examination of possible research and action programs suitable for foundation support in the future. By late 1970 another series of varied investigations was under way, including an inquiry into people's use of time and its consequences both now and in the future and a look at the problems that will emerge from future computer applications. One of the more dramatic concepts now being developed by the institute is a "Future State of the Union Report." The idea is to bring together the forecasts made by the institute during the preceding year, as well as those made elsewhere that have a major bearing on the future of the nation. It will then summarize major future trends by depicting the United States at various intervals in the future. The first report, supported by the Russell Sage Foundation, was released in 1971.

The choice of study areas for the institute is primarily determined by the staff, and, though dependent on sponsors, the plan is to move into new subject areas according to a general list of priorities. Subjects that will be pursued in the near future include the long-range future of the cities, the impact of computers and communications on society, the eradication of starvation, and the future of economically retarded nations. Beyond these are projected studies of new approaches to arms control, the future of the American family, the implications of genetic technology, an attempt to frame a general theory of social conflict, and the interlocking problems of youth, race, and poverty.

Heading this many-faceted probe into the future is the institute's president, Olaf Helmer, who, along with Dalkey and a few others, is considered one of the true pioneers in technological forecasting and futurism. He joined RAND as a mathematician when it started and worked there developing such house specialties as game theory, systems analysis, Delphi, and mathematical modeling. He left in 1968 to help found the institute. Helmer is a tall, imposing man who would rather talk about futurism in general and its promises than about the institute itself. He argues that futurism can help nations set realistic and unifying national goals and rational objectives and that it may become a factor in bringing the U.S. and the U.S.S.R. closer together. As a particular case in point, he thinks that ties with the Communist world may be realized through recognition of common long-term goals. As Helmer stated to the annual meeting of the American Political Science Association in 1969, ". . . a reappraisal of our national goals should include a more future-oriented assessment of our relations with the Communist world. One sometimes wonders whether we have forgotten what the entire quarrel was about. What started out as a difference in ideology on certain economic principles has inadvertently turned into a power struggle for world domination. Our economies, meanwhile, are converging, each adopting some of the methods of the other; what is more, as affluence steadily increases on both sides of the Iron Curtain, we will all, before we know it, be entering the age of post-industrial society, where there will be a common search for new principles by which to order our economic progress, and the old quarrel will have become totally meaningless. This suggests that the proper way to a rapprochement with the Soviet Union may well be via futurism, since our long-range goals are much more compatible than our short-range (and often short-sighted) subgoals."

On another level, Helmer expects futurism to have a subtle but demonstrable and important effect on both the academic and governmental communities in the United States. He says, "Our experience working with the people in Connecticut has shown us that the effect on officials who participate in such studies is that they are never again quite the same. I can't say what the actual impact will be on the state, but I can say that their attitudes have changed considerably: They are very much aware of the future implications of what they are doing today and are thinking in terms of shaping the future of the state by thinking about current actions rather than looking at those actions as discrete events." Helmer contends that bureaucrats are quite ready to accept futurism partly because traditional social science does not provide a sense of direction. The social sciences, moreover, have fallen far behind the physical sciences, and he believes that futurism can begin to close that gap because it is a pragmatic, rather than a theoretical, way to grapple with the application of social science to societal problems. "Disciplined futures research," he says, "takes the strictly scientific and theoretical social scientist and forces him to think practically and look into the long-term impact of trends."

The future of the institute looks bright. It now employs forty and plans to add another 30 to 40 percent to the staff each year for the next several years. It has recently opened a branch in Menlo Park, California, and, according to Helmer, even though there has been a general economic slowdown in the research world, the institute is in constant demand to accept research contracts.

An interesting bit of encouragement for the institute and other futurist groups appears in one of the summaries of a Delphi panel assembled for the Connecticut study, which said:

> Starting in the early 1970's and becoming very noticeable after 1980, there will, in the panelists' opinion, be an increasing search for a new symbiosis between power and knowledge, be it in the form of policy-oriented research, so-called think tank organizations, or new types of professional policy advisors. . . .

The prophecy appears to be coming true as certain government agencies stock up on research adjuncts. One good example is the United States Office of Education, which has been creating a variety of policy research groups in recent years. Two of them have been given the mission of looking into the future.

3. *Educating for the Future*

> . . . *"Exuberant Democracy" is characterized by a mood of exuberant expansiveness, a high degree of confidence in the economy and the political system, an ability of the*

United States to project its influence throughout the world, an actively questing science, and an expanding technology. Identifications with the culture and the nation are positive and proud, and horizons are seen to be unlimited. Americans and their government are extroverted and confident in their dealings with other nationals and nations. However, it seems very unlikely that this state of affairs could come about without an all-out national effort on ecosystems problems (including amelioration of poverty within and outside the nation) of a magnitude approaching that of World War II and with similar unification of national will, launched no later than 1975–1980. It is also probable that the solution to these problems could entail considerable encroachment on individual freedoms, and there would be significant impingement on the quality of life. Furthermore, if this state has been reached through a successful "Green Revolution" in agriculture, thus avoiding widespread famine in the underdeveloped world, population levels are likely to be such as to have resulted in a very fragile ecosystem balance; the prognosis for decades beyond 2000 entails probable catastrophe within another half century.

—One of eleven alternative futures for the United States developed by the Educational Policy Research Center at the Stanford Research Institute

You are likely to miss it when you first come into the room. It is small, made of clear plastic, and sits on a conference table against the wall. It is a replica of a tree and could easily pass for a well-crafted conversation piece. Its title is "Tree of Alternative Future Histories." Looked at symbolically, it represents years of thought and millions of dollars.

The tree is a representation of America from 1960 to the year 2000. A solid trunk extends from 1960 to 1970, at which point the

334

tree develops three major branches that continue to sprout new branches through the '70's, '80's, and '90's. At the top of the tree, which represents the year 2000, there are eleven major branches each representing alternatives for the United States. Each of the branches has a name representing the state of society at that point. They are: Collapse, "1984" Theocracy, Authoritarian Recession, Pollution Stalemate, Welfare Stultification, Garrison State, Philistine Comfort, Socialist Success, Satisfied Plenty, Exuberant Democracy, and Manifest Destiny.

This curious tree sits in the office of Willis Harman, director of the U.S. Office of Education's Educational Policy Research Center, a separate research unit at the Stanford Research Institute. The center is one of over thirty policy research centers and laboratories operated by the Office of Education and one of two centers that are looking at education in the broad framework of the future. The Stanford group began in 1967 and, according to Harman, proceeded to waste a year and half a million dollars trying to get a handle on how to cope with the future.

The staff, which ranges from fifteen to twenty full-time professionals, has followed a course of forecasting that attempts to look at education in the broadest framework of the nation and the world. Harman, a soft-spoken engineer with the ability to discuss possible impending national calamity with the same offhandedness that others use to describe a trip to the store, states his approach to the future of education: "We felt that education couldn't be isolated from the rest of society, so we decided to look at the major alternatives to see how education fits into them. Ours is a holistic approach in which educational policy can be tested in terms of national alternatives and the 'World Macroproblem'—which is a term we use for the total of all the universal problems which have come with uncontrolled technology, application, and industrial development."

The center has no name for its approach to forecasting and, in general, puts little emphasis on dogma and extensive description of methodology. Its method is, nonetheless, complex. It has thus far identified some 20,000 possible combinations of events that could occur between now and the year 2000. Continued re-examination of sets of sequences were made to eliminate inconsistencies and catch missed possibilities. The preliminary result is the tree that decorates Harman's office. The tree represents the most plausible alternatives that the study team could find. The points where the branches begin represent the dates when crossroads between alternative futures meet. The team excluded some possible futures either because they were highly unlikely—such as invasion from another planet—or because they involved such catastrophic developments—like all-out nuclear war or completely debilitating pollution—as to render educational policy considerations irrelevant.

Harman is skeptical of most technological forecasting techniques, like Delphi, because he feels that most of them eliminate changing values from their processes. The center, on the other hand, has not rejected technological forecasts but has tried to keep values and value changes as the primary consideration in its ongoing analysis. Helmer remarks, "If values change we won't develop the technological break-throughs that others predict because we won't want to." And he adds, "With a technique like Delphi you get the bias of experts who are not looking beyond their own discipline."

The center's holistic view of the future has led to broad, dramatic thinking with radical implications. Harman points out matter-of-factly that half the future histories feasible in the year 2000 are highly authoritarian in nature, while most of the others—such as Collapse—portend a variety of unpleasant alternatives. "If the tree is projected to the year 2050," he adds, "more branches appear, and of the forty feasible futures available at that date only a few avoid some period of serious trouble."

Future histories that avoid calamity, according to Harman, ". . . appear to require dramatic shifts of values and ways of seeing the world in regard to the 'World Macroproblem.' " The Macroproblem is composed of a variety of problems that fall into three categories—problems of the ecosystem, the broadening gap between the haves and the have-nots, and the broad range of technological threats (such as thermonuclear weapons, "engineering" of the human body, mental stress, and assaults on privacy and individual freedom). Harman says of the Macroproblem, "Taken as a whole it is nearly unsolvable, but just to live with it will require a cultural revolution of major proportions. I'm not talking about a trivial thing here, I'm talking about radical change in our whole set of basic values."

Research at the center has led to the conclusion that the naïve confidence of the public in the future is completely misplaced *unless*

336

basic premises are changed. Such naïve confidence is expressed in scores of contemporary notions, exemplified by this handful of the many that the center has collected:

"Technological breakthroughs in contraception will take care of the population explosion."

"The deterrence policy will continue to preserve the world from the horrors of nuclear warfare."

"The right programs for urban problems will begin to reduce the severity of the problems of racism in the nation."

"The drastically fallen world image of America, from the hope of the oppressed to the imperialist oppressor, is a regrettable consequence of our involvement in the Vietnamese conflict and can be righted by our finding a satisfactory way to extricate ourselves from that conflict."

"As soon as the Vietnamese war is over, we will begin to make steady progress on the serious social and environmental problems that beset us."

These expectations and others like them appeared less and less probable to the center as it deepened its exploration of the future. Harman and his staff believe that they won't happen because the values at the basis of American society will prevent them from happening. "Pathogenic premises" is the center's term for these values at the heart of the problem. The nine pathogenic premises identified are some of the core assumptions of Western life. It is also intriguing to note that one of them—Number 3—is a direct repudiation of the basic assumption of Delphi—providing a perfect example of the degree to which futurists disagree. As identified by the center, the pathogenic premises are:

1. The pride of families, the power of nations, and the survival of the human species all are to be furthered (as in the past) by population increase.

2. The "technological imperative" that any technology that can be developed, and any knowledge that can be applied, should be.

3. The summed knowledge of experts constitutes wisdom.

4. The reductionist (or machinelike and impersonal) view of man, a premise associated with the development of contemporary science, that lends sanction to dehumanizing ways of thinking about and treating man.

5. Men are essentially separate, so that little intrinsic responsibility

337

is felt for the effects of present actions on remote individuals or future generations.

6. Man is separate from nature, and hence nature is to be exploited and controlled rather than cooperated with.

7. The "economic man" image, leading to a system of economics based on ever-increasing GNP, consumption, and expenditure of irreplaceable resources.

8. The future of the planet can safely be left to autonomous nation-states, operating essentially independently.

9. Disbelief that "what ought to be" is a meaningful concept and is achievable.

These nine premises were spelled out by the center in a report to the Office of Education that brought the premises and the problems they generate directly to the issue of education by concluding, ". . . *education toward changing those premises, directly or indirectly, is the paramount educational task for the nation and for the world."*

Killing those nine premises would be the basis for what Harman terms "the cultural revolution." The refusal of so many young people today to adopt the values of the past and the self-doubt and questioning going on within science lead Harman to believe that the cultural revolution may be starting. "If so," he says, "we will have to make a radical reassessment of all aspects of national policy and, of course, education." An essential part of the revolution will require the destruction of the prevailing feeling that any technology that will make a profit or enable a nation to improve weapons should be applied. Harman thinks this is another idea that is beginning to erode. He says, "For years scientists have insisted that values are relative and that it is hard to attach permanent or nonpolitical values to science. Now there are some within science who are coming to believe that one can put a label of 'wholesome' or 'unwholesome' on scientific developments." He believes that this kind of thinking will have to spread throughout the scientific community and says that as other developments—more advanced weapons and "genetic engineering," to name two—come along, the need will become greater and more apparent.

Acknowledging that his personal assessment is probably a bit on the subjective side, Harman says, "There is a good likelihood that we could be on the road to a better future society, but very basic changes will have to occur within the next five years." He adds, "If we cannot come to grips with these problems, then we're headed for undesirable alternatives of which the most probable would be a totalitarian society." His optimism is based on the assumption that the nation has the ability to take moral charge of its affairs. Summing up this view before the House Subcommittee on Education in December, 1969, he said:

> The Macroproblem which the world faces, and which is rapidly and ineluctably becoming more serious, is at root a problem of value and basic premises—in short, a moral problem. Thus the kind of leadership required is moral leadership. The United States could reassert its role in this domain, but only if we first eliminate our own confusion. It would seem to follow that the paramount educational task for the nation is the fostering of a unifying national purpose, the development of a will to build toward a nation with liberty and justice for all and to take the lead in stewardship of the future.

The broad work of the center is intended to help educational policy-makers shape better plans and decisions. The tree of alternative future histories, for example, is intended as a tool for policymaking. The tree offers three main clusters of national paths between now and the year 1985: One goes through a "slough of despond" or loss of national will and severe economic depression; the second is a long-term projection of present trends leading to several troubled states; and the third is characterized by an all-out national determination to solve the problems of the ecosystem. The tree can be used as a guide for designing policies to increase the likelihood of avoiding undesirable futures. Since the only future histories that look attractive are based on the "war on ecological problems," education should be directed toward the branch of the tree which contains the ecological war without losing sight of the fact that the same policies should also work if the nation travels a different path. Harman points out that education planners should "live imaginatively" in all three of these major alternatives in making policy. Should the nation enter the "slough of despond," for example, educational approaches suited to an affluent and cohesive society will be worthless. Ideally, a policy should fit all three clusters.

In creating its framework for the future, the center has become an

339

advocate of extensive and radical calls for change. The convictions that have resulted from its studies are strong: directly attacking the World Macroproblem; controlling technological development and application; altering values, perceptions, killing old premises; establishing a sense of national purpose and educating people for coping with an uncertain future. Each of these convictions for a more favorable future is being investigated in more detail by the center. Basic suggestions have already been passed onto the Office of Education for making changes in education—among them, specific ideas on changing curricula to meet the problems of ecology and learning to live with an uncertain future.

The Stanford center is supplemented by another with the same name at the Syracuse University Research Corporation. While both centers share the same goal of inventing methodologies for looking at the future, exploring the future and relating it to education, they are approaching these tasks in distinctly different ways. The Stanford group has moved quickly to a major methodology of its own for thinking about the future, while the Syracuse group is developing and applying a variety of methods.

To give the flavor of the kind of inquiry that the Syracuse center is performing, one of its major efforts is a study of the past and future of post-secondary education. The objective of this study is to trace the growth of higher education and consider the alternatives for post-secondary education outside the realm of formal higher education. Using a completed study of student enrollments over the last 100 years, the center has adopted the thesis that ". . . growth in the proportion of the population with post-secondary degrees is about to stabilize unless *basic* changes occur in the character of higher education. . . ." Two key questions derived from this thesis which the center feels are most important and which it is now exploring are: (1) Will the college and university system continue to be the main component of post-secondary education, and what alternatives are open for nontraditional forms of higher education? (2) Since certain goals of the nation's educational policy may be close to attainment— for example, the center estimates that the goal of raising the average citizen's level of attainment to that of the high school will be met by 1975—what alternatives are there for "fresh" educational policy goals?

It is also conducting major surveys of future alternatives and possible goals for both elementary and secondary education, studying work that has been done throughout the world on educational planning, looking at the future of demands on the American educational system, and constructing a set of alternative economic futures of the United States intended to serve as a policy research tool. These economic futures should be able to facilitate specific and systematic conjectures about the relationship of the general economy to costs and demands for education.

The man who was instrumental in setting up the two centers—and who watches over them from the Office of Education—is Hendrik D. Gideonese, Director of Program Planning and Evaluation at the Office of Education's Bureau of Research. Gideonese is an articulate, bearded man touted by many in the world of think tanks as one of the few futurist-bureaucrats around. He says that the impetus to form the futures-oriented think tanks for education began in 1965 when it became apparent to him and others that anything major decided in education was not likely to have full impact on society for twenty or more years. As he explains it: "If in 1965 we were to have decided to change the sixth-grade social-studies curriculum, it would have taken until 1970 before it was ready. The diffusion of the program and all that it entails, like teacher retraining and getting new materials ready, would take another five to ten years. Then it is going to take those students who are getting the new course some years to finish school. The only way to look at this is that a decision like this made in 1965 will first have an impact on students coming out of school in the period around 1985–1990. When we realized this, it was apparent that we had to do whatever was necessary to try to understand the years for which our decisions were really going to get into society."

In 1966 Gideonese and his staff spent eight months talking to policy research experts at such places as RAND, the Hudson Institute, and the System Development Corporation in order to solicit ideas for an educational policy think tank. It was decided that the best way to do this was to set up five pilot centers and pick the most promising as permanent organizations. Centers were established at SRI, Syracuse, SDC, the National Planning Association, and the Western Behavioral Science Institute; the present two survived the final cut made in 1968. It was decided to establish two centers because of the way the Office of Education chose to view the future. Gideonese says: "There is not only more than one way to look at the future but there is more than one future. The future is plural, and the more futures we discover, the greater our capacity to invent a good one. We invent the future whether we want to or not, so we might as well invent a good one. Studying futures becomes in many ways the most powerful of organizing principles."

With the possible exception of the Pentagon, Gideonese feels that the Office of Education is leading among federal agencies in what he terms ". . . analytical, conceptually aggressive, far-reaching policy analysis."

The effect of the two Educational Policy Research Centers on policy will always be indirect but important, predicts Gideonese. "You will probably never find anybody taking their recommendations directly or see their perceptions dictating all that we do. We look upon them as a resource that we use in making policy," he says, adding, "There is no doubt in my mind, however, that they have started making an impact."

4. Futurism and Goals

> It is time we addressed ourselves, consciously and systematically, to the question of what kind of a nation we want to be as we begin our third century . . . virtually all the critical national problems of today could have been anticipated well in advance of their reaching critical proportions. . . . Only by focusing our attention farther into the future can we marshal our resources effectively in the service of those societal aims to which we are committed.
>
> —From President Nixon's announcement of the formation of the National Goals Research Staff, July 13, 1969

The years 1976 and 2000, the nation's 200th anniversary and the millennium, are the focal points for the research of a unique group

342

set up to advise the President and the nation on alternative futures. The idea for it grew from a 1968 proposal originally advanced by Daniel P. Moynihan, then Urban Affairs Assistant, to create a panel of futures-oriented urban researchers in residence. Along with Moynihan, other assistants and consultants—notably, Leonard Garment and the Hudson Institute's Anthony Wiener—worked on the idea. The final consensus was that such a forward-looking group was a good idea, but it should not be limited to urban matters but extended to the boundaries of all societal concerns. The unit emerged in July 1969 as the National Goals Research Staff. The President explained its function: "It is not to be a substitute for the many other research activities within the federal government; rather, it is intended to help us make better use of the research now being done by bringing together, at one central point, those portions of it that relate directly to future trends and possibilities. It will make accessible what has too often been fragmented."

Once it had become well established, the staff was composed of a dozen professionals with varied backgrounds who were lodged in a suite of offices in a new high-rise Executive Office Building a block from the White House. The staff was under the jurisdiction of Garment, and the staff director was Charles Williams, a veteran policy and logistics expert who has done futures work at the Pentagon and National Science Foundation.

In May 1970 Williams described the research role of the staff as synthesizer of futures research which would not contract for futures research but rather draw on the work of others. Williams said, "With practically all major research groups, think tanks and major corporations doing this kind of research, we are assuming a leadership role by bringing all this work together in one central place to be translated for top policy-makers and the American public."

The staff's prime customers were to be the White House and the American public. For the former, its job was to present "policy papers" to the President on future trends. Such papers were presented to the President, according to Williams, but their subject matter—and even their titles—are considered confidential. Besides its role as adviser to the Chief Executive, the staff was also designated as adviser to the nation—a role it was to play in the form of an annual report to the American people to be given on each Fourth of July. The report was to explain the key choices open to the nation and to

343

examine the consequences of those choices. Basic to the idea of the Goals Staff was the realization that for there to be any meaningful work in the future tense it would have to be permanent and continuing. "With the creation of the Goals Staff," said Williams in May before its first report, "ours is the first nation to take the initiative in trying to invent its own future. It is possible that the staff won't survive a change in Administration, but I think that if we can do an excellent job it will become apparent to all that there is a need for this kind of thinking at the highest level."

The "first" report was released in July 1970. It was a flop. It stayed clear of such issues as health, race, violence, housing, militarism, the urban crisis, foreign policy, and national priorities. The issues it chose to discuss—education, technology assessment, environment, population, natural science, and consumerism—were handled in a noncontroversial and self-serving manner. Only a few very general statements of alternatives were made, and no goals of substance were stated. Allusions to and plugs for President Nixon's policies were salted generously throughout the report. One member of the staff reported that the White House had kept the subject matter of the report limited and under control and had heavily edited it. At times this editing was petty and silly, as in the section on consumerism where all references to Ralph Nader were edited out—an action comparable to writing about the future of automobiles and censoring all reference to General Motors. The report was at once forgettable, innocuous, dull, and dishonest. At best, it served to point out a few foreseeable problems such as that of population distribution in the future. Science columnist William Hines summed up what many—including some of the staff and its consultants—felt about the report when he wrote in the Washington *Star*, "A blue-covered National Goals report, delivered to President Nixon the other day with fanfare appropriate to the bringing of the tablets from Sinai, is a bagful of wind."

Although the staff was retained for some weeks after the report was issued, it was disbanded in the fall. Officially the reason for its demise was that of a White House "reorganization," but Williams summed up the reasons as "A combination of difficulties of all sorts, conflicts, and a change of thinking at the White House—in short, it turned into a mushy can of worms."

The failure of this White House think tank may indicate what will be futurism's greatest hurdle: finding a permanent, coherent and powerful vehicle for assessing its findings and using those findings to pose clear alternatives and set firm goals. The work of the futurists is varied—from the disturbing and probably overstated findings of Harman's group at Stanford to the less sensational, more methodologically oriented findings of the Institute for the Future—but all of them have something to say that is worth being listened to, considered, and in some cases turned into plans for the nation. If one accepts the notion that futurists have something to say and that their premises are generally valid, then the need for a super planning group is apparent. It becomes more apparent as inevitably more futurist groups appear, a situation that most futurists are encouraging because of the generally held tenet that futurism calls for pluralism. There are, for example, several federal agencies planning to follow the lead of the Office of Education in setting up futurist groups. Such groups as the National Institute for Mental Health and the Department of Interior have taken an interest in setting up futurist think tanks.

No doubt there will always be commissions, staffs, and task forces assembled from time to time to look at the future and American goals, but these groups are deficient in that they have, at best, only a temporary impact on the system. This deficiency was well summed up in a comment by comedian Mort Sahl, who called for a commission to look into what happened to the recommendations of the commission that looked into "Goals for Americans" during the Eisenhower years.

While the Goals Research Staff never achieved permanence, there are other ideas for futurist-oriented groups operating at the national level which may have better chances to survive and be pertinent. Probably the most ambitious idea for a permanent futures group is that of a national institute for goals and futures research. The idea for a National Goals Institute comes from Arjay Miller, dean of the Graduate School of Business at Stanford and former president of the Ford Motor Company, who sees the need for a "quasi-independent" body that would advise both Congress and the executive branches of government on the futures of American needs and resources.

In contrast to most futures groups that tell us what is possible in terms of trends and technology, Miller's proposed group would say: If you decide you want something as a future goal, we will tell you what it will cost in terms of the resources and manpower needed to achieve it and whether or not it is feasible in the first place. It would be an institute of *applied futures* in which possible goals would be studied in practical terms with strong emphasis placed on the economics of the future, not only looking to see how much goals would cost but how they would be paid for. Miller feels that this kind of analysis is essential because of the gap that often exists between stated goals and the ability to achieve them. He believes that our present attempts to attain future goals are not coordinated, that such patchwork attempts will never amount to much, and that unless we do some analysis of which goals are attainable and which are not, we will be plagued by continued failure which can lead only to discouragement, frustration, and despair.

One way to understand the kind of analysis to be performed by his institute would be to look at the concrete, attainable goals for combating pollution. Miller has explained the dilemma as it exists now: "At the present time, leaders from practically all segments of society are calling out boldly for an end to environmental pollution, yet concrete proposals of exactly what steps should be taken are rare indeed. This should not be too surprising when we realize that no one really knows how to define in objective terms what we mean by pure air or clean water, or what it will cost to attain these objectives. I have heard one estimate that $200 billion would be required to clean up the environment, yet no one to my knowledge has indicated where funds approaching this magnitude will come from. The real character of the problem is brought home when we remember that previously announced national efforts, like the War on Poverty and the call for 2.6 million housing starts a year, are falling far short of their objectives, primarily because of a shortage of funds."

There have been several meetings of leading futurists, interested federal officials and businessmen to discuss the formation of a group along the lines Miller proposes. Reports have it that there is good likelihood that such an institution will be created. Should it be, then it will have to resist strongly the political forces which skewered the White House Goals Research Staff.

One of the men who attended a planning session for the institute in August 1970 was Arthur D. Little's James Gavin. He was encouraged by the idea because he thinks the nation is almost totally devoid of goals at this point in its history and that such an institute might help establish them. But Gavin was appalled by one aspect of the meeting. "Here was a large group discussing the future of goals in our society, presumably the best people to plan the mechanism for a goals institute," he says, "and I just kept looking around the room not being able to get over the fact that there wasn't a black or a woman in the room." Gavin's observation underscores what may well prove to be futurism's severest limitation: thinking about the year 2000 while missing the aspirations, realities, and participatory desires of the 1970's.

That important elements of citizenship have been delegated to and/or assumed by the think tanks is dramatically illustrated by the emerging field of futurism and its stated goal of shaping the future. Futurism is undoubtedly one of the most compelling and heady notions ever to come along for America's policy analysts, and for just that reason they will be giving it more attention in the years ahead. As the evidence grows that these "super-citizens" will continue to gain power over policy, action and all our lives, then the garden-variety citizen must be ever vigilant to what is going on in these privileged preserves called think tanks. Just as with urban problem-solving, military analysis, and other think-tank concerns, the promises and pitfalls of futurism offer compelling reasons for us to intrude to find out what is happening—after all, it is our future they are shaping.

347

ACRONYMS AND INITIALS

Like Russian novels, works about modern institutions and technology are plagued by names that are often hard to keep track of and tend to blur into one. To minimize confusion and save space, the author has bowed to modern custom, mainly in cases where the initials are used more commonly than the full, formal name. For the reader's ready reference, here under one roof are the book's acronyms deciphered.

ADL. Arthur D. Little Inc., a large "Jack-of-all-trades" research and consulting firm.

AIR. American Institutes for Research, a research conglomerate.

ANSER. Analytic Services Inc., a small Air Force think tank specializing in quick answers for military policy-makers.

ARPA. Advanced Research Projects Agency, a research-contracting office working directly for the U.S. Secretary of Defense.

calRAND. California Research and Development Corp., a proposed think tank that would puzzle out problems for the state government.

CNA. Center for Naval Analyses, a policy-research outfit in the Navy's employ.

CRESS. Center for Research in Social Systems, an Army adjunct that probes international issues.

CSIS. Center for Strategic and International Studies, a private advisor on international matters.

FCRC. Federal Contract Research Center, the official title given to institutions that are hired on a long-term basis to help the federal government conduct research.

GAO. Government Accounting Office, the bookkeeper/watchdog in the service of Congress.

HUMRRO. Human Resources Research Office, the Army's behavioral think tank.

348

IDA. Institute for Defense Analyses, think tank to the highest echelon at the Pentagon.

IFF. Institute for the Future, the nation's first think tank totally dedicated to studying the future.

IITRI. Illinois Institute of Technology Research Institute, a large multifaceted research firm.

ILC. Institute for Land Combat, an Army element studying the future of war, specifically its quality and quantity in the 1990's.

IPS. Institute for Policy Studies, furthest to the Left in the political spectrum of think tanks.

JASON. A code name rather than an acronym. It is the name for a group of top scientists at IDA who meet to think about matters of warfare.

LCS-90. Land Combat System—1990, the name of the major study being conducted by the Institute for Land Combat.

MITRE. The name of an Air Force think tank. It is a partial acronym, as its first three letters signify that it was fathered by the Massachusetts Institute of Technology.

RAC. Research Analysis Corporation, the Army's major policy-research firm.

RAND. Research ANd Development Corporation, an Air Force think tank that is considered to be the mother of modern think tankery.

R&D. Research and Development.

SDC. System Development Corporation, an offshoot of the RAND Corp., which today is a major profit-making corporation in its own right.

SORO. Special Operations Research Office, the original name for CRESS.

SRI. Stanford Research Institute, one of the nation's largest all-purpose research contractors.

TEMPO. TEchnical Military Planning Organization, a think tank which is part of the General Electric Company. TEMPO, which now does less military research than it originally did, simply calls itself TEMPO and has dropped the earlier explanation for the name.

TRW Inc. Originally for Thompson Ramo Wooldridge, Inc., now simply TRW Inc. A large West Coast research and systems engineering company.

USA Inc. Urban Systems Associates, Inc., an urban research group.

349

NOTES

With few exceptions think-tank studies are not available from libraries and bookstores but are obtainable only from the institutions themselves or, in some cases, from government agencies. For this reason, informal chapter notes are presented emphasizing how to obtain think-tank documents in order to help the reader wishing to investigate further the topics discussed here.

Chapter II

The Federal Clearinghouse discussed at the beginning of this chapter is perhaps the best single source of think-tank reports. By writing to the Clearinghouse (U.S. Department of Commerce, Springfield, Virginia 22151), one may receive a packet of information explaining how to find what it has to offer and how to order from it.

The facts and figures presented on the federal R&D budget come from two basic sources: the federal budget itself and the publications offered by the National Science Foundation on U.S. R&D. Among the periodical reports of the National Science Foundation used were: *Federal Funds for Research, Development and Other Scientific Activities, R&D in the Aircraft and Missiles Industry, National Patterns of R&D Resources, Federal Support to Universities and Colleges, Research and Development in Industry,* and *R&D Activities of Local Governments.* These publications are available from the National Science Foundation (1800 G St. NW, Washington, D.C. 20550), which will send a catalogue of its publications on request.

Much of the information on R&D in the Washington area was made available by the Science Industry Committee of the Metropolitan Washington Board of Trade (1616 K Street, NW, Washington, D.C. 20006). Of particular interest to anyone wanting more detailed information on the subject is that group's publication *Scientific Resources in the Washington, D.C., Area.* Another valuable source on the Washington R&D

industry is the Washington *Post's Potomac* magazine of Sunday, December 31, 1967, which contains a series of articles on the local R&D boom.

Chapter III

The early history of the RAND Corporation is discussed in detail in *The RAND Corporation: The First 15 Years*, published by RAND in November 1963 and available from RAND.

Additional information on the proposed think tanks mentioned in the chapter can be located as follows:

calRAND—Information is on file at the California Legislature, and the study of the proposal referred to is available from the consulting firm of Baxter, McDonald and Company in Berkeley, California.

Regional Pollution Centers—See *Scientific Research*, September 1, 1969.

Congressional Science Policy Advisory Group—See *Technical Information for Congress*, Report to the Subcommittee on Science, Research and Development of the Committee on Science and Astronautics, U.S. House of Representatives, Ninety-first Congress, April 25, 1969.

The Office of Goals and Priorities Analysis—See *The Congressional Record* of December 18, 1969, page H-12727.

The Inter-American Social Development Institute—See *The Congressional Record* of December 23, 1969, page S-17672.

East-West Think Tank—"A World Think Tank Is Reported Studied by West and Soviets," New York *Times*, December 13, 1969.

National Institute of Education—"Nixon to Seek Educational Institute," Washington *Post*, February 15, 1970.

Chapter IV

Most of the facts used in this chapter come from federal sources, such as *The Congressional Record*, publications of the National Science Foundation, Military Appropriations Hearings, the fiscal years 1969, 1970, and 1971, federal budgets, and agency publications.

Chapter V

The RAND Corporation publishes its own reports, available from RAND itself, the Federal Clearinghouse, and over 100 selected libraries (mostly at universities). Of course, only RAND's unclassified documents are available from these sources. RAND publishes a periodical entitled *Selected RAND Abstracts*, which lists current material available from the corporation. Both the list of libraries which carry RAND documents and the latest *Selected RAND Abstracts* are available from: Publications Section, the RAND Corporation, 1700 Main St., Santa Monica, California 90406. In addition, RAND publishes special bibliographies of its work under a variety of subject headings ranging from Africa to Weather Forecasting, also available on request.

Sources used in preparing the chapter on RAND which would be useful to anyone wanting more detailed information on the Corporation are:

recent RAND annual reports, Bruce L. R. Smith's *The RAND Corporation: Case Study of a Nonprofit Advisory Corporation* (Harvard University Press, 1966), *The RAND Corporation: The First 15 Years* (RAND, 1963), *Independent Public Policy Analysis Organizations—Major Social Invention* by Roger E. Levien (RAND, 1969), and *Policy Analysis in Action,* a paper delivered by Henry S. Rowen at the 1969 meeting of the American Academy for the Advancement of Science.

There have been a number of magazine and newspaper articles on RAND, among which are Saul Friedman's "The RAND Corporation and Our Policy Makers," *Atlantic Monthly,* August 1963; "Special Report on Planners for the Pentagon," *Business Week,* July 13, 1963; Joseph Kraft's "RAND: Arsenal for Ideas," *Harper's,* July 1960; and Gene Marine's "Think Factory Deluxe," *The Nation,* February 15, 1959. A particularly good account of the story of the RAND rumor which leads off the chapter was written by Leroy F. Aarons, entitled "The Anatomy of a Rumor," and appeared in the Washington *Post,* June 14, 1970.

Chapter VI

The Hudson Institute produces extra copies of some of its documents for outside distribution. Information on obtaining these documents can be obtained by writing to the institute at Croton-on-Hudson, New York. In addition, many of the works of Hudson's thinkers are published by major publishing houses.

Three books by Herman Kahn which detail his thinking on defense matters are: *Thinking about the Unthinkable* (Avon Paperbacks, 1964); *On Escalation: Metaphors and Scenarios* (Praeger, 1965); and *On Thermonuclear War* (Princeton University Press, 1960).

Detailed information on the Hudson Institute's run-in with the General Accounting Office is contained in *Observation on the Administration by the Office of Civil Defense of Research Study Contracts Awarded to the Hudson Institute Inc.,* published by the General Accounting Office, March 25, 1968.

Two articles helpful in preparing the section on the Hudson Institute were Byron Riggan's "Where They Think About the Unthinkable" in the Summer 1966 issue of *Horizon* and Arthur Herzog's "Report on a Think Factory" from the New York Times *Sunday Magazine,* November 10, 1963.

Information on the System Development Corporation is mainly available from the corporation, which is quite active in publishing information about itself. SDC publishes an extensive annual report, issues many press releases, and has descriptive brochures and summaries of jobs accomplished on its various areas of interest. Until recently it published the *SDC Magazine,* which described some of its research activities. Unclassified SDC reports can be purchased from the corporation (2500 Colorado Avenue, Santa Monica, California 90406), and those prepared for the government can be bought through the Clearinghouse.

Chapter VII

The most comprehensive source on the military think tanks is a study by John G. Welles, Dean C. Coddington, J. Gordon Milliken, Catherine C. Blakemore, John S. Gilmore, and Terry Sovel Heller entitled *Contract Research and Development Adjuncts of Federal Agencies: An Exploratory Study of Forty Federal Agencies.* The study was conducted by the Denver Research Institute for the National Science Foundation and is available from the institute in Denver, Colorado.

Details on the Camelot incident appears in *Technical Information for Congress* mentioned in the notes on Chapter III. Other information on CRESS was taken from its 1967 annual report and information presented in Senate debate on August 11, 1969. Information on the Logistics Management Institute was gathered from its descriptive brochures and information entered in *The Congressional Record* by Representative Henry B. Gonzalez on January 30, 1969, page E–628.

Information on the Institute for Defense Analyses was gathered from a number of sources, including its recent annual reports, recent Senate and House Defense appropriations and authorization hearings, and speeches and papers authored by its officials. A few of its unclassified reports are available from the Clearinghouse. Useful articles on IDA include: "Think Tank in the Eye of a Storm," *Business Week*, May 4, 1968; Warren Burkett's "IDA: the More It Changes, the More It's the Same," *Scientific Research*, August 18, 1969; and Michael T. Klare's "The Secret Thinkers," *The Nation*, April 15, 1968.

HUMRRO will gladly send out a pile of information about itself on request, including a bibliography of all of its studies (300 North Washington St., Alexandria, Virginia 22314). There is also a revealing portrait of HUMRRO in James Ridgeway's *The Closed Corporation* (Random House, 1968).

Description of the Research Analysis Corporation is based primarily on information supplied the author by the corporation as well as recent Congressional hearings.

Besides documents supplied by the Aerospace Corporation about itself, the article "Aerospace Corp.'s Road Widens" by Lawrence Curren in *Electronics*, September 28, 1970, and *The Aerospace Corp., A Study of Fiscal Management Policy Control* (a report of the Subcommittee for Special Investigations of the Committee on the Armed Services issued August 12, 1965) were used in discussion of the Aerospace Corporation.

Information on both MITRE and ANSER was supplied primarily by the companies themselves. MITRE *Matrix*, MITRE's house organ, is a particularly helpful guide to the corporation's activities.

Chapter VIII

The diverse think tanks discussed in this chapter are masters of brochuremanship and will at the slightest provocation shower one with information about themselves. However, their actual reports are often difficult to obtain except when they are working for federal agencies.

Some specific sources used in preparing the section on Arthur D. Little Inc. include: "The Organic Life of Little" by Brian Loasby in *Management Today*, September 1967; "Think Tanks: One Concern's Work Ranges from Submarine War to Cap'n Crunch" by Richard Reeves, the New York *Times*, June 16, 1967; and an article entitled "What Is Flavor Profile of Artificial Oil of Cinnamon? How Does One Tell a Young Nigerian That Age, Not Environment, Has Reduced His Orgasm Capacity? How Much Marijuana Can a Trained Mouse Absorb? Should the U.S. Sell the Post Office to Private Industry? How Do You Engineer an Entire Seismology Laboratory So That It Will Be No Larger Than a Clenched Fist? What Sort of Life Can a Blue-Collar Negro Family Expect When It Moves Into a Modest White Suburb? What Is the Solution to Algeria?" by Burton Hersh in *Esquire*, June, 1968, and *Crisis Now* by James M. Gavin (Random House, 1968) were also used in preparing the section on ADL.

The SRI Journal, a periodical put out by the Stanford Research Institute, is a valuable source on the institute's major research programs. Larry Schwartz's "War Research at Stanford: Sidestepping the Militants," *The Nation*, March 9, 1970, and C. A. Rosen's "Machines That Act Intelligently," *Science Journal*, October 1968 were both helpful sources.

Chapter IX

Three sources that were used in describing the problems of the urban problem-solvers were: Robert G. Smith's *The Systems Approach and the Urban Dilemma* (a report published by the George Washington University Program of Policy Studies in Science and Technology); James A. Kalish's "Flim-Flam, Double Talk and Hustle: The Urban Problems Industry," *The Washington Monthly*, November 1969; and *The Congressional Record* of December 3, 1969, which from page H–698 on details the problems of the Office of Economic Opportunity.

More detailed information on the Institute for Research on Poverty can be obtained by writing for the institute's annual report, which not only describes its programs but lists papers that are available. "A Think Tank That Thinks for the Poor," *Business Week*, July 22, 1968, is also a helpful source. More information on other urban think tanks is contained in *University Urban Research Centers*, a report available from the Urban Institute.

Publications of the New York–RAND Institute are now available through the RAND Corporation in Santa Monica as well as from the institute itself (545 Madison Avenue, New York, New York 10022). The institute puts out an informative annual report which describes its studies, and institute reports are now being stocked by the libraries which collect the documents of the parent corporation as well as those which specialize in literature on urban problems.

354

The Urban Institute produces lists of its research reports, obtainable by writing to it at 2100 M. St. NW, Washington, D.C. 20037. The institute also produces and gives away a periodic "work statement" that indicates the current status of its projects. One of the few articles on the institute appeared in *Business Week*, September 14, 1968, under the title "Urban Programs Face a Sharper Scrutiny."

Outside of publicity brochures and game manuals there has been very little published by or about Environmetrics.

Chapter X

The "public" think tanks are the major exception to the rule that think-tank material is hard to find in libraries and bookshops. Each of these groups publishes commercially and promotes its work for sale to the public. In addition, most libraries carry at least a sampling of the work of each of them.

The Center for the Study of Democratic Institutions publishes its own materials, offered through its catalogue, which can be obtained from the center, Box 4068, Santa Barbara, California 93103. The center vigorously promotes *The Center Magazine*, which can be subscribed to by writing to the same address. Articles about the center used in the preparation of this section are: Linda Charlton's "Center for Democratic Institutions Widens Scope," the New York *Times*, September 14, 1969; Kimmis Hendrick's "Hutchins Shapes 'True University,'" the *Christian Science Monitor*, July 15, 1969; Ralph Dighton's "Changes Loom at Famed California Study Center," the Washington *Post*, November 9, 1968; Israel Shenker's "Optimism Fills Echoing Think Tank," the New York *Times*, June 17, 1969; and Robert H. Sollen's "Anguish on a Hilltop," *The Nation*, October 6, 1969.

The institutes organized around the Institute for Policy Studies publish with major publishing houses and in leading periodicals. Each institute has descriptive material about itself that is sent out on request. Specific articles about the institutes are: Stephen Clapp's "How the Institute for Policy Studies Tries to Remain Existentially Pragmatic While Subverting the Establishment, *The Washingtonian*, January 1970; Shirley Scheibla's two articles "Radical Think Tank—the Institute for Policy Studies Aims to Disarm the United States"; and "Ivory Tower Activities—IPS Fellows Lead the Radical Thrust for Social Change," which appeared in *Barron's*, October 6 and 13, 1969.

The reports of Nader's Raiders are all published by Grossman in both hardcover and paperback editions.

Brookings publishes all of its own materials and offers a free catalogue (1775 Massachusetts Avenue NW, Washington, D.C. 20036). Three books published by Brookings used in preparing the section on it are: *The Brookings Institution, A 50–Year History* by Charles B. Saunders Jr. (1966), the 1967 *Brookings Annual Report,* and *Setting National Priorities: The 1971 Budget* by Charles L. Schultze, Edward K. Hamilton, and Allen Schick (1970).

All three of the foreign-policy think tanks discussed offer free lists of studies and books published by their authors. These lists can be obtained by writing to the three centers in care of their respective universities. Two articles used in writing about these three think tanks are: Berkeley Rice's "The Cold-War College Think Tanks," *The Washington Monthly*, June 1969; and Don McNeil's "An Analysis of GU's Think Tank," *The Hoya* (the Georgetown student newspaper), September 18, 1969.

Chapter XI

The best periodical sources on futurism are the two journals *Futures* and *The Futurist*. The former is published by Iliffe Science and Technology Publications, Guildford, Surrey, England, and the latter is available from the World Futures Society, P.O. Box 19285, 20th Street Station, Washington, D.C. 20036. *Futures* is the more scholarly and technical of the two, whereas features in *The Futurist* tend to be more general and written for the layman. Both carry news of futurist projects, institutions, conferences, and new publications. In addition, each issue of *The Futurist* carries a list of available books on futurism that can be ordered through the World Futures Society.

Two articles on the futurist movement are "Futurism" by George A. W. Boehm, which appeared in the July–August, 1970 issue of *Think*, and "The Futures Business" by David M. Kiefer, which appeared in the August 11, 1969, issue of *Chemical and Engineering News*. More detailed information on Delphi appears in a series of reports published by RAND and the articles in *Futures* by Norman Dalkey. RAND offers a free bibliography of its Delphi reports.

Studies discussed in the section on the Institute for the Future are sold by the institute, which regularly issues a list of its available publications (care of The Riverview Center, Middletown, Connecticut 06457). The writings of institute analysts appear regularly in *Futures*.

Information on the two Educational Policy Research Centers can best be obtained from the groups themselves. Both centers publish publication lists, and the Syracuse group offers a free periodical entitled *Notes on the Future of Education*, which abstracts the results of its studies. The addresses of the two centers are: EPRC, Syracuse University Research Corporation, 1206 Harrison St., Syracuse, N.Y. 13210, and EPRC, Stanford Research Institute, Menlo Park, California 94025.

The final report of the Goals Staff, entitled *Toward Balanced Growth: Quantity with Quality*, is available from the Superintendent of Documents, U.S. Government Printing Office, Washington, D.C. 20402. The proposal for Arjay Miller's National Goals Institute appears in *The Congressional Record* of March 31, 1970, page E-2712.

INDEX

Paul Dickson

Paul Dickson is a journalist who has reported on science and technology since 1965. For three years he worked as a regional editor for McGraw-Hill Publications, covering space and defense technology. During the academic year 1969–1970 he studied at George Washington University under a fellowship for reporters from the American Political Science Association. It was under this fellowship that he did much of his research on think tanks.

Mr. Dickson was born in Yonkers, New York, in 1939, was graduated from Wesleyan University, and served in the Navy. He has published articles in such publications as *Esquire, Saturday Review, The Nation*, the *Washington Monthly*, the Washington *Post* and *The Progressive*. He lives in Washington, D.C., with his wife, Nancy.